LITERARY GENIUS

A CATHARTIC INSPIRATION
By Gene N. Landrum, PhD

HOW DOES ONE BECOME A LITERARY GENIUS?

For starters it is not inherited. It is acquired. This book is an exploration into what makes the literary genius tick. Is it style, panache, or a way with words? Are the good ones normal, happy, or content? Not so, says Landrum, convinced he knows the pathway to creative expression. The following work delves into the inner drives that motivated Mark Twain, the passions that inspired Dostoevsky, the rebellion found in Shaw, and the sadism of Ian Fleming's James Bond creation. What pushed Agatha Christie to write Detective Mysteries, led Hemingway to become the virtuoso of the short story, made Dr. Seuss the hero of Childrens books, Danielle Steel a Romance Queen, and caused Stephen King to become the Maestro of the Macabre? Cathartic inspiration was a common theme, but he also says, "they were all just mad enough to excite, but not too wacky to get published; passionate enough to titillate, without being decadent; daring without being destructive; imaginative within the bounds of credibility; manic without cracking, mystical within the boundaries of rationality; and driven enough to overcome adversity. But normal or happy they were not."

GENIE-VISION BOOKS
7065 VILLA LANTANA WAY
NAPLES, FLORIDA 34108
E-MAIL: **genelandrum@cs.com**

Published Fall 2000 by Genie-Vision Books
Naples, Florida
E-mail: genelandrum@cs.com

1st edition
10 9 8 7 6 5 4 3 2 1

Copyright 2000
Library of Congress Cataloging-in-Publication Data

      Literary Genius – A Cathartic Inspiration/
      By Gene N. Landrum, PhD

   p.   cm

ISBN# 0-9659355-2-3

1. SELF-HELP, 2. LITERARY 3. CREATIVITY
4. BIOGRAPHY, 5. EDUCATION, 6. PSYCHOLOGY

ATTENTION: BOOK CLUBS, NON-PROFITS & EDUCATORS

COPIES OF THIS BOOK ARE AVAILABLE AT DISCOUNT FOR FUND RAISERS, BULK PURCHASES, SALES MEETINGS & PROMOTIONS.

CONTACT: **GENIE-VISION BOOKS % GENE N. LANDRUM**
              941-597-9545 – FAX 941-597-7347
              E-MAIL: genelandrum@cs.com
              WEB SITE: genelandrum.com

Printed in the United States of America

DEDICATED TO

All the world's teachers, librarians, counselors and book clubs. They have saved more people than all the physicians in history

ACKNOWLEDGEMENTS

Thanks to my wife Diedra Landrum who once again offered a female perspective and scrupulous editing on this book. Barbie Brill of Naples gave valuable insights and former student Becky Quimby provided data on their personal lives. The Naples and International College Libraries, and many friends and fellow teachers were supportive.

About the Author

Dr. Gene Landrum is a high-tech start-up executive turned educator and writer. He originated the Chuck E. Cheese concept of family entertainment among other entrepreneurial ventures. His doctoral thesis was on the *Innovator Personality*. He lectures extensively and teaches in the graduate and undergraduate programs at International College in Naples, Florida. His books look into what makes the great tick, and can be found in most bookstores or on the author's website - genelandrum.com. Titles are as follows:

Sybaritic Genius – Sex Drive & Success (2001)

Literary Genius – A Cathartic Inspiration (2000)

Eight Keys to Greatness (1999)

Prometheus 2000: Truth - Vision - Power (1997)

Profiles of Black Success – 13 Creative Geniuses (1997)

Profiles of Power & Success - 14 Geniuses Who Broke the Rules (1996)

Profiles of Female Genius - 13 Women Who Changed the World (1994)

Profiles of Male Genius - 13 Males Who Changed the World (1993)

Gene N. Landrum, PhD
Fax: 941-597-7347
Web Page: genelandrum.com

CONTENTS

TABLES/CHARTS

"Artists, geniuses, thinkers, inventors, discoverers:
they are the real leaders of humanity – the motive
power in the history of the world"
Alfred Adler, *Social Interest* (1933)

"It isn't Goethe that creates *Faust*,
but *Faust* who creates Goethe. Faust is but a symbol"
Carl Jung, *Symbols of Transformation*

"Writers are made, not born.
To be exact writers are self-made"
Ayn Rand, *We The Living*

"*Each of us are mythological representations of our
inner truth, and our jobs and other mundane experiences
are merely symbols of a larger mythological meaning*"
Joseph Campbell, PBS Special

CHART I
TRAITS OF LITERARY GENIUS

SUBJECT	DOMINANT CHARACTERISTIC
HONORE' BALZAC	RUSHING SICKNESS & MANIC
JOSEPH CAMPBELL	MYTHICAL MEANING OF LIFE
ALBERT CAMUS	SELF-DOUBT LED TO SUCCESS
AGATHA CHRISTIE	SELF-MADE WORKAHOLIC
FYODOR DOSTOEVSKY	CRISES LED TO CREATIVITY
IAN FLEMING	EGOMANIA OVERCAME INEPTNESS
DR. SEUSS [TED GEISSEL]	IMAGINATIVE PERFECTIONIST
ERNEST HEMINGWAY	LIBIDINAL DRIVEN PASSION
STEPHEN KING	TENACIOUS OVERACHIEVER
JAMES MICHENER	PERPETUAL SEARCH FOR MEANING
SYLVIA PLATH	CATHARTIC SELF-EXPRESSION
AYN RAND	INTUITIVE PROMETHEAN VISIONARY
ANNE RICE	SYZYGY – SYNTHISIZED TO SUCCESS
DANIELLE STEEL	OBSESSIVE CHARISMATIC
GEORGE B. SHAW	ECCENTRIC NON-CONFORMIST
MARK TWAIN [CLEMENS]	LIVE-ON-EDGE SOCIAL PHILOSOPHER
VIRGINIA WOOLF	INNOVATIVE DEFIANCE

PREFACE

This book is about the literary arts, books, eminent writers, the methodology of literary genius and the myriad of driving forces behind those who elect to compete in such a demanding profession. More specifically, it is about *success imprints* – indelible influences during their formative years – that conditioned and inspired them. The study delves into the reason behind their success. Was it luck, cathartic inspiration, or innate talent? Even more important, were they normal? And after they got to the top were they happy? They thought so, since they were pursuing their life's dream, but in any traditional definitions of happy they were not. Their sacrifices were such that they had paid a horrific price for their day in the sun. An example is the following findings:

Half were manic-depressive and most were obsessive-compulsive

Finishing school grad Dame Agatha Christie mysteriously disappeared in a bizarre scandal-ridden episode that was never solved

Romance writer Danielle Steel, a socialite, married a convicted rapist and divorced him to marry a convicted drug addict

Balzac, Shaw, Woolf, Rand, Campbell, Michener, and Dr. Seuss were all childless

Twain and Shaw wrote books on philandering when they were still virgins

Michener, Steel, and King have been the most demeaned yet made the most money

James Bond creator Ian Fleming was a sadist and flagrant womanizer

Dr. Seuss and Michener were both renegades and kicked out of school

Shaw never married until age 39 and failed to consummate the marriage during the next forty years

Shaw, Woolf, Camus, Fleming, Hemingway, Plath, Rand, Campbell, King, and Rice were areligious

PREFACE

Romance writers Hemingway and Steel were the most married

Balzac and Steel locked themselves in self-imposed prisons and refused to leave until finished with a manuscript

Stephen King cannot write without hard rock music playing

Occult Queen Anne Rice would like to be a man

Shaw and Twain used wit to keep from getting shot

Camus, Rand and Michener were the most intellectual yet most accepted by the masses

Pathologically shy, Shaw, Campbell & Rand became famous lecturers

GREAT-MAN THEORY. The basis of this study has a genesis in Thomas Carlyle's "Great Man" theory. Carlyle felt "History is the essence of innumerable biographies" and "Worship of a hero is the test of human nobility – there is nothing else admirable."

Studying great authors, therefore may offer valuable insight into their craft. Many of these subjects felt thus. Balzac has been anointed father of the modern novel and much of his success was based on worship of heroes that he labeled, "megalathropologeny." He wrote, "If I am not a genius I am done for." Such egocentrism is pervasive in the eminent. Woolf, Rice and Plath dreamed they were God. Most of the media believed Ayn Rand felt she was god due to her erudite arrogance. Fleming's wife said, "He was totally egocentric and obsessed with himself." Biographer Holroyd said of Shaw, "His greatest creation was himself. He didn't wait until he was famous to behave like a great man" (Holroyd p. 392).

Carlyle's theory was an adjunct to French philosopher Henri Bergson's *elan vital* or "vital force" a concept Freud called "psychic energy." Nietzsche titled it a "will-to-power" and you will find that Shaw in this book called it a "Life Force." Ralph Waldo Emerson said, "There is no history, only biography." Plutarch wrote a book titled *Lives of the Noble Grecians and Romans* 2000 years ago in which he touted the "lives of the greatest men – the poets and inventors of fables."

6

TRAIT & BEHAVIORAL ANALYSIS. The goal of this research was to pick the best writer in each of sixteen genres and see what common characteristics were found that may have been causal to their success. This entailed voluminous reading on the background and experiences of all subjects.

The key factors found to be important to success have been made the subject of one chapter. Examples are the *Cathartic Inspiration* of Sylvia Plath; the *Mythical Motivations* found in Campbell; *Mania* of Balzac; the *Rebellion* of Shaw; the *Egomania* of Fleming; the *Type A* work ethic of King; the *Adaptability (Syzygy)* of Anne Rice; the *Temerity* in Twain; the **Perfectionism** of Dr. Seuss; the *Promethean* **Vision** of Rand; the *Passion* of Hemingway; the *Charisma* of Danielle Steel; and the **Insecurity** of Camus.

NATURE VS NURTURE. Is there any genetic predisposition for greatness in the world of letters? Not based on these findings. Henri Bergson said in *Creative Evolution* (1911), "life transcends intellect." Plath had a 160 IQ and Rand was super bright as was Shaw, but their intellect had little or nothing to do with their consummate success. Money, social status, or formal education, were also of little influence in their trek to the top. They would have agreed with this assessment. Rand wrote in *We the Living* (1937) "No one is born with any kind of talent and, therefore, every skill has to be acquired. Writers are made, not born. To be exact writers are self made."

RESEARCH METHODOLOGY. This book will use one writer to explore the key qualities discussed above. This will allow the book to be read as a proscription for success for any discipline, or be used as a reference work for students, teachers, librarians, book clubs, or as an interesting biography on greatness. It can also be read as a psychobiographical analysis of what makes the successful writer tick.

Virginia Woolf (Essays) is used to explore the importance of innovation to the art. **Agatha Christie [Mystery]** will show the small importance of talent on success. **Dr. Seuss [Children's]** explores the need for imagination over structure. **Joseph**

Campbell [Mythology] is used to show the importance of fantasy hero-worship in removing limits to success. **Dostoevsky [Psychological Novel]** is used to demonstrate how breakdown can lead to breakthrough. **James Michener [Historical Novel]** will demonstrate the significance of travel to success. **Anne Rice [Occult]** is the poster girl for adaptability (syzygy – functioning at various points on a personality continuum). **George Bernard Shaw [Playwright]** demonstrates the power of living outside the box where mediocrity reigns supreme. **Mark Twain [Humor]** offers insight into living on the edge and getting published. **Ian Fleming [Spy Thrillers]** is the poster boy for self-esteem and successful writing.

Sylvia Plath [Poetry] is the quintessential example of cathartic expression. **Stephen King [Horror]** represents the Type A workaholic nature of the successful writer. **Honore Balzac [Mania]** personifies the importance of speed and drive to success. **Ernest Hemingway [Short Stories]** offers insight into the power of passion on the written word. **Ayn Rand [Philosophical Novel]** demonstrates how a holistic vision can enhance verbal expression. **Albert Camus [Non-Fiction]** shows how insecurity can breed greatness. And finally **Danielle Steel [Romance]** shows us how charisma can transcend the spoken word and find its way into the written ones.

WHY SIXTEEN GENRES? Because more would have been unwieldy, less would lack validity. Sixteen individuals are enough to be meaningful yet small enough to be manageable. Eight or ten subjects would have made the task easier, and the book smaller, but it would not have contributed as many interesting stories or the validity needed for many of the controversial issues.

Have some important literary geniuses been left out? No question! Where are the world's great poets Walt Whitman, Kipling, Byron, Keats, Shelly, T. S. Eliot, Dickinson, Maya Angelou, Hawthorne, Frost, and Sandburg? And where are Dickens, Hugo, Tolstoy, Joyce, Fitzgerald, Faulkner, Steinbeck, John Ruskin, Jonathan Swift, Jane Austen, the Bronte sisters, Huxley, Dreiser, Toni Morrison, and Poe? And what about

Yeats, Oscar Wilde, Chekhov, Eugene O'Neill, Tennessee Williams, Jean Paul Sartre, Arthur Miller, and Neil Simon? Expediency rules in such a case. Many of the above mentioned subjects were researched, specifically Maya Angelou, Lord Byron, Oscar Wilde, Colette, James Joyce, Carl Sandburg, T. S. Eliot, and Charles Dickens. These subjects will be discussed and quoted throughout the book.

WHAT IS LITERARY GENIUS?

Using the word *genius* is open to argument. There are as many definitions as there are experts. Howard Gardner developed eight Multiple Intelligences such as kinetic, artistic and verbal. The numbers-happy Western world has attempted to put everyone in a box called a Bell Curve based on their score on IQ tests. Webster defines *genius* as "someone who influences another for the good or bad," someone with "extraordinary intellectual power especially manifested in creative activity" and "those with a high intelligence quotient."

In a world enamored with digitizing everything this definition has prevailed as a universal measure of genius. A score of 140 on a standardized IQ test or 1350 on an SAT test opens many doors, not because of any ability to perform, but because of the score itself. MENSA limits membership to those with an IQ of above 135. Most of those in this book would not have qualified for MENSA, or other definitions of genius. But altering the world through the use of words suffices as genius in the opinion of this author. The definition of genius used throughout this book will be qualitative - ***"to influence others for the good or bad."*** The world is not digital it is analog, it is not quantitative it is qualitative, and that is the logic used to define these subjects in a qualitative manner.

Robert Sternberg, a Yale psychology professor, says it takes a *Successful Intelligence* to achieve in the world. But doesn't offer any measure for use here. He agrees that "The idea that intelligence can be measured by tests is a myth." He wrote, "Intelligence and IQ are modifiable" (Sternberg, *Successful Intelligence*. P. 85). Sternberg agrees with this author's premise that "the true measure of your intelligence is not in a test score;

it is in your willingness to develop your own talents" (p. 150). Validation of this is found from Henri Poincare's experience many years ago when he took his friend Alfred Binet's IQ test and scored at the imbecile level, not once but twice. He did this at a time when his friend Einstein considered him the greatest mathematical genius in the world. The premise in this work is that genius or greatness is not quantifiable. Genius will be ascribed to anyone who has changed their genre in some significant way or have come down as a significant influence in the world of letters. All of these writers qualify by this measure.

SELECTION CRITERIA

Four simple criteria were used to select these subjects. **First,** they had to have made it to the very top of their profession. **Second,** they had to have remained at or near the top for a period of ten years. **Third,** they had to have been personally responsible and not have bought their way in via a mate, family, or name. In other words they could not have been co-authors, had ghostwriters, or married a publisher. Woolf was the daughter of a literary critic and married a publisher Leonard Woolf but neither contributed to her literary appeal or success. **Fourth,** they had to have had some international influence on the genre and or changed the world in some way. This can be arbitrary, but each of these individuals were highly influential. Some excelled through sheer power of numbers like Dame Agatha Christie with over a billion books sold. Stephen King and Danielle Steel have sold close to 500 million. Many were the recipients of the Nobel Prize for Literature or the Pulitzer Prize. Shaw refused his but Camus, Plath, Michener, Hemingway, and Dr. Seuss were all so honored. Others won literary acclaim with Balzac, Dostoevsky, Twain, Campbell, and Rand fitting this criteria. Some literary critics would question the inclusion of Steel, Fleming, Michener, and King due to their lack of literary merit. But the same questions would have been made of Twain and Shaw in their eras. Table 1 outlines their genre, and major contribution.

TABLE 1

SEVENTEEN LITERARY GENIUSES

3 FROM 19TH CENTURY, 7 FROM FIRST HALF 20TH, 7 FROM LAST HALF
10 AMERICANS & 7 EUROPEANS; 11 MEN & 6 WOMEN

LITERARY GENRE	CREATIVE GENIUS	ACCLAIMED WORK
INNOVATOR	VIRGINIA WOOLF	To the Lighthouse (1927)
POETRY	SYLVIA PLATH	The Bell Jar (1961)
CHILDRENS	DR. SEUSS (Geissel)	The Cat in the Hat (1957)
DETECTIVE MYSTERY	AGATHA CHRISTIE	Murder of Royce Akroyd (1926)
HISTORICAL NOVEL	JAMES MICHENER	Tales of the South Pacific (1948)
HORROR	STEPHEN KING	Carrie (1974)
HUMORIST	MARK TWAIN	Huckleberry Finn (1884)
MYTHOLOGY	JOSEPH CAMPBELL	Hero with 1000 Faces (1949)
NON-FICTION	ALBERT CAMUS	The Stranger (1942)
OCCULT	ANNE RICE	Interview With Vampire (1973)
PHILOSOPHICAL NOVEL	AYN RAND	Atlas Shrugged (1957)
PLAYWRIGHT	GEORGE B. SHAW	Pygmalion [My Fair Lady] (1913)
PSYCHOLOGICAL NOVEL	FYDODOR DOSTOEVSKY	Crime & Punishment (1866)
ROMANCE NOVEL	DANIELLE STEEL	The Promise 1979)
SHORT STORY	ERNEST HEMINGWAY	The Old Man & the Sea (1952)
SPY THRILLERS	IAN FLEMING	From Russia With Love (1957)
SOCIAL COMMENTARY	HONORE BALZAC	The Human Comedy (1841)

PROFILES OF LITERARY GENIUS

The following mini-profiles of the subjects offer insight into their selection. It should give the reader some interesting background on those who are unfamiliar and pique the interest for others that are different than imagined. It will also give the reader the opportunity to select a few writers who they admire and to read them alone.

Table 2
PROFILES OF LITERARY GENIUS

HONORE BALZAC – Father of Modern Novel

Mania and excess defined this prodigious producer of French novels that document French society in the 19th century. He was energy incarnate and a zealot who destroyed himself to become a genius. Vitality and excess defined his work as a journalist, novelist, entrepreneur and wannabe philosopher. Everyone and everything paled in his presence and no risk was ever to great for him to take. He is arguably the most manic personality to have ever made a name in literature.

JOSEPH CAMPBELL – Father of Modern Mythology

As a child Campbell was enamored with religious and ethnic icons and the experience transformed his life. It drove him to spend his life pursuing the derivation of myths. In the end he said, "the only way to slay your dragons is to follow your bliss," but his most informative instruction was, "Myths make heroes out those who heed them." Campbell was probably the most erudite of these creative wunderkinds. He believed myths to be the models for understanding your life.

ALBERT CAMUS – Existentialist Novelist

This Algerian born French writer used insecurity and self-doubt to motivate him. He said, "I don't believe in anything" and "to know if one can live with one's passions, that is the question." But central to his work that led to his Nobel Prize for Literature was his aphorism, "I feel one must revolt to arrive at happiness." His philosophy of the absurd built around the *Myth of Sisyphus* was the basis of his existentialism. He became a popular spokesman for the "beat generation" in the 50's and rose to the top by overcoming his battle with TB as a teenager.

AGATHA CHRISTIE – Queen of Mystery

A self-made writer and workaholic who sold 2 billion books in 103 languages without one minute of training in the art. Dame Agatha wrote popular detective mysteries, short stories and plays and proves it is not necessary to have innate ability or formal education to achieve success in the literary arts. A bet with her sister led to her becoming the most prolific writer in British history where imagination proved more important than talent.

FYODOR DOSTOEVSKY – Father of Psychological Novel

Crisis pervaded the life of this man who used a life of trauma as a motivating force to drive him to find what makes man tick. He authored the most famous psychological novel *Crime & Punishment* (1866), demonstrating that one can fool the rest of the world but can never fool oneself. With fewer adversities it is highly unlikely he would ever have become a literary genius. Afflicted with debilitating epilepsy, a proclivity for alcohol, manic-depression, a gambling addiction, and ten years in Siberia he persevered. It is no wonder nihilism and existentialism became his forte. Andre Gide and critic Bennett have called *The Brothers Karamazov* (1880) the greatest novel ever written.

IAN FLEMING – Master of the Spy Thriller

This British egocentric created a fantasy hero James Bond to enact all his own perverse fantasies. His alter-ego 007 was able to go where he didn't dare and to live life on the precipice where he feared. His time as British Naval Intelligence Officer led to insight into spying. When he found his lover pregnant in his early 40's, the bachelor proposed and it drove him to his Jamaican retreat Golden Eye where wrote *Casino Royale*. After that success he wrote one book each year for the next ten years. Unlike Bond, Fleming was a loser who used and abused women. But timing was everything for Fleming who offered a fantasy escape at the height of the Cold War. James Bond was voted the most successful movie series of all time at the millennium, testimony to the impact of the pompous Fleming.

DR. SEUSS GEISSEL – The Maestro of Children's Books

Obsessive perfectionism defined Geissel, a child-man who wrote out his most outlandish fantasies, that appealed to the radical youth of the 60's and 70's. A vivid imagination led Ted Geisel to create *Cat in a Hat* and a *Butter Battle Book* that interested children more than Dick and Jane readers. His off-the-wall with appealed to the renegade nature of children who saw the world in a similar way as Seuss. Geisel's adamant refusal to buy into the adversarial world of adulthood led him to the top. Allowing free-reign to his inner being differentiated Dr. Seuss from the pack. He said, "When I dropped out of Oxford I decided to be a child," and it was that off-the-wall sense of humor that brought a generation of anarchistic children to love books via his zany characters.

EARNEST HEMINGWAY – Brevity of Narrative & Short Story

An obsession with death and the psychic scars of life gave Hemingway an edge in story writing especially when he imbued the stories with his libidinal energy. Hemingway's mastery of narration along with a passion for living life at the extreme led him to success. He won the Nobel and Pulitzer Prizes for *The Old Man & the Sea*, but his edge appears to be the psychosexual energy that pervaded his very being. It was this nature that led his author friend F. Scott Fitzgerald to say,

PREFACE

"Every time he started a new book he had to find a new woman." This psychosexually driven manic-depressive had a gender identity hang-up but it fueled his passionate pathos of words.

STEPHEN KING – Master of the Macabre
The horror-master coupled a kinky imagination with a Type A work ethic to alter the genre. And it has elevated him to what the media calls, "the most commercially successful writer in American history." King's first six novels were rejected but he refused to quit and now is incapable quitting or even slowing down. He writes all but three days each year, Christmas, July 4th, and his birthday, testimony to a man on a mission. Despite earning $30 million a year he still cranks out two to three novels a year. The King paradox is that he has never written for money an says he never will. What motivates him to write such horror? He says, "If I weren't writing I might commit suicide or become a mass murderer."

JAMES MICHENER – The Father of the Historical Novel
This world traveler spent his life in a perpetual search for an identity and heritage. His travels led him to the far ends of the earth and the documentation of diverse cultures and nations. His contribution to historical fiction has been prolific with *South Pacific, Hawaii, Poland, Alaska, Caribbean, Chesapeake, Texas* and *Spacea* among his 90 books. Born a foundling he never had a family and he was inspired to look for that of other cultures and nations. *The World is My Home* (1991) was his memoir that offers insight into a man searching passionately for a destiny.

SYLVIA PLATH – Cathartic Poet
Did self-doubt or cathartic inspiration led this demon-plagued woman to write poems with such passion? Both, but it was words that she loved. She was taught to use words to express emotion and they would become her greatest strength and her greatest weakness. They won her a Pulitzer Prize, but also drove off her husband. They were responsible for her Pulitzer Prize for Literature won posthumously. But they were really used to exorcise those inner demons. It worked for awhile, but ultimately she stuck her head in an oven at age 30 and ended it all. A 160 IQ, Smith and Cambridge education, and a marriage to a man who would become England's Poet Laureate, wasn't enough to tame her tormented psyche. Losing her "colossus" father at age nine had haunting her until she could no longer stand it and wrote it out in a volcanic rush of white passion titled *Colossus, Daddy,* and *The Bell Jar.*

LITERARY GENIUS

AYN RAND – Political Philosophy in Novel Form

This champion of capitalism wrote what is considered one of the world's great greatest philosophical epic novels *Atlas Shrugged* in 1957 to elevate *man* above the *state*. She promised to destroy the despicable system that defiled her family and spent a lifetime dedicated to her cause. Rand is the poster girl for the Promethean visionary, an intuitive-thinking personality type. She always saw the essence of a problem, the "whole" and was able to deal with it rationally, the definition of creative genius. Such people see the big picture and quantify that vision. They are life's "architects of change." Rand's work can be summed up by protagonists Howard Roark and John Galt. Both men were Promethean heroes that would rather destroy their work than have it compromised by self-serving bureaucrats. Rand's message of "rational self-interest" is the underlying philosophy of Objectivism that spawned a political movement Libertarianism.

ANNE RICE – Occult & Surreal Novels

This renegade writer is used to show the importance of adaptability to success. Rice is the consummate model for Jung's Syzygy concept where one is admonished to tap into their opposite gender to optimize their effectiveness. The vampire Lestat is Anne reincarnated, her androgynous double. Rice is able to be feminine while writing masculine, nurturing with an aggressive demeanor, introverted with an extroverted persona. She effectively functions at various points on the personality continuum. In her insatiable search for immortality for dead daughter Michele, Anne created the Vampire Chronicles. As the living dead she became immortal, and the works transformed her from the bottle to fame and fortune. Anne, true to her eccentric reputation, says, "Lestat is the man I would love to be" and "Bloodsucking provides a rush more powerful than any orgasm."

GEORGE B. SHAW – Dramatist

This creative eccentric ignored all experts in his quest for a utopian world. Defiance was his middle name. His renegade nature led him to become an avid atheist, vegetarian, and proponent of free-love despite never consummating his forty year marriage. He was a Marxist and co-founder of the British Labor Party, despite a Irish heritage. This radical was a self-made intellectual who transformed himself into an expert on everything from the theater, books, music, opera, and art. He became a politician, literary critic, playwright, and novelist. Many have called him the greatest English playwright since Shakespeare. He left us with *Pygmalion* [My Fair Lady] as testimony to his eccentric view of male-female relationships. Testimony to his rebellious nature was turning down the Nobel Prize for Literature and Knighthood.

PREFACE

DANIELLE STEEL – Romantic Charisma

The Queen of Romance is personally and professionally charismatic. Her plots and characterizations meet the expectations of her female readers looking for a fantasy escape with little work. Her success is based on those 400 million books sold by the millennium. Steel's romantic plots in exotic locals are spiced with passionate words that inspire and entertain. Her books are regularly aired on TV, in movies, paperback and hardcover. She writes with charm since she is creating a dreamy world that has escaped her in real life. Steel creates escapist adventures replete with dapper men, needy women interfacing in elegant rendezvous like St. Tropez, Rome, Paris and Rodeo Drive. She admits, "I make a world peopled the way I want my life to be."

MARK TWAIN – Americana Wit

Twain was an intrepid warrior who wrote not to make money, or to sell books, but to lead to a successful career on the lectern. His books have become classics primarily because he didn't intend them to be literary masterpieces. Twain had a keen sense of metaphorical reality that he translated into words leading Hemingway to say, "All American literature comes from one book *Huckleberry Finn.*" Twain was a renegade risk-taker who defied the writing establishment. His work was originally banned in Boston but has since been eulogized. Satire and wit from the heart and hearth was Twain's contribution. He married the comic with the tragic in the vernacular making him the chronicler of 19th century Americana. He documented early America like no other writer with witticisms on Virginia City, San Francisco during the Gold Rush, and the Gilded Age.

VIGINIA WOOLF – Essayist & Innovator

James Joyce and Virginia Woolf are both acclaimed for leading the way with a stream-of-consciousness writing style. Her innovative style proved innovative in the early 20th century. A tormented cathartic release of inner torment permeated her work. She had a profound influence on the modern novel, especially with *Mrs. Dalloway* (1925), *To the Lighthouse* (1927) and *The Waves* (1931). Writing "In the lava of madness I found my characters" is testimony to her life on the edge. She tapped into the deepest recesses of her troubled psyche for expression. Molestation, incest, lesbian love affairs, extramarital affairs pervade her work as well as her on-going battle with madness. It is no wonder she wrote with passion.

INTRODUCTION

Environmental Influences on Literary Genius

"Some day there undoubtedly will be a science – it may be called the science of man – which will seek to learn about man in general through the study of creative man."
Pablo Picasso

"Worship of a hero is the test of human nobility – there is nothing else admirable"
Thomas Carlisle's *Great Man Theory* of History

WHAT MAKES EMINENT WRITERS GREAT?

Many things! But most factors are internal not external making them less than obvious to the casual observer. Visionary geniuses are dreamers. But their dreams emanate from some inner sanctum that tells them they are right even when the world tells them they are wrong. What differentiates them from the pack is a prescient ability to quantify that vision.

Literary geniuses are different than the normal population but their difference are strangely similar. Most are driven by a powerful internal force, a force they are trying to placate, but seldom are able to identify. But the truth is that they have this need to tell the world something of a highly personal nature even when they disguise it in some esoteric words like *"The Old Man & the Sea," "Daddy,"* or *"To The Lighthouse."*

The literary genius seldom departs from their internal needs, dreams, fantasies, and imprints. Some merely write to maintain their sanity as Sylvia Plath and Stephen King claimed. Others see it as a passion like Anne Rice who claims, "I write what I am about," or Ayn Rand who said, "I'm a hero worshipper." I call this their cathartic inspirations written as a passionate need to feel whole and to make a contribution to the ways and wiles of the world.

Literary genius has but one master and that is to produce. Such production comes at a high price - health, family, friends, happiness, and any kind of normality. An example comes from an act of the gentlemanly Joseph Campbell. A torrential rain began to come down while Campbell and his fiancé Jean Erdman were walking in Manhattan. The gallant and ever-courteous Campbell tore off his jacket. A smile started to form on Jean's face when Campbell placed his coat gently over his *Decline of the West.* Erdman said after they were married, "I knew what I was in for after that."

Extensive research makes it apparent that there is little genetic predisposition for literary genius. Writers are made not born. Are they special? You bet! Are they different? Unbelievably so! But they are nurtured, imprinted, and conditioned to achieve. They are not born with anything but potential. They are the environment's by-products. Creativity, innovation, a way with words, all are born of *success imprints* and conditioning on the trek through life via the hundreds of thousands of experiential inputs that make us what we are. Is it important to have reasonable health and brainpower? Of course it is but that is not what differentiates the also-rans from the exceptional. This will be the focus of the rest of this book.

SUBJECT DIVERSITY. The subjects in this work were selected from diverse backgrounds and a wide range of cultures. Six were female and eleven were male. Seven wrote during the last half of the 20th century. Another seven wrote primarily in the first half with just three - Balzac, Dostoevsky, and Twain producing most of their works during the 19th century. Ten were American and seven European [Ayn Rand was Russian but she arrived in America in her early 20's and wrote all of her books in English]. Two wrote in French [Balzac and Camus] and all the rest wrote in English although the four Brits [Shaw, Christie, Woolf, and Fleming] would probably have said the Americans did not write in English. Ten were reared in middle class households with two from the lower classes (Camus & Michener) and two from upper class households (Christie &

Steel).   Eight were raised as Protestants, six as Catholics/Orthodox (Balzac, Dostoevsky, Campbell, Camus, Rice, Steel), with one Quaker (Michener), one from Judaism (Rand) and one in an agnostic household (Woolf).

PERSONALITY & LITERARY GENIUS.   How one sees the world and functions within it is critical to getting to the top of any genre or discipline.   Attitude is the result of how we perceive the world.   It can be an asset or liability.   That is precisely why it is the prime focus of this work.

It is imperative we look at the nature of these subjects, their motivations, foibles, dysfunctions and effectively the driving force behind their writing. This cannot be done without looking into the influences of parents, siblings, education, peers, crises, religion, sex drive, and any and all influences that looked causal in their trek to the top.   One example is the maternal influence in the lives of George Bernard Shaw and Honore Balzac. Both were devastated by the treatment of their mothers and at first glance it would appear to highly negative but it proved to be a motivating factor as each drove themselves in a mad attempt to prove they were worthy of their mother's love.

Shaw's mother deserted him at age thirteen to run off with her music-teacher lover.   He was distraught but later moved to London and lived with her until he almost thirty and then lost his virginity to her best friend. And the reason he changed his name from George to GBS was the discovery that his real father was the music teacher who was named George.   Balzac's mother had a similar influence in that she sent him off to a wet nurse and neglected to retrieve him for four years. He was hurt by her preference for an illegitimate half brother Henry motivating him to write to her, "Had you loved me as you loved Henry, I should probably have ended up where he is (he was a flake) and in that sense you have been a good mother to me." Both men had been warped relative to marital relationships. Shaw didn't marry until almost forty and then refused to consummate the relationship despite an ideology of free-love. Balzac didn't marry until fifty and also slept with many women his mother's age, many who were her friends.

INTRODUCTION

VIRGINIA WOOLF - INNOVATOR OF NARRATIVE STYLE

Woolf is used here to demonstrate the importance of innovation to writing. Innovation is key since it is what sets one apart from the pack. Woolf lived outside the box of convention, critical to the innovative process, and her major contribution to literature was a stream of consciousness approach. Her life and work also offer insight into how innovation is often derived from trauma. Virginia was molested early and repeatedly and flirted with insanity much of her life. Writing was therapy for her, a way of coping, and a cathartic release. She was obsessed with telling the world so it wouldn't engulf her.

CATHARSIS & WOOLF'S WORK. Woolf's writing is a study in healing via expression. She wrote to exorcise inner demons and ghosts. She lived in constant fear of insanity. This was apparent in journals and every one of her emotionally laced books and essays. She wrote, "I deal in autobiography and call it fiction" (Gordon 6). Woolf called her style "autoanalysis" – a concept that is quite telling about her. She wrote, "Every secret of a writer's soul, every experience of his life, every quality of his mind is written large in his works" (Woolf pg. 6).

Woolf, like many successful women, was highly influenced by her father Leslie. Leslie Woolf was a literary critic and historian. Virginia grew up wanting to emulate him. Books were the most important thing in his life and became the most important thing in hers as she married a writer and publisher. Virginia's extended family included half-brothers George and Gerald Duckworth, both of whom molested her early. Both appear in her writing since she was screaming out for help. Words were her life and what made her happy. She also turned to them for therapy.

CRISES & CREATIVITY. Woolf's traumatic experiences were not unusual as similar events were found in the life and others. Every one encountered a near-death experience or lost a loved one, sibling, or parent at a formidable age. These traumas led them to consider life's mortality very early and the imprint was telling. In most cases it fueled passions within because they had seen the worst and everything else was a piece of cake.

Trauma appears to contribute to the creative process. Dostoevsky will be the individual used to explore the causal factors in more depth since he led a tragic life that inspired him to greatness. Michener and Rice experienced an epiphany or transformation from tragic experiences that came close to destroying them, but in the end made them.

These epiphanies are referred to periodically throughout the book as *success imprints.* What was the nature of these? They took many different tacks but were manifested mostly as tenacity, temerity, resolve, an indomitable will, insecurity, drive, and often as obsessive or compulsive behavior. The most noteworthy was Dostoevsky. When his mother died he lost his ability to speak. When his doctor father was murdered and castrated by serfs he contracted epilepsy. After being sentenced to death and spending ten tortuous years in Siberia he returned to write *Crime and Punishment, The Gambler,* and his other classics.

PASSION, CREATIVITY & VISION

There have been many explanations for man's passion. Freud called it psychic energy and the Pleasure Principle. Nietzsche labeled it a "Will-to-Power." Shaw married the two and came up with a Life Force concept that can be found in many of his classics. Freud believed that passion, or sex drive is often sublimated into work energy. Balzac, Dostoevsky, Shaw, and Hemingway believed this to be the case and it affected their approach to life and work. Balzac actually donned a monk's robe and locked himself in an attic to avoid wasting his precious energies on women. Dr. Seuss fits Freud's words best.

The important thing is to always remember that passion is critical to all success. No one, and I mean no one, excels in any endeavor without great passion. A person can have great talent but without passion will live life in the middle lane. Talent without passion is like wine without cheese, the world without books, and men without women. Life can be lived but it will be mediocre at best. An example of this is the creator of 007, one Ian Fleming. Fleming was a loser at virtually everything he ever attempted, and by his own admission a man without any literary talent. But he oozed passion and it can be seen in his alter-ego James Bond. Fleming became rich and famous for daring allowing free reign to his most outrageous passions.

Table 3

PASSION & PERFORMANCE

Arousal Theory in Creativite & Athletic Performance
Passion Improves Performance to a point then it interferes with it

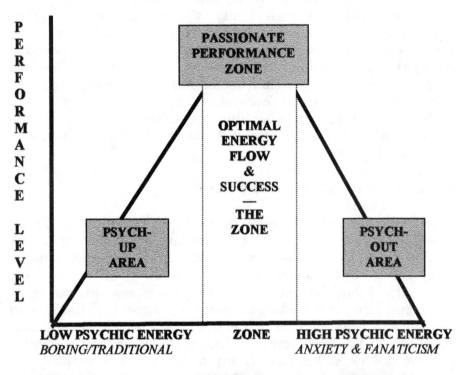

	PERFORMANCE LEVEL	
LOW PSYCHIC ENERGY *BORING/TRADITIONAL*	**ZONE**	**HIGH PSYCHIC ENERGY** *ANXIETY & FANATICISM*
NO PASSION **LETHARGY** *NO INTENSITY*	**FUNCTION** **COMPETITIVE DRIVE**	**EXCESSIVB** **STRESSED** *THROWS GOLF CLUBS*
BORED *UNFOCUSED*	**ATHLETES**	**OVERZEALOUS** *PRESSING*
INSECURE *COMPLACENT*	**WRITERS**	**ARROGANT** *KNOW-IT-ALLS*

Passion is correlated to bipolar illness, high testosterone, risk-taking personalities, and to obsessive and compulsive behaviors. Passion permeated the very existence of Balzac, Dostoevsky, Twain, Woolf, Hemingway, Camus, Fleming, Plath, Rice, and Steel. All were passionate to a fault in their work, words, mates, and dreams.

Arousal theory in sports psychology offers some insight into passion as a catalyst for performance. See Table 3 - PASSION & PEFORMANCE, also known as arousal theory in sports psychology, shows diagrammatically movement from lethargy and boredom through the ZONE and on into a stressed out stage. The Zone is where all athletes and writers want to be. No one is always there and you know it when you are. Those times when you have the ability to write the perfect line to fit the situation and the exact words for maximum effect. We have all been there and we all want to go back. Controlling the elements to allow it is another thing.

The table illustrates how one can get **psyched up** to perform at a higher and higher level as the passion increases. It also shows how performance declines as one passes into the stage called **psyched-out.** Striking a golf ball perfectly is a thrill and when the expectations of that are too great (psyched out) the tendency is to throw the club when performance is bad.

In writing, the tendency is to articulate and perform with inner emotional drive, but when those emotions go over the edge there is a tendency to burn the work as Dostoevsky, Hemingway, and King did, or crawl into a bottle or drugs. Passion is critical to success but as in all things too much will become more debilitating than motivating.

CATHARTIC EXPRESSION. Passionate people write from the soul. And there productions have feeling and come across in their words and actions. There is power in passion especially when it originates from within and that what catharsis is all about. They express inner emotion and are the reason most writers pay the price to pour out their souls into their work.

INTRODUCTION

These seventeen were on a mission to exorcise inner ghosts and it manifested itself in their work. In some cases their words of passion would have succeeded had they not be good at narrative expression. A prime example is Dostoevsky's stories, all imbued with his inner torment. His compulsive gambling found its way into like *The Gambler*. The inner fears of a man who killed and got away with it but walked in and confessed in *Crime and Punishment*, demonstrates his belief that we can kid others but never ourselves. *Notes from the Undergound* is little more than him exorcising his torment of being a prisoner in Siberia. His cathartic novels were a desperate attempt at finding logic in a world he felt had gone mad.

In a similar way *To the Lighthouse* (1927) and *The Waves* (1931) were autobiographical exorcisms by Virginia Woolf. Hemingway wrote out his WW-I injuries in *The Sun Also Rises* (1926) and *A Farewell to Arms* (1929) and used *The Old Man & the Sea* (1952) to cope with advancing age. Fleming creating 007 as an outlet for his sadistic tendencies. Michener wrote historical fiction as a means to find the meaning of lost cultures and heritages. Rice created vampires – the living-dead – in order to immortalize her dead daughter Michele. Steel wrote of fantasy romances that met her ideal since her real world romances all ended up in divorce. Plath used words to express emotion and to write her colossus dad out of her tormented head. Ayn Rand admitted to writing her first book *We the Living* (1936) "to get Russia out of my system." Dr. Seuss drew and wrote for his own childish pleasure, and Mark Twain regressed to a happier youth in *Huckleberry Finn* and *Tom Sawyer*. Stephen King releases his inner fears with words that shock, scare and terrorize. King's make-believe world is but a way to escape the terrors of reality. King told *60 Minutes* in 1998, "We make up horrors to cope with the real ones."

TRAIT ANALYSIS. This book will analyze the behaviors and traits to isolate any and all similarities and differences that appear to have contributed to literary success. The areas explored will be: ***drive, self-esteem, imagination, dysfunctions, hyper-activity, optimism, superstition, risk-taking, charisma, perfectionism, rebellion, tenacity, insecurity, mania,*** and ***vision.*** A surprising number of the subjects possessed all, and most had at least half. Virtually all were egotists. Most were raging optimists and defiant renegades who resisted all forms of conformity. Many were insecure but never allowed it to become debilitating. Most were charismatic and all lived well outside the box.

LUCIDITY & DEMENTIA. Anyone who has ever suffered a panic attack, bipolar symptoms, mania, hyper-activity or bizarre dysfunctional behaviors or shock know that when in a euphoric or elevated state the brain is more aware and capable. Most of these subjects found themselves in such a state one or more times in their frenetic lives. Most were manic and nearly half had symptoms of manic-depression. Almost all had some type of compulsion, obsession, or excessive urge. Dostoevsky 's epilepsy lent itself to many flights of fantasy that appear to have lead to periods of enlightenment. When they didn't they led to debilitating depression. Epilepsy, manic-depression, and risk-taking due to high testosterone (Big T personality types) have all been tied to creativity by the medical community.

Balzac, Twain Hemingway, and Plath admitted to being more lucid when at the very brink. Dostoevsky was more creative when in the horrible throws of an epileptic seizure. Innovative insight lives right at the edge of abnormality. When a person is at that critical point they are often more lucid in a kind of surrealistic way. At the very edge of sanity lies a netherland that can be a scary place. Instant articulation is possible and great insight is possible.

Many of the world's creative geniuses like Sigmund Freud, Carl Jung, Nikola Tesla, Buckminster Fuller, and Walt Disney are testimony to the above. All were in the throws of a emotional breakdown when they made their greatest discoveries. Freud had a nervous relapse when he wrote his landmark work *The Interpretation of Dreams*, and Jung was in a "psychotic state" when he wrote, *Symbols of Transformation* (1913). Alfred Lord Tennyson wrote, "All at once out of the intensity and confused state came the clearest of the clearest, the surest of the surest, and weirdest of the weirdest" (Pickover 271). T.S. Eliot admitted to unique lucidity while recovering from a nervous breakdown during his writing of the classic *The Waste Land.* Lord Byron wrote, "I have a chaos of the mind."

Twain's first book was a by-product of his suicide attempt after being fired from the *San Francisco Morning Call* newspaper. Tesla was in a state of reverie and having a nervous breakdown when he conceived the idea for alternating current and the induction engine. He wrote, "The idea came to me like a flash of lightning...ideas came to me in an interrupted stream." (Landrum 1996 pg. 265).

As mentioned psychotherapist Carl Jung wrote of discovering his most important ideas while in the throws of breakdown. In 1913 he said he was in a "psychotic state" after his break with Freud and had an "intense visionary experience." During this period he conceived the *Collective Unconscious, Active Imagination, Syzygy, Archetypes, Synchronicities,* and the *Personality Types.* Jung said he period transformed him and was "horrible, insightful, and transforming but the most important in my life, in them everything essential was decided" (Storr 92). In a more prophetic moment he said, "One must have chaos to give birth to a shooting star."

Virginia Woolf was interred in an insane asylum when she wrote, *The Voyage Out* (1915). She lived the balance of her life in mortal fear of going back there. Lucidity of ideas and interplay can be found in her work, especially many autobiographical streams of consciousness. She wrote in her journal, "Things seem clear, sane, comprehensible." Her words offer insight into that world on the edge. She said, "I find myself in a state of vibrating." Another line went, "one's lowest ebb is nearest true vision." On writing *The Waves* (1931) she said, "In the lava of madness I found my characters."

CHAOS & CREATIVITY. Chaos can have an enormous impact on the insight of a person, especially those seething with important messages to impart. Eugene O'Neill was a college dropout, transient bum, and alcoholic but when he contracted tuberculosis at 24 he found himself in a sanitarium where he reflected on his life of drunken excess and non-productivity. He said, "I thought about my life for the first time...the inactivity forced me to mental activity" (*IBD* Duff 7-22-99). He was the recipient of four Pulitzer Prizes and one Nobel Prize for Literature. Victor Hugo was arrested for adultery and the trauma became the genesis for *Les Miserables.* He was inspired to cry out against an unfair judicial system.

Such visits to the bottom often mold a person for the tough trip to the top. After one looks in the mirror and sees mortality staring back they come away with an altered perspective on the meaning of life. Suddenly the journey is taken with more temerity and panache. As the story goes what doesn't kill you is destined to make you better. This is certainly validated by the high frequency of near-death experiences and near-mental collapses experienced by these great writers. The traumas left them stronger than before the debacle, more resilient, and fearless. With fewer crises it is quite likely they would have been also-rans in the creative world.

INTENSITY & CREATIVITY. The rabid intensity of these visionaries was amazing. They were zealots living as if double-parked on the highway of life. When the doors were closed they knocked them down. When criticized they assumed it was the carriers, not the message that was at fault. Many lived on the edge more lunatic than normal but that is the nature of innovation. They were renegades looking for a comfortable abode. Not one of these subjects lived or wrote within conventional bounds. Leonard Woolf described his wife Virginia's intensity as "the inspiration of genius and madness." He said, "Out of the sixteen hours of her working day Virginia worked fifteen and I guess she dreamed about writing most of the time when she was asleep."

THEY AVOIDED EXPERTS LIKE A PLAGUE. The literary genius is never too concerned with keeping up with the Jones's. Money is seldom a factor in their actions and they find the pack and head elsewhere. Most had to deal with rejection on a daily basis but refused to believe it was valid. When publishers wrote "not acceptable, worthless or too intellectual" or "without literary merit" they were never deterred from their mission. This is not possible for those not armed with a resilient self-esteem or indomitable will. An awesome optimism pervaded their spirit and allowed them to survive rebuffs that would have driven lesser types into booze. Stephen King wrote six novels before being published. Virginia Woolf wrote for twenty years before being published and her first novel went through numerous drafts over seven years. George Bernard Shaw wrote six novels all summarily rejected as "awful," and eight plays that were all rejected as unacceptable. On average these seventeen were in their thirties by the time they were published and in their forties before realizing and real fame. Despite such a long gestation period none quit. Anne Rice wrote for twenty years without being published but never considered quitting and Dr. Seuss wrote diligently and was in his fifties before he was acclaimed for *Cat in the Hat*.

SYNTHESIS TO SUCCESS

Woolf wrote, "I have the feelings of a woman but only the language of a man." This offers some insight into her need to live outside predetermined gender roles, which contributed to her great success as a writer. She was able to see the world from both perspectives – to be what she was and also what she was not. The experiences gave her tremendous flexibility.

Those able to synthesize into multiple dimensions of their personality tend to be special. They are more adaptable and the flexibility bodes well for a trip in a dynamic environment because the terrain is constantly changing. Those not able to function relative to the conditions are least able to succeed.

The impatient individual must learn to suffer fools. Overachievers must learn to deal with underachievers. The Type A who must deliver on time needs to relax and learn patience. Those individuals with such ability tend to be more successful. Recent research validates the importance of bing what one is and also what they are not. Margaret Thatcher was highly feminine but called the Iron Lady. Why? Because the Russians saw her exhibiting male-like traits that were not like they perceived women.

Less creative people tend to more one-dimensional types. There is nothing wrong with that except they are less capable of dealing with change and tend to function poorly in adversarial environments. Multi-dimensional personalities tend to be able to extrovert even if they are introverted. Such people are able to rationalize logically even if they have a propensity for more feeling or emotional decisions. And the risk-averse are able to take calculated risks.

Consider Dr. Seuss, a visionary incapable of even balancing a checkbook but when it came to his work he was an obsessive perfectionist. His wife Helen said, "He would write 200 words to salvage four." He once turned down 80 different shades of green for a parrot drawing. What does this indicate? He was able to adroitly flip-flop between dimensions of behavior on command and that is what made him great.

SYNTHESIS TO SUCCESS

Creative individuals are more likely to have the strengths of their own gender but those of the other. They escape rigid gender role stereotyping and tend to androgyny and seem to harbor opposite tendencies on the continuum between extraversion and introversion." (Csikszentmihalyi *Creativity* (1996 65-71)

PERSONALITY CONTINUUM. On the personality continuum of extroversion and introversion those in the eightieth percentile of introversion are best served to spend 80% of their time alone or with things. Those scoring at the 80% percentile of extroversion are best served to spend 80% of their time with people since that is how they are energized. Introverts are energized within and with ideas. Extroverts are energized through personal interactions and externally. There is no right or wrong, but creative geniuses appear to have a superior ability for synthesizing and capable of functioning at various places regardless of their normal preference.

One of the more bizarre examples of a writer capable of living at extremes is George Bernard Shaw. He was a paradox in that he had but three years of formal schooling but molded himself into one of Europe's most erudite men. He was also pathologically shy to the degree that he once spent four years alone reading in the British Museum. He was a loner who lived at home with his mother. But when his first six novels and eight plays were rejected he started lecturing to make himself appear an expert to gain respect and mostly to get his work accepted. It worked! Imagine a shy introvert making 1000 speeches. But had he not altered his persona from an introverted writer to an extroverted intellectual playwright it is highly unlikely he would have had a word created – *Shavian* - to describe his methodology.

University of Chicago psychologist Mihalyi Csikszentmihalyi found a similar propensity in 91 subjects studied for his book on *Creativity* (1996). His subjects included Jonas Salk and Linus Pauling. He wrote: (Csikszentmihalyi 1996 pgs. 60-65)

> *The ability to move from one trait to its opposite is part of the general condition of psychic complexity ... creative individuals seem to have relatively complex personalities. They contain contradictory extremes having the ability to move from one extreme to another without inner conflict. Creative people seem to harbor opposite tendencies and express both traits at the same time.*

These visionaries had a propensity for living outside just one dimension of personality. Despite being the quintessential intuitive visionary Ayn Rand spent thirteen years writing her classic *Atlas Shrugged.* She spent two years writing John Galt's radio speech. Hemingway was similar. His son said he rewrote *The Old Man & the Sea* two hundred times despite his big picture view of the world. Woolf had a similar proclivity in that she was highly intuitive, and wrote in her journal that she hated detail with a passion, but when writing her first novel *The Voyage Out* (1915) wrote draft after draft, burning some and rewriting others over many years.

This dichotomy of style separates geniuses from the norm. In this world introverts extrovert, feelers think, visionaries can deal with detail, and the fearful are fearless. The eighty-two percent who were Type A's were impatient to a fault but were able to be patient if the situation dictated. The ability to tap into their opposite gender was also prevalent in Christie, Woolf, Rand, and Rice – all highly androgynous. Conversely, many of the male subjects preferred the company of women and were often described as exhibiting feminine traits. This was true of Balzac, Shaw, Camus, Campbell, and Fleming. Csikszentmihalyi described such behavior as:

> ***Perhaps the most important duality that the creative persons are able to integrate is being open and receptive on the one hand and hard-driving on the other ... When an introvert learns to experience the world as an introvert it is as if he or she discovered a whole new missing dimension of the world."*** (*Creativity* 1996 pgs 360-362)

TIME LINE FOR SUCCESS

The one overriding pattern found in these subjects was their ability to stay the course (see Table 4). The average age for embarking on a writing career was age twenty-one. They averaged age 32 by the time they finally got published and were 42 before producing their greatest work.

The intervening years were ones of struggle and constant rejection. Only after fame hit did they get their early work published although Shaw was never able to despite George Orwell calling them his best work. He was 47 before *Man and Superman (1903)* was produced and 57 when his masterpiece *Pygmalion* hit the stage. Stephen King began submitting articles to magazines in his teens, but had his first six novels summarily rejected. Rice spent fifteen years dealing with rejection before success hit.

Shaw, Virginia Woolf and Ian Fleming waited the longest to find success. All had spent twenty years in preparation. Despite writing a novel at age eleven Woolf was 33 before producing her first book *The Voyage Out*. She was 45 when *To the Lighthouse* was published in 1927. Fleming was 49 when *From Russia with Love* was published in 1957. Dr. Seuss fifty-three when *Cat in the Hat* hit the bookstores in 1957. Mark Twain was 49

INTRODUCTION

when *Huckleberry Finn* was published and Joseph Campbell was 45 when *The Hero With a Thousand Faces* appeared in 1949. Two of the most famous works in this book, books widely acclaimed as true masterpieces, were published when the authors were 58 and 54 respectively – Dostoevsky's *The Brother's Karamazov* and Hemingway's *The Old Man & the Sea.*

Stephen King, Hemingway and Agatha Christie were famous at the youngest age. King was 27 when *Carrie* hit, Hemingway thirty on publication of *A Farewell to Arms* (1929), and Dame Agatha Christie was 29 when her *The Mysterious Affair at Styles* was published in 1920. Dostoevsky first achieved acclaim as a writer with potential when 24 with *Poor Folks.* Danielle Steel was only 24 when her first romance novel *Going Home* was published in 1971. The youngest to produce a novel was Virginia Woolf who at age 10 wrote *A Cockney's Farming Experiences.*

Table 4 will offer some insight into their work and the elapsed time between their first decision to write and their first success and ultimately to their greatest success.

Table 4

TIME LINE FOR LITERARY SUCCESS

ARTIST (AGE) 1ST WRITING	FIRST LITERARY SUCCESS (Pub Date, Age & Yrs to get published)	BEST WORK (Pub Date, Age & Yrs to get published)
BALZAC (22)	Le Dernier Chouans (1829) Age 30 [8 YEARS]	The Human Comedy (1841) Age 42 [12 YEARS]
CAMPBELL (24)	A Navajo War Ceremonial (1943) Age 39 [14 YEARS]	Hero with a Thousand Faces 1949 Age 45 [20 YEARS]
CHRISTIE (23)	The Affair at Styles (1920) Age 29 [6 YEARS]	The Murder of Roger Akroyd (1926) age 36 [13 YEARS]
CAMUS (16)	The Stranger (1942 Age 29 [13 YEARS]	The Fall (1957) – Nobel Prize Age 44 [18 YEARS]
DOSTOEVSKY (21)	Poor Folks (1846) Age 24 [3 YEARS]	Crime & Punishment (1866) 44[23 Y] The Brothers Karamazov (1880)-58
FLEMING (21)	Casino Royale (1952) Age 44 [23 YEARS]	From Russia with Love (1957) Age 49 [28 YEARS]
DR. SEUSS (16)	Mulberry Street (1937) Age 33 [17 YEARS]	The Cat in the Hat (1957) Age 53 [37 YEARS]
HEMINGWAY (24)	In Our Time (1925) Age 26 [2 YEARS]	A Farewell to Arms (1929)–30 [6 YR] Old Man & Sea (1953) Nobel – 54
KING (15)	Carrie (1974) Age 27 [12 YEARS]	The Shining (1977) Movie Age 30 [15 YEARS]
PLATH (14)	Colossus (1959) Age 27 [13 YEARS]	The Bell Jar (1961) – 29 [21 YEARS] The Ariel Poems (1965) – 33 Pulitzer
MICHENER (40)	Tales of South Pacific (1948) Age 41 [1 YEAR]	South Pacific (1949) Age 42 [2 YEARS]
RAND (22)	We the Living (1936) Age 31 [9 YEARS]	Atlas Shrugged (1953) Objectivism Age 48 [26 YEARS]
RICE (11)	Interview with Vampire (1976) Age 35 [24 YEARS]	The Vampire Chronicles (1986) Age 45 [34 YEARS]
SHAW (23)	Widower's Houses (1892) Age 36 [24 YEARS]	Pygmalion (1913) – 57 [34 YEARS] Saint Joan (1923) – 67 Nobel
STEEL (23)	Going Home (1971) Age 24 [13 YEARS]	The Promise (1979) Age 32 [9 YEARS]
TWAIN (28)	Jumping Frog Calaveras (1866) Age 32 [1 YEAR]	Huckleberry Finn (1884) Age 49 [21 YEARS]
WOOLF (11)	The Voyage Out (1915) Age 33 [22 YEARS]	To the Lighthouse (1927) Age 45 [34 YEARS]
17 ARTISTS Avg Age=21	AVERAGE AGE = 32 11 YEARS TO PUBLICATION	AVERAGE AGE = 42 21 YEARS TO BEST WORK

DAME AGATHA CHRISTIE
QUEEN OF DETECTIVE MYSTERIES
b. Torquay, Sept. 15, 1890
d. Wallingford, Jan. 12, 1976

SELF-MADE MISTRESS OF MYSTERY

GENRE & INNOVATION
MYSTERY NOVELS & PLAYS VIA ENTERTAINING PLOTMAKING

MOTTO
"Plays are much more fun than books" - "I regard my work of no importance. I simply set out to entertain. I'm an incredible sausage machine."

GREATEST WORKS
Murder of Roger Ackyroyd (1926)
Murder on the Orient Express (1934)
The Mousetrap (1952)

HONORS/AWARDS
One billion books sold in English; another billion in 103 foreign languages; *The Mousetrap* was most successful play in history of London theater

ECCENTRICITIES
Pathologically reclusive probably bipolar, mysterious disappearance at 35 discovered living alone under alias (husband's mistresses name) in remote spa

LIFE CRISES
Father died when 11; husband's deceit led to breakdown, mysterious disappearance and amnesia state

METAMORPHOSES
Sister Madge bet Agatha she couldn't write a detective story Agatha succeeded with: *The Affair at Styles*

1

Dame Agatha Christie - Mystery

Writers are Made - Not Born

"I regard my work of no importance. I am an incredible sausage machine"

IS TALENT INHERITED OR ACQUIRED?

Determining if success is based on nature or nurture is difficult at best and impossible at worst. But most great writers seem to agree that they were not born with any talent for writing. Balzac firmly believed he molded himself into a great novelist and the data suggests his appraisal was correct. Ayn Rand was adamant about her lack of innate writing skill. In *We the Living* she wrote, "no one is born with any kind of talent and therefore, every skill has to be acquired. Writers are made not born. To be exact writers are self-made." Michener said "I have little skill in psychology of characters, plotting, scenes, symbolism" (Michener 1991 p. 314). Stephen King said, "writers are made not born." Psychologist Alfred Adler validated these assessment with his aphorism, "Anyone can learn anything" (Hoffman p. 133). Serial autobiographer Maya Angelou says, "I am absolutely terrified when I get in a room and look at that yellow pad. I have fooled everybody. Everybody thinks I can write" (Shuker 1990).

Agatha Christie's life and work confirm Adler's admonition "anyone can learn anything." Christie had no formal schooling. She was home-schooled since her parents believed girls should be groomed for motherhood not, a career. This led to Christie being self-taught. As a child she was lonely leading to a voracious reading habit. Like many writers in this work she admitted to writing her first books with little knowledge of her craft and it wasn't until after her sixth book was she steeped in

35

the art of the profession. Her first was written on a bet with her sister Madge, who told her she couldn't concoct a story that she could not unravel. The result was *The Mysterious Affair at Styles* (1920). This first novel took seven years to get published but was the genesis of a long and illustrious career in writing.

Christie was introspective and self-effacing. In her memoirs she wrote, "I regard my work as of no importance. I simply set out to entertain. Once I've been dead for ten years I'm sure nobody will have heard of me" (Robyns 1978 pg. 25). She was wrong; and died the wealthiest writer in the long and celebrated history of English literature.

How could a woman with no formal education, no experience, no formal training, no connections, and an average intellect become a legend in her lifetime? For the same reason many successful people gain fame and fortune. They don't know enough to fail. But Agatha had those qualities discussed throughout this book – tenacity, imagination, passion, drive, temerity and out of the box divergence to rise to the top.

What role did talent play? None! Why? Because talent has little to do with the process, a fact lost on many. And it also didn't have much to do with their IQ, pedigrees, social-contacts, or the amount of money in their war chest. There are millions of talented and bright people living on welfare. And there are many MENSA members and Ivy League graduates working in bookstores. Offspring of eminent people often have trouble dealing with the expectations laid on them by their peers. One reason is they have not had to fight and struggle as much as others and great wins are born of great struggles. If it is too easy it is seldom instructive.

FAME & FORTUNE – NURTURING STYLE. Christie's 100 books have sold one billion copies in English and another billion in 103 foreign languages, a number exceeding the Bard. Her style and success elevated her to the pinnacle of the world of letters. She merely found a niche that had appeal, and pursued it with panache and elegance. The combination made her rich and famous. She wrote *The Mousetrap,* the longest running play in the history of the London theater – a non-stop

38 year run. This simple lady had ten books made into movies and left the world with a $50 million net worth.

In 1955 Dame Christie had the unprecedented success of seeing her name on three marquees in London theaters. She is the only playwright in the long storied life of the London theater to ever have three plays running simultaneously - *Spider's Web*, *Witness for the Prosecution*, and *The Mousetrap*. The Queen of Crime was the most prolific mystery writer in the history of detective stories. She had one new book published each year for 57 consecutive years. Her astounding output consisted of: 150 short stories, 78 crime novels, 26 plays, 7 Mallowan novels, 1 book of poems, and 1 children's book. One London critic wrote, "All she had to do in those last years was to rewrite a page from a seed catalogue and it would have sold. She had become a legend in her lifetime" (Robyn 1978 pg. 24). She had done it on her own and with no training.

THE HISTORY OF MYSTERY

Despite limited schooling, Dame Agatha Christie learned important lessons about her craft from role models and mythical mentors from books. She adored Charles Dickens, Graham Greene and Arthur Conan Doyle - the creator of Britain's master sleuth Sherlock Holmes. Her American father made sure she read Edgar Allen Poe, the father of the very first detective mystery – *The Murders in the Rue Morgue* (1841). Poe originated the "classic form" of the detective genre and was a big influence on Christie's style.

Poe was one of the pioneers in the genre. Soon after came Mary Roberts Rhinehart followed by the master Arthur Conan Doyle. But it would be Agatha Christie who would help raise the medium of the "locked room story" to the pinnacle of popularity. The hard-boiled detective was one of her contrivances and the Belgium egghead Hercules Poirot would become known worldwide. In mid-career she introduced Miss Marple as the female equivalent of Poirot. Others who made contributions to the detective mystery were Dashiell Hammett with his Sam Spade books. Earl Stanley Gardner introduced Perry Mason. Ian Fleming gave us James Bond. And Mickey Spillane created the macho detective Mike Hammer. Other master sleuths in the genre were Ellery Queen (a pseudonym for the creations of Frederic Dannay and Manfred Lee). John D. McDonald, John Grisham and Tom Clancy would introduce contemporary Perry Masons – legal beagle sleuths as savvy detectives. All had a consistent format, a suspenseful story, and unexpected twist that would ultimately be unraveled by an ingenious private-eye.

As a child Agatha Christie adored Sherlock Holmes as a child as well as Charles Dicken's *Bleake House.* Through these authors, she learned the importance of timelessness. The Christie formula was without any topical settings and like Disney, in his animated cartoons, they could be reproduced in any era. This allowed her to cross many eras and transcend generational gaps, an important factor in her long life of writing. This approach kept her books alive for adaptation to TV, movies, and the theater. In her favorite mystery, *Bleake House* she found a role model for Poirot, Sergeant Bucket. Bucket would sire a long line of progeny for Agatha. She also borrowed Dicken's Estella from *Great Expectations,* and she would also adopt the theme of adopted children inheriting the murderous instincts of their real parents.

Suspense fiction evolved out of detective fiction. Fleming used a similar tack in having 007 save the day at the 11th hour. Such protagonists have a prescient intuition allowing them to see through culprits and their dastardly acts. Other superheroes in a savior role were Batman, Green Hornet and Captain Marvel. They always outwit, outfight, and outlast the sociopathic villains. The dark deeds of the culprits in mysteries are central to the making of a hero. We must remember that most of her work was developed during the Cold War between Capitalism and Communism. Surrealism reigns supreme in such a world that spawns great superheroes like Bond, Batman, and Poirot.

Christie's innovative contribution was suspenseful endings that shocked the reader. Her appeal was not the story line. It was the ending. British literary critic Cyril Hare said, "Her formula is the end result is impossible. It is only when you make the closest inspection that you can detect the tiny fallacy which falsifies the equation." (Robyns 1978 pg. 24) The Duchess of Death created two characters that who took on lives of their own. Belgian sleuth Hercules Poirot was a diminutive intellectual detective with an egg shaped head and mustache. Having bequeathed him with the name Hercules she was demonstrating a wry sense of irony in that he was more brain than brawn. He can be found in one-third of her mysteries with her female intellectual Miss Marple in twelve.

SELF-MADE NAÏVE NOVELIST & PLAYWRIGHT

Lack of formal training not only didn't hurt her it was probably contributed to her eminent success. She wasn't so steeped in how a mystery should be written, but more interested in altering the standard approach. In this way she was a maverick. Ignorance is often a benefit when one is breaking new ground. She wasn't so trained to follow any given format to deviate from the norm, so she was able to write outside the box. She had no fear of violating convention, since she didn't know of convention. In other words, tradition was never an inhibiting agent for the Queen of Mystery.

One experience did help young Agatha Miller. Her mother saw fit to send her to Paris to a finishing school to groom her for marital bliss. This training groomed Agatha for the glamorous parlors in which much of her work takes place. Finishing school gave her insight into sitting-room etiquette and social decorum, an environment replete with butlers, chefs, and chambermaids. Th drawing room was central to the Christie mystery and brought her a diverse audience who escaped a humdrum existence into a world to which they aspired.

Agatha Miller volunteered for medical work during World War I. She was assigned to the medical dispensary as a pill dispenser. This was another propitious experience as it gave her insight into how to kill without resorting to guns. Christie detested any kind of violence or weapons of destruction. Pills and poisons were ideal instruments for an overt pacifist to use to kill off their victims. Bullets, guns, and knives were *verboten* in her world of mysterious murder.

Christie had prescient insight into her own limitations. She avoided writing about anything beyond her area of expertise. This included guns and international arenas that she knew were beyond her purview. She admitted, "I could never manage miners talking in a pub because I don't know what miners talk about in pubs." But the English drawing room, parties, and the diabolical social interactions rampant in British society that is so steeped in tradition was her forte.

Early shyness intensified as she aged. Christie began life as a loner but ended up a recluse. As a youth, shyness led her to the safety of books where she escaped into fantasy. A precocious child, she taught herself to read at five. Her mother was well-read and encouraged her reading. Imagination was esteemed in the Miller household and she was encouraged to use it freely and openly as a child. This early freedom to explore and fantasize was a trait found in most of these subjects as well as others like Isadora Duncan and Oprah.

Agatha Miller had an older brother and sister but she was a caboose and was raised effectively as an only child since they were off to boarding school by the time she came along. They functioned more as mentors than siblings. Her dad died when she was eleven leaving her even more alone with her books.

WRITERS: BORN OR BRED? Harvard research psychologist Jerome Kagan says, "No human quality is beyond change...the emotional lessons of childhood can have a profound impact on temperament either amplifying or muting an innate predisposition" (Landrum 1996 pg. 30). Daniel Goleman in *Emotional Intelligence* (1995) described emotions, not IQ, as the true measure of success in life. Frank Barron studied personality for over thirty years and found, "For certain intrinsic creativity, a specific minimum IQ is necessary to engage in the activity, but beyond that minimum, which is often surprisingly low, creativity has little correlation with scores on IQ tests" (Landrum 1996 pg. 40). Washington University Medical researcher Dr. C. Robert Cloninger says, "Character is strictly uninherited. It is shaped by a person's maturity, goal-directedness, and sense of values." Mark Rosenzweig, a researcher at the University of California, "Positive experiences alter brain size" (Hutchison 1986 p. 36), one finding that supports Christie's self-made success since she was reared in an opulent setting that enhanced her set of experience.

EXPERIENCE VS IQ. These seventeen subjects were bright but not brilliant. Tenacity and temerity were far more important to their success than their intellect. Consider Stephen King and Danielle Steel. Are they erudite? Not hardly! But they work prodigiously at their craft and their cathartic insight and inspirations are their tool. The brightest subjects were: Rand, Shaw, Woolf, and Campbell, with Rand and Plath sporting the highest IQ's.

Shaw was the most articulate, Rand the brightest, Campbell the best read, Camus, Plath and Dr. Seuss the most formally educated. Three had masters degrees in literature - Campbell, Michener and Rice. The least educated and most demeaned were ironically the greatest storytellers - Twain, Christie, Woolf, King and Steel. Both Christie and Woolf were home-schooled and both were highly influenced by literary fathers. Woolf was highly influenced by her father and husband, each contributing enormously to her vision, precocity and articulation talents. All agreed they mastered their art by engaging in it and then writing, writing, and writing, and then rewriting.

DYSFUNCTIONAL PERSONALITIES. Christie was a Type A workaholic who overcame deficiencies through sheer effort. She wrote and wrote, and when not writing was busily concocting ideas and contriving mysteries. She was not unique in this as Shaw, Steel, Plath, Twain and King were infamous for writing ideas on napkins, on train tickets, or in Steel's on mirrors all over her San Francisco mansion.

These writers were obsessive-compulsive, manic and into excess. Many wrote to escape a tragic personal life. Balzac trained for the bar with a law degree but refused to practice anything but rhetorical history. Dostoevsky was a military engineer who refused to do anything but write. Twain and Hemingway were both journalists turned authors. Joseph Campbell was a schoolteacher with an obsession for mythical and cultural heritage. TB kept French philosopher Camus from becoming a college professor just as the rigors of English lit kept Dr. Seuss from a similar calling. Music actually played a larger role than writing in some. Shaw, Michener, King and Christie wanted to pursue a career in the performing arts or theater with Christie longing to become a concert pianist. Most were Machiavellian, and all but two were live-on-the-edge rebels. Passion pervaded the souls of all.

CHRISTIE'S CONTRIBUTION TO THE GENRE

The Madam of Mysteries was a masterful storyteller and plot maker. She had a penchant for making murder into an acceptable parlor game like chess. She mesmerized readers with her unexpected endings that had a sensational twist. This would prove to be her signature style and contribution to the genre. Her surrealistic style came from an inner need to escape reality in her work as well as her life.

Christie never took herself or her writing too seriously even after she had achieved worldwide acclaim. She described herself as an "an incredible sausage machine," a writer that just cranked out words without regard for their literary merit. But millions of faithful fans came to adore her work. They escaped into her mysteries allowing them to forget their troubles. The mistress of whodunit mysteries was prolific and that defined her more than most any other factor. She concocted one new mystery each year for 57 straight years. Many years she published as many as two or three.

Christie domesticated murder for audiences looking to escape the Great Depression and then the Cold War. She created fast-paced, easy to read mysteries that took little effort on the part of the reader. Christie was superb at concocting clues around a little suspected villain who was finally caught by an erudite detective. This formula worked in an era of threatened nuclear annihilation where readers wanted to relax into a fantasy world and leave their fears outside the pages. Her characters were never complex and were grounded in reality. They were highly predictable but her endings were not. That is where she became innovative. Her plots were written to entertain, not to inform. And they were never negative. Even her killers were light and frivolous; a necessary component in a world worried about a potential apocalypse.

WRITING AS CATHARSIS

Agatha Christie lived a fantasy life. She was pathologically shy and escaped the need to interact by creating her own drama. She wrote about the life she knew and made up within that arena that was mysterious, possible, and entertaining. Dame Christie was a recluse. When she became a household name she avoided the press like the plague. And she adorned her characters as she would like to have dressed, had them dancing in venues she feared, and had them engage in passionate relationships that were beyond those she would dare. All her fictional characters were steeped in the cultured British life that she knew and loved.

Fantasies were her forte. They made her happy. She once told a reporter that she liked to draw her plots while munching on apples in the bathtub, a telling venue where she could be warm, safe but free without clothes or outside influence. It was through words that she could escape into her make-believe world. In her autobiographical work *Unfinished Portrait* (1934), her alter ego Celia says, "fairy stories were her passion. Stories of real-life children did not interest her" (Gill 1990 pg. 207).

ESCAPE FROM REALITY. Only once did Agatha dare venture out into that surreal world of dance and flamboyant lifestyle of her imagination. And when she got there she came close to being destroyed and never again ventured out into that enigmatic world. It was 1926 and Christie was living a quiet life in a British suburb as mother, housewife, and budding writer. But one day in mid-December she disappeared without a trace. Hints of foul play made her disappearance headlines news.

The Queen of Mysteries had just released her sixth mystery – *The Murder of Roger Ackroyd* - a book that would one day be called her best work. Her mysterious disappearance would have done justice to a character from one of her books. The police were concerned when the 35 year-old's car was found abandoned near a lake. The media would later characterize her disappearance as temporary amnesia, but that was only after the family became concerned when the police were about to ask them to pay for the multi-million pound country-wide manhunt.

Christie disappeared on Dec. 5, 1926. The next morning the headlines screamed, "Woman novelist vanishes! Clothes in abandoned motor car." Weeks later she was discovered living a lavish life of a raconteur in a remote Northern England Spa. She had taken a pseudonym and had ignored the headlines that described her possible murder.

The story is made more interesting because her dashing husband Colonel Archie Christie was the suspected villain. It was known that he was in love with a younger woman and was trying to extract him from his marriage with Agatha. In fact he had told her he was announcing his betrothal to one Miss Nancy Neele the very night of Agatha's mysterious disappearance. Weeks later Agatha would be found living under an assumed name – Miss Teresa Neels – in a remote spa the Harrogate Hydro Hotel in Northern England. In the meantime the police had mounted a nationwide search for her dead body. Archie Christie was the principle suspect.

When an anonymous note to the police turned up her whereabouts, they found her living under an alias, the identical name as her adversary Miss Neele. She had been living secretly in the hotel for weeks while headlines screamed of her murder. Did the Mistress Mystery set up her husband? Or did she flip out and end up in a self-deluded state that psychiatrists label a "conversion? Was she getting revenge, lost in reverie, or in an amnesic state as she told the police? Amnesia appears the least likely scenario. This lonely reclusive woman was about to lose a dashing husband to a young lady and was devastated. In any case she probably wasn't responsible for her actions due to her state of anxiety, but she certainly caused a furor that the police didn't find amusing. The whole episode was a scandal for some time.

METAMORPHOSES

The Mystery Queen first considered writing during a bout with influenza. While bedridden her mother assigned her the task of writing a story. This piqued Agatha Miller's interest in writing. After her father's death she and her distraught mother took a long trip to Cairo, Egypt. On their return she wrote about the experience calling the story "The House of Beauty." It was never published, but set the stage for her transformation when her sister bet her she couldn't write a crime story that she couldn't unravel. This proved to be the genesis of the Christie mystique. She wrote it in just three weeks but *Mysterious Affair at Styles* (1920) would take another four years to get published.

This first book made its way through six different publishing houses before it was finally read and accepted by John Lane of Bodley Head publishing. The book had been lying on his desk for eighteen months before he got around to contacting Mrs. Christie. This book was about a nurse during the war and featured the birth of Hercules Poirot - an unlikely protagonist hero. Poirot was a strange contrast to Agatha's dashing husband Colonel Archie Christie.

She had married Colonel Christie impulsively on Christmas Eve 1914. They had a daughter and lived an uneventful life in a London suburb that infamous December 1926 when he told her he was in love with another woman.

Christie earned but 26 pounds from the serialization rights of her first book. The money was never important to Christie except to buy homes. She owned eight. Christie signed a contract stipulating no royalties until after 2500 copies were sold. It only sold 2000 but she was on her way.

ECCENTRICITIES

The Duchess of Death was easily as mysterious as her multitude of villains. She had more idiosyncrasies than her sociopathic villains. She was fiercely independent, strong-willed, and reclusive. A member of the cast asked her once while rehearsing, "Do you mind if I change this line?" Replying from the audience Agatha yelled out, "Yes I do mind!"

She was unconventional to a fault and spoke of writing while munching on apples in the bathtub. Truth is often stranger than fiction and her disappearance validates this. Her daughter was seven when her car was found abandoned by the lake. The night she disappeared was a day she had met her mother-in-law for lunch. Colonel Christie's mother didn't suspect her son's dubious actions but noticed that Agatha was not wearing her wedding ring. When asked about the ring Agatha just "gazed into space and giggled." That night Agatha left her daughter in the care of servants and drove off alone. It was either a masterly planned revenge or psychotic event.

LIFE CRISES

Agatha Miller's first and foremost crisis was losing her father at eleven. Her traditional mother had told Agatha that formal schooling was not for girls despite the fact her older sister had been given a traditional education. Her mother had told her that too much education was bad for a girls brain and eyesight.

Her mother was permissive in many other ways. She allowed her great personal freedom to explore and live outside the bounds of normalcy. She was taught to sail and was often off to dangerous waters without supervision. Agatha was age 20 in 1911 when she was taken on her first airplane ride further testimony to early training for independence and self-reliance.

Her mother's death in 1926 coincided with her husband's betrayal and the release of what would become her greatest mystery. All together these three events evidently pushed her over the edge. It was her greatest trauma and was strangely left out of her autobiography and she refused to discuss the event the rest of her long life.

POLYPHASIC PERSONALITY

Literary geniuses balance many projects, and adroitly keep from dropping many. Christie had this ability. She balanced many plots in her head simultaneously and even those she didn't have time to develop were filed away for future use.

Multi-tasking keeps the creative interested and avoids boredom, which they cannot tolerate. Such people often are found listening to the radio, reading a magazine, while carrying on a lively conversation. Dame Christie once admitted to having 17 plots in her head that prompted English author Cecil Day Lewis to ask, "Would you sell me a few?" "Certainly not" she responded. "I intend to write them all myself." Another example of her polyphasia was her need to write in many disparate disciplines all at the same time – novels, plays, poems, romance novels, and one children's book.

CRITICAL ACCLAIM

The sincerest form of flattery in the world of letters is sales. Based on books purchased Agatha Christie was truly the Queen of Mystery if not the Queen of Fiction. She was one of the most prolific writers in history with 100 novels and plays to her credit. The Henry Holt Literary Review offered insight into her contributions saying, "She had careful access to all clues; heavy use of dialogue and lightning quick description; which reaches a fast-paced easy read with a constant moral framework. She allowed any character to be guilty, a precedent setting break with tradition." (Frank Magill Reviews 1994)

Christie received many accolades including her election as a Fellow in the Royal Society of Literature. She was given the New York Drama Critics Award for Best Foreign Play of 1955. Queen Elizabeth II knighted her in 1971 and after she became known as Dame Christie. Gillian Gill, writing for Magill Criticisms said, "Christie's unabashedly mass market art in its very contentlessness and anti-intellectualism resonates on the level of fantasy; therefore it is able to express powerful social and psychic movements."

Other literary critics were not as enthralled by her writing. Critic Edmund Wilson once wrote, "I did not care for Agatha Christie and I hope never to read another of her books." After reading one he concluded, "Her writing is a mawkishness and banality, which seem to me literally impossible to read." His friend Nabokov agreed saying "She is unreadable." Smithsonian writer Israel Shenker was more kind in 1990 on the 100th anniversary of her birth, "Agatha Christie has earned her royal rights to immortality."

SUCCESS OF A SELF-MADE WOMAN – What Can We Learn?

Agatha Christie is the quintessential self-made writer. She wasn't born with any special talent other than imagination and inquisitiveness. She was not blessed with super intelligence, had no formal education, and was not helped along by any mentoring or stewardship. The mystery queen created characters that she felt fit the situation, and created plots that intrigued her editors and readers. She opened her own doors and fought her own battles.

Dame Agatha had a prescient sense of life and portrayed it as if it were a chess game being played in an upper middle-class parlor. She deigned to make the game interesting by offering bizarre Machiavellian twists. Such writing demands the author begin with the answer and work to make it plausible and interesting. Christie is proof that there is little or no genetic predisposition to greatness. Her life and work validate early *success imprints* acquired early that molded her into a self-fulfilling adult with passion and perception.

Christie was programmed early to believe she could achieve. As a youngster she was allowed to explore in unknown venues where fantasy lives without fear of retribution. She admitted that her world was replete with a vivid imagination adorned with fairy tales. Such things allow us to reach the penthouse – she owned eight homes at one time - leaving those who bought into their *failure imprints* to live life in the outhouse.

Christie's work ethic was renowned. She told the media "I have stamina." She transformed a weakness, obsessive shyness, into an asset, by going within to find an outlet for her mental images. Her introversion became her strength since it allowed an introspective woman live a life as she wanted.

LITERARY GENIUS

Christie left plots lying around her houses on tables, in the bathroom and the kitchen. Perhaps her greatest talent was the ability to shock the reader by departing from consensus, often the sign of genius. She dared to be different and lived well outside convention. She offers credence to the aphorism that normal people create *normal success* and the abnormal create *abnormal success*. This can be seen in her most famous work *The Murder of Roger Ackroyd.* In her most famous work, she went well beyond convention by having the culprit be the storyteller. This infuriated the world's mystery writers but it made here successful. Critics cried foul. They said it was unfair to cast the villain as the author since the reader would be virtually unable to solve the mystery. The book became an instant best-seller. But headlines shrieked, "She has cheated ... she has broken the Detective Club rules...she hasn't played fair." The *Daily Stretch* wrote, "Tasteless, unforgivable let-down by a writer we had grown to admire."

Christie understood that innovation is little but *creative destruction.* She was always willing to destroy an old concept to launch a new one. Her dramatic masterpiece *The Mousetrap* (1952) gives credence to this principle as well as her last works where she decided to kill off both Hercule Poirot and Miss Marple so that these creations could never again be used after her death. This self-made writer had the insight of a master and the world of letters is better because of her work.

JAMES ALBERT MICHENER
TRANSIENT HISTORICAL NOVELIST
b. NY City Feb. 3, 1907
d. Austin, TX Oct. 16, 1997

TRANSIENCY & SUCCESS

DOMINANT GENRE & INNOVATION
Historical novels with imaginative characterizations

MOTTO
"Entertain and instruct via Honesty – Integrity – Industry"
"Write only for oneself. I never had a childhood and it would influence all I would write"

GREATEST WORKS
Tales of the South Pacific (1947)
The Bridges of Toki-ri (1953)
Hawaii (1959)

HONORS/AWARDS
Pulitzer Prize for Literature 1948 – *South Pacific*
Honorary Doctorates Miami and Nebraska Universities

LIFE CRISES
Illegitimacy and rejection led to a search for "my home."
Almost died in plane crash on New Caledonia Island

METAMORPHOSES
Walked away from New Caledonia Island crash at age 40 and said, "I'm going to spend the rest of my life as if I were a great man. Next day began writing *South Pacific* – his epiphany

ECCENTRICITIES
Vagabond and Type A workaholic, "social misfit" who admitted, "I'm a loner to an extent that would frighten other people. I have always thought of myself as a freak" (Michener 1993 p.viii)

JAMES MICHENER – Historical Novel

Transiency & Success

"By eighteen I had visited all but two states"

CREATIVE SUCCESS & EARLY TRANSIENCY

Michener was a citizen of the world. Not because he wanted to be, but because he had no parents or heritage and the distress, probably more unconscious than conscious, led him to an interminable search for the heritage of others. If he would be denied his own heritage he would find the roots of religion (The Source), Polynesia (Hawaii), cultures (Caribbean), and even outer space (Space).

Those not locked into one given venue tend to be more worldly than those reared in a highly structured environment. Lock your kid in a room and they will never get abducted, but they will never become worldly. They will find security comfortable, too comfortable to forage around in the Netherlands where all greatness is found. Out in the wilds is where fearlessness and innovation are born. Dealing with the unknown early in life arms one for comfort with ambiguity. Removal from safe havens is the one sure way of molding creativity. Michener is the poster boy for such creative inspiration.

TRAVEL & TRANSIENCY & CREATIVITY. Extreme transiency – moving or traveling - as was experienced by James Michener molds a fearless personality and a high propensity for creativity. Why? Because such people are imprinted with feelings of excitement in unknown terrain, while the security driven find such settings frightening. Those who have traveled extensively at a young age learn to thrive on the new. Those who have been over-sheltered fear the new. But it is apparent that in a dynamic world most things are new.

JAMES MICHENER

Michener was a vagabond almost from childhood. An unhappy childhood led him to leave his home in Doylestown, Pennsylvania and hitchhike to nowhere just so it was far away from a place he didn't want to be. He was searching for happiness, but his search led him to what he called, *The World is My* Home (12991) that was his memoir tribute to life on the road. The teenaged Michener left home and spent his life in a perpetual search for some tangible force that was not to be found as a foundling in Doylsetown.

What does travel or extreme transiency have to do with literary genius or creativity. A great deal! Success in the upper echelon no matter the discipline places an individual out in front of the pack with few support groups. Such a place demands a strong sense of self and comfort with ambiguity – the great unknown. When an individual has been in such a venue as a youngster they are far more capable of dealing with it as an adult.

Success has always been, and always will be more a function of inner strength than outer strength. Inner strength emanates from early conditioning and imprints that have left a positive experience, or at least a survival instinct. When a writer finds himself all alone without anyone to come to their aid, they will be forced to fall back on their own sense of self to face adversity. Children who have learned to deal with the foreign, the strange, the unknown or scary are being groomed to face such things later on his life. These seventeen were so conditioned, but few as much as Michener.

Another dimension of early travel and transiency is the fact such people are seldom content later in life to live in one place. They have itchy feet and move more than the average. In the case of authors they tend to write of life on the road as well as living such an existence. Consider the works of Balzac, Twain, Michener, Steel and King. All wrote of strange lands. Actually Twain, Steel and King write of virtually nothing but people out on the highways of life. Every one of Twain's books were based on new venues and read like travelogues. Michener wrote Caravan and The Drifters in addition to his obsession with foreign cultures and heritages.

What differentiates the transient from the protected? Those who have lived out on the road of life have learned to expect rejection, change, roadblocks, and the unexpected, all things encountered in the trek through adulthood. The new can be debilitating or exciting and the only difference in the perceptions appears to be early experiences. Dealing with the new is little more than experiencing the new and those with experience are better equipped than those without.

All innovation comes from living and creating outside the box and that demands early comfort with it. The world of creative writing is a place without guarantees and that is why being comfortable with ambiguity is critical to success in such venues. James Michener learned early to feel comfortable in places he didn't know and was never debilitated by them.

COMFORT WITH AMBIGUITY. How does one get comfortable with strange places? By seeing them as fun and positive not intimidating and negative. Early experiences in foreign venues can teach a child how to cope later in life. Without such experiences they will tend to fear them. Security is a matter of perception. The person raised without any experiences of the new and foreign will grow up fearing them. The child faced with such things early will look forward to them. Security is in the mind of the beholder. One person is devastated by a situation that another finds titillating. Such is the difference that can be imprinted in those who travel extensively early relative to those who live a sheltered life with no risk.

Michener lived in eight different houses on seven different streets before his teens. Contrast that with Margaret Mead who lived in sixty homes before she began school or Frank Lloyd Wright who lived in ten states before age ten. All of these individuals broke new ground as adults and their childhood experiences were just one of the things that gave them comfort with operating out in front of the pack.

Michener's unhappy childhood led to a hitchhiking obsession that kept him on the road except when he was in school. He began his marathon moves as he entered his teens and visited

New York City, Florida and Canada by age thirteen. By eighteen he had visited all but two states. Another example is Danielle Steel who attended schools in Manhattan, Switzerland, and Colorado. She spent her summers spent in Capri, Rome and Paris. She hated the life at the time but all these places are the scenes in her books. Stephen King lived in six states before age eleven. Albert Camus lived in five different foster homes. Mark Twain had worked in St. Louis, New York City, New Orleans, Cincinnati, and Nevada before age 21. Before 30 he had lived in San Francisco, and had visited Hawaii, South America, Europe and the Middle East.

How did vagabond lifestyle influence creativity in these highly disparate individuals? First it molded them to cope with the unknown and foreign. It taught them to deal with new friends, cultures and teachers, and equipped them with an indomitable resiliency. In many ways it armed them for outside threats.

Michener wrote in his memoirs, "The chief characteristic of my childhood was moving. By eighteen I had visited all but two states. By age forty I had worked in 130 sovereign nations" (Michener 1992 p. 437). It is apparent Michener was empowered by what he saw and refused to remain in any one place the rest of his long life. He learned to thrive on the novel.

OVER-PROTECTIVE MOTHERS –THE BANE OF CREATIVITY

Familiarity breeds security and the unknown instills coping. Why is the over-protective mother the bane of creativity? Because locking your child in a safe haven insures they will never face danger, get a bloody nose, or scuffed knees. It also insures they will never learn to cope with the vagaries of adulthood. Adversity is good as long as it doesn't do permanent damage or jeopardize life. In fact, the more dangerous the more learning that takes place. Parental protectiveness has a stifling affect on children that is not discovered until it is much too late. Children become security driven as a function of not being allowed to err. Mistakes are critical to learning and improving mo matter the venue. Over protection merely relegates an individual to seek secure harbors or grooms one for a life in the slow lane.   Employees and children are similar.   Neither will grow into self-sufficient adults if not allowed to err when young.

Many examples of this principle exist. Isadora Duncan lived in a different home every month in turn-of-the-century San Francisco and spoke extensively in her memoirs of roaming alone around the streets at a young age. In her 1926 autobiography she attributed this early freedom to her creation of the modern dance:

> *I could wander alone by the sea and follow my own fantasies. How I pity the children I see constantly attended by nurses and governesses, constantly protected and taken care of. What chance in life do they have? I say fortunately for me this wild untrammelled life of my childhood that I owe the inspiration of the dance I created, which was but the expression of freedom."* (Duncan *My Life* 1927 p. 11)

Diva Maria Callas had a similar background.   She was conceived in Athens, reared in Manhattan, moved every three months for years, and then moved back to Athens at thirteen. Amelia Earhart and Walt Disney each attended three different high schools in three different states.

British billionaire Richard Branson didn't make it through high school.   His mother Eve was asked by the BBC what she felt had made him so innovative. She responded to a shocked host, "At age four, I drove him across London, dropped him off in a park, and told him `find your way home." He obviously made it but he and his mother (*Losing My Virginity* 1998) attributed his phenomenal success to the independence and freedom acquired from a mother with an unusual parental philosophy.

EXAMPLES OF TRANSIENCY ON RICH & FAMOUS. Leonardo da Vinci, Napoleon, and Einstein were constantly on the move. Leonardo was born in Anchiano, moved to Vinci at two, to Florence at 12 and then to Milan. Napoleon was conceived in the hills of Corsica during a revolution. He was sent to France at age eleven and constantly moved back and forth between the two nations. Einstein moved twice in Germany as a child and attended schools in German, Italy & Switzerland. Thomas Edison and Walt Disney were noted for their wanderlust in their teens. Friends Maya Angelou and Oprah Winfrey spent their youths being transported between estranged parents. Maya was born in St. Louis, spent a year in Long Beach, California, traveled the US by train to Arkansas at age four, sent back in St. Louis at seven, back to Arkansas at eight, Los Angeles at twelve and San Francisco at 14. When she and her five year-old brother crossed the United States they had tags hung around their necks for identification since their paternal grandmother in Arkansas had never seen them. What did all this travel and relocation do to young Maya? It imbued her with a powerful sense of self and taught her to deal with the new and unknown and armed her for the life of a vagabond entertainer. Oprah was born in Mississippi and lived in Nashville and Milwaukee on five different occasions.

The eccentric genius Buckminster Fuller was famous, or infamous, for sleeping wherever he found himself. As a teen he lived and worked in he lived and worked in Boston and Canada. During his frenetic life he lived in Boston, Long Island, Chicago, Canada, Maine, Manhattan, Philadelphia, Washington DC, Montana, Los Angeles, and in a Greenwich Village loft. The multi-faceted genius felt comfortable anywhere because he grew up traveling and by twenty-one saw himself as a citizen of the world. Consequently, no foreign assignment threatened him including those in Japan, France, Germany, South America, Bombay, New Delhi and Madras, India.

HISTORICAL NOVEL AS GENRE

Early novels were aimed at recreating everyday experiences and representing the world as it was rather than as it was concocted by the imagination of some writer. They were preceded by Homer's Greek epic stories that were based on mythical gods and spirits. The most famous historical novel ever written was Tolstoy's *War & Peace*. Tolstoy would become one of Michener's early heroes for his style of explaining divergent forces interacting to influence the history of nations and cultures.

LITERARY GENIUS

The Russian novelist effectively developed characterizations to both entertain and inform; in contrast to political ideologies. His protagonists communicated moral messages about life and its foibles. Michener was highly influenced by Tolstoy and attempted to mimic his role model's historical epic style.

Historical fiction aims to educate and entertain. Tolstoy and Michener accomplished this better than most. John Cournas of the *New York Sun* wrote of Michener's influence on the genre at the time he won the Pulitzer Prize for *South Pacific*. He called it "a pleasure as well as an education." Michener admitted in his memoirs, "I aim to entertain and instruct" (Michener 1991 pg. 266). It would take Michener another ten years to settle on the genre that would make him both rich and famous. His second book was autobiographical but a futile attempt to show the vagaries of his life in *The Fires of Spring* (1949). That book showed him that psychological interplay was not his forte.

Michener was without a cultural heritage and adopted those of others in a desperate attempt to find an identity. His search led to many books on the history of national creeds and cultures in which he weaved pioneering people into the trek to the present. These historical explorations led him into a nomadic life that dwarfed his travels as a teenager.

His interminable search for self made him into an itinerant intellectual educator. He wanted desperately to find a home that he never had as a child. His search led him write epic novels on the cultural heritage of religion [*The Source*], societies [*Mexico* & *The Covenant*], lifestyles [*Caravans, The Drifters*], volcanic islands [*Hawaii, Caribbean*], nations [*Iberia, Poland*], immigration [*Texas, Chesapeake*] and *Space* itself. His legacy will be historical novels. His technique was an epic style that would have worn out less vigorous souls. His first book on cultural lifestyles was on the evolution of extended families in *Hawaii* (1959). This book earned him high commercial (not literary) praise, and enormous readership. It established him as a journeyman historical novelist. *Hawaii* blended history, events, and personalities via fictional characters to depict an evolving culture. It was soon followed by *Caravans* (1963), *The Source* (1965), and *Iberia* (1968) all commercial blockbusters.

Michener's books required enormous research and took three years to write. *Texas* (1985] was his biggest seller, followed closely by *Caribbean [1989]*, *Chesapeake* [1978], *Centennial* [1974], and *Space* [1982]. The master of the historical novel was a fastidious researcher. His dedication was boundless. For each new book, he packed up his family and took residence in such diverse places as Poland, Israel, Spain, Hawaii, Colorado, Miami, Maryland, and Texas. He explained his transient lifestyle as necessary for insight into the inner workings of the native cultures and their idiosyncrasies. But it was certainly buried in his inner feelings of isolation and need for closure. He would live in an area for five years and then pick up and move on. He admitted to visiting the Caribbean 32 times prior to relocating to Miami in his seventies where he taught and lectured while writing *Caribbean* (1989).

TRANSIENCY & ADULT SELF-SUFFICIENCY

Michener spoke often about his vagabond childhood and lack of roots. He lived in eight different houses on seven different streets and spoke of being an "itchy foot teenager." Early hitchhiking in neighboring states to Pennsylvania and then to Florida and Canada made him love life on the road.

What did frequent travel have to do with his success? It instilled in him the ability to cope and in his words the freedom "to do pretty much what I wanted. I was a free agent" (Michener p. 122). It also led him to the world of historical fiction. In his hometown of Doylestown he was not a happy camper. He made a big point in his memoirs of having no toys like other children and said, "I never had a wagon, or a pair of roller skates, or a baseball glove, or a tennis racket, or a radio, or a bicycle, or a pair ice skates" (Michener 1991 p. 438). In contrast to an unhappy life in Doylestown life the road was exciting and romantic. And such a vagabond existence dominated his life, books, and entertainment. The trek would not end until his dying breath.

Of his many travels he wrote, "I saw wealth being created, and it shouted back a challenge *be part of this*. Make something important happen" (Michener P. 117). And he did and it made him rich and famous.   He recalled, "I was a happy warrior moving unawares through a succession of mine fields" (p. 120).

COMFORT WITH THE UNKNOWN.   Children growing up in a constant state of flux learn early how to survive with little or no support systems.   They are content with the unknown an actually thrive on it.   Frequent moving forces a child to learn, to adapt, and modify their behavior to fit the new environment. They learn new cultures, languages, friends and attitudes. Amelia Earhart always wanted to be moving.   Much of this emanated from living in three different states during high school.   She told a reporter "I've had 28 different jobs in my life and I hope I'll have 228 more and I don't want anything all the time" (Landrum 1996 p. 200).   Her desire to "go where no one else has" was based on early transiency.

Israeli Prime Minister Golda Meir was even more transient. This indomitable spirit was born in Russia, reared in Milwaukee, attended high school in Denver, graduated in Milwaukee, traveled the United States at 18 and 19 and moved to Palestine at age 21.   It armed her with the belief she could cope in strange environments and empowered her with a self-sufficiency seldom found in more security-bound children.

THE MICHENER HERITAGE.   Michener was born a foundling in Doylestown, Pennsylvania.   His lack of an identity played a major role in his life.   He moved and traveled at the least provocation.   His memoir title is very telling - *The World is My Home* (1991) a book written at age 84. Mabel Michener purportedly took James in as a baby and raised him along with her natural son Robert, who was five years older.   However, it appears Mabel may have been his real mother.

His older brother, on his deathbed, told the media that James was Mabel's illegitimate child by a local married banker.   Mabel was pregnant in 1907 the year of Michener's birth and records indicate that she traveled to Mount Vernon, New York, to have the baby at her brother's home.   Robert told a reporter, "I remember lying on a cot in the same room with Arthur Haddock, mother's youngest brother who was lying on his side and shielding me from the proceedings... It was thus that

James Albert entered this world, so help me God" (Hayes 1984 p. 13). Mabel raised James Albert as a foundling and adamantly refused to acknowledge him as her illegitimate son, not an unlikely scenario in Quaker Pennsylvania. It must be remembered that in turn-of-the-century Doylestown unwed mothers were unaccepted. Acknowledging James could have proved a scandalous admission and more devastating than the lie that it appears she perpetuated.

LITERARY TRANSIENCY. As discussed, Danielle Steel was shuffled between Europe and the United States for much of her youth. She attended boarding schools in Manhattan and Switzerland, and lived occasionally in Spain, Italy, Switzerland and New York. The experience made her fluent in five languages: Spanish, French, German, Italian and Japanese. It also molded an independent and self-sufficient woman capable of writing romances in globe-trotting settings.

Balzac was sent away to a wet-nurse at birth and didn't return home until age four. He was then sent to a local boarding school just a few blocks from his parents home but was visited only twice in six years. Dostoevsky was sent off to a boarding school at age 13 and to a military school at fifteen. Stephen King tells about his father leaving the house for a pack of cigarettes when he was two and never returning. His mother packed up his brother and him and they took off on a gypsy-like existence in six states before he was eleven. Anne Rice lived in New Orleans, Texas, San Francisco and once again in Texas all by 20.

LITERARY INNOVATIONS

Michener's contribution to the world of letters was as an inveterate researcher. Posterity has described him as one of the world's prolific historical novelists. He slaved meticulously over the most trivial and esoteric data in an obsessive need to uncover some nuance of a culture. One literary critic who didn't see him as a literary genius credits him with a prescient vision for detail saying, "Michener appeals to people who don't normally read novels, people who buy books for facts, not psychological insights" (Rosselini June 17, 1991).

What about his books?   He gave us a form of digestible entertainment on history, genealogy, geology, ecology, religion, morals, and anthropology.   He was chastised for his lack of psychological insight but responded to it with introspection, "I am just not interested in analyzing myself, therefore I'm not interested in analyzing my characters" (Michener 1991 p. 314). He seemed to mimic a role model Sinclair Lewis in using the novel as a forum for social ideas.

The Christian work ethic is central to Michener's work.   His Quaker heritage is pervasive in all his characters who worked hard, were honest, had strong ethical standards, and the good guys always prevailed in the end.   One example of his pathological need for detail comes from *Texas* where people complained about learning more than they cared to know about the state's heritage.   Testimony to his anal approach to research can be seen in this statement on his work on *Texas*, "I found a book written in New Orleans in 1848.   It gave me all the cotton prices for all the major markets in the U.S.   It proved to me that the great revolutions in Europe of 1848 had a tremendous impact on the economy of New Orleans.   That so excited me" (Rosselini 1991).

Michener was methodical to a fault.   It took him three years to research and write a major book.   He knew he wasn't blessed with great articulation skills or psychological insights so made up for his failings with diligence.   During one period of introspection he wrote, "I am more academic than almost any successful writer...and I'm probably more academic than any of my critics" (Hayes 1984 pg. 5).   The critics accused him of not writing literature but "money-generating yarns that appeal only to middlebrows."   Lynn Rosselini of *U. S. News & World Report* (1991) described his characters as "one-dimensional and unremarkable" his plots as "contrived and superficial."   She quoted the *Washington Post* who described *The Novel* (1991) as "ghastly."   The *San Francisco Chronicle* labeled it "disastrous." The *New York Times* described the dialogue as "stilted" with "lifeless."   Despite such reviews his legion of fans kept the book on the best sellers list for seven weeks.   His greatest strength was storytelling but without insight into its psychology

WRITING AS CATHARSIS

Literary critic Lynn Rosselini confirms this author's belief that Michener had an obsessive and unconscious need to write historical fiction in order to find out who he was as a human being. She wrote, "He couldn't figure out his own identity so perhaps it would be possible for him to figure out his place in the world by analyzing and locating what he saw around him. He will go out of this world not knowing who he was so he wants to leave something behind" (Rosselini 1991). Biographer John Hayes wrote, "More than anything, Jim Michener writes as a means of attaining immortality" (Hayes 1984 pg. 145).

James Michener perpetually searched for a personal identity and that identity took the form of books about society and the world. He imbued his characters with his own sense of morals, ethics, religious beliefs, and Christian work ethic. Historical truth was paramount in his interminable search for "life's possibilities." He said, "I wrote *South Pacific* primarily for myself to record the reality of World War II" (Michener pg. 266).

Michener's favorite book was *"The Drifters"* (Michener 1991 pg. 393) because "I was the drifter searching the world for enigmatic answers." After Mabel Michener rejected him as her son he took to the road and didn't stop until his death in Austin, Texas, in 1997. He didn't appear to care about the truth of his heritage and accepted Mabel's sentence as a "foundling." But his fear of the truth led him to flee into an internal world of his own where no one else could enter. He was very private and reclusive and it was based on his refusal to speak of what might be the truth. His escaped into books and fantasies and hero-worship resulting in forty books.

METAMORPHOSES

His foster mother Mabel cleaned floors, washed clothes and ran a home for wayward children in Doylestown. It was in this home that he first discovered the magic of books. Mabel was a major influence in this regard, reading to him, his brother and the other foundlings each night. She gathered the children together and read them adventure stories including epic poems like *The Iliad*.   James favorites were paradoxically Charles Dickens and Mark Twain, two authors with tragic early lives who ended up as great storytellers.

Once when Mabel collapsed from exhaustion during Michenr's childhood, he was sent to live with her sister in Detroit.   It was here that he discovered the magic and mystery of words by Balzac.   His aunt owned forty volumes of *The Human Comedy* and the French novelist would become his fantasy mentor:

> *I am indebted to Balzac as I am to any living human being who ever touched me because his books were so filled with violence and compassion and sex and religion and the business of earning a living. He was precisely the kind of person I missed in real life and whom I needed so desperately. By the time I was twelve I had already read forty volumes of Balzac.* "(Michener 1991 pg. 439)

AN EPIPHANY! Michener experienced a life transformation while serving in the Navy at age 40.   He was serving in the South Pacific during the latter stages of World War II and despite a Masters in Creative Writing had still not written one word.   He had decided to become a writer at age ten and that motivated him to work his way through Swarthmore College with a degree in English Lit.   After graduating with a BA in 1929 and armed with a Phi Beta Kappa he traveled extensively through Europe and studied at St. Andrews University.   While in Europe he attended eight prestigious universities aimed at furthering a career in writing.   But he still had not written one literary piece when he almost died in a plane crash.

It was 1944 and Michener was in a plane attempting to land on a tiny atoll called New Caledonia Island. The plane encountered engine problems. The pilot informed him that they might not make it.   After three passes the plane crash-landed.   In his memoirs Michener emotionally about his epiphany and crawling out of that plane and walking back to his quarters a changed man. He sat down and wrote in his journal:

JAMES MICHENER

I swear, I'm going to live the rest of my life as if I were a great man...I'm going to concentrate my life on the biggest ideals and ideas I can handle...I'm going to associate myself with people who know more than I do (Michener 1991 pg. 264).

The next morning he sat down and began writing *Tales of the South Pacific.* In the autobiographical *Fires of Spring* (1949) he commented, "That night I discovered the unimportance of life, that it made no difference if I lived or died, and I passed from callow youth to manhood. Since I was unimportant, I was set free" (Hayes 1984 pg. 69). His life would never be the same after South Pacific was published and he would never work again as a teacher.

ECCENTRICITIES

James Michener was a renegade and never conventional. Biographer Hayes said in his biography of Michener, "Jim is strange, a man who will get up in a social gathering, walk into another room and turn on the TV and watch it alone simply because he doesn't care for the people or the topic of conversation." Hayes said at Swarthmore Michener, "was a social misfit" (pgs. 7 & 34).

Michener admitted to being "thrown out of every school I had ever attended from grade school to college" (Michener p. 327). He described himself as "a difficult young man. I am a loner to an extent that would frighten most people. I was always a diffident, free-spirited don't-give-a-damn sore of guy" (Michener p. 325). He said, "For forty years I've awoke at 4:00 a.m. in a state of dread, nobody will want to read this. It won't work. I'll never fool em" (Rosselini 1991). These are the insecurities of a lonely man driven by self-doubt who uses fears to motivate.

LIFE CRISES

Michener always claimed to be a foundling since that was the story he was told by Mabel Michener. Her denial appears to

have had a debilitating effect on him.   But it did spawn his
interest in heritage and cultures.   An illegitimate child being
raised in the intolerance of a Quaker town was a horrid
experience and he spoke of it for the rest of his long life.   His
memoirs were rampant with rejection and loneliness. He never
recovered from not having a bike or a ball glove and having
been, "evicted six times because my mother couldn't pay the
landlord.   I remembered standing out on the road at dusk
wondering where we would find a place to sleep.   For a child
that was pretty frightening... On many nights we went to bed
without eating" (Hayes 1984 pg 14).   Michener wrote of this
tragic period in his life philosophically:

> *When you grow up at the bottom of the totem
> pole, you see things from a different
> perspective.   Survival was my constant
> companion.   I have lived my life as if it were
> all going to fall apart two weeks from now.
> The urgency stems from some devastating
> experiences in childhood* (Hayes pg. 11)

Michener's traumas were not confined to his youth.   After
finishing his first manuscript *Tales of the South Pacific,* and
contractually agreeing with Macmillan to publish it, he hired a
literary agent.   Now a published author he jumped right into a
new book project, an autobiographical account of his life.   One
morning in 1947 he received a call from his new agent.
Michener said, "He was terminating my contract," and went on
to say, "I had no future as a writer and *The Fires of Spring*
would never be published." (Michener 1991 p. 284).   That very
afternoon George Brett, the President of Macmillan Publishing
came to him and offered him a job in publishing.   Shocked the
new writer asked why and was told, "Because you have no
future as an author."

Both agent and publisher had obviously concluded Michener
was a one-book author.   To add to his misery, literary critic
John Horn Burns, advised him that *The Fires of Spring*
manuscript was "not only unacceptable it was horrible. Most of
the writing is brilliant high school stuff...soggy prose...
embarrassing dialogue." What a day! It was probably the worst

day of his life but the fates intervened. The phone rang the same day of Burns devastating disclosure advising him that he had just been awarded the Pulitzer Prize for Literature for *South Pacific*. He never stopped writing no matter what critics wrote. The Pulitzer opened many doors including ones in Hollywood and Broadway, and he was finally a writer.

POLYPHASIC

Michener always had three books in some state of development at any one time. Like most authors he was never content with working on just one idea. Later in life he would maintain homes in many cities that were the sites of his work and bounced between them frivolously. He lived and taught in Austin at the University of Texas while *Texas* and then taught at the University of Miami while writing *Caribbean*. He maintained a similar vigil in many cities and countries for the last half of life.

The historical novelist was a Type A workaholic. He worked constantly seven days a week most of his long life and never took vacations. Rest was work for this hypomanic and contra to his well being. He had to be at his typewriter to be content. In his mid-80's he wrote, "I can hardly wait to get up in the morning." For Michener morning was 4:00am. Dan Guillory wrote in Magill Book Reviews (1992), "Michener is probably one of the hardest working authors America has ever produced."

His polyphasia included working in many genres. He wrote, "I use writing as convenient shorthand for the entire world of literary expression: poems, opera librettos, novels, drama, essays, biographies" (Michener pg. 361).

CRITICAL ACCLAIM

Michener won the Pulitzer for *Tales of the South Pacific* (1947). His timing was exquisite and attracted the attention of Rodgers & Hammerstein who made the book into the award-winning Broadway musical *South Pacific*. A few years later it would be made into a successful movie and the royalties from these three projects made him financially independent for the rest of his life. President Gerald Ford awarded him the President's Medal of Freedom in 1977 saying, "The prolific writings of this master story-teller have expanded the knowledge and enriched the lives of millions. I, like thousands of others, identify with Michener and feel he has left us with an indelible mark on our literature of this period" (Hayes p. 5). In 1983 the nation's newspaper editors, responding to a survey by *Family Weekly* magazine, voted Michener one of America's living national treasures.

Other honors include twenty-four honorary degrees in the fields of science, humanities, writing, and general citizenship. The one thing that always bothered Michener was being ignored by the educational world despite a Master's Degree in Creative Writing and Bachelor's in English Literature. Why was he snubbed? Commercial success is considered antithetic to much of the literary world who disdain anything accepted by the masses. Having been accepted by the masses he was derided by the classes. And of course he was the first to admit that he was verbose to a fault. When asked to write a brief article of 150 words for *Reader's Digest,* he responded, "I can't even write my name in 150 words."

Michener described his style by saying, "I am not an author. I'm a writer" (Michener p. 314). Lynn Rosellini of the *U. S. & News Report* (June 17, 1991) wrote, "His characters are cardboard and the dialogue is jarringly wooden and cliché-ridden." *Washington Post* critic Jonathan Yardley said flatly, "To suggest that Michener has any place in American literature is preposterous on its face" (Hayes p. 145). What are these critics saying? That his work should adhere to certain literary standards and not just be entertaining and informing. The irony is that most successful authors like those in this book - Agatha Christie, Ian Fleming, Stephen King, Danielle Steel, and Anne Rice were all vilified for daring to be successful without improving the art form. Each of these writers had one thing in common. All were superb storytellers who entertained more than informed. The arbiters of taste tend to be more dedicated to the classes, but as they found, it is never good to irritate the top dog in any profession and Michener was guilty of that sin.

Michener, like many successful writers, hated critics. Why? Because he saw critics as cynics and thought they were expected to demean in order to appear credible. He felt were paid to be adversarial not congenial. Controversy attracts readership and sells copy in the mediums where critics flourish. Critics seldom buy into the truly innovative since it isn't politically correct. Those who dare operate outside the literary box are destined to be denigrated and that is why writers like Mark Twain, Michener, Stephen King and Anne Rice **never** read reviews. Besides, all writing can be improved including Browning's *How Do I Love Thee*, Kipling's *If*, or Hemingway's *The Old Man & the Sea*.

TRANSIENCY & SUCCESS – What Can We Learn?

Michener's success was at least to some degree born of his travels and early transiency. Life on the road taught him how to deal with defeat, accept new ideas, conform to strange cultures, and to live in environs that were foreign.

Given the choice to have your ten year old attend the 5th grade or take a trip around the world, take her around the world. And when faced with discovering the nuances of Rome or Istanbul, one is better served to wander around the city and get lost than taking some guided tour. Getting lost in some diverse district is the charm of such an undertaking and what true learning is all about. To some it is scary, to others it is exciting, but for positive *success imprints* to take place, one must take off on their own and risk getting lost.

Michener would always opt for getting lost over settling for the safe haven. To him it was titillating and a chance to learn about the new and different. Even when he was nearly broke at at 40, and on the brink of total failure, he opted for the road not traveled and came away with a Pulitzer Prize for Literature. Then destiny intervened and Oscar Hammerstien offered him an opportunity to invest in the stage production of his play *South Pacific*. Michener didn't have the money, so Hammerstein lent him $5000 at 6% interest. The success of the play made Michener a rich man. The play ran on Broadway for 1925 consecutive performances and Michener began writing and never stopped. Michener would accumulate a $50 million fortune with $25 million in fine art. As with most creative geniuses money was never important and only gave him the freedom to live life on his terms.

Michener's interminable search for lost cultures left the world with over forty books. His legacy will be his interminable search for the identity behind cultures, even though he never found his own. Living life on the world's highways and byways molded him into an intrepid spirit that found its way into his books. His tomes were often a struggle to get through for his most ardent fans, but most agree they informed and entertained. He was a visionary who was astute at quantifying his vision. He said, "I want to write books that people will read fifty and one hundred years after I'm gone." He succeeded despite his critic's predictions. Posterity was kind to him and he never lost sight of his mission.

It is truly ironic that Michener took more pains in exploring the history of other cultures than his own. It is probably because he didn't want to know the real truth - that his surrogate mother Mabel was in reality his biological mother. Her rejection was too great for him to accept. But it motivated him to write about other lost heritages. Literary critic Doris Grumbach gave some credence to this. She said, "There is every chance that he will be remembered for being not an ordinary, but a highly unusual fellow, almost a Renaissance man, adventurous, inquisitive, energetic, unpretentious and unassuming, with an encyclopedic mind and a generous heart" (Donahue Oct. 17, 1997). It may be added that he was a man in search of an ancestry and since his was too perilous a journey he took one that was less frightening and it led him to a gold mine.

DR. SEUSS – TED GEISEL
IMAGINATIVE CHILDREN'S BOOKS
b. Springfield, MA Mar. 2, 1904
d. La Jolla, CA Sept. 24 1991

PERFECTIONISM & EMINENCE

DOMINANT GENRE
Made reading and humor synonomous to rebellious youth of 60's who identified with his off-the-wall views

MOTTO
"I draw animals because I can't draw humans"
If I Ran the Zoo – coined word NERD

GREATEST WORKS
How the Grinch Stole Christmas (1957) – TV cartoon
The Cat In the Hat (1957) – 1st grade reader
Green Eggs & Ham (1970) – 1st grade reader
The Lorax (1971) – launched the ecology movement

HONORS/AWARDS
1984 Pulitzer Prize; Eight (8) Honorary Ph.D.'s

ECCENTRICITIES
Never had art lesson and "never grew up" according to first wife Helen; passionately private iconoclast

LIFE CRISES
Sister Henrietta died when three; 1953 movie production, *5000 Fingers* "the worst period in my life. It was like the Fall of Rome, and haunted me the rest of my life" – four years later *Cat in the Hat* made him rich and famous

METAMORPHOSES
Adamantly resisted all attempts at thinking like an adult

70

TED (DR. SEUSS) GEISEL – CHILDREN'S

Imaginative Perfectionism

If you want to get eggs
You can't buy at a store
You have to do things
Never thought of before
Scrambled Eggs Super!

PERFECTIONISTS GET IT RIGHT

The poet most known for molding modern German culture was an obsessive perfectionist, a man who refused to complete his work for fear it wasn't flawless. Johann Wolfgang von Goethe completed the first draft of *Faust* in 1874 at age 25 and proceeded to edit it for the next 57 years and was still revising and improving it when he died at 82. Goethe, like Dr. Seuss, was a perfectionist and innovator. Both lived and worked well outside the system and defied convention. Goethe made a pact with the devil in exchange for knowledge. Dr. Seuss stretched logic to the limits and that excited the child within. The ploy worked for both men. Goethe was to Germany what Shakespeare was to England, what Da Vinci was to Italy, and what Dr. Seuss was to generations of children.

Dr. Seuss altered the reading habits of American children by his off-the-wall sense of moral integrity. Perfectionism was his master, but eccentricity was his god. J.R.R. Tolkien had a similar propensity. Attention to detail helped him become the "master of fantasy." He spent 14 years writing and rewriting his classic *Rings* and adamantly refused to trim the 500,000-word manuscript. Seuss had the same indomitable spirit.

Dr. Seuss became an author of children's books in 1937 at age thirty-three. His first creation was *And to Think I Saw it on*

DR. SEUSS

Mulberry Street.   Despite many years toiling as a cartoon illustrator for Madison Avenue ad agencies, where he created off-the-wall jingles and rhymes. As with such people he had a short attention span and renegade nature.

Geisel killed Dick & Jane as readers primarily because he was able to identify with a kids mentality. Most children have short attention spans and love to rebel.   It was these precise characteristics that armed Dr. Seuss for his attack on the traditional world of children's books. By marrying inane, some thought they were insane, words with graphics equally as goofy he was able to capture the imagination of children.

Dr. Seuss was childish. His little protégés identified with his arcane sense of time and place and were delighted by his caricatures.   His love for the absurd endeared him to generations of kids, nurtured on *The Cat in the Hat* and *Green Eggs & Ham.* Biographers described him as childish, a man-child, and unconventional.   There denigration was the very thing that made him a creative genius. And these qualities made him rich and famous beyond his wildest dreams. As an advertising illustrator he dabbled in creativity, but in children's books he allowed free reign to his eccentricities and satire.

Geisel worked as an ad illustrator until his mid-thirties. That was when he began drawing cartoons. He was approaching fifty before he knew any great success. It would be years later before his classic breakthrough *The Cat in the Hat* hit the bookstores in 1957. A few years earlier he had flirted with a similar fantasy creation called *If I Ran the Zoo* (1950).

Ted Geisel wrote over forty-seven books for children in fifty-four years resulting in 200 million books sold in 20 languages. His creative perfectionism would make him the most prolific and revered writer of children's books the world has ever seen. Educators loved his unique and unconventional style.   His method of communicating with children was refreshing and non-threatening while removing the boredom factor so pervasive in that world. And parents loved to see their children having fun reading.   Through it all Geisel never stopped thinking and acting as an adolescent. His vivid if not rebellious imagination was responsible for his creativity allowing him to impart great philosophical truths via zany illustrations.   One incisive example was *Lorax,* a book on ecology written long before such topics were in vogue.   It was so controversial his editors predicted its early demise.   The book was published in 1971 over the hostile objections of the editors at Random House.   But the irascible professor of madcap persevered and proved to be right as he was far ahead of his time with his "anti-pollution and anti-greed" ideology.

The Random editors didn't think a children's reader was the proper forum for spreading the gospel of social philosophy.   But visionary insight was Geisel's style and strength.   This book was a harbinger of things to come.   *Newsweek* (Oct. 7, 1991) described it as launching, "the environmental movement."

LITERARY PERFECTIONIST.   Dr. Seuss thrived on absurd characterizations.   Immense energy was directed at giving children a road map to reading without the boring details.   He got them to read because they didn't think they were reading. They were having fun in a pictorial world of gee whiz.   And they were outside that box where mediocrity reigns supreme.   Seuss was dedicated to protecting children from being adult influence that he thought were debilitating.   He never trusted adults after dropping out of Oxford.   After that he promised himself to "remain a child" so as not to get caught up in a cynical world that he saw as self-serving and mercenary.

The good Dr.'s motto was "might never makes right, the meek inherit the earth, and pride frequently goeth before a fall."   This is incisive testimony to a man who cherished removal of the ego from work and play.   His seven needs of children were: *love, security, belonging, achievement, knowledge, change, aesthetics.*

The zany madcap's number one selling book was *Green Eggs & Ham.* Ironically, this book was created due to a bet between him and the Chairman of Random House, Bennett Cerf. Cerf challenged him to write a book using only 50 words. Brevity is king in the world of children who are easily bored. Geisel won the bet and in doing produced a classic.

DR. SEUSS

Dr. Seuss was a master at reducing the complex to the simplistic while maintaining truth and wit. Hemingway was also a master at this as seen in his classic, *The Old Man & The Sea*. But the consummate example falls to Dr. Seuss's *Green Eggs & Ham* (1970) that had less than fifty words.

Close friends referred to Seuss as the Master of Mishief. He wrote a masterpiece of philosophy at age 85. With mortality staring him in the face, Geisel conjured up a wise old uncle – he was childless and saw himself as uncle to the world's children – as a sage to children. The uncle was Geisel in the guise of a spokesman for human frailty, fear, and failure. In this book he encouraged children to be diligent, work hard, and be honest and all will be well in the end. It would be his last book, *Oh, the Places You'll Go!* It hit the bookshelves in 1990 and became an instant hit if not a publishing phenomenon. It made the *New York Times* bestseller list and within two years had sold 1.5 million copies. He died not long after and testimony to his wit was looking up from his deathbed and asking, "Am I dead yet."

CHILDREN'S GENRE

This is the only genre defined not by its content but by its audience. A paradox exists because many adults read children's books and many of the successful books in history were not even written for children. Think of Defoe's *Robinson Crusoe*, Swift's *Gulliver's Travels*, and Twain's *Huckleberry Finn*. All were written for adults but became classics in the children's genre. Writers like George Bernard Shaw and Dr. Seuss preferred these books to the standard fare.

The first "children's" book was *Mother Goose* written by Charles Perrault and translated into English in 1729. Others in the genre that led the way were *Little Red Riding Hood*, *Cinderella*, *Sleeping Beauty*, *Puss in Boots*, and *Hop o My Thumb*. A separate category was created fifty years later with Mary Cooper's collection of Nursery Rhymes and then came *Grimm's Fairy Tales* noted for their moral messages. It was not until 1907 that Hilaire Belloc wrote *Cautionary Tales for Children* about Matilda who told lies and was burned to death as a moral message. Dr. Seuss credits this work for "introducing me to the hypnotic joys of rhyme." Probably the most famous of all children's books are Lewis Carroll's *Alice in Wonderland* (1865) and *Through the Looking Glass* (1872).

Charles Dicken's wrote his classics *Oliver Twist* and *A Christmas Carol* in the mid 19th century. Robert Louis Stevenson wrote *Treasure Island* in 1882. By the twentieth century the genre was well along with Edgar Rice Burrough's *Tarzan*, Frank Baum's *Wizard of Oz*, and series of action books like *Bomba the Jungle Boy*, *Nancy Drew*, and *Tom Swift*. Illustrations began to appear along with text in the 20th century in the Oz books, Winnie-the-Pooh, Peter Rabbit and Mother Goose. Those that tend to last are the most eccentric, different, unique, and original. They invite the reader to ask questions. This gives credence to Shannon's Law that says, "We absorb information in inverse ratio to its credibility." Based on this Law, it is no wonder the unconventional style of the zany Dr. Seuss has outsold all other children's books in history.

A MAVERICK PERFECTIONIST

Ted Geisel was a pathological perfectionist. He once refused eighty different shades of green for a parrot for one of his manuscripts finally settling on the 81st color submitted by his frustrated editor. Random House was run by Bennett Cerf. His wife Phyllis worked with him in the early days. Phyllis Cerf was really the person most responsible for launching the unbelievably successful Beginner Books subsidiary that published Geisel's classic *Cat in the Hat* in 1957. But when she refused to capitulate to Seuss's demands for total control over his creative style her husband asked her to leave the firm.

Geisel's perfectionism was legend at Random House. His reputation preceded him and each new editor was warned not to mess with his work; and that included one word, color, sequence, syntax, or any illustration. Nothing was to be touched unless the good Dr. agreed. Geisel's power over his work transcended everyone at Random including the Chairman's wife. One editor told the media "It had to be Ted's way." They were aware of his quirks and were instructed to keep their prize author happy at almost any cost.

E. J. Kahn of the *New Yorker* (December 17, 1960) wrote the only feature article on the reclusive whose antisocial attitudes made him infamous as an interviewee. One reason was that he suffered fools poorly and treated muckraking reporters with disdain. Kahn wrote, "Perfectionism is his creed. He insists on retyping a page of copy if one word has been crossed out, and he has spent up to three days worrying about the acceptance of a single adjective." Kahn was stunned when Dr. Seuss told him how he created 100 illustrated images to find one that worked and met his high standards.

Perfectionism in the Literary World. Balzac and Dostoevsky had a similar penchant for perfection. Both were obsessive about their work and refused to allow any changes. They, like Seuss, would go into seclusion until they had resolved some particular scene or word. Agatha Christie, Ayn Rand and Anne Rice had a similar obsession over total control over their work.

Balzac felt he had to be perfect or die. And his needs killed him in the end. The father of the modern novel planned his life's work in his 20's and then worked feverishly to complete it before he died. He barely made it since he died at age fifty from overwork and exhaustion. One of his many mistresses described him as "pretending to be god." *The Human Comedy* is testimony to his need to be perfect. Dostoevsky had a similar propensity and despised everything he wrote. He once demeaned his masterpiece *The Idiot* saying, "My dissatisfaction with my novel amounts to disgust."

Hemingway's need to choose the perfect word and phrase led his winning of the Nobel Prize for Literature for "narrative excellence. But the price paid by Hemingway was 200 rewrites. Control freak Danielle Steel was dissatisfied with anything that wasn't exacting. She described herself as an "extreme perfectionist with a need for detail in everything I do" (Bane & Benet pg. 349). The romance queen admits to controlling every facet of her life and of those around her planning each of her children's schedules six months in advance and her books years in advance. Every single detail is pre-planned in a fastidious need for scrupulous precision.

Random House editors told Ayn Rand that her radio speech by John Galt was far too long. The speech went on for an interminable sixty pages in *Atlas Shrugged* and encompassed 60,000 words. Rand refused to have one word omitted. Anne Rice insists on total editorial control over her work. She says, "I believe in no censorship or editing of my work." She is a classic control freak that is found in the perfectionist personality.

PERFECTIONISM & SUCCESS. Perfectionism pervades other successful domains just as it has the literary world. Darwin's aphorism "It's doggedness that does it," gives some indication of his compulsion for detail. Karl Marx had a similar penchant. The father of Marxism had a singleness of purpose that drove his peers and his wife crazy. He spent the last years of his life in the London Library writing and rewriting his landmark work *Das Kapital* (1867) that even his worst critics called "an epic work of Herculean genius."

Martin Luther King was a fastidious dresser as was Nikola Tesla and Frank Lloyd Wright. These men from different worlds and eras all had a need for perfectionism that contributed to their charismatic style as well as their success. Tesla would wear a white shirt and gloves and discard them after one wearing. Obsession with perfection goes beyond business. When the Olympic champion Babe Didrickson Zaharias decided to take up the game of golf she hit golf balls until her hands bled.

LITERARY INNOVATIONS

Cat in the Hat (1957) revolutionized the reading habits of children in the Western world and was the publishing phenomenon that created Beginners Books. How did it begin? With the zany words of Dr. Seuss who said in a moment of introspection, "I write the verbs and allow the kids to fill in the adjectives." This was his explanation of staying away from too much description since he knew children abhorred being preached to but loved the right to create their own fantasy world of make believe as part of the learning process.

Geisel always maintained that his talent lay in not knowing how to draw. Had he had more expertise, he would have not drawn such arcane and interesting caricatures. His ineptness led to his need to draw unreal, and farcical off-the-wall characters that appealed to the mind of children. It was his child-like imagination that armed him with a prescient ability to speak to children. Had he been more knowledgeable on children's books he probably would have failed. In other words, ignorance proved to be an asset to his innovation.

Geisel was a renegade even in high school. He lasted but one hour in art class. The teacher insisted he draw by the rules and rules were never important to Geisel or any other creative genius for that matter. The teacher explained, "There are rules that every artist must abide by. You will never be successful if you break them." Ted walked out and never returned saying, "I was free forever from art-by-the-rule books" (Morgan pg. 21).

One of Geisel's innovative contributions to the children's genre was humor with a moral spin. Being an iconoclast he refused to comply with convention and was not overly grounded in what could or could not be done. Defiance and a renegade mentality proved to be his nettle especially when appealing to the anarchism of the sixties and early seventies when his three landmark books hit the market - *The Cat in the Hat* (1957), *How the Grinch Stole Christmas* (1957), and *Green Eggs & Ham* (1970). The Cat and Green Eggs were First Grade Readers and the first to stray from the Dick & Jane readers. Their theme was rhyme with nonsensical words that appealed to young kids who could recognize syllables and learn to pronounce hard words. Magill Books critic C. K. Breckenridge (1995) said, "His book have revolutionized the way kids learn to read."

Seuss was the first children's writer to allow the child to become immersed in the action where their vivid imagination could be allowed free reign. His books were also non-threatening and non-educational. He violated tradition, which children love to do, and in doing so gained respect and allegiance. His enormous influence was acknowledged by the *New York Times* when they wrote in 1960, "Geisel has dominated the genre like no one in history" (Morgan 1995 pg. 170). The media was even more gushing ten years later when he dared ignore his literary advisors by writing a polemic on pollution. He was ten-years ahead of his time with this ecological treatise. Lorax became his favorite work.

Geisel's most controversial and consequently most innovative book was written when he was well into his eighties. The *Butter Battle Book* was panned by his editors due to its strong political statement about disarmament, the Cold War, and its prediction of the annihilation of mankind. Was this for children or was the good Dr. becoming senile? His editors thought so and told the media what they thought. They truly believed this book had gone over the edge and attempted to have it killed. Geisel never capitulated even when told, "this book won't sell to juveniles."

The book had been promoted as a tribute to his 80th birthday and was scheduled for release with huge publicity. A media leak led to a reporter demanding to know why Random would publish such a controversial book. They said, "When you're dealing with a genius, and he won't change, you don't change" (Morgan p. 252). *The Butter Battle Book* (1984) was published on his 80th birthday. It shot immediately to #1 on the Best Seller list and was instrumental in his winning the Pulitzer Prize for "a half-century contribution to the education and enjoyment of American children and parents." So much for the opinion of experts.

WRITING AS CATHARSIS

Helen Geisel told the media "his mind has never grown up. He views the world from the wrong end of the telescope" (Morgan pg. 85). She protected him from the world's mundane things like writing checks, which he never mastered, allowing him to spend his time on his toy trains and other childlike pursuits. How could a graduate of Dartmouth not be able to balance a checkbook? Because he had no interest in anything beyond the purview of his creativity. He lived life on his terms and refused to live to the agenda of others. Fun with words and pictures was #1 with Seuss. He said, "My books do not insult children's intelligence ... because I'm on their level. When I dropped out of Oxford, I decided to be a child" (Morgan 248).

Editor Ray Freiman of Random House confirms the cathartic style of Dr. Seuss. He said, "He is his work, all of the whimsy and zaniness of it is part of him, and his constant patter of wisecracks" (Morgan pg. 123). Dr. Seuss was a radical non-conformist. His wacky books depicted bizarre animals in the wrong color and snow that was green instead of white. Had he drawn logically the kids would not have been so attracted. Because he thought and drew outside the box, just as most children do at that age, they considered him their friend. His madcap humor drew both applause and inflammatory invective. This happened early in his career when he was writing political satire for the magazine *Judge* in New York City. The editors received angry letters saying, "hang him." Dr. Seuss was nonplussed and told his editor a twelve-year old asking for his autograph was far more important than the cynical comments of any adult.

METAMORPHOSES

Ted Geisel had what he described as a transformational experience at age four when he was taken to a zoo. He was reared in Springfield, Massachusetts and that trip started him drawing animals. At age six his father took him up a hill to watch Haley's Comet and the experience proved prophetic as it occurred simultaneously with seeing his first owl. This was so memorable he would remember it over 50 years later and described it as the start of his love affair with animals.

Ted Geisel was known in high school and college as the class artist and wit. High school teacher Edwin A. Red Smith became an early mentor. Smith was a young graduate of Dartmouth. Geisel said, "Smith introduced me to the hypnotic joys of rhyme" (Morgan pg. 25). He also introduced him to books by Hilaire Belloc who had written *Cautionary Tales for Children* and the *Bad Child's Book of Beasts*."

The transformation into illustrator/writer occurred at Dartmouth while he was working on the student magazine

Jacko. "It was there that I began to get it through my skull that words and pictures were Yin and Yang ... that married, might produce a progeny more interesting than either parent." He admitted that it took him a quarter of a century to find the correct methodology. "At Dartmouth I couldn't even get them engaged." Sixty years later he would say the *Jacko* experience led him into the field of children's books.

A negative experience completed his transition from wannabe teacher to art-illustrator. Ted matriculated to Oxford with the expectations of becoming a professor of English. The nephew of Thomas Carlyle was his instructor. Carlyle advised Geisel to look elsewhere and reevaluate his career choice. "He told me I was the only man he'd ever seen who should never have come to Oxford." Not much later he found himself in a two-hour lecture on punctuation of King Lear. Right in the middle the light hit and he got up and walked out and never returned.

CAREER DYSFUNCTION. Ted was working on Madison Avenue in New York City as an illustrator. He had found a modicum of success drawing cartoons for commercial ads. While working in the creative department of an ad agency he produced a FLIT bug spray commercial for Standard Oil Company. It was an instant hit and he was given a long-term contract and allowed to function as a free-lance illustrator on a fixed retainer. But on the side he was dabbling with his first love, cartoon illustrations and he had written a book, *And to Think That I Saw it on Mulberry Street.* He had shown it to 27 different publishers and was summarily rejected by all saying "it was too different and lacked seriousness."

Geisel was 33 by now and was itching to write books. A chance meeting with a Dartmouth friend who worked at Vanguard Press proved providential. He was ready to burn the manuscript after having being turned down once more. Mike McClintock asked what he had in his hand and Geisel told him the story of his repeated rejections. McClintock was working as an editor for Vanguard. The President was a renegade editor named Henle who loved the book. In Geisel's inimitable words he said, "If I had been on the other side of Madison Avenue, I'd be in the dry cleaning business today" (Morgan pg. 82).

DR. SEUSS

ECCENTRICITIES

Dr. Seuss not only danced to a different drummer, he saw the world from within the drum. His favorite saying was, "adults are obsolete children." This bizarre sense of humor and zany sense of life in general is what set him apart and led to his success. He was passionately private and according to his first wife Helen had the mind of a child. Testimony to his zaniness was the time as President of Beginners Books in Manhattan he went around and posted bizarre signs on executives doors that read, DR. VIOLET VALERIE VOWEL, DIVISIONAL DIRECTOR OF CONSONANTS. He once drew a picture of Phyllis Cerf with her exclaiming, "WOOPS, I swallowed my word list." Phyllis described him as a "happy genius." Her son Christopher said "He always made me feel great!" When he was forced to send out a rejection letter he concocted a fantasy executive and signed it Dr. Outgo Schmierkase (Morgan pg. 158).

A RENEGADE MENTALITY. It takes a true looney-tune to write an adult book titled *The Seven Lady Godiva's* when your whole livelihood is tied to children's books. This book was a perverse tale of seven nudes and their lovers. He said, "I tried to draw the sexiest babes I could, but they came out looking absurd." It wasn't published. Biographer Morgan described him as a "rowdy and undisciplined revolutionary daring to link drawings with art." At Dartmouth he was voted unanimously "The Least Likely to Succeed."

Logical insanity was his anthem. Novelist Wallace Stegner was with him at a writing conference when he was in middle-age. Stegner said, "I remember him in the pool playing seal complete with barking" (Morgan p 124). When one of his associates asked, "Do you associate yourself with any of your characters?" The ever-honest Geisel responded, "Yes, especially the devious ones" (Morgan p 247). An indication of his mindset was his Christmas request at age 57 for an electric train. Helen bought him a Lionel for Christmas. After *Cat in the Hat* he began collecting hats and had the most unusual collection from Ecuador, Czechoslovakia, New Zealand and wherever.

One example of Geisel's inane sense of humor comes at one of the more serious moments in his bizarre life. When a personal friend questioned his upcoming trip to Reno he responded with classic cynical humor, "My best friend is being divorced and I'm going to Reno to comfort his wife." The truth was that he was on his way to marry his best friend's wife within a year of his wife's suicide. Audrey Dimond and he had fallen in love and it had precipitated his wife's suicide. Audrey was going to get a quickie-divorce in order to marry Ted. He had a knack for finding levity in the strangest situations.

LIFE CRISES

Ted Geisel was devastated at age three when his baby sister Henrietta died at one and a half. Much of Geisel's early life was beset by guilt over a German heritage during an era when America was in a life and death struggle against the Germans. At the end of the war his father with economic disaster when prohibition was voted in and shut down the family brewery.

Geisel escaped into a fantasy world of books and cartoons. Animals and children were safe havens. There were no guns or threats to survival. He found solace in fantasy, words, and stories. Few adults found his zany humor funny and he spent years wondering if he would ever find acceptance in a world steeped in tradition.

He was close to quitting when *Mulberry Street* went through repeated rejections as "too different." But his real trauma occurred in Hollywood in the early fifties. Geisel had been assigned writer and producer of a movie titled *5000 Fingers*. He worked on it diligently, but on opening night it was panned as a miserable failure. In his words, "It was the worst evening of my life. It was like the Fall of Rome" (Morgan pg. 138). The debacle actually became a catalyst for creativity. Within a few years he had produced his masterpiece *The Cat in the Hat.* His first wife Helen told friends "*5000 Fingers* haunted him the rest of his life." But she didn't live to see his worst crisis. He took on enormous guilt over her suicide when she discovered that he had fallen in love with a family friend. She left a suicide note in their La Jolla home saying, "Failure, failure, failure" (Morgan pg. 195). He considered suicide himself or burning down their home. He lost himself in work to forget the horrid experience.

POLYPHASIA

Exploring ideas beyond the scope of the norm demand exploration of many. It takes hundreds to find a few and Dr. Seuss admitted to making hundreds of drawings to find just one that worked.

He also balanced many ideas and concepts in his frenetic brain at any given time. He always had one project in the typewriter, another in research, another in the back of his mind and others floating about in his psyche.

Geisel also flirted in various areas of the graphic arts and entertainment industries. His diverse interests ran to writing jingles, advertising slogans, screenplays, TV scripts, educational books, producing and directing movies, and a multiplicity of drawings for children's toys and radio shows. When not into these he pursued his passion of painting, what he called his "psychosis deterrent."

CRITICAL ACCLAIM

Winning the Pulitzer Prize in 1984 gave Dr. Seuss the credibility he so desperately sought. It had validated him as a legitimate author. He had already found success commercially since his books brought in millions of royalties with 400 million sold. He has been rewarded with dozens of honorary doctorates. The doctorates were ironic since he had made up his pseudonym of Dr. Seuss to "make up for the one I never got at Oxford." When asked why he didn't use his first or last name he said, "Because I was saving those names for the great American novel." When the critics demeaned his work he said, "I am writing for and drawing for kids, not critics" (Morgan pg.247).

The *coup de grace* of acclaim was given by his publisher at Random House, Bennett Cerf. Cerf told audiences, "I have only one genius." The certitude comes from a look at Random House's other writers at the time. They included some of the more brilliant writers in history like William Faulkner, Eugene O'Neill, John O'Hara, Ayn Rand, and James Michener. "Of these, Ted alone is a genius," Cerf said, and he went on to laud his role in changing the way children learned to read. Cerf said, "Beginner Books is the most profitable single publishing entity ever created," adding, "and it was created on the coattails of a cat" (Morgan 158).

SUCCESS BASED IMAGINATIVE PERFECTIONISM

Dr. Seuss was a renegade perfectionist who always allowed free reign to his unconscious fantasies. Few people allow their fantasies to see the light of day. They certainly don't allow them into print. Dr. Seuss had no such reservations.

Tradition is way down the list of importance to the creative genius. Why? Because tradition and creativity are found at opposite ends of the continuum. Such people defy convention, and refuse to bow to the demands of the establishment. Consequently, they are demeaned by the old school and only succeed by refusing to allow the rejection to debilitate them.

Dr. Seuss fits the profile. He was always seen as a self-deprecating personality drowning in self-doubt, flagellating himself for not being creative. He portrayed the establishment as the enemy, a concept the juvenile mind loves, and used adversarial comments to fuel his imagination and for motivation. The establishment saw him as a "weirdo." In the end his ego overcame the rejection and led to his creativity.

Dr. Seuss always questioned his own ideas, but as in most creative geniuses never allowed comments by other to deter him. Without that inner self-confidence he would never have survived in a world that saw him as a reclusive eccentric. Ironically, it was his madcap wit that was so demeaned that is his claim to fame. His outrageousness became his strength. The *New York Times* saw this and called him a "Moppets Milton" (Morgan p. 155). They said of his classic *"Cat in the Hat"* book, "Nobody could possibly have ideas in any way resembling those that occur in this talented man."

DR. SEUSS

The best selling children's author in history was mischievous to a fault. Childish pranks were more important to him than serious dialogue and in the long run it was that impish imagination that allowed him to connect to the children of the world. By the time he saw this important connection he was already fifty years old and earning but $100 a week. Within ten years he had revolutionized the children's book genre and was a multi-millionaire.

Dr. Seuss never took himself too seriously. He ambled through life as a clown prince on a mission to the impossible. All rules and confinement stifled his creativity. He worked seven nights a week until 2:00 a.m. But it wasn't for money it was a labor of love. And anyone who tried to tinker with his work were shown the door. He knew the interrelationship between his words and pictures and no one had better change them.

Dr. Seuss was dedicated to making it easier for children to see the world simply. He said, "If I can be of influence to one child in this great vice-ridden country, my life, I feel will not have been lived in vain." Librarians and primary school teachers viewed him as some kind of assassin for his role in destroying their treasured Dick & Jane books. Dr. Seuss understood the price he had to pay for his innovation and wrote, "I'm subversive as hell! I've always had a mistrust of adults. One reason I dropped out of Oxford and the Sorbonne was that I thought they were taking life too seriously" (Morgan 248). Columnist Anne Quindlen said, "Dr. Seuss wrote words of fun. He will be remembered for the murder of Dick & Jane, which was a mercy killing of the highest order" (Morgan pg. 290).

JOSEPH JOHN CAMPBELL
MYTHOLOGICAL & HEROMENTORING
b. NY City, Mar. 26, 1904
d. Honolulu, HI Oct. 30, 1987

MYTHICAL HERO MENTORS

DOMINANT GENRE
Mythology and its psychological significance and motivating
force on all mankind

MOTTO
"FOLLOW YOUR BLISS" "All our images are masks, our egos
are our dragons. You slay your dragon by following your bliss,
myths are models for understanding your life"

GREATEST WORKS
The Hero With a Thousand Faces (1949)
The Masks of God (1968)
The Inner Reaches of Outer Space (1991)

HONORS/AWARDS
Idolized and worshipped by a legion of intellectuals at Esalen
Institute in Carmel; Filmaker George Lucas admits enormous
influence on the creation of Star Wars movie

ECCENTRICITIES
Spent five years alone in cabin reading Classics; learned to read
and write Sanscrit and Japanese in 40's & 50's to understand
cultural icons, myths, & inherent inner forces driving man

LIFE CRISES
Serious illness in teens and spent whole time reading of Indian
culture; fire destroyed their home and disfigured father

METAMORPHOSES
Wild West Shows at Madison Square Garden at six and New
York Museum of Natural History at ten altered his life

4

JOSEPH JOHN CAMPBELL - Mythology

Mythical Hero Mentors

"All myths make heroes out of those who heed them"

Joseph Campbell is probably the least known of these subjects, however he was probably the most erudite, and will some day prove highly influential to creativity. Campbell spent his life in a small apartment in Greenwich Village with dancer-wife Jean Erdman, a former student he met while teaching at Sarah Lawrence College in Bronxville, New York. Campbell ran on the track team at Columbia while earning a Masters Degree in Anthropology and began teaching at his alma mater Canterbury School. He taught himself Japanese, Sanskrit, German, French, Gaelic, Latin and Spanish. At age fifty he moved to Japan for the express purpose of learning their culture and mythical history. During his stay he studied Zen Buddhism and learned to walk on fire.

When confronted with dealing with the Catholic icons of his religious training and the Indian symbols and rituals of his youth, Campbell embarked on a life-long search for their derivation. The quest led to an inner search into the ego and deep-seated cosmic being pulsating within each of us. The Jungian Archetype became profoundly intertwined in the myths inspiring the intrepid Campbell to delve into Jungian psychology. Every time some new icon or mythg crossed his path he caught a plane and went to the far ends of the earth to find out how they may have impacted that culture or the way we live our lives.

MYTHICAL MENTORS AS MOTIVATORS

In the words of Carl Jung, "It is not Goethe who creates Faust, but Faust who creates Goethe. Faust is but a symbol." There is a vast body of data that would substantiate his view. Frank

Lloyd Wright lived his life in the image of the mythical Welsh God Taliesin. His mother had unwittingly convinced him as a child that he was the reincarnation of Taliesin and above the rules of mere mortals. Wright lived his life as an arrogant know-it-all despite not graduating from high school. He said, "I am a genius" and refused to live by any rules but his own since he truly believed he was special and even if the belief was deluded it armed him with a power that made him great.

Adopting a model or hero can make the road to the top easier. Buckminster Fuller was a true Renaissance man who at age eighty-five acknowledged the importance of early heroes in his life. Fuller had been inspired by the mythical Robin Hood when young but just prior to his death wrote, "Robin Hood became my most influential mythical hero" (Critical Path p. 134).

In Campbell's *Transformations of Myth Through Time* (Campbell 1990 pg 1) he wrote, "The material of myth is the material of our life, the material of our body and the material of our environment. A living vital mythology deals with these in terms that are appropriate to the nature of knowledge."

FANTASY HEROES. Hero-worship and icons permeated the life of Campbell due to his Roman Catholic upbringing and his visits to museums and Wild West shows. Every subject in this work were highly influenced by some mythical hero or fantasy mentor. George Bernard Shaw was enormously influenced at 15 by Goethe's *Faust* and later by Nietzsche's *will-to-power* thesis that he translated into a Life Force. Both Goethe and Nietzsche influenced Shaw more than even he realized. But he did come to grips with the influence of the writings of Karl Marx. After discovering *Das Kapital* in a four year foray in the British Museum Shaw wrote, "Marx was a giant and a genius. He opened my eyes to the facts of history and was the turning point in my career." The influence of Marx ended with Shaw's co-founding of the British Labor Party despite being Irish, and that of Nietzsche is pervasive in his most acclaimed play *Man & Superman*. Don Juan was Goethe's Mephistopheles who defied the establishment similar to Marx, and imbued him with a Nietzschean *will* to rise above mediocre man.

Balzac described his life and work with a colloquialism, "mythomania." Napoleon was his hero and aspired to such power and lived his life in his image. He wrote, "Superstition is the most indestructible form that human thought can take" (Robb p. 369). Balzac was saying that the inner beliefs of man were far more important to his success than talent. He wrote, "I am Napoleon without troops" (p. 121).

Analytical psychologist Carl Jung wrote, "All our concepts are mythological images. All our impulses are instincts." If he was correct it validates the premise of fantasy heroes as motivating forces for greatness. Joseph Campbell was influenced by Jung and resulted in his marrying Jungian mysticism with mythology. Hero worship dominated Campbell's early life. He was enamored of Leonardo da Vinci and Hollywood star Douglas Fairbanks and emulated them in style. "I wanted to be the synthesis of da Vinci and Fairbanks" (Larsen 1992 pg.22).

Early influences in his life were the totems and icons that seemed to bombard his senses and nobody seemed to have any answers for their derivation. In college he came under the influence of Walt Whitman, Heinrich Zimmer and other intellectuals searching for the nature of man. He once wrote, "I'm a maverick scholar in the image of Whitman." In his 30's he met John Steinbeck and James Joyce and became friends with both men. He did a translation for Joyce's *Finnegan's Wake*. He would write later of his influence and their meaning:

> ***Myths are powerful guides to the life of the spirit, our ticket to the passages of life. Each individual must find the myth that is fundamental to his internalized needs. Only a myth can help one live a systematic life with meaning.*** (Moyers, *Power of Myth* 1995 PBS)

As discussed Alexander the Great's mother gave him Homer's *Iliad,* and the fable altered his internal view of his role in life and played a huge part in his destiny. Alexander carried the book to Delphi and then used it as a roadmap to success in battle. Achilles for Alexander was more than just a mythical tale, it removed all internal limitations to what he could accomplish if only he could emulate his great hero.

Superheroes are often elevated to the role of superior beings, mythical ones are that by definition. When Frank Lloyd Wright bought into his mother's prediction that he was the reincarnation of the Welsh God Taliesin, he began to believe that he was above the rules and decorum of ordinary men. He was deluded but in that delusion was able to accomplish what mere mortals could not. Why? Because all internal limits had been removed. He believed he was superior and thus became superior in his creations.

When altering paradigms or conquering the world one must not be constrained and one way is to emulate a hero who is larger than life. Consider the Herculean exploits of Napoleon. The Little Corsican graduated 42nd out of 54 from the Ecole Military Academy in Paris but went on to be called the greatest military leader in history. His hero was Alexander and it is not hard to see the symbolic need for him to travel East and conquer Egypt.

NLP – MODELING EMINENCE. Modeling of behavior was studied extensively at the University of California by researchers John Grinder and Richard Bandler. They gave us the term NLP - Neuro-Linguistic-Programming. It offers some validation of Campbell's work and Jungian Archetypes. They found that following a mentor, especially one with superior talent, can enhance performance. They wrote, "Not all dreamers achieve, but all achievers dream." Their work was aimed at showing the positive results of visualization and mentoring with superior role models. If one wants to serve a tennis ball like Pete Sampras then mimicking his serve is far better than reading all the world's tennis books. You may not achieve his success but you will certainly be better than mimicking a klutz.

DON SUPERMAN'S CAPE & REMOVE INTERNAL LIMITS. When a person models their life and actions after a larger-than-life myth they unconsciously remove the self-imposed inner limits for achievement. Why? Because identifying with a god-like role model causes a modeling of behavior - to be like that superhero - thereby removing the limits that are typically self-imposed by early conditioning. Besides fantasies are more exhilarating than reality and far more desireable to pursue.

Life's limitations are all internal, never external. Those who envision success are successful. Those who become caught up in their own fears will fail. One pursues success the other tries not to fail and that is the only difference. Most people do not see themselves worthy of total success and that becomes a debilitating limitation. We live out our own inner visions of ourselves whether those visions are as President or peddler, Prime Minister or prostitute.

HERO WORSHIP ARCHETYPE & ZEAL. Both Hitler and Picasso saw themselves as Nietzschean *supermen* and lived their lives emulating a Herculean hero. Hitler told audiences, "I myself am fate and have conditioned existence for all eternity." Both were mesmerized by the Schopenhauer and Nietzschen *will-to-power* thesis. Hitler concocted his Master Race theme from Nietzsche and the blond-warrior mysticism of Wagner. Picasso worshipped power and despised weakness and saw himself as the Overman of art epitomized by a teenage self-portrait he gave to his mother signed, *I, the King.*

Ted Turner grew up worshiping military heroes Alexander the Great and Attila the Hun. His office at CNN was nicknamed the War Room by associates based on his military approach to business. When Oprah had to anchor a network show she was scared to death of going on air live. She admitted to mimicking real-life heroine Barbara Walters an said, "I went on air acting as if I were her" in speech, tone, and attitude. Isadora Duncan wrote in her memoirs, "I was possessed of the dream of Promethean creation. I am indeed the daughter of Aphrodite." In a similar manner Madonna carefully modeled her stage persona after Jean Harlow and Marilyn Monroe. Oscar Wilde was similarly inspired by Balzac and wrote, "I cannot travel without Balzac; the *Comedie Humaine* is really the greatest monument that literature has produced."

HEROES OUT OF BOOKS AS MENTORS. Protagonists from books inspire and motivate. Oprah Winfrey told a book show audience, "I owe everything to books." Stephen King who grew up enthralled with *Dr. Jekyll & Mr. Hyde.* Romance novels were the salvation of Danielle Steel's lonely childhood. Many renowned entrepreneurs grew up idolizing Superman, Wonder Woman, Robin Hood, and Tarzan. Even superheroes from Star Trek or Star Wars can remove limitations. Shaq O'Neill, the MVP of the NBA in 2000 and most dominant center in the league sports a Superman tattoo on his right arm, the one he uses to slam dunk the basketball.

HERO PROGRAMMING & INTERNAL SCRIPTING. Adopting a mythical mentor who is larger-than-life suspends belief in the surreal and makes the improbable possible and the impossible probable. When such her worship is so strong as to mesmerize it gets recorded on that unconscious tape that becomes an influence for performance. Brainwashing techniques in wartime have demonstrated this. Superlearning takes place in trauma or while in a theta state. When in reverie or escaping into the mythical world of make-believe we often escape into those images and are able to over achieve.

Campbell was an individual who was programmed early in life to pursue his dream that happened to be the derivation of myths and icons. He referred to these inner symbols on our psyche as "masks" that arise out of IRM's – Internal Releasing Mechanisms. He described IRM's as "behaviors manifested from unconscious hero imprints" recorded earlier in life as Archetypes. And these became mythical mentors or idyllic role models so necessary for overachieving. He wrote, "Masks are imprinted Archetypes. Myths do not just refer to Archetypes, but actually manifest them." (Bill Moyers 1992 PBS TV Special). He went on to say:

> *Each of us are mythological representations of our inner truth and our jobs and other mundane experiences are merely symbols of a larger mythological meaning in our lives.*

This is especially meaningful for writers who are dealing in a world of illusion and make-believe. Imagery is critical to success in such a profession. Campbell admonished us to allow free reign to our imagination and magical imagery or you will "allow your dragons to win" (Moyers p. 150). He said, "Every society invents first magic and then religion and the myth becomes part of its religion."

George Lucas bought into Campbell's idea of myths as motivators and said he would never have been able to finish Star Wars had it not been for Campbell. On release of the movie sequel *Phantom Menace* (Hargrove May 1999) he said, "I consciously set about to re-create myths like Campbell." He described Campbell as his "spiritual godfather, If it were not for Joseph Campbell I might still be writing Star Wars. *Hero* (with a Thousand Faces 1949) was enlightening to me. It is a very old story in a very new costume. When Ben Kenobi says to Skywalker, `Turn off your computer, turn off your machine, and do it yourself, follow your feelings', he was getting in touch with his inner being." (Moyers 1988 p. 179). Executive Director of the Joseph Campbell Foundation told the media, "I do think Joseph Campbell had a profound effect on people's lives."

MYTHOLOGY AS GENRE

Joseph Campbell dedicated his life to finding "mythological representations" or "metaphors of our inner truth." He told Bill Moyers, "only a myth can help one live a systematic life with meaning" (Moyers PBS 1992). Campbell has tied real-life needs to historical myths in what he called, "a common humanity built into our nervous system out of which our imagination works" (Toms pg. 122). He offered the world an intellectual justification for adopting hero-mentors as legitimate role models. Richard Walter says, "I needed someone to champion my understanding that Robin Hood, King Arthur, Superman, Christ and Frodo were really the same person."

Myths were around long before books. They were originally passed down via fables and tales around campfires. Then the Greeks recorded them in the form of great epics like Homer's *The Iliad* and *Odyssey* in which he immortalized mythical heroes like Ulysses, Oedipus, Prometheus, Hercules, Achilles, and Orpheus. The Bible recorded the myths of Cain and Abel, Moses, David, and Joseph. Medieval mythography introduced us to Arthur and his knights of the roundtable, Beowulf, Robin Hood, Taliesin, Faust and Tristan. Mythical heroes from America are Paul Bunyon, Calamity Jane, Tarzan, Superman, Batman, Peter Pan, Captain Kirk, and Butch Cassidy.

Writers have long been enamored with warlords and political leaders like Caesar, Charlemagne, Cyrus the Great, Alexander the Great, Attila the Hun, and Napoleon. All of these heroes have survived as fantasy legends followed recently by Ghandi, Martin Luther King, Babe Ruth, Michael Jordan, Marilyn Monroe, and Elvis. The line between fiction and fact is often obscured in such modern day heroes but Elvis is really dead.

British writer J.R.R. Tolkien was a master of fantasy who created what has been called the world's greatest fantasy *The Lord of the Rings*. This one book has sold 50 million copies in 23 languages making it arguably the most read fantasy of all time. Scott Smith in an article appearing in the *Investors Business Daily* (July 8, 1999) said, "Tolkien set the standard by which all fantasy is judged." Biographer Humphrey Carter called *Rings* "an astonishing project with few parallels in the history of literature. He was going to create an entire mythology" (Smith 7-8-99 pg A8).

FANTASY & MOTIVATION. Alexander the Great was inspired by myths to such an extent he traveled to consult with the Oracle at Delphi to find out if he was predestined for greatness. The Oracle advised "You are invincible my son." That prophetic advice was recorded in his psyche arming him with the supreme confidence to fulfill his destiny.

An even more dramatic example of fantasy heroes altering one's life comes from Homer's Trojan War fable about the lost city of Troy. *The Illiad* was the only book German Henry Schlieman had as a child. Therefore it had enormous influence on him and he grew up mesmerized by Achilles and the city of Troy. Retiring early with a fortune he set out to find the city of his dreams. Trained architects called his search fool's gold, since there research proved the city was but a myth. Schlieman would not be deterred and after years of torment and illness he and stunned the scientific world with his discovery of the ancient civilization buried beneath many other cities in Western Turkey. Without Schlieman's fantasy hero-worship he would have been long since forgotten, but his name is now part of the annals of mythical history.

CAMPBELL'S MYTHICAL HERO IMPRINT.

Campbell's early heroes were Indians and icons. At age six he was taken to a Wild West Show in Madison Square Garden and came away mesmerized. Four years later he visited the Museum of Natural History and came away enamored of the Indians, the headdress regalia, and mythical symbolisms. Native American Indians became his passion and he began to read voraciously on the subject. He said, "I was tremendously impressed with the rooms full of totem poles" (Toms pg. 119). During a serious illness when he became bedridden his father bought him Grinnell's *Indian Love Tales*. Later he enrolled in Dartmouth only because they offered degrees in Indian culture.

He told biographer Michael Toms (1989) "Being brought up Roman Catholic affected me as a boy since their dogma, icons, and other symbols made me take it very seriously" (Toms pg. 119). His father fueled his interest by giving him many books on Indians and American history. Living next door to a library didn't hurt, as he became a voracious reader. During one vacation he met an Indian guide who would become a role model. He was given the White Beaver. He told Bill Moyers:

> *I fell in love with American Indians ... I began to read American Indian myths, and it wasn't long before I found the same motifs in the American Indian stories that I was being taught by the nuns at school* (Moyers *Power of Myth* pg. 12).

By nine was spending all his spare time with books on Indians and icons. He was reading Lewis Henry Morgan's *League of the Iroquois*, and said, "I read and reread it until it fell apart" (Larsen pg. 4). Muses dominated his imagination and he once claimed to have read everything in the library on Indian culture in one year. He told a biographer "When I was a kid I never let anyone pull me off course" (Campbell 1988 p. 147). He spoke of devouring volumes of Bureau of American Ethnology.

WRITERS & THEIR MYTHICAL HEROES

One of the most inspirational stories of books as motivators comes from the life of Maya Angelou. She had been raped at age eight and the trauma caused her to go mute for five years. A teacher decided to bring her out of her self-imposed silence by having her read lines from Shakespeare, Poe, and Kipling. Maya says, "I spoke it. I decided to speak. I haven't stopped since" (Peterson *USA Today* 1992). Bill Clinton gave her the mythical title of Poet Laureate when he had her deliver thehis inauguration poem in 1991. Here is a woman who never attended college, but due to the influence of books has become a tenured creative writing professor at Wake Forest University. She once wrote, "*Crime & Punishment* changed my life." But her most telling comment was to a reporter for *Parade*, "A hero/shero encourages people to see the good inside themselves and to expand it. My heroes were Eleanor Roosevelt, Pearl S. Buck and abolitionist Frederick Douglas." (*Parade* magazine interview 8-6-95 pg. 5).

Dostoevsky wrote in his journal, "I read. I read like a fiend. It was Anne Radcliff novels that made a difference. I would rave deliriously about them in my sleep" (Frank 1969 p. 55). It is not an accident that he would grow up to write highly emotional words of passionate intensity. Stephen King went through a similar transformation from books that he discovered at eight by H. P. Lovecraft. He says, "Lovecraft is the father of supernatural horror. He opened the way for me. It is Lovecraft who oversees almost all of the important horror fiction" (Beahm p. 22). He validated his won inspiration saying, "I discovered Dr. Jekyll & Mr. Hyde and I lived and died with that story."

Anne Rice gave credit for her writing success to the metaphysical stories of Dickens. She said, "I'm overly obsessed with *A Christmas Carol.* I've watched the English film version of it probably more than anyone in history... read and reread the story. I wanted to go into a supernatural persona of Scrooge"

(Riley p. 285). Shakespeare's ghost scene in *Hamlet* also was a huge influence on her.

Hemingway worshipped the work of both Dostoevsky and Mark Twain and emulated their style by concocting stories with moral outcomes. It is interesting that he modeled his career after both his heroes choosing to become a journalist and free-lance writer. Hemingway called Twain's *Huckleberry Finn* and Dostoevsky's *The Brothers Karamazov* two of the best novels ever written. He became to the "Lost Generation" what Twain had been to the "Gilded Age."

Ayn Rand escaped into a hero-worship from French novels while living in St. Petersburg as a child. The conquering hero Cyrus was the most inspirational. She wrote in her Newsletter, "I am a hero worshipper." This is validated by her writing which all centers around some larger-than-life hero - John Galt in *Atlas Shrugged* and Howard Roark in *The Fountainhead*. Rand spent her life writing about people *as they could be* not as they were. She grew up worshipping Peter the Great and Catherine the Great and then fell in love with Victor Hugo's *Les Miserables*. She called Hugo "the greatest novelist in world literature. One does not settle for lesser values, neither in books or life" (Sciabara pg. 82).

LITERARY INNOVATION

Newsweek called Campbell "the rarest of intellectuals in American life; a serious thinker who has been embraced by the popular culture." The Cincinnati Post described him as having a "profound influence on millions." Henry Morton Robinson wrote, "The Hero blends mythology, psychoanalysis, poetry, and scholarship into a compelling narrative and convinces the thoughtful reader that myth and dreams are the most potent and permanent forces in the lives of man. It was an incredible feat" (Larsen pg. 348). Writer Michael Toms interviewed Campbell and wrote, "I was carried into a realm far beyond any of my previous experiences" (Toms p. 14).

Campbell's tied the epic stories of the hero's journey into a purposeful event for the reader. In his words, "Myths are powerful guides to the life of the spirit – our ticket to the passages of life" (Moyers 1992 PBS). His intent was to marry dream-like fantasies with their self-actualizing messages and motivations. He preached, "Archetypes are acquired through identity with myths – they are spontaneous productions of the psyche" (Moyers pg. 61). After a lifetime searching for the meaning of myths he concluded, "the wills of people become inextricably tied to the metaphoric hero who were those who dared "follow their bliss" (Moyers pg. 150). He admonished people to:

> *Follow your bliss for an emotionally stable life. Those who must program themselves to fit the image of others are setting themselves up for a schizophrenic experience. I would never submit and free people do not. They refuse to be programmed by any established order.* (Toms 1989)

Campbell wrote, "If you *follow your bliss*, you'll always have your bliss, but if you follow your money, you may lose it. Make your hobby your source of income, then there is no such thing as work, there is no such thing as getting tired" (Toms p. 126). Campbell believed that to be reborn one must die and reemerge.

Mary Lefkowitz, writing for the *American Scholar* (Summer 1990) concluded, "Campbell is not a historian or critic of religion, but rather a priest of a new and appealing hero-cult – the religion of self-development." That is precisely why he has been included in this work. He studied diverse cultures and found universal messages that translated into ever-evolving success. He was a fan of Jung's and like Jung believed that life's experiences were involved in Archetypes within our unconscious. His work in furthering this concept is his contribution to psychology and motivational theory.

WRITING AS CATHARSIS

Campbell's classic *Hero with a Thousand Faces* was not written until he was in his mid-forties. In this book he said, "Each of us are mythological representations of our inner truth and our jobs and other mundane experiences are merely symbols of a larger mythological meaning in our lives" (Moyers 1992 PBS). That was certainly true for him. He remembered his own myths of Indian culture that he saw "rising from within" and motivating him to find their source. He concluded, "Myths are metaphorical, spontaneous productions of the human psyche, and revelations of the deepest hopes, desires, fears, potentialities, and conflicts of the human will" (Segal p. 221). His cathartic release can be seen in his words:

> *I've been dealing with this stuff all my life, and I am still stunned by the accuracy of the repetitions. It is almost like a reflex in another medium of the same thing. Mythological themes are manifestations of man's character. They inspire the realization of the possibility of your perfection. They grab you somewhere down inside and become revelations.* (Segal pg. 192)

Books were Campbell's passion. When he was dating his young wife Jean Erdman it began to rain very hard. The ever-gallant Campbell ripped off his jacket. Erdman beamed with expectations of having the coat thrown over her for protection. When Campbell covered his precious book *The Decline of the West* she knew immediately that she would always be relegated to second place to books. She said, "I knew what I was in for."

METAMORPHOSES

Campbell lived with an obsessive need to find the answer to life's great mysteries. This need began at age five after that trip to Madison Square Garden to see Buffalo Bill. He was bitten and his youth was spent reading about American Indian culture. At age 80 he still remembered the influence of two books read in his teens, *League of the Iroquois* by Lewis Morgan, and *Book of Woodcraft* by Ernest Seton. He said they were an epiphany during the time he was bedridden with pneumonia. "I read these books and reread them until they fell apart."

JOSEPH CAMPBELL

Other books with a mythical influence were *Indian Love Tales* by George Bird Grinnell, H.G. Wells *Outline of History, Decline of the West,* and *Arnold's Light of Asia* about the life of Buddha. He called the latter "instrumental in my search for the truth of myths." He spent a fortune traveling to the ends of the earth to find the smallest artifact on mythology. While on one trip to Paris he met James Joyce. They became instant friends and he assisted in editing the Irish author's classics *Ulysses* and *Finnegan's Wake.* Both books were a monumental influence on him. He said, "No one knew more about the world I wanted to discover than James Joyce" (Moyers 1988 p. 2). During an early period he spent time in California with John Steinbeck. Whose wife was so taken with him she was willing to leave her husband and run off with the charismatic man of myth.

On one soiree to Europe he met and befriended the consciousness guru J. Krishnamurti. He described the experience "a turning point in my life." At 30 he stopped teaching. He became an intellectual hermit living and reading in a remote cabin in Woodstock, New York. He dropped out for four years devouring the Greek classics admitting, "I read the classics for twelve hours a day in search of the truth of myths."

That period proved to be a reawakening and transformation in his life. On his return to Manhattan, he married ex-student Jean Erdman, who was on her way to a professional dancing career. They agreed to live without the distraction of children in their life. In his words, "We will have earthly children and spirit children – books and plays and creative fosterlings" (Larsen pg. 269). Campbell had married and it would be a wonderful experience, but the two were intrepid warriors pursuing their own careers in far removed vistas. They spent little time together as she was devoted to dance he was in a desperate search for the history of myths.

ECCENTRICITIES

Campbell was a renegade and highly superstitious. He was intrigued with Jung's mysticism, Zen Buddhism, astrology, spiritualism, and the occult. His Roman Catholic upbringing had imbued him with spiritualism, but his heart and head led him to adopt a Buddhist system of god within. He said, "The God we have is the one we're capable of having" (Toms p. 88). He told Moyers on a 1992 PBS Special, "Religion is really a kind of second womb. Everyone is God in their deepest identity. God's in all religions are merely masks of their unique myths."

This was consistent with his belief that "You can't have creativity unless you leave behind the bounded, the fixed, all the rules." An indication of his unconventional and almost mystical approach to things was his marriage ceremony. He insisted the marriage take place precisely on the 5th hour, of the 5th day, during the 5th month, at 5:00 p.m. He believed in Carl Jung's aphorism, "myth is a cycle and this cycle is a symbolic representation of the form of the soul" (Larsen pg. 226).

The master of mythology was a creature of habit. He sat at the same table in their Greenwich Village apartment for over thirty years reading and researching about myths. When his material was depleted he jumped on a plane and headed to the far reaches of the earth to uncover some esoteric artifact or icon to prove a point. On these trips he met with the likes of Jung and Freud. After reading Jung's *Symbols of Transformation* he traveled to Switzerland to meet the eminent psychotherapist. His friends read like a Who's Who including such diverse personalities as Steinbeck, Joyce, Maslow, Jung, Krishnamurti, Fritz Perls, Alan Watts, Jean Houston, Bob Dylan, George Lucas and Jerry Garcia." Garcia told the media, "The Grateful Dead concerts are a recreation of the Dionysian mysteries" (Larsen pg. 540).

LIFE CRISES

After suffering from pneumonia he was weak and debilitated and was taken to a remote cabin in Forest Lake to recuperate. It was here that he met the part-Indian naturalist Elmer Gregor who became his teacher, guide and mentor. Gregor gave him the Indian name White Beaver while they lived and hiked together in the wilderness. Two years later he received a phone call at school informing him that his grandmother had died and his father was severely burned trying to save her. His father was disfigured, but became a hero forever in his son's mind. The family lost everything and his father was scarred for life.

POLYPHASIC

Campbell was an insatiable workaholic who kept volumes of files on every aspect of hundreds of cultures throughout the world. He studied every known religion and their dogmas. He worked obsessively on more projects and books than he could ever hope to complete. His mastery of esoteric facts and their interrelationships was nothing short of mind-boggling, especially when he was in his late seventies and early eighties. At 80 he was living in Hawaii but still traveling the world and lecturing in far-flung places like Greece, Japan, and New York City. While in the hospital for chemotherapy for cancer he was still listening to tapes in order to learn to speak Japanese. This pedagogical vagabond was an overachiever, and validated his own principles of mythical motivation. At the time of his death at 83 he was still busy working on a whole series of new books.

CRITICAL ACCLAIM

On February 28, 1985, the National Arts Club of New York honored Campbell with the Gold Medal of Honor for Literature. This prestigious affair was attended by many celebrities including producer George Lucas, writers Richard Adams and Nancy Willard, singer Linda Ronstadt and many notables from the arts. The Master of Ceremonies was James Hillman, a Jungian analyst and author, who said of Campbell, "No one in our century, not Freud, not Jung, not Thomas Mann, not Levi Strauss, has so brought a mythic sense of the world back into our daily consciousness" (Larsen pg. 545). Adams concluded, "My debt to him is incalculable. He made sense of my life, and he made me an international best-selling author."

The editor of *Psychology Today* San Kan spent time with Campbell at Esalen Institute and said, "Joseph didn't know more than *any* of us, he knew more than *all* of us. I think he was the encyclopedia all by himself. None of us had as much data as he did" (Larsen p. 490). Campbell had a Masters Degree in Anthropology from Columbia, but it was Promethean spirit and obsession with the need to know that led him on an interminable search for the derivation of myths. This search led him to an obscure and esoteric search to remote lands.

Bill Moyers, one of the country's more erudite TV journalists, was enthralled with Campbell's spiritual mysticism. He was interviewed in a highly acclaimed *Power of Myth* PBS TV Special in 1988. It would be one of the most successful cable documentaries ever produced for TV. This breakthrough program married the intellectual and mythical in a manner the layman could understand. Campbell was a master showman, articulate, and never imposing. Metaphors were his forte.

Both Bill Moyers and Michael Toms wrote books about Campbell. Moyers eulogized him in *The Power of Myth* (1991) Toms did so in *An Open Life* (1989). Both Jean Houston and Joan Halifax were on the lecture circuit with Campbell and chose to adopt him as a mentor. Halifax says, "He taught me how to use images, and talk about them." Houston says he transformed "my inner hero" (Larsen pg. 516).

> *He was my hero since childhood. His influence on this human consciousness writer and lecturer was immense. I was ten years old when I read The Hero With a Thousand Faces, and it set me off on all kinds of adventures and challenges that were seemingly inappropriate for a young girl. I decided to become a hero not a heroine.*

Campbell's intellectual explorations into the ethereal world of the unconscious was lost on many critics. They conservatives who require proofs berated him for daring to explore the depths of academic subjects without adhering to scholarly standards and methodology. Other literary critics maligned him for being too metaphysical and too interested in religion. One female critic went so far as to accuse him of being an anti-semite, anti-religious, and an anti-feminist. Morton Adler writing in the *National Review* (Feb. 17, 1992) took great exception to his "Follow your bliss" aphorism calling it "simple-minded hedonism." That is quite provincial considering the essence of

Campbell's whole style was metaphorical and apparently lost on Adler who took his words at face value. Those most critical of his work are those who find fault with Esalen and their New Age messages, although others like Fritz Perls and Abe Maslow were never so demeaned.

SUCCESS & MYTHICAL HEROES – What Can We Learn?

Campbell was convinced that none of us live the life we should or would like. We live the life intended by others or more likely the one preordained by our conditioning. The *will* was programmable for Campbell, as it is for this author, and that instruction set had best not be programmed by someone else's agenda. This was reiterated to Bill Moyers as:

> *Life's potentialities are innately unconscious and myths are powerful guides to the life of the spirit – our ticket to the spirit. Myths are metaphorical references of the will.*

Campbell admonished us to pursue the life that makes us whole and to adamantly refuse to live life as dictated by family, friends, or mates. His recommended a life lived as *controlled introspection.* He believed the literary genius should dare to take introspective journeys that are not safe. He said to "Take a chance. If you lose you are scarcely worse off than before." He wrote, "If you have the guts to follow risk, life opens" (Toms p. 24). Such people were the true heroes for Joseph Campbell.

The successful life and career of Motown founder Berry Gordy offers validity tor Campbell's hero hypothesis. Gordy was eight when Joe Louis won the heavyweight boxing championship of the world. In his memoirs Gordy wrote of the epiphany that occurred that day. He said, "Joe Louis was the first person who made me know what the word hero meant. When he won the heavyweight crown – at that moment a fire started deep inside me, a burning desire to be special, to win, to be somebody. To me he was the greatest hero in the universe. His phenomenal feats had opened my imagination to the possibility of being something in this world" (Gordy pg.11 & 407).

LITERARY GENIUS

In *Myths to Live* (p. 453) Campbell wrote, "All of this life is meditation and most of it is unintentional. All informed species live and model their lives through acts of make believe. A youngster identified with a mustang goes galloping down the street with a new vitality and personality." These words recall the fantasy hero-worship of Ernest Hemingway. When Hemingway was refused induction in the military he was distraught but found a role model in the book *Dark Forest*. The hero was also denied induction but enlisted as an ambulance driver and became a hero and the next day Hemingway enlisted as a Red Cross ambulance driver.

Heroes can empower, motivate and inspire. But their true significance is removal of self-imposed limitations to success. When attempting to push the limits of any art form it is imperative that one believe they can succeed. If that takes identifying with the path taken by others so be it, and even if the belief is deluded it is okay if it works. All great acts or leadership demands consummate belief, pretending you are a greater being is okay if that imagery makes you greater.

Modeling success works. This has been proven with athletes and astronauts. The secret is picking the right horse to ride to grab the brass ring. The more omnipotent the mythical mentor, the better since it makes them larger than life. What is important is to jump into that proverbial phone booth and come out with a cape and the belief that nothing is beyond your talents. The adopted image can transform and inspire from within. Men and women of steel are not born in the physical sense but in the ethereal sense. Their power is within and it is there that transformation must take place. Borrowing the power of mythical imagery is okay.

Writing with a big red S on your chest is acceptable but just don't try to go beyond the edge where reality and possibility meet. Grand achievement is there for those who believe, and pretending to be Superman can help in the trek. The secret is in selecting the ideal fantasy hero that best fits your needs.

FYODOR DOSTOEVSKY
FATHER OF PSYCHOLOGICAL NOVEL
b. Moscow, Russia, Oct. 3, 1821
d. St. Petersburg, Russia Jan. 28, 1881

BREAKDOWN & BREAKTHROUGH

DOMINANT GENRE
First novelist with psychological underpinnings that delved into the inner mind of protagonists to find motivations for actions

MOTTO
"Self-purification through suffering"

GREATEST WORKS
Crime & Punishment (1866)
The Idiot (1869)
The Brothers Karamazov (1880)

HONORS/AWARDS
Nietzsche, "I learned more about psychology from Dostoevsky than any other person" - Gide/Bennett wrote, "The Brothers Karamazov is the greatest novel ever written"

ECCENTRICITIES
Manic-depressive, epileptic, compulsive self-destructive gambler

LIFE CRISES
Mother died at 15, father murdered when 17 triggering epilepsy, rebellion, arrest, and death sentence for sedition; reprieve at 11th hour led to epiphany in Siberian prison that spawned many books on the psychology of man

METAMORPHOSES
Imprisonment led to transformation: "The escape into myself from bitter reality did bear its fruit – the individual triumphs only through his loss of individuality."

5

FYODOR DOSTOEVSKY– Psychological novel

SUCCESS IS OFTEN BORN OF TRAUMA

"Prison destroyed many things in me and created the new"
"SELF PURIFICATION THROUGH SUFFERING!"

Success is born of tragedy just as breakdown precedes breakthrough. Few individuals in history demonstrate this better than Fyodor Dostoevsky who was transformed by the negative life forces that nearly destroyed him; but ended up remaking him into one of the great novelists in history and as father of the psychological novel. The irony of his dysfunctional life is that the psychological symptoms that plagued him and made his life a living hell were the catalyst for his great insights into the plight of man.

DYSFUNCTIONAL CATALYST. The father of the psychological novel suffered from obsessive-compulsive disorder and bipolar illness. He was suicidal, epileptic, a compulsive gambler and had many emotional breakdowns. These problems contributed to his metamorphoses from journeyman writer into a master at portraying characters of unbelievable realism. Many of his famous characters were cathartic representations of his own emotional dilemmas and dysfunctions. Four of them had seizures that he labeled "Mystic Terrors."

TRAUMATIC TRANSFORMATION. Dostoevsky's traumas were far worse than the plights of his protagonists. Letters to his brother document his transformation. His elegant existentialist style didn't materialize until after he had spent ten years exiled in Siberia and endured the tortures of epilepsy, obsessive gambling, manic-depression, nervous afflictions, manias and compulsions. Excess defined him, but it appears to have been exacerbated by his crisis-ridden life. It began with his mother's premature death, was worsened by his father's murder and castration, became manifest with his arrest and death sentence for sedition and found it full fury after he lost his daughter while in Geneva fleeing from debtors prison.

Words of passion erupted out of those demons buried deep within his troubled psyche. How so? It appears the tormented become more introspective when lie is held in the balance. Inner turmoil can destroy or lead to ardor. In Dostoevsky's case he attempted to write out his worst fears and compulsions in hopes the despicable "fiend" would go away. The fiend was his bouts with epilepsy, compounded by his mania, obsessive behaviors and compulsive gambling.

Dostoevsky came to believe he was a visionary and in some respects he was. Consider the insightful words written on the coming of the Bolshevist Revolution. They were written in 1870 about an event that occurred in 1917. He had Pyotr Stepanovich Verhovensky in *The Possessed* (1871) say, "There's going to be an upset as the world has never seen before. Russia will all be overwhelmed with darkness, the earth will weep for its old gods" (Gide pg. 167).

Dostoevsky spoke of Mohammad's religious conversion, saying, "Mohammad assures us in the Koran that he had seen Paradise. He did not lie. He had veritably been in Paradise in an attack of epilepsy, from which he suffered as I do" (Pickover 268). Dostoevsky's long vigil in a Siberian prison made him introspective to a fault. He wrote of being buried underground and "enduring cold, hunger, sickness and the hatred of companions." The other prisoners disliked this educated man who could read and write only pushing Dostoevsky further into his inner sanctum. This is how he survived.

On release from prison he wrote to his brother saying, "the escape into myself did bear its fruits" (Gide pg. 63). The traumas led him into a lifelong search to justify such beastly brutality and personal anguish. Such introspective probing was at the root of his psychological novels that portrayed mankind in a perpetual struggle with their own inner drives, wants and needs.

CRISES & TRANSFORMATION. Many writers, including Nietzsche, have suggested that a great problem doesn't kill you makes you stronger. Aristotle wrote, "No great genius is without some mixture of insanity." Vision and insight are often a function of personal crises or what Van Gogh characterized as "the storm within." Goethe said, "whatever was destroying him also fueled his creativity" (Pickover 1998 pg. 264). Clifford Pickover in *Strange Brains and Genius* offered numerous examples of genius being molded by "losing a parent shortly after birth" (260). He cited many examples of scientific genius being afflicted with manic-depression, epilepsy (TLE), or OCD - obsessive-compulsive disorders.

Creative inspirations often occur only after we reach the breaking point. Why? Because trauma enhances focus and lights some inner fire that inspires and motivates. Staring at our mortality tends to remove the natural roadblocks within our psyche that can block creativity. When we have been stripped of all fears, personal and professional, we experience a transformation. Psychologists have found that "super-learning" takes place in the midst of chaos. When we become transfixed or in a state of shock we become more conditioned to change. It is in the theta (trancelike) state that we alter our perspective. That is why behavior modification tapes have us listening to tapes just prior to sleep. Life-threatening experiences put us in this hypnotic state. Children are often in this state. It is the reason for their superior learning ability.

When a person faces a death-threat or tragic loss they tend to see the world through a different filter. They are often transformed by the experience and often perform Herculean feats like lifting a car off a child. An unusual number of these writers reached the pinnacle of success only after some life-threatening event or the tragic loss. The visit to the bottom appears to have groomed them for the top. Dostoevsky, Michener and Rice experienced epiphanies.

Instead of a crutch tragedy can became a catalyst. Is the transformation always for the better? No! Virginia Woolf spent much time in an asylum, never had children, and lived a life fearing the next incarceration. Dostoevsky never quite knew when the next epileptic fit would befall him and he spent much of his life in mortal fear of his "mystic terror." Woolf vacillated between sanity and creativity during which she wrote her classics but in the end suicide won out. Plath and Hemingway ended their turbulent lives in the same way. After her daughter's death at age five from leukemia Anne Rice crawled into an inebriated existence with a case of beer daily to mask the pain until emerging as the Queen of the Occult. James Michener was a reclusive personality due to his lack of a childhood or any parental guidance. Ted Geisel remained a child, preferring not to deal with adulthood because it was mean and lethal. He wrote, "I've always mistrusted adults, one reason I dropped out of Oxford. They took life too seriously. When I dropped out of Oxford I decided to be a child."

DOSTOEVSKY – CRISES & CREATIVITY

Dostoevsky's life reads like a Greek tragedy. The father of the psychological novel led a rather uneventful early childhood. When 13 his mother became terminally ill and died of TB within two years. He suddenly lost the ability to speak. This was the first sign of internalization of grief. Then his domineering father sent him off to a military engineering school in St. Petersburg despite his desire to pursue a life in the literary arts. Dostoevsky once again repressed his feelings and obeyed his dictatorial father. They never spoke for months. Then when his father was murdered and castrated by servants Fyodor experienced guilt beyond his comprehension, since his wish for his father's demise had come true. Freud concluded this in his famous analysis of Dostoevsky.

Biographer Frank spoke of a drastic personality change and the onset of his epilepsy after his mother's death. That precipitated a severe reclusive nature and unhappiness. He "escaped into books, vodka, and a renegade lifestyle." The ensuing darkness led to a turbulent life leading to arrest for political anarchy, near-execution, imprisonment, exile, compulsive gambling, heavy drinking and a tormented life.

AN EPIPHANY! The master of the psychological novel was transformed from a promising young military engineer into a renegade writer with his father's murder. The transformation proved advantage for his career but devastating for his personal life. He would spend the rest of his life searching for logic in a Christian world that could allow such tragedy to happen. He became enamored with death, murder, sickness, and unhappiness and especially the cause of the "fiend" (epilepsy).

Dostoevsky's early crises armed him with survival instincts and led him to analyze the cause of man's inhumanity to man and its meaning. He had what Freud described as "a very strong destructive instinct, which might have made him a criminal but had been directed mainly against his own person (inward vs outward) and thus found expression as masochism and a sense of guilt." (World Literary Critiscim 1992 pg. 973).

Dostoevsky was a self-destructive personality. He was a slave to his dysfunctions. He was unable to relax for fear of a seizure, could not stay away from roulette tables, and drank to excess to escape a horrid world, and lived life on the edge. It is amazing he was able to function at all with such a plethora of afflictions. Most people would have crawled into a bottle or just ended it all. But Dostoevsky used his afflictions to further his insights into mankind. The result was the first books that looked within and came to be known as psychological novels.

Dostoevsky didn't hit bottom until his arrest for espionage in his late twenties the budding young writer was a member of the Petrashevsky Circle, an elite group of intellectuals arrested for subversion. He was given a death sentence commuted by the Czar at the 11th hour. But he was sentenced to five years in Siberia at the height of his career. And when released was forced to served five more years in a Siberian military compound. Those ten years completed his transformation from idealist to nihilist released in a torment of creative energy that became magnificent treatises on the meaning of life.

ENTROPY? Entropy means general disorder, conflict, social disintegration, chaos or crisis. Webster describes it as "a measure of the unavailable energy in a closed thermodynamic system or a measure of disorder." Nobel Prize winning biologist Dr. Ilya Prigogine describes it as "general disorder, conflict, social disintegration or environmental depletion." Prigogine won the Nobel Prize in Biology by demonstrating that emotional systems living "close to equilibrium will be completely predictable" and those of "ever-increasing complexity (entropy) is the mechanism that brings about chaos" (Capra 1996 p. 185). In other words, the non-chaotic system is highly predictable but never capable of true creativity because in his system all things approach chaos, what he termed the "bifurcation point" at which point it self-destructs or reemerges better than prior to the crises. Prigogine said, "many systems of breakdown are actually harbingers of breakthrough" (Pearsall 1991 p. 238). That would explain Dostoevsky's success.

Prigogine said, "all structures are teetering perpetually between entropy and negentropy, between chaos and information, self-destruction and reorganization to a higher plane" He wrote:

> *It is out of the chaos and turmoil and disorder that higher levels of order and wisdom emerge. The more unstable the more likely it is to change – to evolve... In the field of psychological activity this is perhaps the main experience we have – every artistic creation implies a transition from disorder to order* (Hutchison p. 267).

HISTORICAL EXAMPLES OF CRISES & CREATIVITY. One example of this Prigogine's theory at work is the reemergence of Japan and Germany from the devastation in World War II. Do you think they would have the most powerful currencies today had they not been destroyed? Not a chance! Had they not been thrown into chaos and forced to rebuild every factory from scratch they wouldn't be nearly as strong today. When starting from the bottom a nation or individual must try harder and work harder. That is why the sons of highly successful people seldom have similar success. It is not because of talent or opportunity but due to having it too easy.

DISSIPATIVE STRUCTURE THEORY. Prigogine's Law of Dissipative Structures is what happens when one faces a tragedy. They either die or reemerge. Prigogine called it chaos or reincarnation. At the *Bifurcation Point* men like Dostoevsky either breakdown or experience a breakthrough. An example is breaking a bone in your arm. You can never break it in that spot again. Why? Because it heals stronger at the break than if it had not been traumatized. Prigogine applied this law to emotional systems. In his profound words, "Psychological suffering, anxiety, and collapse can lead to new emotional, intellectual and spiritual strengths – confusion and death can lead to new scientific ideas" (Prigogine 1984).

Therevore, *it isn't what happens to us that counts, only how we deal with the experience*. Those who allow tragedy to overwhelm them crawl into a bottle and self-destruct. The creative genius tends to use the tragedy to motivate them to greater success. Dostoevsky appears to be a poster boy for the latter. He wrote to his older brother Mikhail from prison saying as much. "Prison destroyed many things in me and created the new. The escape into myself from bitter reality did bear its fruit – the individual triumphs only through loss of individuality" (Gide 1961 pg. 66).

PSYCHOLOGICAL NOVEL GENRE

The Greeks were the first to write about human behavior. Socrates said, "The life which is unexamined is not worth living." Plato wrote, "The soul knows who we are from the beginning." Aristotle wrote, "Man is by nature a political animal, our character is the result of our conduct." Later Shakespeare became a master of insight into the plight of man. Balzac and Hugo delved into the machinations that motivated man. Both Dickens and Scott influenced Dostoevsky. Henry James and George Eliot carried the torch further with their prescient views on man and the reasons for his actions. The genre was furthered by the writings of Joseph Conrad, James Joyce, Virginia Woolf, and William Faulkner. They had man's motives play a key role in their stories.

Behavior for Dostoevsky was based on unconscious drives that were difficult if not impossible to control as seen in Roskolnikov in his classic *Crime and Punishment* (1866). It is interesting that Dostoevsky suppressed his father's murder (it was not known publicly until the early 20th century), despite his repeated use of parricide in his work. Oedipal themes were also quite prevalent in his writing with psychological themes pervading *Crime and Punishment* (1866) and *The Brothers Karamazov* (1880). The inner motives of man are also quite prevalent in *House of the Dead* (1860), *Notes from the Underground* (1864), *The Gambler* (1867), *The Idiot* (1869), *The Possessed* (1871). Freud validates this with his comment, "Dostoevsky illustrates psychoanalysis in every character and every sentence" (Joseph Frank 1976 pg. 379). This is interesting since it implies that Freud believed Dostoevsky had anticipated psychoanalysis as much as he did existentialism.

PSYCHOLOGY AS A THEME IN DOSTOEVSKY'S BOOKS

Psychologist Alfred Adler was highly influenced by Dostoevsky as indicated by the following statement: (Adler, 1925 pg. 283)

Dostoevsky's achievements as a psychologist have not yet been exhausted. He must be hailed as our teacher. His creations, his ethic, and his art take us very far in the understanding of human cooperation.

Freud said "Dostoevsky `assumed the burden of parricidal guilt' over the death of his father. The Father of Psychoanalysis wrote, "Dostoevsky punished himself by his first epileptic seizures" (Frank 1976 pg. 383). Biographer Frank used the Adlerian "inferiority complex" concept to draw out the parallels between Dostoevsky's early traumas and his creative genius. He said, "only through the abolition of serfdom could the trauma of his guilt be assuaged" (Frank 1976 pg. 88).

Dostoevsky spoke eloquently about man's freedom to kill due to an omnipotent power that emanates from within a superior being. In Raskolnikov, Dostoevsky creates a superior intellect capable of killing impassionately. His free-will theme was drawn out in *Crime and Punishment* (1866) with Raskolnikov as a renegade intellectual who dispassionately murders a miserable wretch to depict *will* as superior to *emotion* especially for the superior man. Dostoevsky is depicting an *internality* of the will in contrast to its *externality*. Raskolnikov is able to fool the police and even his family but in the long run he is incapable of dealing with his own inner guilt that motivates him to turn himself in to the police.

Dostoevsky's message is loud and clear. Even a super human being can dupe the rest of the world but they are incapable of duping themselves. He was also attempting to depict a super hero who may inherit the kingdom of God by denial of the mind, will, and by surrendering his will to a higher power. He was really attempting to find the source of his own inability to control his urges, compulsions, gambling obsession, epileptic fits and need to live life on the edge.

Historical Examples of Crises Leading to Creativity. It is quite unlikely that Alexander the Great would have conquered the world had his father not been assassinated when he was twenty or had he been more normal (psychologists say he was M/D). Would Leonardo Da Vinci have been able to create the *Mona Lisa* or *Last Supper* had he not been born illegitimate? Unlikely! Similar traumas are found in the life of Michelangelo whose mother died when he was six. Mother Teresa lost her father at eight. Madam Curie lost her sister and mother by fourteen and had a nervous breakdown at 15 and another just prior to her second Nobel Prize. Of the seventeen subjects in this book twelve (76%) lost a parent and the rest had near-death experiences early in life.

Literary Examples of Crises & Creativity. Each of the subjects in this book experienced some horrible trauma or lost a parent or sibling at an impressionable age. A few had near-death experiences that appear to have transformed them. French novelist Balzac had a life-long love/hate relationship with his mother writing of his "desertion" and to his mother, "Had you loved me I would probably have ended up a failure." Samuel Clemens lost his father, sister, and brother before age twelve. Michener had to experience an airplane crash to launch his writing career. Ayn Rand had to leave Russia and write the Russian Revolution out of her system with cathartic novels. And had Anne Rice's daughter not died the vampire books would have never been written.

FYODOR DOSTOEVSKY

LITERARY INNOVATIONS

Crime & Punishment (1866) is considered one of the world's great psychological novel.   Philosopher Frederick Nietzsche claimed, "I learned more about psychology from Dostoevsky than any other person." Freud called *The Brothers Karamazov* (1880) a great book.

Literary critics see Dostoevsky as the creator of "moral horrors" – or what biographer Frank termed his ability to show "human relations as a struggle for psychic domination." Frank also called him the "chronicler of the moral consequences of flux and change; and of the breakup of the traditional forms of Russian life (serfdom)" (Frank 1976 pg. 6).   Hemingway said, "No one lasted more than three rounds with Dostoevsky."

WRITING AS CATHARSIS

All the Dostoevsky characters were imbued with his fantasies and dysfunctions.   The interpersonal dialogue that gained him the label *existentialist*, were based on his obsessive fascination with mental disorder, religion, ethics, and man's will to power. His personal problems in the caste system prevalent in Russia also pervaded his writing.

It is no coincidence that his works are rampant with abnormal people. He was abnormal and that is how he peopled the world. Epileptics, gamblers, hypomanics, pathological liars, thieves, and fringe members of society permeate his work.   His internal search for what made him tick made his books tick.   He was on a mission to find his own identity and that search proved providential for his writing.   Most of his heroes were in a life and death struggle to find the meaning in their life.

Dostoevsky's most autobiographical work was *The Gambler* written ironically, to help him rise above massive gambling debts.   It was a traumatic period for Dostoevsky written during his four years outside Russia.   It spoke of his experiences with his true love, Polina Suskova, a lover he met in Paris and traveled with to Italy.   It was a romantic period in his life that he used to cope with an unhappy marriage to an ill wife in Russia. Dostoevsky escaped to a fantasy world that would never materialize. Ironically, his second wife would play stenographer and take the notes for *The Gambler*.

Notes from the Underground was an anthology of the time he spent in a Siberian prison. *The Idiot* dealt with his execution experience. *Crime and Punishment* was written about his struggle with omnipotence - the superman persona (himself as the rebel Raskolnikov) and egoism versus his Christian ethic.

Dostoevsky's self-destructiveness offered him insight into his character Raskolnikov – a man torn asunder from within. Both paradoxically destroyed what they loved. Biographer Frank said, "Raskolnikov represents in some ways his own diabolical and uncontrollable urges and obsessions to gamble and drink. It is his pathological psychic predisposition to kill conditioned by ideological self-intoxication" (Frank 1995 pg. 102). In many respects, Raskolnikov was Dostoevsky, a man incapable of coping with his own dysfunctions. It was through Raskolnikov that Dostoevsky released his own pent-up emotions against ignorance that dictated his own life and turmoil.

METAMORPHOSES

Dostoevsky escaped into books early. He admitted to reading "like a fiend" as a teen. His mother pushed him into books and he was reading by age four. By age eight he had read the whole bible. An introverted and highly intense child, he escaped into the fantasy of books, especially novels by Ann Radcliff. He became emotionally addicted. "I would rave deliriously about them in my sleep" (Frank 1969 pg. 55). This internalization of emotional words led to the violent swings in temperament that today would be diagnosed as bipolar disease. But it was in books that he found solace, and escape from a dictatorial father. Only when reading or writing did he find peace.

ARREST & SENTENCING. Dostoevsky was arrested as an anarchist at age 28 and was condemned to die before a firing squad. He was marched to the wall and was awaiting death when the Czar suddenly appeared and commuted his sentence.

He was sent to Siberia for five years of hard labor, but would not return for ten. His survival caused him to retreat into an inner world where he found solace in spiritualism and became philosophical about life. Life was suddenly much cheaper in one sense and dearer in another. A free-spirited youth had been transformed into a nihilistic adult.

He wrote to Mikhail with emotional relief, "Never has there seethed in me such an abundant and healthy kind of spiritual life. Now my life will change. I shall be born again in a new form" (Boorstin 1992 pg. 662). Intense introspection saved him while in Siberia. He deplored the cold, lice, cockroaches, chains and hard labor and would later describe them as "four years being buried alive and closed in a coffin" (Gide 1961 pg. 67). But he saw the benefits in the change in him and would write his brother later, "Prison destroyed many things in me and created the new. I won't even tell you what tranformations were undergone by my soul, my faith, my mind, and my heart in that four years." (Frank 1990 pg. 66).

A WRITER IS REBORN. On his release from prison he was assigned to a remote Siberian village Semipalatinsk for military duty. There he met and married a widow suffering from tuberculosis, the same malady that had killed his mother. He soon joined his brother in a publishing house and wrote *The Insulted and Injured* and *The House of the Dead* to purge his head of the Siberian experience. He then wrote *Notes from the Underground* and worked as a journalist for his brother. *Notes from the Underground* was his cathartic release of the good experienced in Siberia. His wife Marya died in April 1864, and even though they were estranged it was difficult. Within three months his beloved brother Mikhail died and he never recovered. He agreed to assume his brother's huge debts for the magazine *Epoch,* but it was nearing bankruptcy. It took only a few months for *Epoch* to become completely insolvent and Mikhail's widow tried to destroy him. He began gambling in a misanthropic approach to crawling out of mountains of debt but only succeeded in becoming so deep he had to flee the country to keep out of debtor's prison. He wouldn't return for four years. In the midst of all these traumas his epilepsy worsened. He had hit bottom and wrote: (Frank 1995 pg. 54)

My epilepsy has worsened. If I work for a week without interruption I have an attack and the next week I cannot work because of the result of two or three more attacks. It is impossible to finish. The more one pays the more insolent they (creditors) become.

This period produced his most famous novel *Crime & Punishment*. The first draft was written in a fit of mania. It was dictated to 20-year old Anna Snitkina who he would later marry. He destroyed the first draft saying, "I burned it all. I didn't like it" (Frank 1995 pg. 42). During this time he was close to suicide, worked a demonic schedule, proposed to three different women, and spent his spare time gamling. Within five years his bouts with trauma found their way into words. His crises fostered literary masterpieces *Crime and Punishment, The Gambler, The Idiot,* and *The Possessed. The Gambler* was him as a self-destructive roulette addict. It was written in twenty days. *The Idiot* was about his own near-execution. *The Possessed* was based on a revolutionary man attempting to survive by life-denying forces beyond his control – the story of Dostoevsky's life in a nihilistic society.

ECCENTRICITIES

Dostoevesky was different. He was one of the first existential writers and a model for what the *beat generation* called unsociable and mysterious. He was afflicted with wild swings of temperament that sent him into deep depressions followed by feelings of euphoria and omnipotence. Vitality and egoism defined him. His brother described his intensity saying, "he works all night, never goes to bed until five in the morning and then gets up and works all day on editorials. He is the unhappiest of mortals" (Frank 1995 pg. 3). The man was a compulsive gambler in cards, roulette, billiards, and business. He tempted lady luck and lost. He not only lost his money but his sense of worth. Once in Geneva he pawned his clothes for food so he and new wife Anna could eat.

Suffocating debt threatened him with debtor's prison causing him to flee Russia for Europe. But he always felt lady luck awaiting him in a casino. He only succeeded in going further and further in debt. In one obsessive move he sold off all his future royalties to pay his debts and then lost it all in one sitting at the tables. Another time he sold off the advance royalties for three books for 1000 rubles, and the next day wrote to his friend Turgenev saying, "I have lost everything. I am completely broke. I even gambled away my watch" (Boorstin pg. 666). Such experiences sent him ever deeper into depression. His despair he went days without food.

Dostoevsky described his epileptic fits a "mystic terror." They dominated his life and work and were horrific experiences to be endured by both wives and friends. He was also beset by extreme perfectionism. He was a fastidious dresser and a fanatic for details. On finishing *The Idiot* he said, "My dissatisfaction of my novel amounts to disgust" (Gide pg 26). He rewrote *Crime and Punishment* and *The Brothers Karamazov* numerous times. He preached the need to never "sacrifice artistic integrity for editorial expediency" (Frank 1995 pg. 87).

LIFE CRISES

Dostoevsky's life from thirteen on was traumatic. It began with his mother's premature death, his father's murder and his own incarceration and near-death experience. After graduation from military school he turned to a writing career in St. Petersburg. At age twenty-four he became involved in a political revolutionary group known as the Petrashevsky Circle and when he was 28 was arrested for anarchy. He and the others were condemned to die by the firing squad. The next day he was led blindfolded and listened to the words, "ready, aim" when the Czar intervened. He told his second wife Anna, "If not for the providential accident of my arrest in 1849 I would certainly have gone mad."

Epilepsy plagued Dostoevsky throughout his adulthood. These emotional episodes were horrible. But in one moment of introspection his said, "the fiend is party to every work of art." To Dostoevsky the "fiend" were seizures and panic attacks. But he was also obsessive-compulsive disorder, bipolar, and had a foot fetish. Normal he was not.

POLYPHASIC PERSONALITY

Manic personalities tend to polyphasia. They are never content with doing one thing at a time or working on just one project. Dosteovsky fit the profile. He worked on many different manuscripts simultaneously. And speed and work were his escape from the fears of failure.

An example of his multi-tasking work ethic took place during the height of his traumas. At the time he was in his mid-fifties and the editor of the *Epoch*. He not only wrote editorials for the magazine at the same time he was busy writing his classic, *Crime & Punishment*, he began a new novel *The Gambler*. During this same period he got married, filed bankruptcy and slept but a few hours each night.

CRITICAL ACCLAIM

Nietzsche said, "Dostoevsky was the only psychologist from whom I had anything to learn" (Gide pg. 96). The master of psychological innuendo, Sigmund Freud wrote, "The *Brothers Karamazov* (1880) is the most magnificent novel ever written; the episode of the Grand Inquisitor, one of the peaks in the literature world. His magnificent characters are tendencies within himself" (World Literature Criticism 1992 pg. 972). Andre Gide agreed with Freud about *The Brothers Karamazov* being the greatest novel ever written (Gide 1961) as did critic William Bennet. Gide described Dostoevsky as wanting to see man ascend to a superman state of total will-to-power in the Nietzschean sense.

Most critics credit Dostoevsky with writing impassioned novels of rare psychological insight that had lasting influence on literature. It was Dostoevsky's legacy to search for internal freedom where he married the psyche with cognitive insights. Man's autonomy was of the highest importance for Dostoevsky.

FYODOR DOSTOEVSKY

SUCCESS OUT OF TRAUMA – What Can We Learn?

Dostoevsky transformed inner anxiety into passionate words and scenes. His many traumas were cathartic inspirations. Many of crises would have destroyed a lesser man, but he used them as a catalyst for creativity. His afflictions were beyond what most people would consider tolerable. During that era little was known about obsessive-compulsives, mania, depression, epilepsy, gambling addictions, or Type A behavior. It is no wonder he lived life on the edge.

The anguish Dostoevsky had to bear due to his many physical afflictions, the bitterness over imprisonment, gambling to try and get out of debt, and the tragic death of his beloved brother, wife and daughter all contributed to a tormented life. These scars left their mark on him and helped him try to find an answer. It is ironic that when Dostoevsky finally earned enough money from *Crime and Punishment* (1866) to pay off a number of his most vocal creditors it so infuriated them he was forced to flee St. Petersburg to escape indictment. While out of the country Dostoevsky wrote some of his most cherished works - *The Idiot* (1868) written in Geneva and *The Eternal Husband* (1870) and *The Possessed* (1871) written in Dresden.

Dostoevsky offers great insight into crisis and creativity. When trauma finds its way into our lives we can use it as a crutch or as a catalyst and there is only a fine line between the two extremes. We can crawl into a bottle or say to hell with it and go for broke. That is what most of the subjects in this work did. Trauma can empower or impoverish and only the individual has control of those alternative outcomes. The minute our traumas become catalysts the difficult becomes easier and all else is a piece of cake. Doors close will suddenly open. Crises is never recognized as a catalyst when at its peak. Only after it has past does the individual emerge better or crawl into the gutter as a victim. The only difference between winners and losers is the mental fix on what has transpired. And the winners always see trauma as temporary roadblocks on their trek to the top.

GEORGE BERNARD SHAW
RENEGADE PLAYWRIGHT & ESSAYIST
b. Dublin, Ireland July 26, 1856
d. London, England Nov. 2, 1950

SUCCESS & DARING TO BE DIFFERENT

DOMINANT GENRE
Independent non-conforming dramatist & essayist

MOTTO
"A reasonable man adapts to the world. An unreasonable man attempts to adapt the world to him. Therefore all progress depends on the unreasonable man."

GREATEST WORKS
Man & Superman (1903) [Don Juan & the Life Force of Nietzsche]
Pygmalion (1914) [My Fair Lady – most popular play & movie]
Heartbreak House (1919) spiritual bankruptcy – his favorite play
Saint Joan (1923) practical genius & inspired heroine Nobel Prize

HONORS
Nobel Prize for Literature (1925) which the iconoclast refused

ECCENTRICITIES
Renegade atheist, vegetarian, pacifist, faddist, and cynic who never consummated a forty year marriage to a socialite; he was Professor Henry Higgins

LIFE CRISES
Real father was his mother's music teacher/lover whom she ran off with to London, leaving the 13-year old with his alcoholic biological father; bout with death led him to marriage at age 39

METAMORPHOSES
"*Das Kapital* was the turning point in my career, Marx was a revelation"

6

GEORGE BERNARD SHAW – DRAMA

AN OUT-OF-THE-BOX DISSIDENT

"Some men see things the way they are and ask, Why?
I see them as they are not and ask, Why not?"

INNOVATIONS EMANATE FROM THE FRINGE

The Irish dramatist is the quintessential example of a radical reshaping the world. Shaw was described by one London critic as a "terrorist," whose words were "weapons of humour." (Holroyd 1989 pg. 247). Shaw would have agreed since he believed "Almost all of my greatest ideas have occurred to me first as jokes" (Holroyd p 240).

Shaw was an iconoclast who defied all tradition and convention. He had some inner need to rebel and destroy and turned to words to exact his dirty deeds. He worshipped at the altar of literary heroes Marx, Schopenhauer, and Nietzsche. It was their influence that led him to his *life force* theme a cousin to Nietzsche's Superman.

The writing methodology of Shaw was synonymous with rebellion and few were safe from his cynical invective including medicine, religion, music, politics, restaurants, politics, and the literary community. One example is his inflammable words:

> *"I regard current morality as too economic*
> *and sexual relations as disastrously wrong;*
> *and I regard certain doctrines of the Christian*
> *religion with abhorrence. I write plays with*
> *the deliberate object of converting the nation*
> *to my opinion in these matters. I have no*
> *other effectual incentive to write plays."*
> (Holroyd 1989 pg. 80)

GEORGE BERNARD SHAW

Shaw, the revolutionary and self-proclaimed scholar, said, "I am a specialist in immoral and heretical plays" (Holroyd pg 239), a vehicle he used to inform and entertain. Unconventionality defined this man who was revered and feared. Few were on the fence as people loved him or hated him. His acidic tongue was intemperate. Everyone was fair game.

Shaw viewed the world through a unique filter. The power of the *will* was the thing critical to all success in any venue and he lived his life as if he were a Nietzschean Superman and above the rules of ordinary man. All of his work is imprinted with the "overman" view of the world. It left many fans in a state of shock or wonderment.

In many respects Shaw was the Irish Nietzsche. And in the likeness of his mythical mentor he aroused the ire of conservatives, liberals, the Left, the Right, Communists, Catholics, Jews, Protestants, Faddists and the art world. Even agnostics were not safe around his flaming invective.

Shaw's life and work offer credence to *innovation emanating from radical ideas*. It is almost axiomatic that *few wins are born within the pack*. That is why *paradigm shifts* are created by individuals living outside the box. Most people fear the unknown and refuse to operate in any arena they deem unsafe. This can be seen by how few truly great things are ever originated by Fortune 500 firms. Why? Because such organizations are too mired in protecting their asset base to take the degree of risk necessary to change the world. That is why Steve Wozniak's employer Hewlett-Packard, a wonderfully progressive firm, told him they had no interest in his programmable computer. Their refusal forced Wozniak and his friend Steve Jobs to found Apple Computer. It is why Bally turned down the first video game Pong and why no bank would finance Disney's first animated film *Snow White*. It is also why mother Church imprisoned Galileo, and why it took a billboard salesman like Ted Turner to create CNN. Shaw said it best, "Reasonable men adapt to the world. Unreasonable men persist in adapting the world to them. Therefore all progress depends on the unreasonable man."

RENEGADES - THE CREATIVE DESTROYERS. The academic definition of innovation is *creative destruction*. This means that one must be prepared to destroy what exists to innovate. Change can improve one's life or destroy it. But those individuals who refuse to destroy anything are those that also never achieve anything. In a dynamic world one must be dynamic or pay the price of mediocrity, and dynamic demands operating contra to the status-quo. Even an adolescent is unable to matriculate to adulthood if they don't destroy their frivolous youth. That happens to be the nature of things and why all great innovation comes from those mavericks who dare to be different. Renegades are comfortable with ambiguity and thrive on the new and different, and thrive in risky venues.

Renegades are always willing to destroy tradition. Sam Walton created the largest retail firm in the world by daring to be different. When dying of cancer he was asked to document his formula for success, and the wise old man of retailing offered the world his views on what it takes to build the largest retail behemoth in history. He said, "I always swam upstream, broke the rules and admired those in my firm who did so."

George Bernard Shaw and Walton viewed life through a similar filter. Thee were rebels and always willing to violate tradition. Shaw was in his mid-eighties when he shocked the British conservatives during World War II by telling a reporter:

> *I would welcome a German attack on London. The Germans are knocking down a good many things that we ought to have knocked down ourselves many years ago. I should hate to see them bomb Westminster Abbey, but I should be happy for them to bomb some of the monuments in it.* (*Smithsonian*, Nov. 1990)

Shaw attacked politicians unmercifully especially after he was older and above needing to comply with anyone for money or publishing. He called them imperialists in print and supported Ghandi's Indian uprising. He described their move a "stupid blunder of Right-wing diehards." Shaw was cantankerous but harmless other than with words. Staid old England was not pleased that an Irishman dared lambaste their most sacred icons. But Shaw could care less and refused to bow to the power elite throughout his long life.

Shaw was a Creative Evolutionist, a thesis derived from his avid support of the Darwinian movement. He was still in his teens when he refuted organized religion and became an avid life-long atheist. By twenty he had become a vegetarian and remained so the rest of his life. He never drank or smoked and always slept with the windows open even when the weather was frigid. His cynicism included demeaning traditional family values and marriage. He was an avowed bachelor until age 43 when he finally married the woman who had cared for him during his serious illness. But he never consummated the marriage during the next forty years.

THE PRICE OF BEING DIFFERENT. Shaw, like most artists, paid dearly for defying the established way. Virtually every novel, essay, and play was demeaned or summarily rejected by the experts. Until age forty he was a hard-working but barren author with little to show for his Herculean efforts. Rejections plagued all of his work. But he used the rejection to fuel his resolve rather than allow it to victimize him. He never stopped writing even after most of his work was never published. King Edward II called him "mad" for his anarchistic play *Arms and the Man* (1894). At least twice he was forced to quit the literary field in order to begin over as a critic, journalist, and essayist.

Between 1879 and 1885 Shaw's first six novels were rejected. And after he met with a similar fate at the hands of producers of plays he turned to journalism and lecturing to make his mark in the world. He spent a number of years as a music critic, art critic and journalist. In the 1890's he wrote eight plays all of which were dismissed as failures. It wasn't that they were bad as they were later praised, but the fact that they violated the hollowed traditions and beliefs of editors and publishers who relegated them to file thirteen. Ultimately, Shaw turned to humor to mask his defiant words and ideals.

NON-CONFORMITY – A PANACEA FOR GREATNESS. The irony of Shaw's early writing is that they were ultimately hailed as creative genius. Eccentricity was his enemy but it also proved to be the foundation of his later literary success. His plays were permeated with dialogue and scenes so controversial they bordered on heresy in staid England. But it was his intellectual jargon and idealism that have come down as his contribution to the world of letters. His short tenure as a politician - vestryman for his district - led to his breakthrough as a serious dramatist in 1903 with *Man & Superman.*

George Bernard Shaw is not unique as a literary renegade. Victor Hugo violated every rule of writing and the theater in his first play. Dr. Seuss was rejected prior to becoming the benchmark for children's readers. The same happened to Mark Twain who was castigated by the 19th century traditionalists for daring to write in the vernacular of the common man; and they banned his books for the very thing they are noted for. Agatha Christie was almost run out of the industry by detective writers who took great offense at her daring to use the villain as the storyteller in her first acclaimed novel *The Murder of Roger Akroyd.* Joseph Campbell said, "You can't have creativity unless you leave behind the bounded, the fixed, all the rules." Biographers described Virginia Woolf's success as, "a revolt against the narrative style of novel writing."

Non-conformity has a long history in the arts. Leonardo da Vinci violated most traditional forms of painting in creating his own style and it wasn't long before his innovation became a standard to emulate. The same was true of Michelangelo in sculpture and Isadora Duncan with dance. Duncan virtually annihilated traditional dance and ballet by refusing to acknowledge them as worthy of her or any other self-respecting artist. By daring to be different she is now considered the Mother of Modern Dance.

Few individuals would dare stray so far from tradition as Picasso. The Father of Cubism dedicated his life to the destruction of the status-quo and when his friend Matisse was appalled by his great masterpiece *Les Demoiselles d'Avignon* he put it in a closet for three years. Picasso wrote of his style. "I am against everything. The painter must destroy. He must destroy to give it another life" (Landrum 1996). The very essence of Cubism is the violation of sensibilities. The shock is the message. Only a small percentage of the population see beyond what they can touch or understand. When Picasso painted outside the realm of understanding his paintings stood dormant for years waiting the world to catch up with his prescient vision.

Maria Callas had a similar influence on opera as did Madonna for music-video, Michael Jackson for pop, and Berry Gordy for mainline soul. These artistic renegades all paid a high price for daring to be different. People do not like to have their cherished icons destroyed but it is incumbent on the innovators to do so if they are to lead the way. The world fights change. Why? Because the so-called experts and keepers of tradition have such a psychological investment in what *is* they cannot see the possibilities of what might *be*. They are caught up in the box of conformity while creative geniuses like Shaw must operate in that void where the meek fear to go.

HISTORY OF DRAMA GENRE

Drama is only one genre that Shaw participated in but it is the one for which he is best known. He wrote novels, essays, poetry, literary criticism and was a master letter writer. His Nobel Prize was for drama as was his classic *Pygmalion* (My Fair Lady. *Wit* was the vehicle he used to communicate his moral messages. He used it adroitly to disarm critics and adversaries.

Drama and wit were originally married in Greek Comedies. The Greeks used the two to inform while entertaining. The word *drama* comes from the Greek verb *dran* meaning "to act" or "to do." Drama is synonymous with the stage, a theatrical setting with spectators looking to be entertained by a comedy or tragedy. The origins of drama were centered in Greece and their Tragedies and Comedies are still with us, especially those written by the three great Greek playwrights Aeschylus, Sophocles, and Euripedes. They produced many plays that can still be seen on college campuses. The most famous were *Antigone* (441 BC), *Medea* (431 BC), *Oedipus* (429 BC), *Cyclops* (423 BC), *Electra* (418 BC), and *Helen* (412 BC). The Romans continued the Greek tradition with the two major playwrights Plautus and Seneca. One wrote comedies the other tragedies.

The next era of drama came with the Renaissance and the appearance of Shakespeare, the greatest playwright in history. His innovations in tragedy, comedy, romance, and history have yet to be surpassed for their daring and achievement. His 38 plays display the imagination and insight of an intellectual with a sense of humor and the daring of someone who could identify simultaneously with the educated and the masses. Shaw had an imaginative sense of the tragic and the ability to describe it for a large cross-section of society.

Second to Shakespeare in Elizabethan comedy was Ben Johnson, followed by Frenchman Voltaire and Diderot. The German's were mesmerized in the theater by Goethe and Schiller. Yhe 19th century witnessed the emergence of Victor Hugo and Alexander Dumas. They paved the way for the Father of Modern Drama Norwegian Henrik Ibsen. His *Pillars of Society* (1877), *Doll House* (1879), and *Ghosts* (1881) had enormous influence on 20th century dramatists including Shaw. Shaw was friends with an equally rebellious Oscar Wilde whose scandal-ridden wit brought us *The Picture of Dorian Grey* (1891). Russians Turgenev and Chekhov contributed to the advancement of the genre although Ibsen led the way in the 20th century.

In America Eugene O'Neill, Arthur Miller, and Tennessee Williams made the greatest impact in mid-20th century. O'Neill was also a renegade alcoholic who was unceremoniously kicked out of Princeton, tried to kill himself, and left his pregnant wife for a mining expedition in Honduras. Neil Simon and Andy Warhol came along with the baby-boomer generation.

The three dramatists in this work were Christie, Camus, and Michener. All had more success in other genres but were quite successful with smash hits. Christie led with *The Mousetrap*, *Spider's Web*, and *Witness for the Prosecution*. Michener's *South Pacific* won a Pulitzer Prize and had a successful movie run. Camus made his impact with existentialist plays like the *The Stranger*, *The Plague*, and *The Fall*.

GEORGE BERNARD SHAW

A RENEGADE INNOVATOR WHO DARED BE DIFFERENT

GBS, as he called himself at the turn of the century, was a radical by almost any definition. Why did he choose GBS instead of his given name George? Because George was not only the name of his alcoholic father, a loser in his eyes, but it was also the name of his mother's lover George Lee, his purported real father. After Shaw figured out he was illegitimate he came to hate the name George motivating him to change his name to Bernard Shaw then GBS.

Shaw used words to shock and to communicate. His life and work validate Shannon's Law, an electronic communications principle that says, "the absorption of information is inversely related to its credibility." In laymen terms, the Law means to effectively communicate one must be prepared to sensationalize via shock, outrage, fright and terror. The muckraking journalism of the early and latter 20th century is testimony to this type of journalism. Titillation and sensationalism elicit passion in the reader. In other words, it is best to flaunt tradition if one is desirous of optimizing the communications process. It is the pathway to recognition in the literary arts, journalism, and politics as well as most innovative ventures.

It is a sad commentary that a writer must shock to get recognition. But it is a fact of life that sex, sensation, and trash sells better than more idyllic messages. Just look at the success of books by shock-master Howard Stern, O.J. Simpson, Dennis Rodman, and Monica Lewinsky. Their political incorrectness made them millions, a far more appealing attraction than literary merit. Arrogance reigns supreme at the very top of most firms, and the publishing industry is no exception. If controversy sells, it will be published regardless of the merit. In the long run the Shavian way tends to open more doors that the traditional way.

Most manuscripts are relegated to young inexperienced journalism majors who seldom have a clue about any work that is innovative or esoteric. If you are writing about some obscure or innovative business concept, human relations breakthrough or philosophically abstract, or mythical concept beyond their purview there is little chance of it being understood or accepted. Shaw faced this 100 years ago nothing has changed.

CATALYST TO THE TOP. After Shaw's first eight works were summarily rejected, he gave up trying to go through the front door and went through the back. He knew it would be futile to try and win over a system ill-suited to accept his intellectual precepts. He found a job as a literary critic and music critic for a daily paper and then started lecturing extensively to build his reputation as an expert on cultural and intellectual matters.

Ironically, it was only after he took up with some sophisticated women who opened important doors did he make it. In the interim he made 1000 speeches, a real challenge for someone pathologically shy. His objective was to get acclaim from the masses who could influence the classes. His ploy worked! He was finally published and his plays were produced. One biographer described this self-proclaimed methodology as: "Shaw's greatest creation was himself by setting himself up in London as a man of genius" (Holroyd p. 246).

What do I bring to the party? An important question that should always be asked but seldom is. Am I a superb wordsmith? Am I steeped in philosophical truths the world is waiting breathlessly to hear or read? Am I just interested in seeing my name in print? Do I have a passion to impart some truth about myself or my path? Am I salacious enough or into romance? Am I a storyteller? For those attempting to appeal to the mass market publishers it is critical to impart a mass-market message of high sales to large audiences without a whole lot of downside risk. If those are not in a proposal the publication will not see the light of day. Give them what they want and they will give you what you want. GBS recognized this earlier than most and departed convention to get himself accepted and produced.

Shaw's sixty plays have flourished because he persevered. He was almost fifty before he had success. To his stead he never once stopped writing during those long years of rejection. Tenacity was his forte. He was turned down by sixty publishers for various reasons, most notably for being too intellectual, for anti-capitalism, anti-marriage, anti-religion, anti-colonization, anti-war, and anti-romance. But he never quit.

Shaw's early writing was aimed at attacking Shakespeare in order to draw attention to himself. He believed that any press was good even if it was negative. This was one of the reasons he paid Rodin to sculpt him and engaged famous artists to paint him. He never became self-deluded even when he became famous. He wrote, "I am overrated as an author. Most great men are" (Holroyd 1989 p 147). He believed rejection was only part of the game and never allowed it to discourage him saying, "The violent attacks convinced me that I was born to be a dramatist." His persistence won out.

ECCENTRICITY. His marriage to socialite Charlotte-Payne Townsend as he approached age forty was one of convenience. He felt sexual gratification was a kind of loss of freedom and women used this power to control their men. He retaliated as only he might by refusing to consummate the marriage. He and Charlotte lived together in a platonic state of intellectual harmony for over forty years. Now that is eccentricity. Shaw viewed doctors as quacks and felt they should be avoided at all cost. He called them self-serving money-suckers incapable of curing man's illnesses. Another enlightened rebel, Leonardo da Vinci had similar feelings and warned kings to "keep clear of physicians." Shaw went so far as to write a play warning people about doctors as social predators. He mercilessly attacked the medical profession in *The Doctor's Dilemma* (1906

EGOMANIA ENHANCED HIS INSECURITIES. Shaw believed all men had innate potential and the Superman or Life Force in all of us was waiting to be tapped. He said, "I branded myself a Creative Evolutionist" but his real hero was the Nietzschean will-to-power thesis. His strong sense of self allowed him to co-found the British Labor Party, a remarkable feat considering he was Irish. This group was originally known as the Fabian Society a fringe group of socialists who were fans of Marx.

How was an Irishman able to do this? By daring to rebel and communicate on an intellectual level in rhetoric often lost on far more educated people. He always walked that fine line between radical eccentricity and innovative genius. Friends were unsure whether he was a genius or a psychotic and friends tended to the former and enemies the latter. His cynical diatribe and eccentric lifestyle were never understood. Therefore, the traditionalists panned his work and described him as a crank. Both intellectuals and eccentrics understood him and for the most part loved him. The establishment neither understood nor liked him. And most came to fear him. He made himself acceptable by playing the intellectual critic, erudite lecturer, and worldly raconteur roles that elevated him above his adversaries from the establishment. Only then was he recognized, published, and produced.

AN ACERBIC WIT. Levity and cynical humor were Shaw's trademarks as both critic and playwright. He used facetious wordplay to disarm his adversaries and philosophic syllogisms to communicate his intellectual ideology. He admitted this in comparing his style with Mark Twain. "Twain is in very much the same position as myself. He has to put things in such a way as to make people who would otherwise hang him believe he is joking. Telling the truth is the funniest joke in the world." He went on to say, "If you want to influence people insult them first, win them afterward. Then you can say anything you like as long as people think you don't mean it." In another aphorism he said, "Most mocking when most serious, most fantastic when most earnest." (Holroyd 1988)

HISTORIES RENEGADES. Few great people are traditionalists. The pathway to greatness lies outside the box. Mediocrity lies within. Even the spiritual Mother Teresa refused to conform. She dropped out and formed her own order, an unheard of thing in the dogmatic Catholic Church. Einstein was kicked out of high school as was James Michener. Buckminster Fuller got kicked out of Harvard and came up with a term for the successful labeled *antiestablishmentariansism.* Babe Didrickson Zaharias, arguably the greatest female athlete in history, had three people at her funeral because she was so hated on the golf tour. Freud was the most hated man in the latter 19th century and had three former associates commit suicide. Even the loveable Babe Ruth was suspended many

135

times by the New York Yankees. He was suspended five times. French writer Colette is arguably the most radical female writer in history. She scandalized the Moulin Rouge, not an easy achievement, with an on-stage nude love scene with her female lover while married to a French socialite.

A true renegade was Frederick Nietzsche. He gave credence to rebellious behavior as a catalyst for success in his classic *Thus Spake Zarathustra* writing, "Whoever wants to be a creator in good and evil must first be an annihilator and break values. Thus the greatest evil belongs to the greatest goodness; but this is being creative." Playwright Oscar Wilde was imprisoned for daring to challenge the English system of morals for having an open affair with the son of the Marquees of Queensberry. He wrote, "Art is individualism" in defense of his behavior. Both Carl Jung and Bertrand Russell supported open marriage, polygamy and free love. Philosopher John Stuart Mill adds credence to this saying, "That so few dare to be eccentric marks the chief danger of our time."

Einstein was a renegade who said, "I was an upstart heretic who violated the existing dogma." And he would later say, "Few people are capable of expressing with equanimity opinions which differ from the prejudices of their social environment." Psychiatrist writer Anthony Storr described Einstein's success saying, "Einstein provides the supreme example of how schizoid detachment can be put to creative use." (Storr 1993)

Isadora Duncan wrote, "I'm a revolutionist. All geniuses worthy of the name are. Every artist has to be one to make a mark in the world." Stephen King's best friend told the media, "His abnormal behaviors were important in making him what he became. He always loved the chance, bet, and risk and theatrical experience for high stakes." King said, "I make up horrors to help cope with the real ones." James Michener was even more radical than King saying, "I had been thrown out of every school I ever attended." A biographer described him as a "social misfit" in college and a "campus radical."

Biographer Chris Sciabarra wrote a biography on Ayn Rand titled *The Russian Radical* (1995). Sciabarra went to great length showing how Rand aroused anger in all factions including the left, right, liberal, conservative, religious, agnostics, mystics, homosexuals, feminists, educators, and even the pornographers. It is ironic that her heroic pathos was akin to Shaw's despite their opposite political ideology. Rand was a rabid capitalist and right of Attila the Hun. Shaw was a fanatical socialist and strong advocate of Marxism.

SHAW'S LITERARY INNOVATIONS

Shaw was the first to write popular plays using intellectual and philosophical ideology. Many of his lines have made their way into our daily conversation like Eliza Doolittle's line "Not bloody likely." Prior to Shaw the word *bloody* didn't exist in colloquial English. It is now impossible to walk the streets of London and not hear the word. Another of Shaw's innovations was his attempt to create a whole new English alphabet with forty letters instead of twenty-six. His effort proved unsuccessful but would become the genesis of *Pygmalion* (1912).

The intelligencia understood Shaw but didn't like him because his "certainty was annihilating." (Holroyd 1988 p 217). Literary critics didn't understand him and were appalled by his irreverence. One critic wrote, "Shaw is a terrorist." Another described his play *Androcles and the Lion* (1916) as vulgar, childish, and blasphemous that "will scandalize" and "this work of the prince of hypocritical egoists is a disgrace" (Holroyd 1988 p. 323). Even his friends in the radical Fabian movement saw him as an eccentric. Holroyd says, "he was admired, not liked, and not loved" (Holroyd pg. 217).

ERUDITE & SELF-TAUGHT. How did a man with only two years of formal education and none in the literary arts find such success in literature? How did such a man get called the greatest playwright since Shakespeare? An inveterate imagination helped. But in the end it was his inner power to believe he was right and ability to defy convention. Shaw was an Irishman from a working class family and was never respected by the landed elite. He didn't know enough to know he wasn't capable of becoming an intellectual so he was.

GEORGE BERNARD SHAW

Shaw was raised in the middle class but lived much of his adult life among the upper classes. He lived, loved, and partied with the well-read and well-bred gentry. He socialized with the likes of Oscar Wilde, Bertrand Russell, Ellen Terry, W. G. Wells, Sidney Webb, and Leonard and Virginia Woolf. Shaw was extremely erudite on a wide range of subjects. He was articulate and charismatic. His intellectualizing transgressed many disciplines including art, music, philosophy, politics, marriage, religion, health, medicine and the general nature of man's ability to cope in a changing world. He was an interesting Renaissance man drawing upon his experiences and philosophies to preach his gospel of the heroic man.

Shaw wrote on many esoteric subjects. He was a bold raconteur. His aphorisms were noted for their insight and wit like, "Life does not cease to be funny when people die, any more than it ceases to be serious when people laugh" (*The Doctor's Dilemma* (1906). Shaw was a self-proclaimed pedagogue who made himself into an expert on the arts and life. Testimony to his influence occurred when all lights on Broadway were dimmed with his passing in 1950 at age 94. This revolutionary scholar of the arts created a mystique beyond his own comprehension, which never ceased to amaze him.

Once Shaw had gained fame he became judge, jury, and intellectual arbiter of all within his purview. As a journalist, critic, and essayist he was able to articulate his knowledge with passion and panache. Few dared debate him in an area of his expertise since he was famous for a caustic tongue that could destroy with words. He was able to seduce with words and admitted to having a talent for "a wicked tongue, a deadly pen, and a cold heart" (Holroyd 1988 p 101). His flare as a witty philosopher struck a note with thinking people and attracted many disciples who were not appalled by his banal humor. He was admired, sometimes hated, but almost always respected.

Shaw's mother Bessie was an enormous influence on her son. She was an iconoclast of the first order. She had the audacity to move her lover and music teacher George Lee into their house in what Shaw described a *"menage a trois* existence."

LITERARY GENIUS

After watching his mother thumb her nose at societal tradition, Shaw learned early that one doesn't need to conform.

WRITING AS CATHARSIS

Shaw wrote to exorcise the ghosts of his mother's desertion at 13 and his father's alcoholism. He wrote to prove to his mother he was deserving of her love. When she left him in Dublin with his father and ran off to London with her music teacher/lover he was emotionally devastated. He would join her a few years later but the damage was done. Later he would write to soulmate Ellen Terry, "My success is due to my mother's complete neglect during my infancy."

Inner turmoil molded him into a manic overachiever and perfectionist. Rejection led him to a life of rebellion in which he refuted all tradition and social convention. If his mother could get away with flaunting the sanctity of marriage in front of the world then so could he. The defiance of family values can be seen in his plays that made fun of marriage and love.

Shaw was Professor Henry Higgins in *Pygmalion* – My Fair Lady. He had borrowed the idea from British philologist Henry Sweet, a friend who helped him with his ideas on linguistics. The lead role of Eliza Doolittle was played by his great love Mrs. Patrick (Stella) Campbell a woman who had rejected him. Despite great pressure from the literary community, Shaw adamantly refused to have the story end with his alter-ego Higgins marrying Eliza to legitimatize her in society. As Professor Higgins, Shaw played his most enjoyable role as the omniscient arbiter of English values and deportment with Eliza his protégé.

Cathartic inspiration pervades all of Shaw's work. His female protagonists were real-life lovers or wannabe lovers including Florence Farr, Janet Achurch, Ellen Terry and Stella – Mrs. Patrick Campbell. All were depicted in roles as iconoclastic heroines in context of his Life Force theme such a pivotal part of his whole existence. A Superman-like *will* permeated their characters in the likeness of Bergeson's *Elan Vital*. Shaw believed his life and success were a direct result of this mystical Nietzschean inner energy source.

The Life Force imagery and political ideology are pervasive in his work. *The Philanderer* (1893) was a comedy based on female liberation depicting marriage as an antiquated form of religious servitude. *The Devil's Disciple* (1887) was a religious melodrama advocating capitulation to one's instinct or Life Force. *Candida* (1895) was a mockery of Victorian domesticity (his mother's unconventional behavior) as well as a denunciation of religious dogma. *Man & Superman* (1903) was his first great success and testimony to his use of intellectual concepts - the Life Force in Don Juan – to entertain and amuse. This is the work most critics acclaim as his best in addition to being the consummate expression of his philosophy and epistemology. It uses the theme of "creative evolution" to show man's potential rise to the pinnacle of his power. It is based on the Don Juan legend and is witty, farcical, and conveys a strong philosophical Shavian message of energy incarnate.

Pygmalion (1913) is Shaw's most successful play and his last romantic comedy. It attempted to show the absurdity of class distinction. The transformation of Eliza Doolittle from flower girl to society lady was important to Shaw since she was his metaphor for Stella his real-life love goddess. However, once she transformed herself into his ideal he didn't want her. Psychologically, he was rejecting her just as his real-life love interest Stella had rejected him. This was portrayed in My Fair Lady when his alter-ego Professor Higgins says, "Why can't a woman be more like a man."

Shaw's pacifism peaked during the WW-I atrocities that he immortalized in *Heartbreak House* (1916). This play released his pent-up Fabian radicalism spawned by the collapse of civilization during the war and Russian Revolution. Shaw considered *Heartbreak House* his best play. Shaw spoke far too much about the *menage a trois* relationship of his mother, father, and her music teacher/lover George Lee not to have it deeply imbedded in his tumultuous psyche. Out of his trauma came the need to revolt, defy, and take the other road.

METAMORPHOSES

As discussed, Shaw's unconscious anxieties were all molded by his mother's abandonment. Shaw shared his inner turmoil with actress Ellen Terry and in one letter described the even as "abandonment." After she had left him with his father he attended a play that transformed him. He and his father attended a performance of Goethe's *Faust* when he was 15. George returned home and decorated his room with symbols of Mephistopheles. We now know that our memorable experiences are those that take place during periods of emotional turmoil or trauma. It is telling that Goethe's classic play would become a central theme in Shaw's later work - *Man & Superman.* Mephistopheles was resurrected 30 years later as Don Juan. Later he would write the time alone changed him. He wrote, "My struggle afterwards was to become *efficient* in real life" (Holroyd 1988 p. 51).

A later transformation took place in the British Museum as Shaw sat reading Marx for years. Marx would become a mythic like mentor and his favorite book became *Das Kapital.* This proved to be a synchronistic event since Marx himself had sat in this same revered hall some thirty years earlier researching his classic work. Urging "workers of the world to unite" appealed to the rejection felt by Shaw. He would write, "It was the turning point in my career. Marx was a revelation. He opened my eyes to the facts of history and civilization" (Holroyd 1988 pg. 129). The evils of slum landlordism that he saw in London would become an intellectual rallying point for his first play *Widowers Houses* (1892).

Shaw wrote plays about heroes as he was a hero-worshipper. His work was about Greek mythical gods and heroes like Androcles, Pygmalion, Faust, Don Juan, Julius Caesar, Joan of Arc and Napoleon. These larger-than-life characters all lived out the Nietzschean Superman theme he called the Life Force.

ECCENTRICITIES

Bernard Shaw started out in life as a maverick. He was purportedly illegitimate causing him to refuse to use the name

George when in his twenties. But strangely, he lived with his mother until almost thirty. He became an overt atheist by his teens and a vegetarian in his twenties when he adopted Marxism. He was against marriage, an advocate of free love, and a food faddist. Testimony to his eccentricities was a penchant for sleeping with the windows open in severe weather. He ate only brown bread, wore only Jaegger wool suits - what he labeled "hygienic dress" - and refuted all forms of Capitalism. And even though he saw himself as a philanderer he admitted to being a virgin until age 29. He finally lost his virginity to a matronly friend of his mother one Mrs. Jenny Patterson. She was his first true love but for the renegade Shaw love and romance were not synonymous. In almost any definition Shaw was a radical eccentric who was intent on destruction of all forms of existing dogma. Refusing to consummate his marriage to wealthy socialite Charlotte-Payne Townsend is further testimony.

One of Shaw's most defiant acts was his refusal to accept the Nobel Prize for Literature, the British Order of Merit, and Knighthood. Brutal honesty caused him much chagrin. Friends were often turned into enemies due to his acerbic wit. He described the emerging medical profession as "witchcraft," and became infamous for preaching against vaccinations as the work of the "money-sucking devils." His diatribes can be found in his play *The Doctor's Dilemma* (1906).

Short story *Don Juan Explains* (1887) "showed my indifference to conventional opinion." Late in life he became immersed in a highly controversial affair with a young American wannabe actress who was forty years his junior. He was 65 when a brazen Molly Tomkins approached him for the role of Eliza in his award winning play Pygmalion. Shaw was smitten with the 24 year-old Molly. The long torrid affair was tolerated by Shaw's wife Charlotte. They would take a vacation to Italy and Charlotte would find Mollly ensconced nearby. After Charlotte's death Molly proposed they live together but the 90-year old Shaw turned her down.

LIFE CRISES

Shaw was devastated psychologically when his mother ran off with her lover. When he finally left Dublin for London Lee moved out and he ended up living with his mother. Her misdeed left him with deep-seated insecurities that plagued him for the rest of his life, but it also armed him extremes self-sufficiency and the knowledge that he could be different and not pay a very dear price. Of course a huge ego offset those who detractors who saw his divergent as bizarre.

Shaw wrote to Ellen Terry and said, "My success is due to my mother's complete neglect of me during my infancy – it taught me independence and self-sufficiency" (Holroyd pg. 18). Even more telling was his statement, "In the lost childhood of Sonny the philosophy of GBS was conceived (pg 19). Love and relationships had little meaning for Shaw due to his childhood.

His work is pervaded by the love-hate relationship with his mother. He wrote, "Love is a permanent relationship akin to the socialist hatred of private property" (Holroyd p. 152. His definition of property was a wife. He said " I was never duped by sex as a basis for a permanent relationship" (Holroyd pg. 162). Biographers referred to him as being "emotionally lame, and unable to come to terms with women except in a make-believe world" (Holroyd pg 107). The truth was he was in love with love and sometimes lust but never relationships. He wrote, "Love does not last because it is not of this earth; and when you clasp the idol it turns out to be a rag doll" (Tehan 1990 pg. 2).

On his arrival in London his sister Agnes died which gave him a greater sense of mortality. His first serious illness that he saw as life threatening, coincided with his classic *Man & Superman.*

POLYPHASIC

Shaw was multi-faceted. He worked as a journalist, playwright, novelist, music and literary critic, politician, editor, social reformer and lecturer. In some ways he tried to cram two lifetimes of work into one admitting, "I want to be thoroughly used up when I die" (Horloyd pg 251). Shaw was a manic creator writing plays on trains, in cars, while walking in the park, at dinner, and while attending the theater. No venue was out of bounds for this overachiever. Whenever the mood hit he wrote. He wrote *Man & Destiny* (1896) while a female artist, and ardent fan, painted his portrait. Shaw wrote *Man & Superman* while functioning as music and art critic for a newspaper and simultaneously fulfilling a political office as vestryman. At no time in his long life did he work at one thing. Eighteen-hour days were normal fare. He wrote, "Work is my mistress" (Holroyd pg 74) and later "Like Prometheus we must work to make new men" (Holroyd pg. 10).

CRITICAL ACCLAIM

During the last quarter of Shaw's long life he was regarded as the "sage of the Western world." Critics agreed that *Saint Joan* (1920) was his best play and it resulted in the Nobel Prize for Literature. Author Ruth Adam calls it the "greatest play of the twentieth century." *Man & Superman* (1903) is considered his most intellectual achievement with Don Juan trying to trick the world by jousting with the devil. *Pygmalion* (My Fair Lady on the stage and screen) was his greatest commercial success and elevated him to international acclaim after which he became revered as the most capable playwright in England. Shaw's death elevated him to sainthood. India's Nehru wrote, "Shaw was not only one of the greatest figures of the age but one who influenced the thoughts of vast numbers of human beings during two generations" (Adam 1966 pg. 11).

World Literature Criticism described *Man & Superman* as "superb interplay of intellectual communications for the purpose of entertainment while informing." They wrote, "No where in the English language during the 20th century has there been a more dazzling sustained discussion of ideas in dialogue form." Literary critic Homer Woodbridge called it, "a sparkling comedy, featuring skilled comic characterizations." Biographer Holroyd (1988) described Shaw's magic as "his ability to show man's passions as the driving force behind his heroic actions – ala the Life Force – as a philosophic episode."

LITERARY GENIUS

Critics have called him the greatest English dramatist since Shakespeare. Others found him irascible and ruthless and in some respects, a mystic. He was certainly an influential luminary with few peers. His forte was combining symbolic farce with inner integrity and comedic passion. Shaw's *great man* pathos leaves us wanting a heroic ideal.

SUCCESS & REBELLION – What can we learn?

Shaw was both a visionary and a renegade and in his view the two concepts were inextricably intertwined. He gave credence to this with, "I write plays as they come to me, by inspiration and not by conscious logic. The progress of the world depends on people who refuse to accept the facts and insist on satisfaction of their instincts" (Holroyd pg. 106).

Shaw rebelled but chalked up the rejection to myopic ignorance by the uninitiated or those locked into a world of logic. But we can learn from him that one man's innovation is another's ridicule, with the only difference timing and delivery. Violating convention is important, but it must be constrained by timing and intent. Shaw disguised his dissidence in humor and those laughing are hard pressed to shoot the messenger. There is a fine line between grabbing the brass ring and following off the horse. Shaw was adroit at destruction via tasteful dialogue.

GBS defied the establishment and lived to enjoy the experience. He used adversity as motivation. After many rejections he wrote, "My reputation grows with every play of mine that is not performed" (Holroyd p. 383). At one time he had 10 plays sitting on his shelf that had never been produced. His solution? Alter his reputation? Despite being pathologically shy he went out redefined his image by making 100 speeches.

The London Times *(1899)* said, "Shaw is quite unable to take even his own work seriously." That was because he had been ridiculed and derided to such a degree he was shell-shocked. He was 50 before he finally was produced and age 57 before he made any real money despite a number of dramatic masterpieces. It was 1913 when Pygmalion was first produced in London.

GEORGE BERNARD SHAW

Shaw's aphorism to defy and march to your own drum is instructive. Followers live in the shadow of leaders who dare to be different. The only way of getting in the lead is by dropping out and starting your own band, blazing your own trail, and living by your own creed regardless the consequences.

For writers this means believe and never allow a detractor to dissuade you from your vision. This will always demands a resilient will and indomitable sense of self. Fear cannot intervene or you will capitulate to those who would destroy you. Shaw never did and he won out in the end although it took many years. In his inimitable words, "The people who get on in this world are the people who get up and look for the circumstances they want and if they cannot find them, make them." That is *Shavian* - what the Oxford dictionary defines as a "unique way of looking at life."

Few of us will ever have a word named for our preference for dealing with life like *Shavian*. Shaw did because he was determined to be what he was or die. In the eyes of the masses he was a misunderstood intellectual being thwarted, not because of talent but because he was a maverick. Radical would have been more exacting. Due to his branding stint he became known as authority rather than aspirant, a slight change but critical to getting published. Shaw was a master of hype and he was the protagonist in his life-drama. His rise to fame and fortune was a study in branding himself as worthy of more. But he never capitulated to the so-called experts while altering his image, he just made himself into his own expert.

IAN LANCASTER FLEMING
MASTER OF SPY-THRILLERS
b. London, England, May 28, 1908
d. Mayfair, England, Aug. 12, 1964

BELIEVE & THE WORLD WILL FOLLOW

DOMINANT GENRE
Spy thrillers for adults wanting a fantasy escape into hero-worship with 007 – the man that Fleming could never be

MOTTO
"I believe in Bonds, Blondes, & Bombs – I must be able to live as I want, with no restrictions, or I don't want to live at all. I must be able to live as I want or I don't care to live at all"

GREATEST WORKS
From Russia with Love (1957)
Doctor No (1958)
Goldfinger (1959)

HONORS/AWARDS
Sold 30 million books in first ten years; 80 million since ; Most successful movie line in history:"Bond, James Bond" - *Dr. No*

ECCENTRICITIES
Sadistic womanizing who did everything in excess smoked three packs of cigarettes and bottle of gin daily

LIFE CRISES
Father killed in WW-I when nine and raised by permissive mother; almost buried in avalanche while skiing the Swiss Alps

METAMORPHOSES
Never wrote until age 43 when his long term mistress Ann Charteris Rothermere became pregnant and he broke down and proposed; the anxiety led him to escape into the Bond fantasies

IAN FLEMING – SPY-THRILLERS

EGO CAN OVERCOME INEPTITUDE

"I only believe in Bonds, Blondes & Bombs"

SELF-ESTEEM - THE PANACEA OF GREATNESS

Believe and the world will follow; sometimes to their death, as was the case with Napoleon, Hitler and cult leaders Jim Jones and David Koresh. Even if you don't know where you are going, people will follow if you are convincingly positive and endowed with self-confidence. Self-esteem isn't everything, it is the only thing in the world of letters.

Ian Fleming is the poster boy for ego overcoming weakness. He was a failure at almost everything he ever tried except golf, women and booze. But he blamed others for his ineptitudes and wore an exterior of pomposity and arrogance that held him in good stead. An omniscient attitude hid the raging insecurity that raged within and he overcompensated with a haughty exterior that opened many doors to boardrooms and bedrooms.

James Bond was Fleming's only viable success. He flunked out of a series of schools, failed as a stockbroker, banker, correspondent, and then as husband and father. He kept getting new positions due to his charisma and confident exterior. His supremacy was imbued into Bond – the romantic raconteur afraid of nothing and superior at all. The dashing 007 was the man Fleming so desperately wanted to be. Bond smoked Fleming's brand of cigarettes, made love only to gorgeous women, drank the same chic gin, drove the same fast sports cars, and played only prestigious golf courses. Biographer Lycett (1987) called him a "prima donna totally obsessed with himself."

Fleming' was a flake with charm. Confidence was used to defuse his insecurities and to mask his laziness. Fleming imbued Bond with his own strong sense of self that oozed style, flair, British decorum, dashing elegance, and a flippant charisma. The international intrigue was the perfect setting for his Cold War sensational dramas that came precariously close to comic book type fantasies. Believability was questionable but time saved Fleming due to the Cuban Missile Crisis and the spy plane by Powers getting shot down over Russia. The daily fear of a potential nuclear war in the 50's and turbulent 60's gave Bond credibility to a world looking to escape in fantasy. And 007 was just romantic to temporarily suspend believe.

In a millennium vote Bond was voted the number one box office hero for the 20th century. Why? Who would not want to identify with a debonair *bon vivant* living and loving in the fast lane, driving an elegant Aston Martin attired in $1000 suits, and playing golf at Royal St. George's, skiing the Alps, when not betting the house at baccarat tables in Monaco. Bond was the romantic flake males admired, and females dreamed of loving.

ARROGANT LOSER & BOND. Fleming flunked out of Eton, Sandhurst Military Academy, Munich University and the University of Geneva. Every job he attempted was a disaster. He earned a reputation as the world's most inept banker and the world's worst stockbroker. His personal life was just as bad. Fleming's wife and lovers spoke of him as "an amiable eccentric." Those abused and used by him called him a "ruthless bastard."

Fleming's only real success was Bond. He began writing the 007 books as a lark in his early 40's. Fleming had broken down and proposed to long-time mistress Ann O'Neill, who was married to a friend but pregnant with his child. The guilt led to a proposal, but in a state of anxiety he fled to his Jamaican retreat Golden Eye and in six weeks hammered out *Casino Royale* (1952). For the next twelve years Fleming would leave his wife and son in London and leave for the Caribbean where he wrote one new novel each winter.

Fleming's snobbish arrogance knew few bounds. He liked to tell his golf and drinking buddies, "The only two people you should ever call are God and the King." This rogue was pretentious, grandiose, and flamboyant far beyond his talents, a snob who believed only in "Bonds, Blondes & Bombs."

Fleming failed as businessman, politician, journalist, correspondent, and as a mate. His talents were as lover, gambler, golfer, partier, and philander. Fun and frivolity were his forte. Sex and sin topped his list of priorities and dependability and ethics were at the very bottom. He was an incorrigible playboy who believed that work entailed being seen in casinos, country clubs, yacht clubs, and ski resorts. Biographer Lycett (1995 p. 66) said, "Ian merely wanted a job which would give him leisure money enough for an entertaining life." It is easy to see why 007 was a fantasy.

Fleming was a hedonist without a heart, a romantic gigolo who disdained work and marriage. On one New York business trip he told his boss he was too ill to attend an important meeting. When his boss Hugo came by to check on his sick employee he found him ensconced in St. Regis Hotel with a blonde and bottle of booze – pure Bond. Ian was incorrigible. He often slept with the wives and daughters of his best friends. One of these women, the wife of his best friend said, "If he saw a woman he must have her. He thought he could get away with murder" (Lycett p. 69). One lover was Mary Pakenham – the model for Pussy Galore in *Goldfinger.* She said, "No one had sex on the brain as much as Ian." (Lycett p. 85).

Fleming was groomed to be a playboy by a permissive mother who sent him off to a Swiss resort to make him into an independent male. It backfired. He became a party animal in Apres ski bars and lived a life of debauchery between London and Geneva. He was well-read and well-bred and the time on the continent enhanced his proficiency in five languages. The experiences found their way into the Bond books. The master of spy thrillers had panache, class and style but little integrity.

GENESIS OF BOND. Writing had never been a consideration for Ian since his older brother Peter was a writer. But Ian loved books and would later become a book-aphile. During the war he had thought of writing about the sinister intrigues he saw as a Navy Intelligence Officer but never quite got around to it.

Casino Royale was a pillow fantasy as he described it. He never expected it to be published. When finished he went through with the marriage with his pregnant girlfriend. Anne O'Neill Rothemore called it "trivial trash." Both were shocked when the book became a huge success.

WRITING INEPTITUDE. Ian's boss at his first job at Rowe & Pitman in London had asked him to write a short story. Since Ian's brother Peter was already a successful writer it was assumed Ian had a similar proclivity, especially since Ian loved books. Hardly! The boss was in shock at the story and filed it away with the succinct comment, "no good." In 1939 Ian was asked to write a story for the *London Times*. The story was rejected as "unacceptable journalism."

How could someone with so little apparent talent at writing sell 80 million books? Easy! He wrote fantasies for the masses not literary works for the classes. He adroitly stayed well within his area of expertise. Fleming knew his literary limitations and never ventured beyond calling his books "Fairy tales for grownups." His flare was for the spy intrigue for which he had some insight due to his wartime experiences and his greatest area of expertise was in womanizing, drinking and living life as an international playboy.

Many of the Bond scenes were plucked right out of Ian's life experiences. The love affair on a train in *From Russia With Love* was something that he had experienced many times. Fleming had few peers as a libertine womanizer and admitted to a need for sadism with his many lovers. Those qualities can be seen in the Bond works. Playing golf at Royal St. George, skiing in the Alps, gambling at Monaco, and romance were all part of Fleming's life and he made them part of Bond's. 007's bizarre and titillating exploits were entertaining even when they stretched the limits of believability.

CATHARTIC INSPIRATION. Underlying the baser drives of Fleming was an ego bigger than God. He and his fantasy hero were both armed with egocentric habits that knew few limits. An indomitable sense of self was at the seat of all Fleming's writing and a lesser ego may never have pulled it off.

Bond was Fleming with more guts, connections, and talent. But the Fleming mystique is rampant in every scene. The fantasies were endemic to Fleming. Acquaintances and associates at Naval Intelligence described him as "crazy" and with "enormous imagination." His wild explorations into the surreal proved to be his strength, although his detractors saw them as a weakness. But his self-esteem always won out when rejected. He never stopped believing in himself even when called a flake or nuts by his many adversaries. He rejected all advice from even the most revered men. He didn't listen to editors or publishers. When friends Noel Coward, Somerset Maugham and Lord Beaverbrook made suggestions he ignored them. Ian responded to their allegations with "You can't have a thrilling hero eating rice pudding." He proved right.

Fleming's friend and biographer Joseph Pearson (1966 p. 176) called *Casino Royale* "an experiment in the autobiography of dreams." He described the cathartic style of Ian and Bond smoking the same number of cigarettes daily - an incredible 70 and having them removed from an identical gunmetal case. Both men wore the same loafers, dark blue Sea Island shirts and ate the same scrambled eggs, coffee and orange juice breakfasts, steaks with bernaise sauce, vodka martinis, and each had a proclivity for fast cars and fast women. Both Bond and Fleming had lived life in a devil-may-care style of "my way or the highway." Both men were effete snobs.

TIMING & SUCCESS. Timing is critical to all success in any venue. It certainly intervened in the enormous success of James Bond. The Cold War was at its zenith and the international intrigue pervading Bond's assignments played well in a world fearing an apocalypse. Bond at the millennium would not have gotten off the ground, but he still sells since the spell has been cast. 007 is a superhero of mythical proportions that is easy to idolize at a time when struggling young men and women need to escape out of the reality of the moment.

Fleming's most noteworthy books *Casino Royale* (1952), *Live & Let Die* (1953), *Moonraker* (1954), *Diamonds are Forever* (1955), *From Russia with Love* (1956) appeared during the Cold War era. The spy wars had peaked when Gary Powers was shot down spying on Russia. This made the Bond fantasies plausible. And then the Cuban missile found Kennedy, a Bond fan defying Kruschev. The two were playing chess with the world as the pawn and this all played well for the Bond series.

Bond was the dashing espionage agent that Fleming fantasized about when he was Assistant to Admiral John Godfrey, the Director of Naval Intelligence during World War II. Biographer Pearson described Fleming as a man who saw himself special, a man who hung out with diplomats, generals, and royalty during the war. Fleming fantasized about winning every fight, seducing every beautiful girl, and breaking the bank at Monte Carlo. Few men could have conjured up the Bond fantasies as well as Fleming. He had just enough information and imagination coupled with a sado-masochistic urge to pull it off. One of the most psychological telling factors is his choosing the "M" for the head of Naval Intelligence Admiral Godfrey and Bond's boss as well. It was what he called his controlling mother Eve as a child.

Fleming always pushed the window of believability. Critics of the time actually denigrated his writing as being comic book hero kind of stuff. Many of his love interests described him as "an enigma." Many of his golf buddies saw him as a "maverick."

James Bond lived on-the-edge as did his creator. His exploits were immersed in a life and death struggle with the hated Russians to save the West for Communist rule. The evil villain was SPECTRE (Special Directorate for Counter-intelligence, Terrorism, Revenge, and Extortion). In some books it would be the Mafia, terrorists, and deranged criminals. All these plots gave Fleming' an outlet for his sadistic tendencies. None were so blatant as the scene with Bond tied to a chair and beaten about the genitals with a carpet brush in *Casino Royale*.

HISTORY OF SPY-THRILLER GENRE

Espionage and spy books have a long history starting with Edgar Allen Poe, the acknowledged father of mystery, suspense, and detective fiction. Spy thrillers began as detective stories like Poe's *The Murders in the Rue Morgue* (1841) and the *Purloined Letter* (1844). Later Arthur Conan Doyle created an adventure series aimed at the British upper classes. Belgian writer George Simenon and Agatha Christie were masters detective mysteries. In the United States Perry Mason, Ellery Queen, The Thin Man, Sam Spade and the Maltese Falcon became popular followed by Mike Hammer.

Fleming's Bond books pushed the envelope. He found a following with his fists, wits and tits motif. Such an approach leaves little room for literary expression or innovation but they titillate and entertain. In the words of critic George Grella, "Bond lives in the dreams of countless drab people, his gun ready, his honor intact, his morals loose: the hero of our anxiety-ridden, mythless age; the savior of our culture."

Friends and critics chastised Fleming for writing adolescent fantasies. But as is often the case his failing proved to be the very thing that launched him to the best-seller lists. Bond was always pushing all reasonable limits with his daring and ephemeral exploits. Bond was not just any old hero. He was risking his life to save the world from Communism. This is what differentiated Bond from Sherlock Holmes, Hercules Poirot, Perry Mason, and Mike Hammer. These heroes pushed the limits through cognitive insights. But Bond pushed them technologically, intellectually, sexually, and politically.

EGOCENTRIC & NARCISSIST

James Bond was an unpredictable rogue, dashing flake, and debonair cad, but he had nothing on his creator. Fleming abused women with wanton abandon. In many ways, Fleming was an effete bore, but his on-the-edge lifestyle was provocative and attractive to women. He was every woman's fantasy – handsome, sophisticated, elegant, and daring.

155

After his controlling mother broke up Ian's first true love he decided not to marry but to use women as objects of passion. He was just 21 when he made this Machiavellian pact with himself. He said, "Some women respond to the whip, some to the kiss. Most of them like a mixture of both." (Pearson pg 69).

Ian was an egocentric who refused to be part of anything if he was not center stage. His hedonism and self-indulgence transferred to Bond's proclivity for same. Who was more steeped in wine, women, and adventure than the arrogant and licentious Fleming? He became spymaster extraordinaire only because of his lecherous and egoism. Fleming's style is the Bond Archetype, whether playing golf with arch-villain Goldfinger at Royale St. George, skiing the Alps to recover military secrets from a mad Russian, seducing Pussy Galore, or dueling with Dr. Goodhead.

FLAMBOYANT USER OF WOMEN. Ian Fleming was a horrible student, worse businessman, and unable to stay focused on anything other than golf, booze and women. He was a guy's guy who never lost touch with his Eton cronies. Adoring women talked their husbands into giving him jobs for which he was ill suited. An early love affair with Maud Russell, a woman 17 years his senior, led to his job at Reuter's News Agency. Maud worshipped Ian and opened many important doors for him. She was instrumental in getting him a job as a bank vice president, a job that he also lost for incompetence. Then another intimate acquaintance persuaded her husband to hire him as a stockbroker. His boss said he drank more than he sold, and years later only remembered that he "was the world's worst stockbroker."

One of Ian's many conquests was a vivacious young married socialite named Anne O'Neil, who would later be known by her second husband's name Anne Rothermere. The two carried on a blatant affair over a 14-year period through two of Anne's marriages and a plethora of Ian's liaisons. When she became pregnant with his child in 1952 she divorced her husband and married Ian. He was 44. She never understood why he was unfaithful, and the marriage in reality was short-lived.

Fleming treated his wife in the same brutal manner as the many lovers he had used, abused and discarded. After his son Casper was born in August of 1952 he found solace in the arms of a long-time Jamaican mistress Blanche Blackwell.

Ian had a low opinion of women. He told his neighbor friend Noel Coward, "Women are not worthy of emotional hits like jealousy." These feelings are pervasive in the Bond books and movies. The Bond mystique is a sexual profligate, insensitive and ruthless. During the war he told Alan Schneider, a personal assistant in Naval Intelligence, "women are like pets, like dogs, men are the only real human beings, the only ones capable of true friendship" (Lycett pg. 151).

The only time Ian showed any emotion was when his long-time lover Muriel Wright – the model for Pussy Galore - died in a London bombing raid. He had treated her cavalierly, but was devastated at her untimely death causing a friend to say, "You have to get yourself killed before he feels anything." After his death, Anne wrote, "I know he is a child, but I love him." Fleming admitted to his childishness saying, "James Bond is like a Walter Mitty syndrome resulting from an adolescent mind which I happen to possess" (Lycettt pg. 220).

LITERARY SELF-ESTEEM. Great books demand great egos, or at least, authors who believe they are special. Balzac wrote "I am a brain and other lives must contribute to mine. If I'm not a genius I'm done for." Dostoevsky said, "I am a braggart" and biographer Holroyd said of George Bernard Shaw, "His greatest creation was himself." Anne Rice and Sylvia Plath dreamed they were god and lived their lives as if it were true. Plath wrote, "I have a terrible egotism. I wanted to be God" (Stevenson pg. 16). Picasso offers further credence. When he was leaving Barcelona for Paris at nineteen he decided to leave a painting of himself for his parents and titled it *I the King*.

FLEMING'S INNOVATIVE CONTRIBUTION

Fleming was not innovative in the sense that he pushed the window of literary expression. But he was a master at concocting narrative events with intrigue, passion, and panache. He pushed the boundaries of believability with Bond jumping between planes and off perilous cliffs, and landing unscathed. His books were but 70,000 words, half the size of this work, and he wrote 2000 words per day. Once a book was finished he would only do one rewrite. This strategy insured flow, continuity and originality.

Fleming's legacy is in films. The first one was a raving success. The animal magnetism portrayed by Sean Connery insured the success of *Casino Royale.* The combination were the most successful British export since the Beatles. Connery's role was bequeathed to Roger Moore, George Layenbry, Timothy Dalton, and Pierce Brosnan. Exotic special effects and outrageous scenes made them special. Anthony Weller (*Forbes Nov. 22, 1993*) wrote, "It is difficult to exaggerate the phenomenon of these movies, the most popular film series ever, and not just as financial blockbusters. In every man born after 1930, there surely still exists a part of his psyche which dreams of being James Bond."

Noel Coward told Fleming, "Bond is too far-fetched." He was correct, but Fleming was more attuned to the needs of a world trying to escape reality. Bond fans were never told that 007 had been lifted from a German diplomatic code broken by the British Naval intelligence during WW-II. Author Raymond Chandler wrote, "Bond escapes conventional English, daring to use sense of place and acute placement of events."

WRITING AS CATHARSIS

The plot of *Casino Royale* was based on an event in a Lisbon casino where Ian and his boss Admiral Godfrey had stopped on their way to New York City during WW-II. One night while playing baccarat they were at a table with a group of German officers. Fleming imagined a diabolical scheme for breaking the bank and the Nazi's and running off with their beautiful women. Biographer Pearson said Godfrey looked at Fleming and saw this "glazed look in his eyes" (Pearson pg. 96).

Fleming played golf to a 7-handicap as did Bond. John Pearson wrote, "When Bond looks at himself in a mirror...James Bond is simply Ian Fleming daydreaming in the third person. Bond is essentially this odd man's weird obsession with himself" (Pearson 1975). Other biographers spoke of the almost surreal likeness of Fleming to Bond. One wrote, "he never got on any train without getting laid."

Fleming had a bad habit of using friends as models for both protagonists and villains. When he didn't care for a relative or acquaintance he took delight in casting them as hoods, using Blanche Blackwell's cousin as *Goldfinger*. In the golf scene Bond won by default when Goldfinger hit the wrong ball.

Golden Eye was prophetically Fleming's last book. *You Only Live Twice* (1964) was an eerie premonition of his premature death. Pussy Galore was long time love interest Muriel Wright. Ian treated her as a veritable slave according to biographers. Muriel was an attractive athletic woman who was an avid Alpine skier, champion polo player, and successful model. She was immortalized in *Goldfinger*. Fleming's most successful book was *From Russia With Love* (1956). It was born of a conversation Ian had with Truman Capote on a flight to Jamaica. Capote had just returned from Russia and his stories inspired Fleming. *Diamond's Are Forever* (1955) was spawned by Ian's numerous trips to Saratoga Springs and evenings spent with De Beers diamond dealers. Many of the horse races and gambling scenes were lifted from those experiences.

METAMORPHOSES

Fleming was bibliophile who loved books and wanted to write of his war experiences but never quite got around to it until those black days when his lover found herself pregnant and in a moment of guilt he proposed. Once he thought about the loss of his independence he ran off to Jamaica and in seclusion wrote and wrote to forget about his impending marriage.

Fantasy is often an escape from the real world that is too difficult or too awful to comprehend. It was 1952 and the 42 year old was in a state of anxiety over his upcoming marriage. He sat at his battered Royal typewriter and produced *Casino Royale* in a torrent of words aimed at forgetting about his future. The book was completed in March 1952. He married Anne three months later when she was four months with child.

ECCENTRICITIES

Biographer Lycett called Ian "an amiable eccentric" and a "chameleon like showman." His friend John Pearson called him, "the most eccentric young man in London" (Parson 66). Ian was licentious, a flake, womanizer, self-indulgent, morose, flippant, arrogant, and probably bipolar. He suffered from hypochondria and "egocentrism." He never lived life as it was, but as he hoped it might be, and that escapist attitude proved providential to his writing style.

Fleming died young due to a dissipating lifestyle. He did most things in excess. He drank a fifth of whisky each day while smoking 60 cigarettes. Seduction was important, but so were golf, fast cars, and gambling. He was reclusive and anti-social. Few men have such voracious appetites. Life in the fast lane caught up with Ian at age fifty-six when his heart gave out from a life of debauchery.

A DEATH-WISH MENTALITY. Ian lived fast and died early. When 19 he drove a Bugatti 100 mph and lost a race with a train and he and he car were dragged fifty yards. He walked away unscathed. Once while skiing at Kizbuhel he refused to comply with out-of-bounds signs and lost a battle with an avalanche and was rescued in snow up to his shoulders. Pearson wrote, "He loved taking risks." But it was his disdain for any form of moderation that led to his early demise. The vast quantities of gin and bourbon finally caught up with him in 1961 when he suffered a massive heart attack.

Fleming like Bond had sadistic tendencies. Pain excited him and giving it to his lovers titillated him. Anne Rothemere submitted to his need for cruelty but others were not so disposed. His S/M fantasies did find their way into Bond's world. Ian lived life on his terms or he didn't care to live it at all. No one ever knew which Ian would show up. His moods vacillated between exuberance and withdrawal suggesting a bipolar personality. His excessive drinking exacerbated fits of depression and black moods of melancholia. He was often rude to guests and reclusive with friends, and an enigma to friends and lovers. He was a flippant flake who never quite grew up.

LIFE CRISES

Ian lost his father Valentine at age nine during WW-II and was raised by a controlling mother. Her permissiveness proved lethal. Eve Fleming was the primal influence in his life. She indulged his whims, coddled him, and molded him into a self-centered man-child. He grew into a spoiled and arrogant adolescent. Later she would push him to achieve but it was too late. The die was cast. He was on his way to life as an irresponsible hedonist. The tragedy is that his only son, Casper didn't have a father, and took up drugs in his teens, and died of an overdose at seventeen.

Hypochondria pervaded Ian's life. He suffered from migraines and would retreat into his own inner sanctum, turning to alcohol to relieve the pain. It only exacerbated his problem. His relationship with his Anne lasted but weeks after the birth of their child. She delivered by caesarian section and it left scars that Ian found ugly and a turn off. They stopped sleeping together and the marriage was over in fact even though it lasted until his death. The irony is that she was interesting to Ian as the wife of another man, but once she was his he lost interest. Anne was but another female looking to impede his need to be free and naughty. Within a year they both had lovers.

POLYPHASIC

Fleming was never in any one profession. He was a banker, stockbroker, journalist, and writer. He relished juggling many things at once including female relationships. Seldom did Fleming have fewer than four women in some state of an intimate relationship. The child-man was easily bored. He was always playing cards, golfing, skiing, drinking, or chasing. His one and only professional passion was Bond.

IAN FLEMING

CRITICAL ACCLAIM

The literary community disdained Fleming's work to the same degree the public embraced it. Self-promotion was key to his early success. But it was his outrageous action scenes and salacious dialogue that made him rich and famous. He was loved by the common man and castigated by the literary elite. *From Russia with Love* was his most respected work since it depicted the fight between Russia and America in an exciting and surreal way. James Bond was his most successful creation. He was every man's hero, and every woman's fantasy.

Critics called Bond "boyish, charming, unflappable, heartless, sadistic, and even misogynistic." The *New Statesman* (1958) called his Goldfinger book, "Sex, snobbery, and sadism." They panned Fleming for developing "unrealistic plots" that were pure fantasy. One writer said, "He has really gone off the rails in the matter of murders, beatings, and tortures, impossibility and lust" (Lycett p. 333). But it was daring to write what others could only imagine that made him successful. Had he been more believable, it is likely he would have had a short career.

Presidency John F. Kennedy was asked by the media to list his top ten favorite books during his push for education. When Bond turned up on the President's list, Fleming gained immediate credibility. When Sean Connery said in *Dr. No (1962)* "Bond. James Bond!" the words became forever imprinted in the movie lexicon. The Associate Press wrote on October, 23, 1998, "those words went down as smoothly as a vodka martini." The line was reused in the next 17 Bond films.

In *Diamonds Are Forever* his blatant sadism peaked. In *From Russia with Love* he described blood dripping from a girl's exposed breasts. This motivated British critic Paul Johnson to call *Dr. No* "the nastiest book I ever read. Mr. Fleming has no literary skill, the construction of the book is chaotic, and entire incidents and situations are inserted, and then forgotten in a haphazard manner" (Lycett pg. 331). Fleming referred to his dashing alter-ego as a "cardboard dummy." But that dummy made him rich and famous. To his credit not one of the Bond movies flopped and most have been box office bonanzas.

SUCCESS & SELF-ESTEEM – What Can We Learn?

Fleming was obsessed with himself and that proved to be the genesis of Bond. That was the opinion of both his wife and mistress Blanche Blackwell. Both women agreed that his personal vitality and intrepid view of life were the magic that carried over into his writing. His female lovers called him "attractive" and "fascinating." Mistress Blanche Blackwell described him as "self-centered, vain, arrogant, with a rugged vitality and blue eyes that were pure Bond." The cathartic inspiration of Fleming was right on when he said, "An author must be in a state of lustful excitement when writing of love."

Fleming's success offers hope for all writers. Here was a man who couldn't write and was basically a flake. But he refused to be a failure and gave free reign to his imagination and it led him to create an institution in the spy-thriller genre.

Fleming's ego was super-imposed on 007. Both were dashing international playboys. Bond was chic and hip and appealed to the struggling working classes. In some respects Fleming was able to appeal to men like Danielle Steel has appealed to women. They have created a fantasy world of escape and the reader need not work hard but can still come away titillated by the experience. There is something intriguing about escaping on a yacht, or snacking on caviar with gorgeous women getting into fast sports cars and surviving death-defying exploits. Fleming gave audiences what they wanted and in return they gave him what he wanted – adulation, acceptance and success.

Fleming was helped to the top with important people opening important doors. Noel Coward, Evelyn Waugh, Somerset Maugham, Lord Kemsley and Lord Beaverbrook helped him get published. Lord Beaverbrook called *Casino Royale* a "grand slam" giving it instant credibility. Why did such a literary man say such a thing? Lord Beaverbrook owed Fleming a favor. Fleming was shrewd enough to write a piece and have it published on the famous man's 75th birthday. Fleming described him as, "one of England's greatest bridge players" and had it published in the *Sunday Times*. Fleming was a master at using people to his advantage. His charismatic style carried him much further than his writing. Most of his books would not have made it past the acquisitions editor today.

Biographer John Pearson called him "irrisistible to both women and the intellectual elite" (Pearson p. 30). Raymond Mortimer, the literary critic of the *Sunday Times*, wrote that Fleming was a "craftsman with consummate skill in creating a cultural hero. James Bond is what every man would like to be, and what every woman would like between her sheets. But only in their daydreams" (Lycett pg. 416). The same critic called *You Only Live Twice* "Ghastly!" Testimony to Fleming's charismatic style and luck the book became his most successful commercially.

Fleming never rewrote one scene in any book. He was afraid if he returned to a scene it would destroy the moment and he would hate it, therefore he never edited anything. "I couldn't possibly go on if I read what I had written." He had a mortal fear of his eroticism and re-reading would force him to deal with that and he didn't dare.

Fleming entertained via thrilling adventure scenes and unimaginable feats. It took an arrogant man to live so far out on the edge of believability. Belief in himself rather than any intellectual insight made it work. Fleming unwittingly wrote his own epitaph in his notebook after his first heart attack. "Gamblers just before they die are often given a great golden stretch of luck. They get gay and young and rich and then when they have been sufficiently fattened by the fates they are struck down." Within months of writing these terse words John F. Kennedy included *From Russia With Love* as one of his top ten books and American sales took off. A movie deal was signed for *Dr. No, From Russia With Love* and *Goldfinger*. All three were made into films during the next three years. On March 25, 1961 Fleming suffered a massive heart attack. He didn't die until 1964 but the chivalry was gone. During this period something motivated him to write a children's book *Chitty, Chitty, Bang, Bang*. The egoist's last book published while he was alive was *You Only Live Twice*, a book that would be his obituary.

SYLVIA PLATH
CATHARTIC POET & NOVELIST
b. Boston, MA Oct. 27, 1932
d. London, Eng Feb. 11 1963

CATHARTIC EXPRESSION WORKS

DOMINANT GENRE
Ariel and *The Bell Jar*, cathartic representations of a tortured inner-self attempting to cope in a cruel and treacherous world

MOTTO
"Only achievement can get rid of the accusing, never satisfied Gods who surround me. I walk the razors edge of tragedy"

GREATEST WORKS
The Bell Jar (1961) Autobiographical purge of her unconscious
The Colossus (1957) Book of poetry-rage against father's death
The Ariel Poems (1965) Collection of poems on inner fury

HONORS/AWARDS
Pulitzer Prize for Literature 1957 *Ariel Poems* first posthumous winner ever

ECCENTRICITIES
Pathologically perfectionism & a bipolar personality. A control freak with need to be perfect or be dead, she chose dead

LIFE CRISES
Father died when eight; she spent rest of life attempting to write it out of her psyche - *Colossus (her dad); Daddy* 1957- nervous breakdown in college and attempted suicide

METAMORPHOSES
Introspective need to exorcise inner demons in words
"If I didn't write, I felt nobody would accept me or love me"
Epiphany in 1959 with *Electra on Azalea Path*, pregnancy, and discovery of Jung and Roethke

8

SYLVIA PLATH – POETRY

Cathartic Expression Sells

"Writing was a substitute for myself"

Words made Sylvia Plath and they destroyed her. They were lightning rods that kept her from electrocution by a tormented psyche. She used words to defuse that inner turmoil, but also used them as weapons of destruction. Her acidic tongue was lethal. Casualties included college roommates, friends, mother, and her husband, British poet Ted Hughes. Her inflammatory words and deeds drove him into the arms of another woman. Unable to deal with the loss, she placed her head in an oven and turned on the gas. Ted published her Ariel poems, written in the middle of those last days of anguish, and won her the Pulitzer Prize of Literature posthumously.

Sylvia was the product of a New England family, a mother school teacher/librarian Aurelia, and Polish immigrant father Otto, a professor who became her colossus. The family was steeped in words as vehicles of communication and the way to deal with emotion. Plath was super bright (160 IQ) and articulate, but used words as a release of inner turmoil more than as a means of communication. *The Bell Jar* was the consummate anxiety mind-dump, to such an extent she used a pseudonym. They allowed her to matriculate through Smith and earn a Fulbright Scholarship to Cambridge where she met and married Hughes who would one day become the Poet Laureate of England. They married while she was in graduate school and her two children Frieda and Nicholas were born in London only a couple years before her tragic death.

WORDS – EMOTIONAL RELEASE

To Plath words were pleasure, a means of releasing those inner torments that plagued her from the day her father Otto died when she was eight. She wrote, "I'll never speak to God again." Her words were ferocious outpourings in her verse, one novel and as a free-lance writer for magazines. They were written in a volcanic white heat in a desperate attempt to avoid the psychotic urges that scared her. It didn't work. She disappeared in high school, attempted suicide in college, and completed the job at age thirty while living in London. Plath was an addictive personality plagued by manic-depression, hyper-active drive, a Type A behavior, and was a mystic looking for the secret to her manias. Cathartic inspiration and expression was her forte.

INNER PASSION CAN BE PROFOUND

Allowing inner emotion to flow into words is often therapeutic for the writer and may be a source of inspiration for the reader. Bearing one's soul in print is never easy but is often preferable to the alternative. This was never more apparent than in the tumultuous life of Plath who released a plethora of emotional invective through verse. It kept her sane and made her message more believable. In her case she had to die to have her words become immortal.

How many of us have the guts to say what we really think or to reveal our deepest anguish? Plath was such a person and her feeling dialogue in *The Bell Jar* and *The Ariel Poems* offered insight into her inner suffering and anguish. She spoke often and candidly of her torment in a way not dissimilar to Virginia Woolf half a century earlier. Her desperate words were passionate pleas for help that often crossed over into inflammatory accusations against those she loved. It is obvious she was attempting to exorcise those inner demons that plagued her from the day her father died at age eight.

CATHARTIC REALISM. Writers are only able to write from a conscious or subconscious perspective. They tap into their wellspring of experiences and often embellish those for affect and to fantasize or titillate. But ultimately, the words are not far removed from inner needs for expression, an escape from a reality that is too difficult to tolerate.

Dostoevsky, Woolf, and Hemingway also had a preoccupation with death and emotional dysfunction and those feelings made their way into their characterizations. Woolf wrote, "I deal in autobiography and call it fiction; every secret of a writer's soul, every experience of his life, every quality of his mind is written large in his works" (Gordon pg. 6). Camus's nihilistic view of the world found its way into a life of existential philosophical invective. King, Steel and Rice all wrote in a Woolfian stream of consciousness aimed at relieving their inner turmoil. James Michener' admitted in his memoirs *The World is My Home* (1991), "I wrote *South Pacific* primarily for myself."

Stephen King has always recognized that he is but writing out his greatest fears and embellishing them for the reader. King said, "Writing is necessary for my sanity. I can externalize my fears and insecurities and night terrors on paper, which is what people pay shrinks a small fortune to do" (Contemporary Authors New Revision Series Vol 52 pg. 241).

Dr. Seuss didn't want to act as an adult and chose a career that allowed him to be frivolous, inane, and the clown prince of cartoons. Ray Freiman, Dr. Seuss' production manager at Beginner Books said, "He is his work, all the whimsy and zaniness of it is part of him" (Morgan pg. 123). When a friend asked, "Do you associate yourself with any of your drawings?" Geisel responded "Yes, especially the more devious ones" (Morgan pg. 232).

Hemingway wrote short stories to get even with lost loves (Jane Mason) and her cuckolded husband. In fiction he was able to call his mistresses bitches and the males he couldn't stand wimps. His major books were *The Sun Also Rises* (1926) and *A Farewell to Arms* (1929), furious attempts to remove that brush with death in an Italian foxhole during WW-I. *The Old Man & the Sea* (1953) was his struggle with aging and losing his virility and ability to write.

George Bernard Shaw had virulent and deep-seated frustrations over Victorian hypocrisy and British decorum. This led him to spend his life and work trying to destroy them. He saw himself as the *Life Force* or "great man" in his classic drama *Man and Superman* (1903), Napoleon in *Man of Destiny* (1895), Sir Andrew Undershaft in *Major Barbara* (1909) and the elocutionist Professor Henry Higgins in *Pygmalion* (1913). Shaw saw himself as man's savior as a modern day Prometheus.

Every passionate word in Rand's two classic works *The Fountainhead* (1943) and *Atlas Shrugged* (1957) was an attempt at destroying communism. When she left Russia for America she promised to let the world know and did she. She spent the rest of her life getting retribution through words and became known as the Mistress of Capitalism. Rational self-interest became an alternative to a centralized system contra to freedom. The Russian Radical admitted "I write to get Russia out of my system" (Sciabara pg. 99). Every philosophic diatribe was aimed at purging her rage against an insidious system that had stolen her father's business and destroyed his will to live. Her revenge were epic novels - *The Fountainhead* and *Atlas Shrugged* – the foundation of the Libertarian Party and Objectivism. She said, "Dagny is myself with any possible flaws eliminated" (Sciabarra pg.244.

PLATH – POSTER GIRL FOR CATHARTIC EXPRESSION

Plath's verse earned her a cult following of rebellious 60's and 70's revolutionaries. Like another cult-hero James Dean, she died young but left a legacy of anger at a system that didn't understand or appreciate her. Her anger and passionate rhetoric became a rallying call for the disenfranchised youth of the 60's. Her blatant honesty and rage over her inability to control her emotional urges was aligned with the counter-culture era. Her outbursts on human frailty and brazen intensity shocked and alarmed a spirited generation. Her last poems titled the *Ariel* poems are a tribute to her ethereal spirit.

In college, Plath fell in love with Shakespeare's *The Tempest* because it paralleled her own chaotic and fear driven existence. She feared falling off a horse, a poetic metaphor for falling off life. It was her way of conveying a misanthropic struggle for survival. These words are found in *Ariel*, a *tour de force* that mentor George Steiner said "had a vivid and disturbing impact, and a desperate integrity" (Contemporary Authors p. 355).

Ariels poems were ferocious and vicious, an incisive reflection of her inner rage, and a futile attempt at saving herself from self-destruction. It didn't work as she became so caught up in her spiraling world that became a vortex that engulfed her. Mentor A. Alvarez called them "metaphors of the terrifying human mind." He described her emotional rhetoric as "anonymity of pain, which makes all dignity impossible" (Contemporary Authors – New Revision Vol 34 pg. 356). Biographer Stephenson said, "Every time she put pen to paper she began to analyze herself" (1989 pg. 33).

The *Ariel* collection was published two years after her death. Her tragic suicide made her into a martyr as often happens. Fury and emotion dominate work aimed at placating an enigmatic inner muse. It revealed her life creeping ever closer to the precipice. These poems were emotional and savage, offering insight into her crumbling world. Robert Lowell called her last works "controlled hallucination, the autobiography of fever" (Contemporary Authors Vol. 34 pg. 356). It was a valiant attempt to exorcise those inner ghosts described in her autobiographical novel *The Bell Jar* (1963).

This novel was written anonymously while pregnant in what she called a period of "transformation." She had discovered Jung's *Symbol's of Transformation* and Roethke's *The Waking,* two books that had an enormous influence over her thinking and writing. *The Bell Jar* was an attempt at her own transformation out of a world of flirting with insanity into rationality. Because of the work's brutal honesty she published it using a pseudonym. It was a vicious attack on everyone she loved including her mother and husband. It offers insight into her flirtation with insanity. Her verse play *Three Women* was written with insight on her Oedipal and Electra hang-ups.

POETRY - A PRESCRIPTION FOR SELF-DESTRUCTION

Sylvia Plath was a self-destructive teenager. She grew up to be a nihilistic adult with suicidal tendencies. Poets have a long history of bipolar illness and suicide including the likes of Lord Byron, T. S. Eliot, Dickens, Poe, Blake, Keats, Shelly and Dylan Thomas. It is interesting these people must use emotional words to express passion for life, yet are destroyed by what makes them successful.

Obsessive people turn to obsessive acts just as desperate people do desperate things. Such people have an inordinate degree of pathology and dysfunctions. They are driven, obsessive, compulsive and prone to excess. Manic-depression is highly prevalent in such individuals as is Type A personalities. Alexander the Great has been classified as bipolar as has been Napoleon with their military success a function of their euphoric stages and their defeats associated with their depression. As a teen, Napoleon wrote these profound words in *The Sorrows of Young Werther.* "Life is a burden to me, because I taste no pleasure and all is pain."

POETRY AS GENRE

Poetry is an instrument of creative expression for vital individuals, but is often created by those on the edge of normalcy. It appeals to the introspective and emotional personality. The genre has a following of people in touch with their inner selves. Such people have a holistic view of the world and like to marry the emotional with cognitive expression. This ability to synthesize the emotional with the rational is what makes them some of the world's great communicators. The Greeks defined poetry as *poiein* meaning "to make" or one who invents or makes things up. Myths were the genesis of Homer's stories that had originated in fable.

Poetry is a genre dominated by people who worship at the altar of "I." Why? Because one must be engrossed with their onw reason for existence and be introspective to a fault. Egocentrics and manic-depression dominates the genre. Sylvia Plath was both. While at Smith she wrote in her journal, "the girl who wanted to be God."

Poetry is any rhymed or metrical composition carrying with it a value judgment. Therefore, any artist who creates or innovates can be labeled a poet as long as they make a philosophical statement via verse. Poetry comes in many forms including Ode, Sonnet, Elegy, Ballad or Drama and may take on many styles such as Epic (heroic action), Lyric (singing), or Satire (moral censure). The verses of Plath were what the Greek poets Homer and Hesiod claimed were inspired by the Muses. In Greek mythology, the daughters of the goddess of memory were Muses, inspirational characters who could charm with words. Virgil and Dante are Roman and Italian examples.

PLATO & PASSION. Plato was one of the first writers to define poetry as a "supernatural force" where the audience is bound to the play. He banned poets from his Republic because they and their work lacked ideological meaning. He saw passion as being inconsistent with rational ideology. *Ideas* dominated all thinking at Plato's Academy. Wisdom was godly and poets were but interesting and entertaining gadflys but not considered serious imparters of knowledge.

EPIC POETRY. Homer's *Iliad* was one of the first great epic poems written. It's equivalent was not seen until the end of the Dark Ages when Omar Khayyam wrote the *Rubaiyat* in the early 12th century. Dante's *The Divine Comedy* (1321) came later and was soon followed by Shakespeare's output of 154 Sonnets. John Milton's *Paradise Lost* was written in verse form in 12 books followed by *Paradise Regained* in the 17th century. Great lyric beauty came in the form of John Keat's *Endymion* (1818). *The Song of Hiawatha* by Longfellow was a 19th century epic poem followed by Rudyard Kipling's Nobel Prize winning *Kim* and *If.* The 20th century brought us Emily Dickinson and T.S. Eliot's *Waste Land* (1922). Eliot and Ezra Pound were expatriates writing of spiritual loss and fragmentation fraught by WW-I. They influenced Robert Frost and Carl Sandberg followed by A. H. Auden, Anne Sexton, and Stephen Spender.

PLATH'S CATHARTIC VERSE

Plath's poems and novel were both acclaimed for their cathartic release. Her seething unconscious produced *The Disquieting Muses* (1957), a poem of love and hate doing battle in her diabolical unconscious. *Daddy* was written in 1957 as part of her *Colossus* collection, a tribute to her heroic father, the only Colossus in her life. Otto had the audacity to die and leave her alone in the world without a *Daddy*. Her father pervaded her writing with words like "Daddy, I have had to kill you, You died before I had time" (Stevenson pg. 264). She recognized her Oedipal Complex and described herself an "overexposed X-ray" (Stevenson pg. 303). Passion spawned emotional outbursts of those inner demons that permeated her life and work. They were self-destructive. When Ted Hughes was detained from some meeting she assumed he was with another woman and went into a violent rage and would destroy his work. Often she destroyed his most precious works that had taken months to finish. She actually destroyed precious and rare Shakespearian books that he cherished. She justified her act as "punishment for his missing lunch" (Stevenson pg. 206).

Catharsis was central to all her writing. This was never more apparent than the autobiographical *The Bell Jar*. She wrote it in one last valiant attempt to survive in what she considered an unfair world. It described her life and death struggle against the forces of evil. But it was in her journal that she wrote of the deep-seated anxieties that plagued her. One 1950 journal entry declared, "I'm lost." In *Disquieting Muses* are the telling lines, "an old need of giving my mother accomplishments, getting reward of love" (Stevenson pg. 126). On December 28, 1958 she wrote of her failed 1953 suicide attempt saying, "I felt if I didn't write nobody would accept me as a human being. Writing was a substitute for myself: if you don't love me, love my writing and love me for writing (Stevenson pg. 128).

These words are a pretty sad commentary for an attractive and talented young female of 26 with an IQ of 160 about to embark on her life's work. But she had long been a slave to her inner demons, most of which were self-induced. They kept her from living any semblance of a normal life. Like Balzac she believed she had to be a genius or die humiliated. Sylvia graduated *summa cum laude* from Smith College in 1955 and received a Fulbright Scholarship. She had already been published, but insecurity lay buried in her and refused to let her relax. She had to be perfect or die trying.

CATHARTIC WRITING. A willingness to write from the soul and heart, regardless of the consequences, is the hallmark of genius, especially if one is writing poetry. But it is also critical to other genres. *Publishers Weekly* described the Queen of Romance's work as "Steel's cathartic drama." Steel is writing about love she has never found in real life. She very adroitly escapes into fantasy stories where life meets the perfection that she wants but can't find. She told the media, "I'm terrified of not writing. I make a world peopled the way I want my life to be" (Bane & Benet pg. Pg. 186). Second husband and ex-convict Danny Zugelder told the media, "She creates the fantasy she wants to live and that's how she lives. And if any little thing doesn't fit into that fantasy, it either doesn't exist or she changes it to fit her fantasy" (Bane & Benet p. 148).

Anne Rice offers prescient insight into her own catharsis:

> *I write to explore my worst fears, then I take my protagonists right into situations that terrify me. My characters all represent longings and aspirations within myself"* (Ramsland pg. 295)

Ian Fleming wrote the Bond fantasies as an outlet for his sadist needs that were stifled in the real world. He had to create an intrepid warrior like 007 to explore his deepest nees. Fleming was Bond as he wanted to be but could not.

POETIC INNOVATIONS

Cathartic realism was Plath's innovative contribution to the genre. She never hesitated to write of her flirtation with dementia. In many respects, she sacrificed her life for her art. Her poetry clearly demonstrates that inner truth communicates quite effectively. Plath gave us seething words of passion from her troubled psyche. Critic Charles Newman said, "She evolved a poetic voice from the precocious girl; to the disturbed modern woman; to the vengeful magician; to – *Ariel* – God's Lioness." He said *The Bell Jar* was "one of the few American novels to treat adolescence from a mature point of view... chronicling a nervous breakdown and consequent professional therapy in non-clinical language" (Contemporary Authors Vol. 34 pg. 356).

WRITING AS CATHARSIS

Plath was the master of self-doubt. She escaped into her own world of insecurity and used passionate words to exorcise the inner ghosts that plagued her daily. Few things describe her cathartic release as these lines from *The Bell Jar*:

> *I saw my life branching before me like the green fig tree in the story. From the tip of every branch, like a fat purple fig, a wonderful future beckoned and winked. One fig was a husband and a happy home and children, and another fig was a famous poet and another fig was a famous poet and another fig was a brilliant professor, and another fig was Ed Gee, the amazing editor, and another fig was Europe and Africa and South America, and another fig was Constantine and Socrates and Attila and a pack of other lovers with queer names and offbeat professions, and another fig was an Olympic lady crew champion, and beyond and above these figs were many more figs I couldn't quite make out – I saw myself sitting in the crotch of this fig tree starving to death, just because I couldn't make up my mind which of the figs I would choose. I wanted each and every one of them, but choosing one meant losing all the rest, and, as I sat there, unable to decide, the figs began to wrinkle and go black, and one by one, they plopped to the ground at my feet.* (The Bell Jar *USA Today* 10-24-96 pg 6D)

Plath's suicide is testimony to her emotional instability. Her life had been destroyed at age nine when her father died. Then her husband left her with two small children for another woman, a poetess. It was all just too much for her to bear even though her violent outbursts had driven him away. In her soul Ted had replaced her Colossus father as an adult hero to worship and respect. When he walked out she lost all will to live. But even her last act was dramatically staged and meant to save her at the 11th hour, but it went awry due to the vagaries of London traffic. Her London maid was due to arrive within minutes so she turned on the oven and placed her head in it, but only after meticulously placing cookies and milk on the table for her two small children. Had the maid arrived anywhere close to the appointed hour she would have found Sylvia and all would have been well since Ted would have been tormented by guilt and hopefully returned to her open arms. But when the maid entered the apartment Plath was dead at age thirty.

METAMORPHOSES

Each year at Christmas, Plath's teacher-parents gave her a diary in her stocking. She was expected to write in it and tell the story of her life – her foibles and fears. When eight her godlike father was diagnosed with diabetes and died within two years. His death shocked her to an extent that she made her mother promise to never marry again, and wrote in her journal, "I will never again speak to God."

Her emotionally strong mother didn't cry at the funeral infuriating the little girl. Her Colossus was dead but she never allowed him to die in her heart. Biographer Stevenson wrote, "Her real idol was the *Colossus*, her dead father, and every man she chose for a lover had to be somehow cast in his mold" (p. 104). Plath's first publication was titled *Colossus* (1960) and he is ever-present in much of her writing. She spent her life in a mad attempt to live up to his expectations.

Plath was a second born child. Her older brother Warren, was sickly and always the focus of attention in the Plath household. Soon after her father's death Warren became seriously ill and Sylvia was sent off to live with her grandparents. This trauma reinforced her use of words to communicate as she wrote to her mother daily despite being only blocks away. During another of her brother's illnesses Sylvia was sent off to a Girl Scout camp for the summer where she was also forced to communicate with words. Words were an outlet that always seemed to be at a time of crises.

Plath wrote *Daddy* when approaching 30. The poem was a stream of cathartic words as follows:(Stevenson 264-265).

Daddy, I have had to kill you
You died before I had time
...
I was ten when they buried you
At twenty I tried to die
And get back, back, back to you
I thought even the bones would do
...
So Daddy, I'm finally through.

When she wrote these words she was pregnant and going through a transformation of the mind after absorbing the passionate words of Jung and Roethke. She and Ted were on vacation in Saratoga Springs, New York and she wrote of experiencing a metamorphoses of the mind, body, and spirit.

ECCENTRICITIES

Idiosyncrasies defined Plath. She was bright, a perfectionist, obsessive, and had a penchant for the arcane. She was bipolar although at the time had not been diagnosed as such. Today she would be on Prozac. She did little in moderation. Plath believed she was "precognitive" and "psychic" and turned to Ouija Boards, Astrology, and Tarot Cards to find her way.

Plath was alternatively grandiose and despondent. When up she was able to outwork and outthink her peers and was highly productive. When depressed she was debilitated and incapable of doing anything. She experienced euphoric flights of optimism that turned into a *tour de force* of verse. But when she came down was prone to suicide. She described her intensity as "electric" and the mood scared her. Her journal entries offer insight into her turmoil. She wrote "I have violence in me." Signs of a dual personality exist and she wrote of "two electric currents – joyous positive and despairing negative – dominate my life" (Stevenson pg. 134). In 1958 she wrote "I am now flooded with despair, almost hysteria, as if I were smothering." In *Witch Burning* (1959) she wrote, "I am lost, I am lost, in the robes of all this light" (Stevenson pg. 171).

She was vindictive, paranoid, hysteric, volatile and often self-destructive. Husband Ted Hughes was her all-everything hero in one moment, and a despicable wanton lecher in the next. Her jealous rages knew no bounds. When he was away she imagined him running off with some bimbo and would go through his desk to find his most precious poems not yet published and burn them in a symbolic act of immolation. Such behavior is a horrid act against any writer who has toiled to create and to have it burned is tantamount to sacrilege. She once tore up all his poems and placed the little pieces and placed them carefully on his desk for him to see.

In one violent rage Sylvia tore the telephone from the wall and burned valuable Shakesperian books. She had crossed the threshold and her acts drove him off into the waiting arms of poet Assia Wavill. The irony is that Wavill would also gas herself in a macabre reenactment of Sylvia's death.

Sylvia's compulsions and passion for books offers further insight into her eccentricity. A college roommate borrowed a textbook and returned it with some words underlined. Plath went into an uncontrollable rage and began screaming at the unsuspecting coed who thought she had committed some sacrilege. Plath documented the event in her journal writing, "I was furious, feeling my children had been raped, or beaten by an alien. I felt as if I had been intellectually raped" (Stevenson p 80). Another roommate dared rearrange her clothes initiating a violent attack and emotional outburst.

LIFE CRISES

Otto Plath's death was the defining moment in Sylvia's life. She was emotionally devastated and would never recover. One reason was her mother refused her to look into the casket, an act for which Sylvia never forgave her. She then demanded that her mother "never marry again" and prepared a formal note for her mother's signature and insisted she sign it. The repression of her own grief surfaced later when she attempted to kill herself. On one occasion she disappeared in New York City and was reported missing by friends and family.

Perfectionism was one of the ways she overcompensated for inner insecurity. Like most Type A personalities, Plath confused self-worth with achievement. And since her scholarly father Otto was an intellectual - a PhD of entomology at Boston University – she lost herself in books and epistemological pursuits. She drove herself and the intensity took its toll on her health and emotional well-being. And during her Sophomore year at Smith, she broke down under the pressure of trying to be the perfect girl, student and writer.

In her novel *The Bell Jar* she wrote of the time as she saw herself slipping slowly into mental illness. Fearing insanity and life in a mental institution she decided to end it all in "one final act of love." After days of vigil her family discovered her lying unconscious, near death, in the basement of their home. She had overdosed on sleeping pills but fortuitously had vomited them up while in a coma. She would spend the next four months recuperating in a Boston hospital. This eerie experience haunted her for the next ten years. She lived in mortal fear of her own volatility and self-destructive potential.

Her last emotional trauma precipitated her demise. In the fall of 1962 she was the mother of two and trying unsuccessfully to get published. When her volatile temper drove her husband out the door she fled to the safety of writing. Sylvia never did anything in moderation, but now she became manic and wrote as if her very life was in the balance. The result was the *Ariel* poems written in a furious *tour de force* – forty cathartic poems that left her emotionally drained, and physically exhausted.

By January 1963 she was in a feverish white heat of emotion and anxiety when she wrote a verse play *Three Women* with all three voices dimensions of herself. In the *Second Voice* she wrote of the anguish she was experiencing. She wrote, "This is a disease that I carry home, this is a death." It was her voice calling out for help, the voice of a daughter of the beekeeper (her father's dissertation was on bee-keeping) that pervaded her very being. Biographer Stevenson called *Three Women* "the first great poem of childbirth in the language" (Stevenson pg. 232-234). Weeks later, on a dark dreary morning in a lonely London apartment Sylvia Plath decided she couldn't cope anymore. Ironically, her masterpiece of autobiographical insight – *The Bell Jar* – had just been released.

POLYPHASIC

Plath was polyphasic in the sense she could work on a number of poems simultaneously, all in a different state of completion, and rather than get confused, relished the task. She would schedule much more than was possible to complete like a woman on a treadmill. She always attempted to achieve more and more in less and less time. Sylvia was determined to be the perfect wife, mother, student, writer, poet, Ted's editor, and the one to promote their work. The pressure was too much for a mother of two, especially one who was emotionally and physically drained.

Plath bombarded editors with a steady stream of manuscripts from her and Ted. She was a wife, mother, and writer while finishing up a Masters program at Cambridge. Friends and family were astounded at her whirlwind lifestyle and ability to keep so many balls in the air without breaking. Manic-depressives have an unusual capacity to maintain a vigil that would kill ordinary people. But when the bubble breaks so do they. During their first year of marriage Sylvia was in her final year at Cambridge and studied constantly, took up Oriental cooking, had a baby, became pregnant with the second and wrote poetry incessantly. Ted Hughes told a friend, "Sylvia sits and writes for about twelve hours at a stretch and gets too excited to sleep" (Stevenson pg. 124).

CRITICAL ACCLAIM

Critics love Plath's work or hate it. Why? Because it was pure cathartic release, unencumbered passion, unconventional, and radical. Ted Hughes described her style as "clairvoyant and psychic." She is now considered one of the first of a new school of poetry known as the *Confessional School* along with her friends Robert Lowell and Anne Sexton.

SYLVIA PLATH

Twenty years passed between Plath's death and her Pulitzer Prize in 1982 for *Collected Poems.* About her death, the *Observer* (Feb. 1963) wrote, "The loss to literature is inestimable" (Martin p. 245). Biographer Stevenson in *Bitter Fame* (1989) wrote, "There is almost no one writing poetry today who has not been affected by the power and passion of Plath's poetry" (pg. 303). Andrea Sachs in *Time* (April 18, 1984) called her a "fierce accomplished poet," and one who "has endured" with "harsh, brilliant, astonishing" words.

Frances McCullough, who collaborated with Hughes in the publication of her journals, wrote in the Forward, "she sacrificed everything for a new birth." George Steiner said, "It is fair to say that no group of poems since Dylan Thomas's *Deaths and Entrances* has had as vivid and disturbing an impact on English critics and readers as *Ariel*" (Contemporary Authors Vol. 34 pg. 355).

Many contemporary critics place Sylvia Plath with the greatest poets in the 20th century. That says a lot considering the presence of Frost, Dickinson, Sandburg and T.S. Eliot. Further testimony is the massive appeal of *The Bell Jar,*.a book that took on cult-like status with annual sales numbering 100,000. The book offers a lurid insight into the mind of a woman balancing precariously on the abyss of madness. It demonstrates the high price a person pays for allowing emotional dysfunction to dominate their life. It offers insight into the terrible emotional cost of repressing the self. Living for achievement is costly indeed and her poetry and novel are testaments to a driven personality.

SUCCESS & CATHARSIS – What Can We Learn?

Plath divulged her deepest hatreds and fears in verse. Such expression of inner thoughts is never easy, but can prove therapeutic. Sylvia had a sense of the tragic and her work had panache and daring. Tragedy in the theater and life demands we die to gain immortality and this was the case with Plath.

Plath's journals and poems reveal a very unhappy woman searching for a way out of a dysfunctional world. Demons plagued her turbulent soul. Was her torment worth her success? She would have said yes. But she probably wouldn't have taken drugs to tame her raging manias. Research shows that most artists, especially poets, forego the use of drugs to find normality since they reduce their emotional edge.

Cathartic expression has never been more graphically or literally obvious than in those last twenty-four tormented months of Plath's life. During this period she produced her best and most enduring work. Her rage was out of control as was her ability to slow down. She turned to writing to find inner peace but it was not enough to remove the anguish. Typical of Plath's approach, was her retreat into the vegetable garden to burn the love letters she had found from Assia Wevill to Ted. She burned them in a kind of satanic ritual and then wrote the whole affair out of her system in a poem titled, *The Other* - "Words Heard by Accident, I have your head on my wall." Then in a self-destructive rage she burned an entire new novel she had written dedicated to Ted. The tragedy is the novel *Falcon Yard* has been lost forever. Did this purgative move placate her? No! She ended in all six months later.

In poet Horace Walpole's prophetic words, "Those who *think* see life as a comedy, those who *feel* see it as a tragedy." Those words sum up Sylvia Plath's tragic existence. Addictive personalities suffer a similar fate. But if such individuals can learn to introspect and not destruct they will prevail. Plath sensed this writing, "I shall perish if I cannot write," and that defined her. This girl who dreamed she was Joan of Arc set out to be a maiden of verse and her work will remain a strong statement for introspective writing. That will be her legacy.

MARK TWAIN (Clemens)
AMERICANA HUMORIST
b. Florida, MO Nov. 30, 1835
d.CT, April. 21, 1910

RISK-TAKING & SUCCESS

DOMINANT GENRE
Humorist with penchant for tragedy of the human condition in the vernacular

MOTTO
"No man will dare more than I"
"If everybody was satisfied with himself there would be no heroes"

GREATEST WORKS
Tom Sawyer (1876)
The Prince & the Pauper (1882)
Huckleberry Finn (1884) sold 10 million

HONORS/AWARDS
Honorary Doctorates from Oxford, Yale, Missouri
"All American literature comes from one book *Huckleberry Finn*" (Ernest Hemingway)

ECCENTRICITIES
Renegade risk-taker who was bankrupt in mid-fifties fleeing to Europe to avoid creditors; wore white suits all year: "I had certain peculiarities and customs (manic-depressive)"

LIFE CRISES
Sister, brother, and father died before he was 12; adult brother died on Mississippi; first son died while he was in a reverie

METAMORPHOSES
Fired from San Francisco newspaper; attempted suicide, and revived via writing novel on mining - *Jumping Frog of Calaveras County* (1867)

9

MARK TWAIN (Samuel Clemens) – HUMOR

COMFORT WITH AMBIGUITY

"No man will dare more than I"

RISK-TAKING & SUCCESS

Helen Keller wrote, "Life is either a daily adventure or nothing." Mark Twain lived by that aphorism. As all students of entrepreneurship know, breaking new ground on anything is little more than an adventure in risk-taking. In fact, no word is more synonymous entrepreneurship than risk, and a career in writing is little other than operating your own enterprise.

Few things are more important to literary success than creativity. And creativity depends on temerity. Why? Because to be creative one must break new ground and that takes guts. Anyone defying convention, and the top dogs in any venue, will require a strong sense of self, because everyone, including family, friends and even mates will say you have lost your way. True innovation and creativity will demand audacity and the refusal to allow fear to be part of the journey. Writer George Gilder said it best in *The Spirit of Enterprise* 1984):

> *The investor who never acts until statistics affirm his choice, the athlete or politician who fails to make his move until too late, the businessman who waits until the market is proven – all are doomed to mediocrity by their trust in a spurious rationality and their feelings of faith."*

Agatha Christie risked a blossoming writing career when she thumbed her nose at convention and had the storyteller be the culprit in *The Murder of Roger Achyroyd.* Her daring made her many enemies, but it also allowed her to become the Queen of Detective Mysteries. Mark Twain said, "Courage is mastery of fear. No man will dare more than I."

RISK BIG & WIN BIG. Why are these two concepts tied together? Because risking small results in small wins. In other terms, you can only win the amount you are willing to bet. Bet big win big, and bet little win little. Playing penny ante poker results in winning and losing pennies or at worst a dollar. Playing big stakes poker results in winning and losing thousands. This is also true of any professional venture. Allowing fear to dominate any decision only guarantees moderate success. Prudence insures no great losses, but also insures no great wins.

Personal and professional risks are treated in a similar manner. People and firms tend to risk less when there isn't too much to risk, but once they have accumulated many assets they have tendency to risk less and spend more time and energy protecting their asset base. The exception to this axiom is the world's great entrepreneurs and visionaries. Mark Twain, Frank Lloyd Wright, Thomas Edison, Picasso, Bucky Fuller and Ted Turner always bet it all to win it all, even after they had already made it. That is the nature of the visionary genius. Twain, Edison and Wright were bankrupt when they were in their late 50's. But all died rich due to their temerity.

RISK & REWARD IS A ZERO-SUM GAME. It has been shown that *removing risk removes rewards in the same proportion as the mitigation of risk!* Living on the edge and a willingness to bet the farm on your prescient ideas is critical to success in virtually any venue. Why? Because risk and reward are inextricably intertwined in the battle for success. Twain lived life right on the edge, refusing to bow to the pressures of the establishment. Ayn Rand had a similar proclivity. She was rewarded with a ten foot $

sign on her casket in 1982. When publishers and editors recommended she lighten up her rhetoric and shorten it for a mass market, Rand ignored them and followed her own path. She was rewarded with 25 million books sold that the experts said wouldn't sell at all.

Gamblers like Dostoevsky, Hemingway, Camus, and Fleming lived life on the edge. Were they fun husbands? Hardly! Did their temerity improve their craft? Probably! Life outside convention tends to be eminently more interesting and significantly more dangerous. But danger and creativity appear to be strange but willing bed fellows.

Should a writer ignore the advice of experts or literary sacred cows? There is little question that allowing free reign to one's creative juices is far preferable to bowing to any ritual from any authority. Imparting one's inner dreams and actions without regard to outside interference is always the best advice. Life, and especially creative life, is far too short to live by another's agenda. One must believe and follow their own path or not go at all. Confirmation comes from Harvard scientist Burton Klein who wrote in *Dynamic Economics* (1977), "The more certain an environment, the poorer will be the incentives for risk-taking and the less certain an environment, the higher will be the incentives for risk-taking" (pg. 77).

FEAR – THE ENEMY OF SUCCESS. Fear is by far the biggest enemy of creativity. Fear of trying anything new, fear of failing, fear of embarrassment, fear of looking stupid, fear of offending loved ones, fear of not conforming to those in power, all guaranteed to destroy creativity. Such fear is debilitating. Winners fear little. Losers fear most everything. Winners only strive to win. Losers strive not to lose. A fine difference, but the only one separating two people with similar talent.

Successful people thrive on the unknown. They love new and abstract problems to solve and new terrain to conquer. Risk titillates such people while it debilitates the also-rans. That doesn't mean to imply that creative people

187

do not question their moves or shake when facing intense danger. They do but are not so incapacitated to freeze and allow the situation to take control. Dr. Seuss was unbelievably insecure. He once said, "I'll never write anything." At age 36 George Bernard Shaw wrote, "I wish I could write a play but I have not the faculty." But these words were but self-imposed motivational talk aimed at inspiring them onward. Shaw wrote, "No child should be shielded from danger, either physical or moral," his admonition for using self-doubt and danger as the territory for growth and learning.

Far too many young people worship at the altar of fear. The unknown is scary, but that is also true of the creative genius. The only difference is attitude. One repels from the foreign. The other attacks it with great anticipation. The fearful tend to conform and consequently live a sheltered, non-risk life with a highly predictable result. The intrepid warriors are not so safe but tend to find some wonderful nuggets on those dangerous trails through life. The fearful look for confirmation and security, but the only true security comes from within, never from without. Fear and uncertainty are the masters of those who allow outside forces to control their destiny. Creative insight is the destiny of those living outside convention.

CREATIVE DESTRUCTION & INNOVATION. The term "creative destruction" is synonymous with innovation. Nothing creative is achieved without destroying what went before whether that is a new idea, manuscript, product, house, or transition to a higher state of being. A new house is out of the question if one is not predisposed to tearing down the old one. And the adolescent in all of us will never give way to the adult without the destruction of teenage behaviors. A new product cannot replace the tried and true one if the firm is unwilling to risk losing some customers tied to the old. Innovative people must break down traditional barriers to create a new paradigm.

When a person is out in front of the pack, territory often tread by the creative genius, they are faced with the novel and foreign. It is never safe territory when out in front and that is why one must find comfort with ambiguity or lose all chance for creative endeavors. This is why creativity and risk-aversity are diametrically opposite concepts. It is impossible to be creative and security driven. Innovative people live life on the edge and Twain was the consummate example, a man who was truly a creative destroyer. That is why his classics were banned in Boston. The father of 19th century Americana dared write in the vernacular. It was dangerous but made his work great. Twain's temerity earned him the enmity of the literary elite, but it also made his work a lasting bastion of creative splendor.

Mediocrity lives inside the box of mediocrity. Creativity is having the guts to live outside that box where innovation reigns. A willingness to violate tradition is critical to creative success. Twain was vilified for his daring. Educators and librarians labeled his writing the work of the devil, describing it as "vile, vulgar, rough, trashy, inelegant, irreverent, course, and vicious." Louisa May Alcott suggested he stop writing if "he cannot think of something better to tell our pure-minded lads and lasses" (Kaplan p. 268). Alcott detested *Huckleberry Finn* (1884) and *Tom Sawyer* (1876) two books now acclaimed as classics. Both books are responsible for replacing the British literary style with a purely American one.

It is truly ironic that the very group who benefited the most would be the one vilifying Twain's work. Literary critics have since eulogized Twain as the single individual who ended the British domination of American literature. Twain's down-home colloquial humor was considered nothing more than gutter tripe by his American peers, but ironically, was revered by British critics. George Bernard Shaw saw Twain as a "pathmaker," saying:

> *Mark Twain is by far the greatest American writer. He is in very much the same position as myself. He has to put things in such a way as to make people*

189

MARK TWAIN

who would otherwise hang him believe he is joking.   Telling the truth is the funniest joke in the world. (Kaplan p. 382)

Twain was *persona non grata* in America's drawing rooms but a huge hit in farmhouses, working communities, and in the hinterlands. Political and social correctness was not high on Twain's list of priorities. He used wit to disarm his critics. His dime novels were his salvation. They separated him from the stilted drawing room books that were aimed at the refined set. He became known as the People's Author by his slice of life approach. He was not steeped in formal education and as a self-educated commoner had more insight than the so-called experts.

Twain was known in the 19th century as the Wild Humorist of the Pacific Slope due to his adventurous travels to foreign lands and his writing about the great unwashed and unkempt. He lived of what he wrote and the imagery of the Wild West pervades his work. As in most creative geniuses, Twain had an affinity for misadventures and made and lost millions on wild schemes that wouldn't have happened to the less risky.

Many who live life on the precipice as Twain fall into it. But those that live to tell of their adventures are better for having taken the risk. Many of these writers have become immortal due to their propensity to risk – namely Balzac, Camus, Fleming, Plath, Rand, and King.

Others like Woolf, Hemingway and Plath took their own lives. Steel has had five divorces and King is a recovering drug and alcohol addict. But even these experiences were tame compared to some of the debacles of Samuel Longhorne Clemens. Mr. Clemens, aka Twain, lived life as a high-roller, betting millions on nefarious schemes that led to bankruptcy and a flight to Europe in his 50's.

Creative geniuses are always willing to bet it all on their dreams. Nikola Tesla stood on stage at the 1893 World's Fair in Chicago and allowed 1 million volts of electric current pass through his body to prove that he, not Edison was right. Why would a rich talented inventor risk his life in such a stunt? To validate his thesis, the driving force of the creative, who would rather die than see their creations destroyed. Other creative geniuses with such a penchant were Margaret Mead who traveled to the jungles of New Guinea to write her innovative books; Sigmund Freud who went well outside the bounds of medical decorum to write *Interpretation of Dreams;* and one of the world's great innovators, Leonardo da Vinci whose biographer said, "Leonardo was an enlightened rebel who did not give a whit about careful wording" (Zubov pg. 53).

LITERARY SUCCESS & AN AUDACIOUS MENTALITY

Twain always pushed the windows of opportunity in literature and investing. He always chose the adventurous road to the safe one. To him there were no risky situations, only interesting ones to challenge one to be better. He lived life with abandon and paid the price for his temerity. But he also broke new ground. At the millennium the irreverent humorist is universally acknowledged as the father of modern American literature and is particularly remembered for *Huckleberry Finn* (1884). Hemingway wrote, "All modern American literature comes from one book by Mark Twain called *Huckleberry Finn*...there was nothing before, there has been nothing since" (World American Criticism pg. 3713). Faulkner praised him as an American original, influencing his work more than any other writer.

If breaking with tradition is what risk-taking is about, then Samuel Clemens is the poster boy. He continually experimented with the new and different, marrying wit with tragedy in the vernacular of the common man. In this way he captured frontier America like no one before or since. But this strength proved to be his greatest weakness. He paid the price and was called, "crude and uncultured." Part of Twain's magic was his irreverence and fearlessness.

Twain has outlasted his critics and has come to be known as the consummate American writer, a man who documented the Gilded Age, dared challenge the Boston and New York elite, and offered insight into America's frontier. Without Twain we would have lost much of our history including life in covered wagons, on mountain trails, on the raging rivers, gold and silver mines of the old west, on riverboats, backyards, front-yards and saloons. Twain's words made frontier life real. Clemens was especially proficient at describing life in pre-civil war America. His stories captured the essence of that period. He wrote for the working classes and that is what he has characterized for that era.

His words and deeds were of covered wagons, the gold rush, wild Indians, itinerant miners, riverboat gamblers and the disenfranchised. By age thirty he had seen much of the world and had a penchant for documenting what he saw in the words of the people he saw. He had been to Central and South America, the Caribbean, Hawaii, worked in the Nevada silver mines, and California's gold mines. He had lived and worked in San Francisco at the height of the Gold Rush, had been a riverboat captain on the wild Mississippi, and traveled to England, Italy, Greece and the Holy Land.

Twain was constantly making fun of himself. It proved to be an endearing quality for devoted fans and adversaries. Today he is criticized for making fun of American pioneers and minorities, a true irony since he preached far and wide on the sins of hypocrisy and oppression. A satirical style set him apart. Many harrowing escapes armed him with insights not available to less adventurous writers. Near-death experiences allowed him to see life through a unique filter. He spoke in his autobiography of coming close to drowning seven different times and of nearly dying of measles that caused him to quit school.

POSTERITY - KINDER AND MORE ACCURATE. Twain's books are now used to illustrate the early Americana spirit of pragmatism, egalitarianism, and honesty. Despite being banned, Twain is likened to an American Cervantes, Homer, Tolstoy, and Shakespeare due to his witty insights. Franklin Delano Roosevelt admired Twain to such a degree he borrowed liberally from his work. The words "NEW DEAL" came from Twain's *A Connecticut Yankee in King Arthur's Court* (1889). Twain's first novel the *Gilded Age* (1873) gave an entire era its name. You can visit Tom Sawyer's island in Disneyland or visit Twain's likeness in Disney's Animatronic's studio. Twain's influence is pervasive in American culture with tributes found in Las Vegas, Lake Tahoe, and in TV ads. How did an uneducated frontier man make himself into a celebrated man of letters? By worhsipping at the altar of words – the only possession he carried west in his youth was a dictionary – and the daring to write what he saw and heard without fear of derision.

GENESIS OF TWAIN'S WRITING CAREER. Twain's writing career was a fluke. He loved to tell stories about his Gold Rush mining town experiences. They were so hilarious a publisher asked him to write them down and he would publish them. The man had lied but it motivated Clemens to write *The Celebrated Jumping Frog of Calaveras County* in 1865 as a colorful view of frog-jumping contests among the miners in a god-forsaken place called Jackass Gulch. When the publisher declined his offer Twain self-published the book, in an era when such a thing was unheard of. In a moment of candor he admitted the book was never written to make money, it cost him $2000 out of his pocket, but to get him a job as a writer or journalist. Twain's use of the pseudonym Mark Twain was also an unintended ruse. In his first attempt at writing, letters to the editor in Virginia City, Nevada, he used the name Twain – a river term meaning two fathoms deep – to keep from getting killed.

HISTORY OF HUMOR GENRE

Humor is synonymous with both "wit" and "comedy." Both terms have been used over the decades to define the genre that has found its way into novels, plays, philosophy, poetry, psychology, and even tragedy. Henri Bergson suggested in *Laughter* (1900), "comedy is created by substituting mechanical and predictable events for natural and spontaneous ones." This was never more apparent than in Freud's *Jokes and Their Relationship to the Unconscious* (1905), in which he says, "humor provides infantile gratification by disrupting the adult world that is often too serious." Twain couldn't have said it better than the father of psychoanalysis.

Comedy began with Greek epics and plays, and moved on to the Romans, finding its soul in Shakespeare's *The Comedy of Errors* (1590). One of the first writers to experiment with satirical comedy was Ben Johnson who wrote *Every Man in His Humor* (1598) and *The Alchemist* (1610) aimed at showing characters being defined by their obsessions or "humors." Oscar Wilde's *The Importance of Being Ernest* is a comedy of manners satirizing middle-class respectability and the audacity of aristocratic snobbery. George Bernard Shaw's *Man and Superman* (1903) was written as a comedy of ideas with a Nitzschean hero whose ego and will are destroyed by his own omnipotent opinions.

WIT. The name Twain, is synonomous with humor and wit. The word "wit" comes from the Old English, meaning "to know," and is often used in context with a kind of mental capacity. A derogatory usage has been "half-wit" or "have you lost your wits?" The word *wit* has come to mean astute vision or special insight. Twain and Shaw were masters. Due to Twain's extensive travels and jobs he acquired a jaundiced view of human nature. He had worked in such diverse places as New Orleans, Cincinnati, Sacramento, Virginia City, San Francisco, New York City, Honolulu, Athens, and London. This myriad of experiences gave him a unique perspective on life and its inhabitants. He became a master storyteller, and used the talent as a lecturer, journalist, and free-lance writer.

The Laughing Philosopher led a life that was one long adventurous struggle for survival. He was born as Haley's

Comet sailed overhead. This convinced him that he was predestined for greatness. Mimicking Haley's Comet he led a vagabond life. An example of his risk-taking style comes from a letter written as a hoax to promote one of his books. He had just completed *Innocents Abroad* (1870) and thought he might just use some provocative mudslinging to give it some free press. Twain sat down and wrote a tongue in cheek letter to the editor of the London *Saturday Review*. In the letter he referred to the book as callous and scandalous. To his shock and amazement the paper picked up his cynical diatribe. The paper picked up his words intact writing, "the insolence, the impertinence, the presumption, the mendacity, and above all, the majestic ignorance of this author." His joke had came back to haunt him and despite all attempts to squelch the bad press no one believed anyone would have had the guts to write such a thing as a joke. Twain did.

AN UNCONVENTIONAL ADVENTURER

The media called his books, "trash and suitable only for the slums." Twain predicted the Boston banning was a blessing in disguise and would double sales. He wrote:

> *They have expelled Huck from their library as trash and suitable only for the slums. That will sell 25,000 copies for us. And when libraries can't buy it then another one hundred will be sold since the public does not have access to it free, while the publicity gained will cause the purchasers of the book to read it out of curiosity (Kaplan pg. 269).*

History proved Twain correct. Huck went on to sell ten million copies before he died. The banning validates Shannon's Law - an electronic publishing principle that says, "the absorption of information is inversely related to its credibility." This was certainly the case for Twain whose sales increased when his credibility was questioned and only succeeded in gaining him more visibility.

DARING ENTREPRENEUR. Twain was an inveterate pioneer in writing and investing. He was the first writer to produce a manuscript on a typewriter, the first homeowner to install a telephone in his home, and the first person to use a phonograph to dictate a book. His work would set the stage for dictating machines. Clemens always dared what others feared. It led him to bankruptcy and the loss of millions, but also led to his greatness.

Numerous investments in nefarious schemes almost ruined him. His most infamous investment was in the Paige Typesetter Company. By 1880 he had invested and $30,000, but instead of writing it off he kept on investing and by 1890 had invested $150,000. By this time he was age fifty-five and filed for bankruptcy protection. By sixty he was still over $100,000 in debt.

Twain was as much entrepreneur as author. He started many new ventures the most infamous the publishing firm Charles L. Webster and Co. This enterprise was used to publish the Twain books. But the one that proved his downfall was *The Grant Memoirs* on the life of President Ulysses S. Grant. This enterprise turned him bitter and caused him to leave the country in 1891. Three years later he filed bankruptcy. The risk-taker also invented his own board game played out as the history of mankind. The game was educational as entertaining but proved to be a miserable failure that he labeled his "fatal addiction."

HISTORY OF CREATIVE RISK. History is resplendent with examples of risk-taking and success. Amelia Earhart lived life on the edge. Just prior to her record-breaking trek across the Atlantic she wrote, "Courage is the price that life exacts for granting peace" (Landrum 1996 pg. 189). Howard Hughes had a similar penchant and paid the price, but accumulated a billion dollars in the process. Had these two adventurers been less prone to bet the farm they would have had a more normal life but one eminently less exciting and rewarding. Was their risk worth the gain? If asked they would have said yes. But looked at

196

objectively, most normal people would have questioned Earhart's premature death and Hughes life on drugs due to his seven major crashes. Martin Luther King probably said it best, "Courage faces fear and thereby masters it. The price of freedom is death."

Catherine the Great wrote in her memoirs, "I have the most reckless audacity. No woman is bolder than I." Leonard da Vinci had a similar predilection. He was one of the first scientists to climb mountains in search of scientific evidence for his theories. It was reckless daring that led Dostoevsky to the firing squad and it also helped him write his classics, *Crime & Punishment*, *Notes from the Underground*, and *The Brothers Karamazov*. Had Dostoevsky not been a compulsive gambler he would have led a more normal life but would probably never written *The Gambler*.

LITERARY INNOVATIONS

Twain documented an America in transition and did so in the vernacular of the old West. His renown as a humorist has survived a number of eras making him an American treasure. He portrayed 19th century America via the tragic and comedic. His was a talent and style that few writers master. Clemens satirical wit had few peers, best illustrated by his cynical humor about lying. "How easy it is to make people believe a lie and how hard it is to undo that work."

WRITING AS CATHARSIS

Clemens wrote of himself and his deep-seated needs and cravings. By documenting his most grievous misgivings about society he was purging his own inadequacies. After he had became famous as an author he lectured to sell his books. Twain was a manic-depressive personality. For him words were a therapeutic medium aimed at calming his raging psyche. When in the manic state he turned to words as a release especially when depressed. His words always conveyed passion and energy often found in bipolar writers like Hemingway and Plath.

Clemens often admitted to writing as a means of maintaining his sanity in a world he found less than rational. Words were weapons used to convey his philosophy of life. Would any other writer dare say, "I don't give a damn for any man who can spell a word only one way" (Twain 1917). Could you dislike a man who said, "I was seldom able to see an opportunity until it ceased to be one" (Kaplan pg. 227). Such introspection is not only humorous but a path to mental health. Clemens wrote for *everyman* and in the process was writing to understand himself. In an introspective moment he said, "We are all alike so by studying carefully and comparing myself with other people, I have been able to acquire a knowledge of the human race" (Twain 1917 pg. 133).

METAMORPHOSES

In his autobiography, Twain wrote of contracting measles at twelve and quitting school to work as a typesetter. He said the job forced him to study the meaning of words, a passion that remained with him the rest of his life.

But it was working as a reporter in San Francisco that transformed him from itinerant vagabond to serious writer. At the newspaper Bret Harte became his mentor. Twain wrote, "Harte trimmed and trained and schooled me patiently until he changed me from an awkward utterer of coarse grotesquenesses to a writer of paragraphs and chapters that have found a certain flavor" (Twain pg. 124). Later Harte would become an enemy but the early experience proved providential. When the *San Francisco Morning Call* fired him he attempted suicide. Failing that he went off to Jackass Gulch to salve his soul. As is often the case the firing closed one part of his life and opened another that he did not recognize immediately.

Life on the frontier was cheap and colorful and he became a social commentator, and often told of the stories in those mining towns. His experience in Calaveras County proved so hilarious he took to lecturing and resulted in *The Celebrated Jumping Frog of Calaveras County* (1867). As is most often the case, the book was not written for the money but to open doors. It did and he was hired by the Sacramento Union as editor allowing him to sail to Hawaii that would culminate in *The Innocents Abroad* (1869).

ECCENTRICITIES

Clemens was a character and renegade. Newspapers in 1867 described him as "The son of the devil" because of his renegade style and refusal to conform to the rigors of journalism. He wore white linen suits all year round and it became his signature dress. The need to be different led to his insightful comment "I have certain mental and physical peculiarities" (Twain 1917 pg. 209). Manic-depression or bipolar illness was not a diagnosed illness in the 19th century but Clemens was a classic case based on his mercurial swings of temperament as described in his memoirs. He had all the symptoms including the suicide attempt in San Francisco.

Biographer Kaplan described Twain as experiencing "obsessive and chronic rages and depressions" (Kaplan pg. 199). In his autobiography he admitted to doing most things "excessively," and as having been "born excited." He wrote, "The resulting and periodical and sudden changes of mood in me, from deep melancholy to half-insane tempests and cyclones of humor, are among the curiosities of my life" (Twain 1917 pg. 209). Such mood swings are the symptoms of bipolar personalities. Twain wrote manically as did the other bipolar personalities Balzac, Hemingway, Woolf, Steel, and Plath. He typically produced 3000 to 4000 words every day and once in a fit of energy wrote 200,000 in sixty days.

LIFE CRISES

Death and tragedy dominated Twain's life from a child to his marriage. He lost a sister, brother, and father before age twelve. As a child in Hannibal, Missouri he had many brushes with death. He wrote, "I almost perished from measles at ten... I drowned seven times before I learned to swim" (Twain 1917 pg. 78). Of his mane debacles he wrote, "Once I had been underwater twice and was coming up to make the third and fatal descent when a slave woman pulled me out." (Twain pg. 72.) At 14 Twain fell into an icy river with friend Tom Nash. Nash would become the model for Tom Sawyer, who would save Twain from death, but who would become deaf over the incident.

One of Twain's most traumatic experiences was the death of his Henry in a Mississippi steamer explosion. The *Philadelphia's* boiler exploded killing him instantly, but Twain had dreamed of the event the week before and had asked his brother not to go on the trip. Twain was devastated and wrote of it in *Life on the Mississippi* (1883).

Twain's greatest personal tragedy was the death of his first son due to his own negligence. It would become the catalyst of his greatest works but at the time devastated him and his wife Livy. His wife was always ill and left their infant son Landon with Twain. The boy was two but suffering from a bad cold at a time when the Twain's were living in Buffalo, New York. On one bitter cold day Twain and the boy was on carriage ride when his blankets fell off. Twain was off in one of his famous "reveries" a function of the manic personality, and the boy caught pneumonia and died within days. By the time the coachman saw what had happened Langdon was nearly frozen. Years later Twain admitted to a friend that he had been responsible and felt he had killed the boy. His life hit bottom. His career as a publisher of newspapers had gone awry, his wife was perpetually ill, his writing had hit a wall, and Langdon died. He wrote later, "I had rather die twice over than repeat the last six months of my life" (Kaplan 135). It was June 1872. Within the year he had written *The Gilded Age* (1873) and two years later *Tom Sawyer* (1875). His crisis had turned to creativity.

POLYPHASIC

Twain always had four books in his head at any one time. He began writing Huckleberry Finn in 1876, stopped, and began anew in 1878, stopped, started in 1880, then stopped again. His classic took him eight years to write during which time he wrote seven other books. He finally completed the book in 1884. He wrote in his memoirs:

> *There has never been a time in the past thirty-five years when my literary shipyard hadn't two or more half-finished ships on the ways, neglected and baking in the sun; generally there have been three or four, at present there are five* (Twain 1917 pg. 264)

Clemens was incapable of sticking to just one profession. He worked at various times as a printer, riverboat captain, newspaper reporter, silver and gold miner, sales agent, lecturer, journalist, editor, publisher, author, inventor, lecturer, entrepreneur, and book publisher. As a writer he covered the waterfront. He wrote biographies (Joan of Arc & The Gilded Age), travelogues (Innocents Abroad), history (A Connecticut Yankee), humor (Tom Sawyer), and satire (Huckleberry Finn). Twain was impatient to a fault.

CRITICAL ACCLAIM

Literary critic Russell Baker wrote, "Mark Twain is the most readable of writers even when not in top form." *American Literature* (1968) called *Huckleberry Finn* "a masterpiece. It is probably the one book in our literature about which highbrows and lowbrows can agree" (American Literature 1968 pg. 226). Testimony to Twain's literary success was the three honorary doctorates. In his inimitable style he wrote, "Yale made me a Doctor of Literature. I was not competent to doctor anybody's literature" (Twain 1917 pg. 347). He was honored with a Doctor of Laws from the University of Missouri and remarked, "The only thing I knew about laws was how to evade them." But when Oxford made him Doctor of Letters he was too impressed to make any disparaging remarks since he believed that he had finally been given the ultimate acclaim for his contributions to literature.

During Twain's life he was held in higher esteem in Britain than in America. The Brits felt Twain was a positive influence on humor. On one trip to London he was met at the ship by literary icons Robert Browning, Lewis Carroll, and Anthony Trollope. This was at the same time New York and Boston critics were describing his work as vulgar. One critic gave insight into this dichotomy writing, "What would have happened had Twain fallen under the influence of the *New Yorker's* editors with their institutional contempt for the old lady from Dubuque?" (Baker Oct. 1993). Humor is often a product of the fringe not the sanctified halls of ivy. Had Twain been steeped in such rhetoric it is highly unlikely he would ever have had such widespread influence on his era.

SUCCESS & RISK – What Can We Learn?

Mark Twain became an American icon due to daring. He went where others feared and enjoyed the experience. Most people would not be able to live with such defiance of establishment. Did he pay a price? He sure did and it was high but his rewards were also high.

How many writers would dare bear the wrath of the literary elite? Or go deeply into debt to self-publish or to establish a publishing empire that seriously detracted from his time on the typewriter? But such is the price of greatness. He paid it willingly as do most creative geniuses, but turned to wit to disarm his detractors. One of his aphorisms offers insight into his style. "The human race has only one really effective weapon and that is laughter." But his most audacious comment was when asked about the notice of his death in a London newspaper in 1897. He wrote a terse telegram in response, "The report of my death is greatly exaggerated."

Twain's promotional skills and verbal sagacity leave us a legacy on the genre. He knew his market better than most and directed his words to that audience. That infuriated the establishment who believed that books should be found in drawing rooms not card rooms.

Twain's colloquialisms have made him one of the most quoted authors of all time. He had a way with words that belied his education. He played the media like a piano while ignoring the literary elite like the plague. They didn't like him or understand him and he didn't understand them. He knew his strengths and weaknesses and said, "I wrote for the working classes. I never cared for the cultured classes since they had no use for me" (Kaplan pg. 43).

Courage conquers all and Twain proves it. He dared say what others would not and his words have made him great. He remains a model for today's aspiring writers because he had a mania for facts, but a prescient vision of their meaning in the larger sense. Twain once told Rudyard Kipling, "I never care for fiction or story books. What I like to read about are facts and statistics of any kind." Such is the nature of the Promethean personality, those entrepreneurial types who pursue knowledge for the sake of knowing.

We should learn from Twain's need to live on the edge and follow his example of how not to fall into that precipice. There are no great wins in life without great risks and individuals like Twain will always grab the brass ring because of their brashness.

ANNE (HOWARD ALLEN) RICE
MISTRESS OF OCCULT & SUPERNATURAL
b. New Orleans, LA October 4, 1941

SYNTHESIZING TO SUCCESS (SYZYGY)

DOMINANT GENRE
Occult & Existential Mysticism in an entertaining medium

MOTTO
"Bloodsucking provides a rush more powerful than any orgasm;" "I definitely believe in no censorship of any kind and I am a writer obsessed with horror and with the erotic"

GREATEST WORKS
Interview With the Vampire (1976)
The Queen of the Damned (1988)
The Mayfair Witches (1994)

HONORS/AWARDS
Publishers Weekly, "Interview is an extraordinary first novel"

ECCENTRICITIES
Androgynous with a gender identity crisis; loves cemeteries
"Lestat is the man I would love to be. If I had one wish it would be to be a man"

LIFE CRISES
Mother died when 14; daughter Michele died of leukemia (1972) at age five; Anne quit job, dropped out, and started drinking spawning her breakthrough book *Interview*

METAMORPHOSES
Interview with a Vampire written to exorcise inner ghosts and to immortalize Michele; Her work is mystical, supernatural, occult

10

ANNE RICE – OCCULT

SYZYGY–Synthesis to Success

"I've always loved the images of androgyny"

BE WHAT YOU ARE AND ALSO WHAT YOU ARE NOT

The Queen of the Occult entertains her fans with surrealistic stories of the occult. Cathartic androgyny is her medium. She has always lived life on the edge but with her Vampire Chronicles she has had her feet firmly planted in space for some time. Rice seems to live life as she writes, outside the mainstream just far enough to be interesting but close enough to be believable. She synthesizes all things including her own behavior, a woman who can be tough and nurturing at the same time. In many respects Rice is quite feminine, in others she comes across as a spokeswoman for androgyny. Her demeanor is ladylike and submissive and in a nanosecond she can be masculine and aggressive. She once admitted, "I don't know most of the time what gender I am" (Ramsland p. 148).

Rice has a penchant for detail but a disdain for objectivity. She is a devoted mother but writes pornographic books. On-the-edge defines her. Rice is a mixed bag of messages, a dichotomy that defies logic. She is an introvert capable of extroverting on command. Such is the nature of many creative geniuses, individualists capable of being what they are and in the next moment of being what they are not.

The Queen of the Occult sees the big picture but can go into analysis-paralysis on the most inane subjects. She writes about bizarre, ungrounded subjects, but is such a control-freak she refuses to allow one word of her manuscripts to be changed. On one hand she is a space cadet, on the other she is precise to a fault. Rice is obsessive and into excess. When she took up an interest in violins, she read every book in the library. When she began a doll collection, it dominated every aspect of her life, with 1000's of dolls found in every nook of her grandiose homes. When she wrote a book on vampires, the project resulted in a whole series titled the *Vampire Chronicles*.

Rice is highly intuitive and mysterious but very grounded. This ability to be what she is and also what she is not makes her poster girl for Jung's concept of Syzygy, the focus of this chapter. Her statement, "I'd be a man in a minute" (Ramsland pg. 222) offers credence to her adaptability. Rice is an interesting study and an anomaly, a woman armed with a chameleon-like temperament that has led her to the top.

FIND YOUR WEAKNESS & ATTACK. The ability to adapt to various environments is found in the behavior of the creative genius. Such people are highly adaptable, more than most. They run into a brick wall in most dimensions of their life and change to fit the needs of the situation. Rice identified her weakness and attacked it as did most of the wunderkinds in this book. Her writings attack the very fears that would debilitate her. She told *Rolling Stone* (July 13, 1995) "I think all my writing has been part of a battle with my fears. When I write, I explore my worst fears and then take my protagonist right into awful situations that I myself am terrified by. And I think that the act of putting all that fear and terror and confusion into an orderly, plotted story has been very therapeutic for it definitely helps me to continue through life."

We should all learn by this. Fear of Alpine skiing can only be removed by skiing down a hill. The fear of water can be removed by sticking your head in it. The fear math is overcome by passing a math class. If you can't hit a tennis backhand down the line you must hit enough of them to know your probability of success. Psychologists have proven that until the belief in success exceeds 50% the chance of success increases. That means one must practice what one fears until they believe they can achieve and then, and only then, it is no longer a weakness, but a strength. All limits come from two parts of the anatomy - the *heart* and the *head.* Remove those from the head and all else will prove easy.

SWITCH GENDERS AS WELL. Joan of Arc cut her hair and donned a male uniform to lead French soldiers into battle against the hated English. How many men would have followed the Maid of Orleans into battle had she mounted her horse sidesaddle attired in a dress? None! In a male-dominated environment she functioned as expected of a leader. Any other approach would have ended in failure. Cite Catherine the Great, a very feminine woman who had to act like a man to defeat her imbecile husband. Catherine was about to be arrested and place in a convent when she donned the uniform of a male colonel replete with sword and boots, mounted her white steed like a man (full-saddle) and attacked her husband. Catherine defeated her husband and went on to become the Empress of Russia despite being German. Catherine's temerity and willingness to become what she wasn't, not only saved her life, but catapulted her to the throne. Had she remained the subservient female wife she would have been dead.

ADAPT OR DIE. Napoleon became the greatest military leader in history, not because of any talent, but because he molded himself into what France needed in a time of chaos. He arrived on the scene from Corsica just after the French Revolution. He was Italian not French, but during that period the nation needed a captivating leader and he became a captivating leader, despite speaking broken French. Few people realize the Little Corsican was really an unflagging agnostic, a fact he kept secret until he wrote his memoirs in St. Helena, since he had to conform in a Catholic country. Even more incredulous is the fact he took over France on the basis of nationalism. Napoleon adapted to the role needed in order to achieve.

MULTI-FACETED PERSONALITIES. A wealth of data exists on people can function in one dimension and then become their opposite. This has nothing to do with split or multiple personalities. It has to do with what psychologist Mihaly Csikszentmihalyi of the University of Chicago type cast as "operating at various points on the continuum.'" He wrote, "Creative people are complex – differentiated and integrated at the same time" (Csikszentmihalyi 1996 pg. 362). What does this mean? The ability to be both feminine and masculine, introverted and extroverted, or risk-taking and risk-averse.

Examples of females and males reversing roles to gain control are legion. Do you think Margaret Thatcher made decisions on the same basis as the majority of women? No way! Thatcher earned the nickname Iron Lady and what Reagan called her, "The best man in England" through sheer force of an indomitable will or she would have been eaten alive in the chauvinistic Parliament. The BBC described her as such writing, "Mrs. Thatcher does not have one traditional feminine cell in her body." French President D'Estaing was not nearly so complimentary. When the media asked this chauvinist what he thought of her he said, "I don't like her." "Why, they asked?" "Because she is not like a man nor like a woman." The truth was that she was not functioning in the stereotypical role that he deemed correct for a woman. David Ben Gurion said, "Golda Meir is the only man in my cabinet" when she was the only woman. On the other side of this argument are Carl Jung and Walt Disney who had many female qualities.

JUNG'S SYZYGY. Eminent people adapt to the needs of the moment including tapping into their opposite gender. This arms them to do battle on most any front. Such people, even if quite masculine are able to tap into their feminine side when the situation dictates such behavior. Carl Jung coined the term Syzygy to mean the "conjunction of the inner feminine or inner masculine" that he believed lies dormant within the unconscious of every person. His term for the femaleness within each male was the *Anima* [Soul & Eros) and the maleness in every female the *Animus* (Logos & Spirit).

Psychologist Nathaniel Branden wrote in *Pillars of Self-Esteem* (1994) "The most creative individuals are those who can integrate both male and female aspects of personality." What was he saying? That people capable of tapping into their opposite gender are far better equipped to cope and adapt and will able to come away with a higher degree of self-confidence. This means that men who can be more nurturing and women who can be more rational, especially when operating in an arena dominated by the opposite gender are better equipped to cope. This would say that to be successful *introverts* should be able to *extrovert, control freaks* should be able to *let go,* the *cautious* should take some *risks, visionaries* should *suffer the details,* hard-core *rationalists* should listen to their *gut,* and *numbers-crunchers* should look at life's possibilities. University of Chicago psychologist Mihalyi Csikszentmihalyi wrote:

> **Perhaps the most important duality that creative persons are able to integrate is being open and receptive on one hand and hard-driving on the other ... When an extravert learns to experience the world as an introvert it is as if he or she discovered a whole new missing dimension of the world and we double and double again the amount of life. Keep exploring what it takes to be the opposite of who you are.** (*Creativity* 1996 pgs. 360-362)

Anne Rice validates the Syzygy concept. She was expert at tapping into her male nature or *Animus* as it armed her with a unique ability to identify with male vampire alter-ego characterizations. She told a biographer, "I've always felt very uncomfortable in the role of being a woman. I feel like my intellect is masculine, or androgynous" (Ramsland p 234). And her androgynous characterizations, especially the vampire Lestat, her fantasy hero, reflect her inner feelings as indicated by her statement, "My characters all represent longings within myself. Lestat was me (Ramsland pg. 14 & 327).

Virginia Woolf was even more androgynous than Rice. She was a bisexual who never came to grips with her true gender. She wrote, "I have the feelings of a woman, but I have only the language of man." She had an affair with her sister Vanessa's husband who after he death said, "She was more lesbian than heterosexual."

ATTACK YOUR OPPOSITE. If you are merely what you *are* the best you can hope for is to optimize that dimension, but it will be the limit of your progress. To move to another dimension greater than what you are, it is imperative to add a further dimension and become when necessary what you are *not.* This entails transcending a single dimensional personality, finding your weaknesses and mastering them while optimizing your strengths. How can a person be both without betraying their own inner self? How can an extrovert become an introvert or vice versa? These are the tough questions that separate the world's superstars from the also-rans.

Anne Rice validated this dimension in a *Rolling Stone* (July 13, 1995) interview. She said, "I think all my writing has been part of a battle with my fears. When I write, I explore my worst fears and then take my protagonist right into awful situations that I myself am terrified by... it has been very therapeutic for it definitely helps me to continue through life." Rice feared the dark yet wrote of dark eerie places and fell in love with the "cities of the dead" – those New Orleans cemeteries.

Csikszentmihalyi studied ninety-one creative subjects including writers and scientists like Linus Pauling and Jonas Salk. He found they were able to flip-flop between different dimensions of personality on command. Sophocles described this quite eloquently when he wrote, "When woman becomes the equal of man she becomes his superior." What was he really saying? That by adding male qualities to the already strong feminine ones a woman would be capable of getting through the glass ceiling. Jung described his Syzygy concept of gender role reversals as that "inner place where all of woman's ancestral experiences of man exist." He said the female Archetype in males was where "all of man's ancestral experiences of woman could be found" (Storr 1996 pg. 98).

Most of the writers in this book were able to tap into their Syzygy. Balzac complained of his "highly effeminate nature." Virginia Woolf wrote, "It is fatal to be man or woman pure and simple; one must be woman-manly or man-womanly." Sylvia Plath said, "My life is is run by two electric currents, one joyously positive, the other despairingly negative." French writer Colette wrote, "I struggle to be a real woman while feeling like a mental hermorphodite." Her diverse lifestyle led to the strong woman, weak man dichotomy in her masterpiece *Gigi*. Csikszentmihalyi discussed this in *Creativity* writing, "Creative and talented girls are more dominant than other girls, and creative boys are more sensitive and less aggressive than their male peers" (pg. 66).

210

Anne Rice validated his thesis with her statement "I'd be a male in a minute." And even though Catherine the Great wasn't quite so blatant she admitted in her memoirs, "There is no woman bolder than I. I have the most reckless audacity." Csikszentmihalyi said it best in *Creativity* (Pg. 65-71):

> *Creative individuals are more likely to have not only the strengths of their own gender, but those of the other. Creative individuals escape rigid gender role stereotyping and tend to androgyny. Creative people seem to harbor the opposite tendencies on the continuum between extroversion and introversion, and express both traits at the same time.*

Fortune magazine wrote in 1996 "Female entrepreneurs are more like male entrepreneurs than they are like other females," adding credence to the duality of gender roles for the adventurous.

HISTORY OF OCCULT GENRE

Early writings on the supernatural can be found in the Greek Classics and Homer. It evolved through the Dark Ages and finally found its roots with Shakespeare during the Renaissance. The supernatural is a cousin to mythology and horror, and is differentiated by the metaphysics found in *Dracula*, *Faust*, and Shakespeare's *A Midsummer Night's Dream*. Probably the first ghost-like stories can be found in the Waverly novels written by Sir Walter Scott in the 1820's. The supernatural and spiritualism found in this genre can be traced to Charles Dickens, Nathaniel Hawthorne, Henry James, Edgar Allen Poe, Saki, and Algernon Blackwood. Nathaniel Hawthorne's *The House of the Seven Gables* (1851) was an early novel with an occult-like plot. Marlow' and H.P. Lovecraft were also practitioners who influenced the current writings in the genre of Rice and King.

The works wielding the most profound influence on Rice were *Hamlet* and *A Christmas Carol*. The ghost scene in Shakespear's masterpiec "obsessed" her. In Dicken's work the "supernatural

211

persona of Scrooge" overwhelmed her. She wrote, "I've adopted Charles Dickens as my guardian angel and mentor. I've always been obsessed by Dickens" (Ramsland pg. 17). Edgar Allen Poe's macabre stories also influenced her writing that was enhanced by New Orleans "cities of the dead" cemeteries that she thought "were beautiful." Fantasy and metaphysical themes intrigued her from a young age, but never more than in Shelley's *Frankenstein* (1818) and Stoker's *Count Dracula* (1897). She loved the concept of the living dead.

AN ANDROGYNOUS WRITER

Rice began life with a gender-identity crisis that set the stage for her later unconventional behavior. Her father was not to have a son and christened his little girl Howard Allen O'Brien. She would become his alter-ego and surrogate son. She told the media her bookish dad and wannabe writer of poems was her greatest influence. She said, "My father was a terrific influence on me" (Ramsland p. 24). Little Howard Allen became the male child he never had, but on her first day at school told the teacher her name was Anne, and the name stuck.

But the ambiguous gender identity had already formed. Anne admits she always felt as much male as female and told a reporter, "I've always loved the images of androgyny. I think I have a gender screwup to the point that I don't know most of the time what gender I am" (Ramsland pg. 148).

Part of her gender ambiguity stems from her youth spent in ritual-bound New Orleans. Growing up in the Garden District forced her to walk past all those above ground tombstones and cemeteries. The Roman Catholic icons and ritualistic spiritualism took their toll with their mythical symbolisms from the Mass to the ritualistic dogma. Rice often speaks of the androgyny that pervades her native religion, nuns in asexual habits, sans lipstick, and their disdain for displaying any facet of femininity. In interviews she described the statues in Church as "androgynous such as Christ weeping with defined hips" (Ramsland pg. 30).

As a child Howard O'Brien was already a renegade. Her iconoclastic mother allowed she and her sisters free to scribble on the walls, draw on the floors, and to roam unencumbered throughout the Garden District. Her life was beyond free, it was permissive to a fault.

Her mother Katherine Rice was well-read and well-bred, but a rebel and alcoholic. Anne grew up a free soul with little structure and no restraints about expressing her innermost passions. She describes her early childhood as "ordered chaos." Fantasies, castles, and make-believe were the cornerstone of her youth. And much of this came out of the Roman Catholic dogma that she describes as "mystical, transcendent, and supernatural where miracles could transform" (Ramsland pg. 19). She escaped into an inner world of surrealism and fantasy enhanced by her first movies like *Hamlet*. Forty years later she would recall her imagery of the ghost scenes when "Ophelia floated on the streams with flowers coming out of her hair" (Ramsland pg. 17). On the release of her book *The Vampire Lestat* she said, "Lestat is the man I would love to be" (Riley pg. 14).

Anne grew up obsessed with writing. She wrote her first novel at eleven, and had already decided to become a writer. She later said, "My father was living proof that a person could write" But his male influence left its mark on her. She told Katherine Ramsland, "I would cheerfully be a six foot blond-haired man wearing a size thirty-eight" (Ramsland 222). She went on to say, "A trickster lays inside us. If we ignore it, we may be destroyed. If we face it, we may experience real transcendence" (R-327). It is obvious her Trickster is male. She said, "I've always felt uncomfortable in the role of being a woman. I feel like my intellect is masculine" (Ramsland 234).

HISTORICAL EXAMPLES OF SYZYGY. What separates the successful from the average is an ability to function in more than one dimension. Napoleon was both a Type A and Type b as were Freud, and Mao Zedung, Howard Hughes and Walt Disney. Shaw spent five years as a virtual hermit in the British Museum, but when he was unable to get published he went out and made over 1000 speeches to promote himself. The extraverted Joseph Campbell sequestered himself in a remote cabin for four years to read the Greek Classics. Inventor Nikola Tesla, Frank Lloyd Wright and Martin Luther King were macho men who dressed in sartorial splendor that would have done most women proud.

Buckminster Fuller was pathologically shy to the point he once spent two full years without saying one word to anyone including his wife. But when someone asked about his Geodesic Dome or other creation he would start talking non-stop for hours. On one occasion Fuller was invited to meet Prime Minister Nehru. Nehru walked into the room, sat down, and asked one question and Fuller started talking and didn't stop for an hour and a half. The astonished Indian leader left without the chance to respond. Fuller was also a puritan when it came to sex but was a philanderer. Despite a penchant for order he made intuitive decisions that he labeled "Teleology - intuitive conversions of the brain of gut-like feelings" (Hatch pg. 283). He even named his boat *Intuition,* strange for a man who worshipped at the altar of reason and numbers.

LITERARY INNOVATIONS

Rice is famous, or in some ways infamous, for marrying the salacious with the sadistic in the metaphysical quasi-religious. She has adroitly tied the supernatural with the perverse, in what some critics label "sexual fantasies." Rice creates metaphysical concepts with sexual metaphors and somehow sells them to a mainstream audience. Most probably don't see through her subtle analogies and metaphors. She justifies her style as necessary to the immortality theme where spirituality and perversity reign supreme. She says, "there aren't too many people on earth who could pass up immortality if it was offered to them. It wouldn't take me long" (Ramsland pg. 322).

Rice's major contribution to the world of letters is this tie between the arcane with the real. It is easier to sell a fantasy than a reality and she knows it. She first married sex with spirituality in *Cry to Heaven* (1982) and *The Claiming of Sleeping Beauty* (1983). When asked why she says, "I don't believe there's any moral, aesthetic, or psychological limit to supernatural fiction" (Ramsland pg. 248). For her, sex and art are one. She told *W* magazine (Dec. 12, 1985) "bloodsucking provides a rush more powerful than any orgasm."

Irma Heldman writing for the *Village Voice* said, "She has created a preternatural world that parallels the natural one that is spellbinding, eerie, original in conception, and deserving of popular attention" (*Contemporary Authors* pg. 401). Donna Tartt writing for *US* magazine in Nov. 1998 (pg. 84) said "She receives far less credit than she is due for almost single-handedly rescuing the American novel from the doldrums of meta-fiction and minimalism and restoring it – with gallop and glitter – to the fine old bracing art story." Others refer to her style as existential mysticism – horror and surreal eroticism.

One of Rice's major innovations is the transgender quality manifested in her characterizations. An obsession with the occult and supernatural allows her to "move back and forth through time, to really talk about things like death and mortality and God" (Tartt 1998). This allowed her to synthesize diametrically opposite concepts such as the occult with the norm, eroticism with religion, supernatural with verity, and the mystical with the logical. In her interminable search for gender identity she has crossed into a foreign land of imagery that is often lost on the critics and without the entertainment value can be easily described as perverse. *Contemporary Authors* (pg. 399) wrote, "Rice is a beautiful writer, her prose glitters and every character in Lestat's dark odyssey is unique."

CATHARTIC INSPIRATIONS

Rice was a mistress of introspection and escape. She wrote, "I write about what I am about, and I'm obsessed with horror and with the erotic" (Ramsland pg. 222). She says, "My characters all represent longings and aspirations within myself" (Ramsland pg. 349). She says that vampires validate her and that "Lestat is the man I would love to be" (Riley pg. 14). Her books are little more than inner exorcisms, vacillating between the erotic and spiritual. She claims that growing up in a city like New Orleans with its Roman Catholic symbols and icons were instrumental in her surreal imagery.

ANNE RICE

Rice told the media, "I'm obsessed horror, the erotic and death" (Ramsland pg. 212), and needs to write it out of her system. Lestat was a hero that she needed as an identity model. Louis was her alter-ego in *Interview*, but his role has been taken by Lestat. In the early years she wrote to deal with the death of Michele, since she has been searching for an identity. But in it all she has been looking for the nature of life and her place in it.

The living-dead world has brought her fame and fortune and she is reticent to move out of that surreal vista. Spiritual truth gnaws at her and the ageless question of, How does one live after death? Is there an afterlife or eternity? Rough questions for a woman who is no longer steeped in Roman Catholic dogma but is unable to shake its spell. She admits to being curious on a religious level but has not taken sides.

Rice believes she is precognitive. Her first encounter was when she dreamed of Michele contracting an incurable disease a year before it happened. She says, "I dreamed my daughter was dying – that there was something wrong with her blood." (*Contemporary Authors* pg 400). Two years later she created Claudia as a mythical reincarnation of Michele as the young girl in *Interview with the Vampire*. She told *People*, "it was written out of grief in five weeks of white-hot access of the subconscious. Claudia is beautiful and blond but is granted eternal life at the age of six."

METAMORPHOSES

Even as a young girl Rice was of the mystical and arcane. She recalled the many books, movies, and icons in New Orleans that altered her into what she is today. One book she says changed her was Richard Matheson's *Dress of White Silk* featuring a young girl who turns into a vampire. Anne read this at eleven and remembered it forty years later. She told Ramsland, "I never forgot that story. I wanted to get right into the vampire." (Ramsland pg. 40). A short time later she saw the movie *Hamlet* and was taken with the ghost scene. Then came *Dracula's Daughter*. She says, "I loved the tragic figure of Dracula." But her most transformational experience was the book and movie, Dicken's *A Chrismas Carol*. She became obsessed with it and said, "I've watched the English film version of it probably more than anyone in history ... read and reread the story. I wanted to go into a supernatural persona of Scrooge" (Riley pg. 285).

Her mother Katherine raised Anne to be a genius. But Anne admits wanting to be a nun as a young girl. Then in her teen years she wanted to be a saint and dreamed of being God. As an adult she wanted to be a man. As a writer who dares be different she has made an attempt at marrying all these concepts into one heroic omnipotent being that is both male and female, religious and anti-religious, real and surreal.

By age nine Rice had written in her journal that she would be a writer. Each day at school she would make up a different story and work out a plot. This led her to major in English at Texas Women's College just north of Dallas. She earned a Masters Degree in Creative Writing from San Francisco State University in 1972. While working on her thesis she and husband Stan Rice were living in the Haight-Ashbury district of San Francisco. It was in the middle of the *flower child* era when love and revolution ruled the world. When she found herself pregnant, Stan got a job at UC Berkeley, and they moved their to raise their daughter.

It was in Berkeley when tragedy struck and transformed her life. When Michele died at five Anne became despondent, started drinking excessively, quit her job and the marriage almost ended. That was when she got an inspiration to write the horror of her life out via vampires, the living dead that would grant Michele immortality as the young girl in the book.

The creatures of the night never died and they would be the genesis of *Interview with the Vampire* (1976). The book was aimed at both mitigating the pain and the reincarnation of her dead daughter as Claudia. She admits to tapping into the depths of a screwed up psyche to preserve the memory of Michele. Anne had somehow tied the death of her mother from alcoholism to the blood disease of Michele, both fluids that could kill and preserve life and used them as an inspiration.

217

Louis was the vampire, both hero and victim, but never the villain. She empathized with a hero not a villain. It is through Louis that Anne released her innermost demons. Claudia would take on the idyllic doll-face imagery so important to her sanity. She later said, "Claudia is the embodiment of my failure to deal with the feminine. She is the woman trapped in a child's body. She's the person robbed of power" (Ramsland pg. 154). *Interview* was Anne's desperate attempt at creating a supernatural world where immortality reigns supreme, a world where Michele could never die. She was now in her mid-thirties and had never been published, but her cathartic release changed all that.

ECCENTRICITIES

By any definition Anne Rice is weird. She dresses like no woman nor any man. She is obsessive-compulsive, erotic, a type A, and a female who says if she had one wish it would be to be a man. She does all things in excess. Moderation is not in her vocabulary and when she decided to collect dolls, she was not content until she had the world's largest collection.

Rice is obsessed with the mysticism of cemeteries and all things occult. He male friends are mostly gay. When asked why she wrote pornography, she told *People* "I wrote about the fantasy that interested me personally and that I couldn't find in bookstores. I wanted to create a Disneyland of S&M" (Contemporary Authors pg. 402). She wrote these under a pseudonym A.N. Roquelaure. It was a means of releasing her sexual fantasies. These were written while living in Haight-Ashbury during the turbulent 60's when leather and flowers adorned everything and actions were done in the name of love.

Nothing could be weirder than a multi-millionaire buying her clothes at Goodwill, an agnostic buying a former Catholic orphanage, and a caring mother wanting to be a man. Such is the nature of a woman writing of supernatural while raising a teenage son. Testimony to her eccentricity is her comment, "I'm sure now of one thing, if I get as weird as I want to get, and as crazy as I want to get, readers will go with me" (Riley p.132). In an interview with the *Washington Post* she said, "I think sometimes that if I had had perhaps a few more genes, or whatever, I would have been truly mad, a multiple personality whose selves didn't recognize each other" (Ramsland 1991).

LIFE CRISES

Anne was fourteen when her mother died of chronic alcoholism. A short time later she was pulled out of her New Orleans home and moved to Dallas, Texas. This was a traumatic experience, not appreciated by people not from the Crescent City. New Orleans people seldom, if ever, get the city out of their system. Her unhappiness would dissipate when she met a renegade boy named Stan Rice. The two ran off together to San Francisco.

She returned to Texas to finish her bachelor's degree, but in the interim married the wannabe poet and returned to live in the City by the Bay. They stayed for 27 years, not returning to New Orleans until 1989. Anne desperately wanted to be a published author but rejection letters told her that her dream was not meant to be. Stan was a struggling poet teaching at San Francisco State during a period of acid, grass, week-long parties, hippies, and Fritz Perls.

It was the drop-out and turn-on generation of free love and spiritualism to combat a system that had no meaning. The whole period was a crisis looking for a cure, pure insanity that cannot be totally appreciated in retrospect. Anne was now in her 30's with a young child and watching life pass her by. She desperately tried everything to get published when Michele was diagnosed with leukemia. Anne's life came crashing down. When her daughter died Anne wanted to follow her into the grave. She quit her job, stopped writing, and her marriage nearly broke up. She was morose and crawled daily into a twelve-pack of Miller's Light. During this period she was diagnosed with Guillain-Barre Syndrome called "mock-polio" a serious viral infection that affects the nervous system. She had a mild paralysis that would take years to completely heal.

After Michele's death, Rice took refuge in the immortal world of vampires that proved to be the rebirth of Michele and her own. As with Type A's Anne wrote all night in a furious attempt at finding reincarnation for her dead daughter. It happened with Claudia's birth as an immortal Michele. Louis was Anne thinly disguised as a male vampire.

Rice's epiphany occurred when she crawled out of her self-imposed stupor and started writing *Vampire*. Looking back Anne said that the time was "lightning striking twice" – her own terminal disease coupled with Michele's death. But involvement is critical to outlasting such trauma. She lost herself in *Interview with the Vampire* in 1972. It would not be completed until 1974, and not published until 1976. Rice had longed to be a writer, but it took a calamity to get her published. Had Michele not died the vampire series may never have been born. Literary success also proved to be a healing balm as her body slowly healed of the *mock polio* diagnosis.

POLYPHASIC PERSONALITY

Rice describes herself as an "indomitable spirit." She is an obsessive zealot with a radical nature, a woman capable of pursuing many things at once, admitting, I work best when I work fast., extremely rapidly in long uninterrupted periods" (Ramsland pg 275). She told biographer Riley "No one has ever called me dull or static." Type A's like Rice arae impatient and impulsive. She edits one book while writing another and fabricating a third. She can mult-task and is often found carrying on a lively conversation while eating and watching TV. She is woman with passion for life with few limits.

CRITICAL ACCLAIM

Rice is Queen of the Occult and Mistress of the Macabre. She has a wide readership. Fans pant for her next new supernatural novel. Literary critic Edith Milton says, "To hell with literary pretensions and Gothic formulae, *Interview with the Vampire* is an erotic novel where the sucking of blood has replaced more reproductive activities" (*Contemporary Authors* p. 362). Milton said the book was silly. "It is not that the erotic content is so explicit, but that the morbid context is so respectable." Brain Johnson of *Macleans* (Nov. 16, 1992) says "Anne Rice has blossomed from cult writer to literary star." Her

Lestat character is a Promethean hero who has become the 007 of vampires. Stan Beeler writing for *Contemporary Popular Writers* says, "Anne Rice is one of those rare phenomena; a writer who has been able to attain a level of success in more than one genre. She has done well with novels that appear on bookshelves with works of fantasy, historical fiction, and erotic fiction" (*Contemporary Popular Writers* pg. 337).

Rice has also left her mark in the high-tech world of the Web. She has gained widespread recognition via a state-of-the-art Internet creation. Two of her books have made into high budget movies - *Interview* (1994) and *Exit to Eden* (1994). She now has 20 books published with adoring fans always longing for her next weird fantasy.

SUCCESS BASED ON OUR SYGYZY – What Can We Learn?

The refusal to be but one type, culture, gender, or personality began with the Greeks. They started the tradition of living a bisexual existence and admonished us to "know thyself." They believed anything was possible if we would but look within. Rice has lived her life by those rules.

In many books Rice has thrown tradition out the window and lived right on the edge of decorum, a lifestyle preference portrayed vividly in her book *Feast of All Saints* where she explores the *castrati*. The gay lifestyle has always interested her and her best friend was gay writer John Preston. Her favorite entertainer is the androgynous David Bowie.

When questioned about editing her work she says of editors, "You can take in a chunk of Dosteoevsky's *The Brothers Karamoazov* and they'd tear it to pieces. That's their business" (Ramsland p. 138). She admonishes us to "write what you are about ... and don't clutter up your brain with opinions of people you don't respect" (p. 138). Her editing philosophy:

> *I don't like anyone changing my words. I don't think an editor should go over a manuscript, and change things any more than I think a gallery owner should heat up the*

paint on a canvas and go around smudging it.
If I change something for an editor, that
means I've failed. It's the writer's obligation
to protect the integrity of the manuscript from
everyone. (Ramsland pg. 190).

This shows that she knows who she is and is not about to allow anyone to change her or her work. Anne Rice is the quintessential example of a woman living life at various extremes. She sees herself part male, part female, an atheist who questions her belief, and a risk-averse person who dares more than most. She is a conservative radical who says she writes to get into those inner demons that confront us. "We all wear a clock of respectability while in our hearts we are all monsters" (Ramsland 1991).

Rice describes her writing as "loquacious philosophy for the tormented." Others call it escapist and "Everyman Eternal." She identifies with vampires as heroes, a writer who dares allow her imagination run amok and lead her into uncharted territory. To her heroes are monsters and villains are heroes. What a dichotomy! Rice has unique ability to tap into Jung's Syzygy concept, allowing herself the liberty to be both man and woman in her life and work. She has the imagery of a female transmitted via an aggressive male drive.

The ability to live and write in absolute defiance of the establishment is a Promethean trait that will destroy you or make you great. Rice is such a person. She dared to defy the masters and paid the price for her rebellion with critical bashing. But she has persevered and now has brought light to millions of adoring fans. She sees through an iconoclastic filter but her lens is holistic and this has brought her fame and fortune. Her philosophy is inextricably tied to characters and scenes articulately portrayed to fit her imagination. They are not always logical, but are entertaining and interesting. If we can suspend our belief system like Rice and allow our imaginations to delve into our opposite, the total will add up to more than the sum of the parts.

STEPHEN KING
MASTER OF THE MACABRE
b. Portland, Maine Sept. 21, 1947

TYPE A'S ARE PRODUCTIVE

DOMINANT GENRE

Horror – The Sultan of Shock depicting a world that is scary but possible; innovated on $1 per installment of 2000 Internet serialization of *The Plant*

MOTTO

"We make up horrors to help us cope with the real ones"
"I believe that writers are made not born"
"I'm an addictive personality"

GREATEST WORKS

Carrie (1973) – Top film of 1976; $200,000 paperback rights
The Shining (1977) – 1980 movie with Jack Nickolson
The Stand (1978) his masterpiece of Good vs Evil
Riding the Bullet (2000) Innovative Internet serialization

HONORS/AWARDS

First to have three books on Best Seller List at same time in 1998; Called "World's Best Selling Novelist" and "Greatest Selling Horror Writer in History" with 500 million books sold

ECCENTRICITIES

An addictive personality; writes to music while drinking, rides Harley and loves to shock. "I try to terrorize the reader."

LIFE CRISES

Father disappeared when two; escaped into books and movies during whirlwind journey in six states

METAMORPHOSES

Ray Bradbury's "Mars" radio show when 7 and then the Sputnik launch while he was in the theater at 10

11

STEPHEN KING - HORROR

Type A's Are More Productive

"I'm an addictive personality"

Industriousness prevails for all disciplines. In the words of Stephen King, "Hard work is the only thing that separates the talented from the successful." Such is the style of a man who writes every day of every year except three – his birthday, Xmas, and July 4th. Work and writing is a way of life and money is not the reason. With King the drive is deep-seated as it is in most creative geniuses who must produce or perish. But the bottom line is that work overcomes most other deficiencies.

Those who are more productive, even when the output leaves something to be desired, give themselves the best chance of real success. Why? Because increased output enhances the chance one of the productions will be extraordinary. Breakthroughs always increase in direct proportion to the number of attempts as is proven in business. Marketing experts have found it takes 3000 new ideas to create one "successful new product." In other words, failure begets success if one perseveres.

Psychologists know that perfection is a by-product of a heuristic – trial and error learning – approach. Creative people must overcome self-doubt and that can only be achieved after repeated trials that reinforce confidence. Success improves with each word written, tennis or golf ball struck, and each dance step taken. Athletic trait-anxiety tests show that the probability of success only comes after there is a 50 percent belief that it is possible. Until that happens we are all buried in our own deluded sense of self-doubt.

Success is never a linear process. It is a broken line of success, failure, greater success, more failure, etc. in an iterative process that ultimately makes achieving a greater probability than failure. Hopefully, we will not be destroyed in the process of learning how to fail successfully. But it is fear that is the mortal enemy of anyone attempting to achieve great things. Those who allow fear and uncertainty to dominate their lives are destined to become the pawn of fear. They have no chance of real success until they cast fear aside. Why? Because failure is born of fear, not inability. The eminent never allow fear to dominate their life or work.

King questioned his writing ability early when he was continually rejected. And shockingly, he questioned it again after his tragic 1999 accident that almost cost him his life. But the Master of the Macabre never won out over his inner resolve. He began three new books in 2000 after having lost 100 pounds while ensconced in a wheel chair and altered the distribution of books with his Internet serialization. Then enraptured he offered the world books by chapters on a pay-as-you-go by using the honor system.

The only people who do not experience failure are those who don't expose themselves. Exposure to ridicule and rejection is part of the process of growing and King is a master at this. An Alpine skier who never falls down while skiing is never pushing the limits and consequently will never improve and that is true of musicians, golfers, entertainers, and writers. King's early life was an example of a man not sure and at times he crawled into a bottle to drown out the inner demons that kept telling him he was a flash-in-the-pan success.

Everyone who makes it to the very top pay a very high price for success. Even a genius of narrative like Ernest Hemingway had to work diligently to achieve the brevity of expression for which he is famous. Papa wrote and rewrote *The Old Man & the Sea* 200 times before he dared release it. With each rewrite any manuscript will be improved, it is merely a matter of what level of perfection one demands and can tolerate. Each rewrite improves, but at a diminishing rate. The first one improves the work by approximately 50% improvement, the second 25%,

226

third 12.5%, and fourth 6.25%. At what point does the writer say, enough! Agatha Christie admitted that she didn't really become a writer until after her sixth book.

Charles Darwin organized and reorganized his research data on animals for 20 years before he drew some insightful conclusions and documented them in the *Origin of the Species*. Thomas Edison failed at over 1000 experiments prior to his incandescent light bulb innovation. Carl Jung spent his life looking into the motivations of mankind prior to his insightful conclusions. Biographer and associate Barbara Hanna (1997) said, "Jung's most creative period and most important books were not produced until age 70" (Hannah pg. 288). Jung's one-time mentor Sigmund Freud was even more a slave to his work and research. Freud was a total unknown until his mid-forties, quite old for a scientist, when he published his landmark *Interpretation of Dreams*. The book was a compilation of his research on dreams and their meaning to every day life. Freud's instant success was really a by-product of a life's work.

MONEY AS MOTIVATOR. Stephen King is the consummate workaholic. Money does not motivate him. Most great people disdain money including callous businessmen with a reputation aggressive tactics. Did Bill Gates ever do anything for the money? Not a chance! But he is the richest man in the world because we keep score in capitalism with money and when you execute well the money comes in baskets. Money should never interfere with the writing process.

King writes constantly despite having more money than he can ever spend. Michener did the same as do all great people. Workaholic geniuses like Picasso, Bucky Fuller and Oprah Winfrey all disdained money as a motivator. Prodigious wordsmiths like Christie, Rice, and Steel, were prodigious producers, but money was never behind their stories. Money is often confused with wealth. Money is but an extrinsic reward for superb execution. Bucky Fuller said, "I didn't take out patents to make money but I have proven that one can be world-effective while eschewing money" (Fuller 1981 p. 149). The euphoria of *doing* is the magic, never *completing*. But such a revelation is never evident during the creative process. Every author in this book would have written without pay and many did. But the one constant is their passion for their chosen field and that passion superceded family, health, friends, and family.

THE KING OF WORKAHOLICS. Most eminent have a propensity for Type A behavior. They are in a hurry, not to produce as much as to appease an inner drive that pushes them to excel. It was true of Alexander the Great, Darwin, Lord Byron, Einstein, Freud, Shaw, Michener, and Woolf. Whatever the calling, to be the *very* best entails outworking your ineptitudes and your adversaries. This is axiomatic whether writing verse, hitting golfballs, or painting the Sistine Chapel.

Thomas Edison had already etched his name as a genius in the world of invention. But at age 65 his journal shows that he spent an average of 120 hours per week in his lab. What prompted him to work rather than take a walk on the beach? It certainly wasn't money. Edison was already wealthy. It wasn't notoriety. He was already world-famous as the Wizard of Menlo Park. It was an internal need that he was driven to appease.

For the same reason Ayn Rand spent two and one half years writing one speech for her classic *Atlas Shrugged.* The book would take the perfectionist 17 years to complete. The same driving force led Buckminster Fuller to concoct a theory of *Dymaxion Sleep.* The brilliant innovator would work for six hours non-stop and then take a 30-minute self-induced nap. He would wake and work another six hours and place himself in the trancelike state once again for 30 minutes and he did this for days. He could go to sleep in 30 seconds allowing him to outwork men years younger all the way into his 70's.

Eighty-percent of the subjects in this work were classified Type A personalities with King the poster boy. What is a Type A? IT is someone who confuses self-worth with achievement. Such people feel guilty when not productive. They are incapable of resting and practice their craft more than others. They write more words, think of more plots, hit more tennis or golf balls, paint more pictures and live more. Danielle Steel would take her children to a picnic and relax while writing a novel, turn over and be writing another at the same time. Such people take on more projects than any sane person could possibly contemplate. They tend to be impatient, intolerant, and impossible to live with. But they get more done than a whole room full of normal people. Many suffer fools poorly and are not too into the little stuff. They become so consumed with the whole they often lose sight of details picked up by others who see them as flaky and irresponsible.

Stephen King said, "Hard work is the only thing separating the talented from the successful" (Beahm pg. 27). Work was his only master and it has made him the most read writer of the 20th century and arguably the most successful writer in history. Schoolboy friend Chris Chesley described the Master of the Macabre as a "frenetic workaholic and Type A."

RUSHING SICKNESS. Research indicates that the overachievers tend to live life in a hurry. It as if they feel they may perish before completing some important work. They live and work as if double-parked on the highway of life and tend to drive fast, speak fast, think fast, eat fast, and even sleep fast. They are more prone to speeding tickets and traffic accidents. George Bernard Shaw rode his bicycle at precarious speeds through downtown London. Carl Jung rushed through life at a frenetic pace. Frank Lloyd Wright was involved in numerous automobile accidents. Amelia Earhart's favorite pastime was racing fast sports cars and planes and testing their limits.

Speed is one of King's penchants. He owns a Hog – a classic Harley-Davidson motorcycle and rides it with disdain. He writes faster due to listening to hard rock on the radio. When his favorite station was about to close, King bought it to maintain his lifestyle. Virginia Woolf and Sylvia Plath, both Type A+'s, wrote with an intensity that drove their mates mad. Ian Fleming drove fast and sleek sports cars and imbued 007 with his need for speed.

Most of these writers wrote in white heat, not to meet any deadline, but to appease some inner need to produce. Most disdained vacations since they interrupted their daily routine. Michener refused to take a vacation for years. Danielle Steel was notorious for using her lipstick to write plot ideas on the mirrors around her palatial San Francisco mansion.

HISTORY OF HORROR

The Horror genre has not been the same since Stephen King. He has become known as the father of the supernatural novel that is rooted in the genre's history. The history of horror is closely aligned with the modern Gothic novel, the occult and the supernatural. The ghost scene in Shakespeare's Hamlet was one of the first modern uses of metaphysical and paranormal phenomena. Soon after Marlow produced *Doctor Faustus*," that introduced the devil into popular literature, then Goethe gave him the name Mephistopheles.

The Gothic Romances followed including Edgar Allen Poe's *The Raven* and Bram Stoker's *Dracula*.. This was advanced with Mary Shelley" *Frankenstein* and the *New Prometheus*. Stevenson's *Dr. Jekyll & Mr. Hyde* and Dicken's *A Christmas Carol* set the stage for H.P. Lovecraft and Henry James. Lovecraft's horror was an early influence on King. King still touts him as the master of horror saying, "He opened the way for me. It is Lovecraft who oversees almost all of the important horror-fiction. His *Rats in the Wall* and *Supernatural Horror in Literature* struck me with the most force, I still think, for all his shortcomings, he is the best writer of horror fiction that America has yet produced" (Beahm 22). Soon after King saw Ray Bradbury's *Mars is Heaven* demonstrating that "fantasy can also be a visual medium" (Beahm 16). King heard the *Mars* radio show when he was seven and never forgot it.

KING – MR. PROLIFIC

King must write or die. To him writing is an all-consuming passion. It is the driving force from within that is number one reason he gets up each morning. The workaholic has published one new book each year for almost thirty years and this prodigious productivity has kept him in the mainstream of popular mass-market books and movies for that whole period. His need to write every day comes from what he calls his "fearsomes." He says, "If I weren't writing I'd commit suicide"

(Beahm 136). King's "marketable obsession" for writing can be seen in *Skeleton Crew*:

> **You don't do it for money, or you're a monkey. You don't think of the bottom line, or you're a monkey. You don't think of it in terms of hourly wage, yearly wage, even lifetime wage, or you're a monkey. In the end you don't even do it for love, although it would be nice to think so. You do it because to not do it is suicide.** (Beahm 203)

Is that the philosophy of a Type A? He told *60 Minutes* (8-2-98) "I believe writers are made not born." He compulsively writes for eight to ten hours all but three days each year and there is little indication he will slow down until forced to.

HISTORY'S WORKAHOLICS. Writers might pay attention to the admonition of Thomas Edison, "Creativity is 99% perspiration and 1% inspiration." Leonardo Da Vinci was also a tireless workaholic who left a legacy of his work in 15,000 pages of notes very meticulously written in a mirror image. His remark "Death rather than weariness" gives some idea of his intensity. He admitted, "No work is capable of tiring me" (Zubov pg. 209). Buckminster Fuller had a similar penchant with 37,000 entries in what he called his "Chronofile."

Catherine the Great and Napoleon were notorious for dictating to two or three secretaries simultaneously. Napoleon's valet Constant said of his vitality. "I never saw a man with so much personal activity. He had the energy of a whirlwind." Agatha Christie appeared to be a passive British housewife but she was driven. The Queen of Crime wrote one new book a year for 57 straight years. During many of those years she wrote two or more plus a play. Albert Camus was a social party animal but still outworked his peers. He suffered from a fear he might die before documenting his ideas. He wrote to a friend, "Sleeping is a waste. I have a mad and avid thirst for everything ... Man's most dangerous temptation is inertia" (Todd 220).

231

Magill Books said, "Michener is probably one of the hardest working authors America has ever produced" (Guillory 1992). Anne Rice says, "I'm obsessed. I work best when I work extremely rapidly" (Ramsland 1994). Few writers have the drive of Danielle Steel. She admitted to the media. "I work pretty much around the clock. I'm sure I'm a workaholic. When I get a new idea I become totally crazed, in a trance and will go a month without leaving the room" (Hoyt 326). Quite the schedule for a mother of eight who admitted to the media, "I work ten hours a day and spend ten hours with my seven kids. That leaves me four hours to sleep. I'm a workaholic" (Hoyt 326). A servant told the media, "She is always in a hurry." Steel admits, "I sit at my typewriter and type until I ache so badly I can't get up, sometimes for as much as 18-20 hours. I have fainted when I stood up and other times have fallen asleep face first in my typewriter and awoke the next morning with the keyboard marks on my face." (Bane & Benet 1994 p. 243).

Balzac was truly driven. He believed he would die if not successful and drove himself with a vengeance. The Father of the Modern Novel produced almost 100 novels in less than twenty-five years. His price? Premature death at age fifty. He lived at the mercy of his inner demons. One night when ill he managed to write 15,000 words and this was in an era sans typewriters and electricity forcing him to write by candlelight. Balzac wrote much of his all-night beginning at 1:00 am in the morning and continuing unabated until eight o'clock. He took an hour and a half nap, consumed vast amounts of coffee, and began writing non-stop until 4 o'clock in the afternoon. He then had dinner and went to bed for an hour only to awake for his 1:00am writing binge. Balzac repeated this unbelievable schedule seven days a week for months at a time until he would break down and be forced to take a rest.

KING'S CONTRIBUTION TO HORROR GENRE

King's contribution has been an ability to write bizarre tales that are just within the realm of possibility but bizarre enough to be mystical. He writes page-turners with supernatural themes, stories that are possible, but not probable. In this way he piques the imagination of *everyman's* internalized fears. He has successfully married the weird with the unbelievable and made it almost real. His ability to mix metaphysical themes like telekinesis, extrasensory perception, and parapsychology with contemporary action is entertaining and scary. His scenes border on alchemy. Everyone can identify with his arcane sense of suspenseful chaos. King's absorption with the fears of the common man has made him readable and successful. He marries the surreal with the real while striking fear in the mind of the reader. This separates him from other writers in the genre. This was never more evident than in *Dark Tower* (1982), a book spawned by the Texas gunman, who sat in a tower picking off students like in a shooting gallery.

King's forays into the supernatural began with *Carrie*, a telekinetic girl who could reek revenge on her adversaries. He followed this theme with a foray into ESP in *The Shining*. He created an infectious disease for *The Stand*. It would be pyro-kinises in *Firestarter*. In all of these books King explored the deep-seated fears in his own psyche while tapping into the fears in his readers. He says, "I try to terrorize the reader, if I can't I try to horrify, if I can't I'll go for the gross out," adding "The novelist is God's liar and he can sometimes find the truth that lies at the center of the lie" (Beahm 193).

Critics say King's talent has been to bring horror out of the closet and into the mainstream. *People* magazine selected him as one of writers who defined the decade of the eighties. Walter Kendrick of the *Village Voice* (April 29. 1981) said, "No matter how hard you fight he's irresistible." He "writes with such fierce conviction, with such a blend of brutal power." King has reestablished horror as a viable literary genre. How? By spinning superior stories with a universal theme of fear with universal appeal. His stories are real making the reader buys into the mysticism or suspend their belief. His innovative style comes from "visual movies in my head." It is this ability to use vivid imagination intuitively that permits him to write fiction of the fantastic. He marries science fiction with irrational fantasy saying, "What I write comes from the gut instead of my head, from intuition rather than intellect," (Beahm 151).

STEPHEN KING

WRITING AS CATHARSIS

King admits to escaping into word fantasies to maintain his sanity. "Writing is my cathartic release. If I weren't writing I might be a mass murderer or commit suicide" (Beahm 136). He admitted to the media that early religious experience helped mold him, "I was raised Methodist, and I was scared that I was going to hell. The horror stories that I grew up with were biblical stories" (*Contemporary Authors* p 238). It isn't a coincidence that his success has been in depicting children dealing with fears as he had done as a fatherless child in abject poverty. He says, "I externalize my fears and insecurities and night terrors on paper, which is what most people pay shrinks a small fortune to do" (*Contemporary Authors* pg. 241).

King told *Playboy* "I'm like a kid. I like to make believe". He described going into a state of "auto-hypnosis" where he dredges up autobiographical material. He told the *New York Times Book Review* it is only through writing that, "I maintain my sanity.at people pay shrinks a small fortune to do." In *Danse Macabre* he says "we make up horrors to help us cope with the real ones. Fear and death are two of the human constants giving us an opportunity for identification and catharsis." His *The Shining* (1977) was based on his inner fears of alcoholism and childhood rage. When his cat was killed on a road near his home, and his daughter nearly came to the same fate, he wrote *Pet Sematary*. It was so real it scared him and he stuck the manuscript in a drawer for three years.

METAMORPHOSES

As a child the Titan of Terror escaped into fantasies in the form of weird comic books, sci-fi radio shows and movies and any other medium that was out of the ordinary. His father Don had been an aspiring writer who did not persevere. His mysterious disappearance when Stephen was two left a void that Stephen continues to fill with words and actions. His mother Ruth took to the road to find her way. Stephen and his adopted brother David lived in six states in six years. Stephen escaped into books and movies like *Earth vs the Flying Saucers, the Invasion of the Body Snatchers,* and *The Creature from the Black Lagoon.*

They made an indelible imprint on his psyche. When the family returned to Maine King discovered a cache of his father's books by H. P. Lovecraft buried away in a box. These books would prove to be a lasting influence on him. He devoured them and found his hero. "Lovecraft struck me with such force. I still think for all his shortcomings he is the best writer of horror fiction that America has ever produced" (Beahm 220. His earlier escape into comic books like *Weird Science, Tales from the Crypt* and *Tales from the Vault* had awakened an interest in the occult that horror writer Lovecraft completed.

King wrote his first story at age seven and sold his first short story to a magazine at 18. All were about horror despite his interest in science fiction. They were published in upscale men's magazines like *Cavalier, Swank* and *Cosmopolitan*. He was paid $250 a story. When he decided to switch from short stories to novels he wrote science fiction and all were summarily rejected. His forte has turned out to be horror not science fiction. He said, "It never occurred to me to write a horror novel. It's odd because I had never actually sold anything but horror stories" (Beahm 59). *Sword in the Darkness* (1970), *Getting It On,* (1971), and *The Running Man* (1971) were all rejected prior to him becoming famous.

When he began writing Carrie he was not sure he could write. He tore up the first draft in total disgust saying, "I might just be chasing a fools dream." His wife Tabitha retrieved it and saw something in the plot. He agreed to rewrite it as horror rather than science fiction. The family had hit bottom, living in a house trailer without a phone, two kids, and walking to his job as English teacher since he didn't have a car that worked. By this time he was drinking a case of beer daily. He altered the Cinderella story of the teenaged Carrie into a supernatural theme with *Carrie* a tormented teenager with telekinetic powers. He finished it and sent it off to Doubleday fully expecting another rejection letter. He said, "I felt I had written the all-time loser," (Beahm 59). In 1974 Bill Thomson called and said he would buy it for a $2500 advance. This was a fortune at the time for the King family, and would soon turn to $200,000 for the paperback rights sold to New American Library.

STEPHEN KING

ECCENTRICITIES

The King of Kooky was always unique. He was an introverted loner and considered a nerd in his Maine high school and in college. King is a paradox in that he doesn't fit the model of a writer. He played football in high school, played in a rock band, wrote constantly, but never allowed rejection to deter him. High school and college teachers described him as "different," a guy with a paperback in his hip pocket, cigarette in his mouth, and his newly acquired guitar slung over his shoulder. Testimony to his eccentricity is the 126 year-old Maine mansion he purchased replete with bats and a 40 foot swimming pool. It is an eerie sight with 23 rooms located in Bangor, Maine. Spider webs and bats adorn the iron fence with his Harley sitting at the ready. Kin is an ungainly six foot three, beer drinking, guitar-strumming, author of supernatural fiction.

LIFE CRISES

King's early life was a series of crises. It all began with the mysterious disappearance of his salesman father when he was two. His mother spent the next few years struggling to survive. The family lived in Maine but took to the road with residences in Chicago, Wisconsin, Indiana, Connecticut, and Massachusetts. They returned to Maine when Stephen was eleven. He attended many schools but spent much time in books and movies. Ruth King worked two and three jobs to feed his older half-brother David, who was adopted, and Stephen. This vagabond period left a mark on King that has found its way into his novels. King writes about long rendezvous across America with scenes in areas he had visited in those vagabond years. By age eight he had escaped into comic books and a fantasy life and began writing by age seven.

After graduating from the University of Maine King found a job teaching English at Hampton Academy. By this time he had a daughter Naomi. She had been born out of wedlock but he soon married Tabitha Spruce, an aspiring poet he met in the stacks at college. He occasionally played in a band in the evening to help pay the bills. He was drinking heavily, playing poker and spent little time at home except to write. The family was living in abject poverty in a trailer home when he sent the Carrie manuscript to Doubleday. His car was sitting on the front lawn and they didn't have a phone. When Bill Thompson of Doubleday called he was unable to reach King and sent a telegram to inform him of the good news.

With the paperback right sale of $200,000 King went out and bought a red, white and blue Cadillac. The family moved to an apartment and he began work on his second novel *Salem's Lot*. *Carrie* was published in 1974 and in May the paperback rights were sold to New American Library for $400,000. He was 24 and so excited and unsophisticated he went shopping to buy his wife a memento of the occasion. The new author returned with a $16.95 hairdryer from the local drugstore.

In a TV interview in early 2000 King admitted that he was an "addictive personality." He said, "I would drink a six pack before dinner and finish the case before I went to bed." He finally turned his own demons into words with *Dolores Claiborne*. King is a country boy at heart and quite candid about his life and dreams. It makes him readable and endearing. But no one has ever accused him of being normal. He is obsessive, compulsive and does little in moderation.

A POLYPHASIC PERSONALITY

Addictive personalities tend to thrive on too much to do in a given amount of time. King is no exception. He keeps many plots in his head at any given time. King has a need to keep many balls balanced and the challenge is inspiring and motivating. Most Type A's like King are unable to sit and do nothing. In fact, it is difficult for them to sit and do just one thing. In King's case this has led him to work on one project in the morning and another in the afternoon. Testimony to his multi-dimensional needs are the nearly forty novels, five short stories, and ten screenplays he has produced since the early 70's. At his present pace he will be the first American author to sell a billion books.

During the 1980's he wrote 14 novels, poetry, short stories, and screenplays. When not writing King is busy with his many hobbies including amateur softball games in his hometown, football games at the local tavern, lecturing, listening to rock and roll, riding his Harley, doing book tours, and playing in pickup bands. An example of his polyphasia occurred in 1997 when he had the #1 book on the annual Best Sellers List – *Desperation* with another book *Regulators* by his alter-ego Richard Bachman in the #2 spot. The first printing on the two was 3 million. He told *Playboy* "I work on two things simultaneously." But he insists that what he is working on in the morning demands his undivided attention and by afternoon he is either editing a past work or conjuring up something new.

CRITICAL ACCLAIM

The TV show *Sixty Minutes* (Aug. 2, 1998) called King the most successful writer of horror in history based on his 300 million book ales in 25 years. The workaholic is now working on the next 300 million. He has been acclaimed as one of the world's great storytellers with A&E proclaiming him to be "the wealthiest author in history" (Jan. 17, 2000). Despite incredible commercial success he is still demeaned.

At a mid-90's book show (ABA) the President of the American Booksellers Association introduced King as "America's horror writer Laureate." He is the first writer to have three books on the Best Sellers List at the same time (1980 – *Firestarter, Dead Zone, The Shining*) and this soon became four and then five. During his first eight years as a published author he sold 22 million books. During the 80's King had seven of the top selling twenty-five novels in America and has remained on the *New York Times* Best Sellers List continuously for over a decade. He has shattered all records for any genre. Not bad for a writer the critics abhor. But King has finally transcended literary criticism as one of the chroniclers of 20th century Americana.

Literary critic Burton Hatlen wrote, "Few writers have such a clear sense of the demons that lurk within the American psyche" (Beahm 66). Orson Scott Card wrote in *Contemporary Authors* (pg. 236) "nothing is as unstoppable as one of King's furies." He went on to say, "If someone in the future wants to see what American life was like, what Americans cared about, what our stories were in the seventies and eighties, they'll read Stephen King. In fifty years King will be regarded as the dominant literary figure of the time." Pepperdine University professor Michael Collings wrote, "The Stephen King phenomenon is a one person entertainment industry."

King told *USA Today*, (Sept 17, 1998) "I am a salami writer. I try to write good salami. You can't sell it as caviar. It is the literary equivalent of turkey rice soup. Nourishing but not actively offensive." This only succeeded in fueling his critics. But a USA Today article stated, "If forced to choose between good storytelling and good writing I will settle for a good story. Literary critics who praise gorgeous writing without a story are like some guy dating a model, saying she's dumb as a stone boat but is great to look at" (USA Today 9-17-98).

SUCCESS & THE WORKAHOLIC – What Can We Learn?

Speed wins. And Stephen King is the personification of the concept. *Rolling Stone* (May 13, 1993) wrote, "Stephen King is a one-man horror industry." *Time* called him "the world's oldest teenager." But the forty books in his repertoire say one thing. The man is driven to write and he writes every day and that is one of his secrets. He never stops and doesn't appear that he ever will. King doesn't need to ever write another word to live the good life but that never was and never will be a motivating factor in his life. He is about improving on his past performance and writing that truly great novel. His goal is two long novels a year.

King is a driven writer. His drive has left an indelible mark on the world of fiction. Every single book is still in print, and half have found their way into movies or TV. He is now the most economically successful writer in America with earnings from movie royalties alone in 1997 estimated at $50 million. He took a big cut in 1998, but it won't land him in the unemployment lines, since he still earned $40 million. When *USA Today* (Sept. 17, 1998) asked about his productivity he responded, "When you've written 35 books you can never work too fast." I see another 35 before he shuts off his word-processor.

HONORE BALZAC
MANIC FATHER OF MODERN NOVEL
b. Tours, France May 20, 1799
d. Paris, France June 28, 1851

PASSION OVERCOMES ADVERSITY

DOMINANT GENRE
Serial Biography of 19th century French Society; the first to couple political commentary with serious fiction

MOTTO
"My soul thirsts for immensity, for the infinite, for nature en masse"; "Genius is the alternative to death"

GREATEST WORKS
The Human Comedy (100 novels between 1831 - 1850)
The La Peau de Chagrin (1831) "psychic autobiography"

HONORS/AWARDS
Engels wrote, "I've learned more from Balzac than all the professional Historians, economists, and statisticians put together" Hugo hailed him as the father of the modern novel

ECCENTRICITIES
Manic-depressive who was excessive in everything; obsessions caused him repeated breakdowns; often wrote 50,000 words in a few days sleeping little with demonic work ethic

LIFE CRISES
Mother sent him to a wet nurse and left him for four years; numerous nervous breakdowns due to hyper-kinetic behavior

METAMORPHOSES
First attempts at philosophy and historical non-fiction (Cromwell) ended in disaster causing him to pursue a career as a novelist that culminated in him altering the novel form

12

HONORE BALZAC – MANIC

HYPERACTIVE OVERACHIEVING

"If I'm not a genius I am done for"

Balzac dreamed of becoming a world famous author, trained for the law, had to be a genius, and played at entrepreneurship with wild schemes and acquisitions in the printing and publishing industries. All together these needs fashioned him into a manic overachiever the likes the world seldom sees.

His mother, Anne-Charlotte Balzac mother married a much older man and their first-born died thirty-three days later while she was nursing him. Paranoid over the death, she refused to nurse Honore when he was born the next year. Instead she sent him to a wet nurse, but failed to fetch him for four years. His father was thirty-two years older than his cuckolding wife who had taken up with a younger lover leaving Balzac the tragic refuse who was more in the way than wanted. During the time she produced an illegitimate son named Henry. By 13 Balzac was feeling the torment of rejection and lack of parental love and was sent home from school with a nervous ailment that was threatening his ability to study. By age 15 he was having serious emotional problems and attempted suicide. The lonely boy escaped into books and Napoleon became his ideal father.

Balzac told of his early plight in his autobiographical novel work *La Peaud de Chagrin.* He wrote, "My mother hated me before I was born." Later, he would write of the neglect saying, "My mother happened to notice I was missing." When he finally came home, he was allowed to stay but for a few months before being sent to live in a boarding school, only blocks from the family home. Balzac wrote later, "In six years she visited me twice." His escape into books earned him the nickname The

241

Poet. He devoured history, dictionaries, etymology, and a nervous affliction he labeled "intellectual congestion." He was asked to leave school in what his sister Laure described as a "coma," a nervous breakdown. It would be the first of many due to overwork in the name of showing his mother he was worthy of her love.

After graduating from law school Balzac locked himself in an attic and vowed not to leave until he became a famous author. He gave himself two years. The project would take ten. Balzac described his isolation as a gamble of "death or glory" (Robb p. 55). To him his isolation took on the guise of a romantic mission. He wrote, "I loved my prison, for I had chosen it myself." During his vigil he wrote an esoteric work titled *Discourse on the Immortality of the Soul*. It was not good. His next foray was serious biography, *Cromwell* (1820). It was also a miserable failure.

Balzac's childhood led to a life-long love hate relationship with his mother. During his struggle to become a writer she told him to get a real job. He ignore the advice saying, "The author should do anything he likes, but not literature" Robb p. 60). But his early failures led him to his calling and he outlined his life's work that would become *The Human Comedy*.

A MAN OF EXCESS. Balzac lived life in the fast lane. Everything he did was larger than life and done in excess. He had huge appetites dwarfing the norm – an all-consuming need to be the brightest, biggest, funniest, and loudest. He ate and drank prodigious amounts of food and wine and worked as if he would die the next day. He ate fast, drank fast, talked fast, slept fast, loved fast, thought fast, and worked fast. He was a maniac on a mission to be genius fearing that if he failed he would die. And the truth was that he was unable to function normally since he lived in constant torment over his mother's treatment. The irony is that the super-heated vitality molded the father of the modern novel but the price was his health and life. His manic lifestyle led to premature death at age fifty.

MANIA. Balzac was addicted to caffeine. He began drinking coffee in his teens to sustain him and his habit became a compulsion then an obsession. It worked! He could stay up for days, fueled by the magic of caffeine. Workaholic is too soft a term to describe this zealot who normally worked 18-20 hours a day seven days a week. Many days passed when he didn't make it to bed. Work led to a prolific output, but the price he paid was a dastardly life and early demise. But he felt the price was worth the cost as he wrote, "If I'm not a genius I'm done for." This human dynamo worked harder and harder, drank more and more coffee, until his engine was working overtime. This ever-spiraling cycle becomes a self-fulfilling prophecy and caffeine led to more energy and the need to write more and more until his life was lost in a compulsive reverie.

BALZAC & ROMANCE. Balzac's frenetic work schedule left little time for traditional romance and no time for a full time wife. But even if it had he believed that each liaison detracted from his creativity in a kind of zero-sum game where each encounter with a woman lost one creative expression. This led to a Freudian type sublimation of libidinal drive into creative ones. Such drive led to quick romances with married women who could open important doors but demanded little else than occasional stroking. He gave them what they wanted and they gave him what he wanted – quick sex and no commitments.

At 23 he took up with a 45-year old grandmother Laure de Berny. She would become the consummate *Balzacian* female – a lonely older woman looking for romance and finding it with a younger man. De Berny loved him, coddled him, advised him, and financed his work. She opened many important doors and in return he immortalized her in his works. Balzac understood the needs of women, especially the older, sophisticated, and lonely ones. He wrote for them and they responded in kind by buying his books and becoming adoring fans. Balzac had a long line of mistresses, always older and well-married women.

Balzac's sensitive portrayal of these lonely women won undying love. They gave him sex and he responded by granting them immortality. According to author friend George Sand, Balzac had many more female friends than male, and their feedback became fuel for his work. Balzac was obsessed with sex and eroticism but never married until three months before his death. Why? Because he was convinced that sex and literary output were a game with one detracting inextricably from the other. He wrote, "My orgies take the form of novels."

MOTHER FIXATION. Balzac's liaisons with older women were a function of a mother who had deserted him. His love-hate relationship with his mother was also tied to the birth of a love-child named Henry. She openly favored Balzac's illegitimate half-brother. It motivated him to prove that she was wrong and he would prove it if it killed him. And it did, but also succeeded in making him into the author he desired to be.

Balzac's contribution to literature was immersed in the life of the family and especially the French wife and mother. He offered insight into their needs, passions, and loneliness. He was aware of what made these women tick and let the world know of their plight. The French housewife would become his greatest supporter and made his books successful beyond his own wildest dreams. They recognized him as a man who understood them. During his lifetime they buried him in 12,000 letters applauding him and many with offers of seduction. He had become their hero. One of these letters arrived when he was half through his monumental work *The Human Comedy*. The letter arrived from the Ukraine, from a lonely woman whose marriage of convenience to a much older man offered little solace to her needs. Her letter was signed The Stranger. This stranger turned out to be Evalina Hanaska, a woman who would become his wife just months before his fires were extinguished.

HYPOMANIA & CREATIVITY. According to the American Psychiatric Glossary on DSM-IV "*hypomania* is a mood disorder characterized by excessive elation, inflated self-esteem, grandiosity, hyperactivity, agitation, and accelerated thinking or speaking." Hypomania defined Balzac, and fueled his success. He would lock himself in a room and refuse to come out until he had mastered a scene, chapter, or concept.

In order to remain chaste, Balzac donned a monks robe to remind him to remain faithful to his work and not waste his limited energies on anything but writing. Psychiatrist Julian

Lieb wrote "Hypomania is of special value to poets, humorists, entrepreneurs, inventors, scientists, and others whose work requires creativity" (Hershman & Lieb pg. 22). Goethe validated this with his statement, "In my 75 years I have not known four weeks of genuine ease of mind." Danielle Steel wrote, "When writing I become totally crazed, go into a trance, and will go a month without leaving a room" (Hoyt 324). Her boss said, "She is a woman with astonishing energy. She was ten times faster than anyone I know" (Bane & Benet pg. 33).

Bipolar writer and research psychologist Kay Jamison says, "High energy levels and boldness are clearly essential to virtually all creative endeavors. Mild mania is the best state for creativity because it increases both the quantity of completed work and its quality." Jamison found, "In periods of intense creative episodes virtually all creative writers and artists (89%) experience intense, highly productive, and creative episodes" (Jamison 1993 pg. 105).

BALZAC – TYPE A PERSONALITY. The Type A personality is defined by DSM-IV as "A temperament characterized by excessive drive, competitiveness, a sense of time urgency, impatience, unrealistic ambition, and a need for control." This defines Balzac as well as the majority of the writers in this work. In *Paradoxes of Creativity* (1989) Jacques Barzun wrote, "Mad passion and passionate madness is the reason why psychopathic personalities are often creators and why their productions are perfectly sane."

Speed, impatience, and intolerance are the qualities of the Type A. They fear not being loved and misinterpret self-worth with achievement. Balzac felt he would never gain his mother's love if he was not a genius and it pushed him to the limits. He confused work with affection, as do most Type A's and such people often alienate their loved one's because they are always preoccupied with their work and are seldom available.

Like all Type A's, Balzac had a very short attention span, was bombastic, finished people's sentences, scheduled more than was humanly possible to finish, and flagellated himself for not being diligent. He was always early and was impossible to please.   On beginning *The Human Comedy* at age thirty he planned an epic that would take a lifetime to complete.   One night while ill he wrote 15,000 words explaining, "demons drive me."   When he finally proposed marriage when nearing fifty he didn't buy one wedding ring, he bought three.

ADD & DRUGGING.   Had Balzac, Goethe, or Lord Byron lived today they would have been drugged with Ritalin for being afflicted with Attention Deficit Disorder.   So would have Mark Twain, Walt Disney, Einstein, Sylvia Plath, Dostoevsky, Hemingway, and Ian Fleming.   All were disruptive in school due to hyperactivity.   All would have been diagnosed with ADHD or ADD.   The drugs would have slowed them down to a more normal nature, but the truth is their success was highly tied to their hyperactivity.   In retrospect, had our Type A forefathers been on Ritalin, America would not have been developed, Cubism and Relativity might never have happened, and Mickey Mouse and the Geodesic Dome may not have been.

Conformity is desirous for the development of an orderly system, however great creativity is antithetic to order.   The creative child has a disdain for useless conformity.   It is the reason Edison, Einstein, Frank Lloyd Wright, Walt Disney and Bucky Fuller all dropped out of school.   Had these eminent writers been conformists they would not be in this work.   To conform is to chase mediocrity.   Is that the objective of education?   I think not.   Forcing students to conform is placing them in a box where mediocrity reigns supreme and drugging them achieves the same result.

MANIA & SPEED.   Balzac went through life in triple-time.   The speed allowed him to create prodigiously, and it also led to premature death.   By age fifty he had burned himself out.   He had lived life in a perpetual hurry.   His vitality was his strength and also led to his demise.   Balzac didn't publish the first edition of his monumental work *The Human* Comedy until age thirty.   By fifty he had completed 92 novels, numerous short stories, six plays, plus fifty novels left in draft form.   Few writers can even conceive the plots for such a massive output, let alone create them in an era before typewriters or PC's.

Balzac was a study in passion at the service of literature. His hyperactive life would have been amusing had it not been so tragic. He sensed what he was doing to himself. He wrote, "the days melt in my hands like ice in the sun. I'm not living. I'm wearing myself out." (Robb p. 25). Such comments came after being chained to his desk for days with only catnaps to reenergize him and numerous cups of coffee to sustain him. He once produced 15,000 words while seriously ill and was incapable of relaxing. His was a kind of death-wish fanaticism.

Passion was pervasive in Balzac's world. His energy was legend. When he entered a room it exploded with his presence. When he laughed the walls literally shook from his energy. Women were attracted to such verve despite his ungainly size. When he began speaking people stopped to listen. Such energy is both overwhelming and disarming. People loved him or hated him and no one came away neutral. His personality bordered on the psychopathic.

Writers like athletes often outrun their mistakes. Agatha Christie and Michener are examples. Balzac believed he had to keep on producing more and more or he would die. Coffee sustained such drive, but it also became addictive. The caffeine altered his personality while transforming him into a prodigious wordsmith. He was able to outwork others but the need for more and more led him to hashish. Then he turned to alcohol to bring him back down. This became a never-ending battle of ups and downs that took its toll on him. By forty he had another emotional relapse.

BI-POLAR PRODUCTIVITY. Only two writers in this book did not have the symptoms of hypomania – Joseph Campbell and Bernard Shaw. All experience volatile emotional swings. When up they were euphoric and capable of conquering new worlds. When down they were debilitated. Virginia Woolf's husband Leonard said his wife would go into "rages" when writing and sleep but four hours each night: (Hodges 1992 pg. 254)

Virginia would write it, and rewrite it again and again from end to end five or six times... Out of the sixteen working hours she worked fifteen and I guess that she dreamed about it most of the time when asleep. Her behavior is the inspiration of true genius and madness.

Fleming's biographer Lycett said, "Ian had a chronic inability to stay still." Sylvia Plath's husband, poet Ted Hughes, wrote to a friend saying, "Sylvia sits and writes for twelve hours at a stretch and gets too excited to sleep" (Stevenson 1989 p. 124). Danielle Steel was hyper at writing and romance. A boyfriend she befriended in prison told a biographer, "I once received seventeen letters in one day from Danielle" (Hoyt 1994 p. 324). Steel once wrote a novel in nine days while caring for a brood of seven kids. The Romance Queen averaged two novels a year as did Christie and King. She slept but two or three hours a night and admitted, "While working on a book I pretty much work around the clock. Every 20 to 22 hours I take a two or three hour sleeping break then I go back at it" (Hoyt 326).

HISTORY OF MANIA & OVERACHIEVING. It isn't just creative writers who use speed to succeed. Leonardo Da Vinci wrote, "No labor is capable of tiring me." Darwin's motto was "Its doggedness that does it." Both Catherine the Great and Napoleon were famous, or infamous, for dictating to three or four secretaries simultaneously on different subjects without missing a beat. Napoleon once destroyed four horses in a mad dash across Europe. His valet said, "I never comprehended how his body could endure such fatigue. I have never seen a man with so much personal activity" (Landrum 1996 p. 129). Hitler's mania was legend. Dr. Hermann Rauschning, president of the Danzig Parliament said, "He neither tires or hungers; he lives with morbid energy that enables him to do almost miraculous things". Like Balzac, Mao Zedung stopped bathing since he felt it was a waste of time and relaxed him too much.

SOCIAL COMMENTARY GENRE

Social commentary is writing about the plight of man struggling to survive in a dynamic social world. The style originated with the Greeks with Socrates aphorism, "Know thyself." Plato continued the method with his *Dialogues,* followed by Chaucer's *Canterbury Tales.* The genre stalled after Chaucer. With the Renaissance came Cervantes who produced *Don Quixote* (1615) as a commentary on chivalry in Spanish life. Henry Fielding's *Joseph Andrews* (1742) and *Tom Jones* (1749) then spoke of the trials, tribulations, and moral implications of the 18th century. Jane Austen contributed to the genre with *Sense and Sensibility* (1811) followed by Balzac who was influenced by Voltaire, Dante, Rabelais, Cervantes, Rousseau. Balzac became a self-proclaimed scriptwriter of the age saying, "French Society was to be the historian, I was only its secretary" (Robb p. 1994).

Writers most influenced by Balzac were Tolstoy, Dumas, Hugo, Sand, Oscar Wilde, Dostoevsky and Hemingway. But his greatest influence would ironically be on Marx and Engels in *Das Kapital.* Strange that a wild entrepreneur like Balzac who worshipped at the altar of free enterprise would become the role model for the Bible of Communism. Engels wrote, "I've learned more from Balzac than all the professional historians, economists, and statisticians put together." Balzac's work also proved inspirational for Oscar Wilde's *Dorian Gray.* Rodin saw Balzac as a real-world Prometheus and sculpted him for posterity in the role. James Joyce gave credit to Balzac for his style in *Ulysses* where he attempted to "convey a passionate tone to the pathos and anguish of Dubliners."

BALZAC - A DRIVEN GENIUS

Balzac said, "I was intoxicated with the desire for fame. Genius is the only alternative to death" (Robb pg. 34) and proceeded to dedicate his life to the task of achieving glory. The price? He led a miserable personal existence and shortened his life. Excess dominated every aspect of his tormented soul. He once wrote 50,000 words in ten days. Virtually every day was dedicated to 18-hours of intense writing. He feared that if he slowed down he would miss his self-imposed deadline of documenting every aspect of French Society in 100 volumes.

Was Balzac aware of his mania? Of course he was, but he was incapable of changing. The result was the 100-volume epic *The*

Human Comedy. He was impatient and impulsive and these traits helped and hurt him. He wrote, "I am incapable of waiting. It is an incorrigible fault in my nature" (Robb pg. 379). **ENTREPRENEURIAL MADMAN.** Balzac's heroes were always mimicking his own nefarious schemes. He had his protagonists overcoming the chaos and strife in their life to live happily ever after. Balzac was never so lucky. His gambling and wild investments caused him continual pain and many bankruptcies. He was a gambling fool who saw great riches resulting in his crazy ventures. When unable to get published he bought a printing company. And when it failed he threw good money after bad and kept leveraging his losses until they strangled him. He often considered fleeing the country to get away from his mounting creditors. But Balzac rationalized his losses by writing in his journal, "No education is complete without suffering" (Robb pg. 25.) In another moment of introspection he wrote, "Debt is a countess who is a little too fond of me" (Robb p. 128).

HISTORICAL MANIA & CREATIVITY. History is full of manic people who parlayed a modicum of talent into huge success. How? They turned to intensity and verve to overcome their adversaries including those within. Such people are afflicted with a kind of "rushing sickness." Pete Rose of baseball fame is such an individual. Rose was cut from his high school baseball team and was blessed with very mediocre talent but went on to break Ty Cobb's all-time hit record in the major leagues. How did someone with little talent become the most prolific hitter in all of baseball? His nickname tells it all - "Charlie Hustle."

Work made made Margaret Thatcher. She admitted she had no more than four hours of sleep a night for thirty years. Nikola Tesla, the father of alternating current slept but two hours a night. Edison refused to leave his lab and had food shoved through the door. A *Fortune* executive Mitch Davenport described the hyper-active lifestyle of Buckminster Fuller as "bubbling like a fountain. He had so many ideas he never ran dry. Never!" (Hatch 1974 p. 150). Fuller was convinced that speed was critical to all success and coined a word for it - *Ephemeralization* or "The acceleration of doing more with less" (Hatch p. 237). Fuller concocted a sleep system that allowed him but 30 minute naps around six hours of work that he managed to maintain around the clock. He did this well into his seventies and was thus able to outwork much younger men. Psychologist Kay Jamison in *Touched with Fire* (1993) researched the benefits of bipolar illness for creative writers and found, "The mind of Lord Byron was like a volcano. It ran swift as lightning from one subject to another, and occasionally burst forth in passionate throes of intellect, nearly allied to madness." (p. 105). She spoke of Virginia Woolf's hyperactive verbosity, "Virginia talked almost without stopping for two or three days, paying no attention to anyone in the room or anything said to her" (pg. 29).

LITERARY INNOVATIONS – THE MODERN NOVEL

Balzac altered the novel to such an extent he has come to be known as the father of the modern novel. He had an unusual insight into the machinations of French society and documented it with passion. He "made the reader think." Balzac was the first author on the European continent to serialize his novels in newspapers. He used the serialization as a marketing tool to create a demand for the book prior to its release. It also provided excellent feedback on scenes and controversial topics that allowed him to alter the final manuscript before printing. Periodicals demand succinct dialogue. Balzac learned to write better and more succinctly by writing for the newspapers. The experience made him more to the point with fast-paced and informative dialogue.

Balzac was a shameless self-promoter. He finally concluded that writing a good book was second to being able to promote it. He said, "There is no point in knowing how to write if you don't know how to talk, and talk at great length, talk volumes, in order to attract a buyer" (Robb pg.108). One of his major contributions was in making bureaucracy and business the subject of serious literature. He considered himself more philosopher than author and in that sense was able to document for posterity the psyche of 19th century French Society for both the masses and classes.

NOVEL AS INSPIRATION. Novels were only read by women in France prior to Balzac. In that era – 19th century women were housebound and after their children were raised had time to read. While their husbands were out and about cavorting with their mistresses the women lost themselves in the fantasy of novels. It was their escape and Balzac filled that void better than any marketing person in history. He did so by altering the nature of the novel and aiming it directly at the target market. But to sate his own intellectual needs he made them into a statement on the nature of the social mores of French society. In so doing he successfully tapped into the sensibilities of his audience and attracted legions of faithful female fans that could not wait for his next new volume in much the same way Steel and King do today.

Balzac was a wonderful storyteller. He mastered the nuances of human nature, lonely women, and the more banal sides of life. He often walked alone on the streets of Paris in the middle of the night consorting with nefarious low life's to discover their motivations and needs. He was inquisitive to a fault and dallied with princesses and prostitutes, aristocrats and trollops, the erudite and the unwashed, making little distinction between social breeding and friendship. This gave him a prescient insight into the machinations of life on the street as well as in the drawing room. This proved to be an invaluable advantage for document 19th century society. He had a penchant for drawing out the philosophical and historical nuances of all classes and wrote in the dialect of the common man. This endeared him to his target audience like few other writers. His use of phrases like "a woman is a well-served table" was a hit with the cultured set. His long-term lover Madame de Berny became the prototype for the older, lonely, married woman and he immortalized her in many of his books.

WRITING AS CATHARSIS

Social commentary came naturally to Balzac because he had an unconscious need to get even with a mother who had deserted him. He felt abandoned and wanted to understand that in the larger sense. His autobiographical *Lys dans la Vallee* was dedicated to that early period in his life that he never forgot. "I was an object of such indifference that the governess often forgot to put me to bed" (Robb pg. 9). The early rejection left a mark and molded a bitter and solitary boy who escaped into books. And he would spend the rest of his life attempting to write out his mother's mistreatment. His books are rampant with statements like, "I never had a mother."

Like most successful authors Balzac observant and imaginative. He saw what was happening in his world and used creative expression to place it in context for the world to enjoy. Balzac was preoccupied with fame, fortune, and sex. His pursuit of fortune kept him one step ahead of his creditors and his work bears the imprint of his sexual and entrepreneurial drives. He wrote incessantly about his poor investments saying, "I am more a great financier than a great writer, for I have settled my accounts with my pen" (Robb p. 117).

His classic work *La Peau de Chagrin (1831)* was autobiographical. It documented his excess and abstinence. He yearned for sex but feared it would drain him of creative output. Biographer Robb said, "He was obsessed with sex. Sperm for him was an emission of pure cerebral substance, filtering through the penis a work of art" (Robb p. 179). Fear of being robbed of creative juices by female intrusion into his life is defined with a comment he made to his literary friend Alexander Dumas after a liaison, " I lost a book this morning. No woman alive is worth two volumes a year" (Robb p. 179).

METAMORPHOSES

Balzac went through a transformation from a wannabe writer into a world- renowned novelist when his first attempt at writing, *Cromwell* was ridiculed when released in 1819. He could easily have returned to law and left the world of letters behind. But the failure only increased his determination to succeed as a writer. He recognized his weaknesses and concentrated on his strengths and went where he felt comfortable, novels with a moral.

But in order to make some money to finance his passion he became a publisher. Once again he was a miserable failure and lost everything. But Balzac was intransigent. He then acquired a printing company to help pay off his publishing debts that had grown to 70,000 francs. By 1829 that number had doubled and led him to pursue even wilder schemes to gain solvency. He considered leaving France to stay out of debtor's prison. Ironically, his mother loaned him money and he stayed and began writing for the masses, not his first choice, but as a way of eating. He wrote furiously and used the money to pay off his creditors but the money just paid the interest leaving him with 150,000 francs of debt. History has labeled him an "obsessive gambler." Irrational risk-taker would have been more accurate. But financial crises transformed him from inept philosopher to prolific novelist who may never have achieved such success had he not been such a miserable failure.

CRISES – THE MOTHER OF CREATIVITY. Balzac began life in trauma and it followed him to his death. He was never able to get over the early rejection of his parents. He wrote, "I never had a mother. My mother hated me. Marat was an angel compared to her" (Robb p. 40). His revenge was sweet in his autobiographical work *La Peaud de Chagrin* when the protagonist hero Raphael de Valentin pays off his debts by selling the island Loire on which his mother is buried. As an adult he wrote a cynical letter to her saying, "Had you loved me as you loved Henry," his flaky and totally inept illegitimate brother, "I should probably have ended up where he is and in that sense you have been a good mother to me" (Robb pg. 30).

Biographer Robb implies that most of Balzac's 2000 characters and countless female lovers resulted from the "inner-emptiness" resulting from his traumatic early life. Balzac flirted with suicide from his teens until his premature death. He was lonely and despondent. His first suicide attempt took place during the birth of his illegitimate half-brother Henry. At age 25 he wrote, "I'm watching the Seine and thinking about crawling under its humid sheets" (Robb p. 121). He liked to refer to suicide as "an old mistress" that for him was a series of five-year cycles that tormented him to the point of visiting that mistress.

AN EPIPHANY. Failure dominated Balzac's life. He failed as a philosopher, publisher, printer, investor, entrepreneur, and newspaper journalist. At age 33 he was at a crossroads in his writing when he had a bad fall and struck his head on a rock. He fell unconscious and for many months lingered in a schizoid state during which he concocted the theory "mythomania." He escaped into a surreal world where his imagination ran amuck and he came up with the idea to document all of French society in a monumental work consisting of 100 books. He came to see his life-threatening fall as providential. Always superstitious, he wrote, "The artist is not privy to his own intellect. He operates under the influence of certain circumstances whose precise combination is a mystery" (Robb p. 195). *The Human Comedy* then took form and his transformation turned him from an ambitious writer into a master. Biographer Robb described his uncannily accurate premonitions materializing better than he could ever have imagined.

ECCENTRICITIES

Balzac was a maverick and highly eccentric. His approach to life was weird at best and eerie at worst. Conventional and normal were words never used to describe his life or work. He saw the world through a different filter and was at various times a psychic, mystic, and visionary. A passion for excellence defined him and drove him. His need to excel led him to extravagance beyond any normal definition. His motto was "dissipation is a way of life."

Balzac roamed the streets of Paris while the city slept. He normally wrote all night but when stuck he go out and live with the nocturnal world that in Paris could be stranger than fiction. He mingled with the denizens of the night, street people, pimps, and prostitutes. One reason for Balzac's nocturnal lifestyle was the debtor's law. French law restricted arrests for debts between sunset and sunrise and made him into a vampire-like Prometheus who hide during day and roam at night. The street people found themselves in his characterizations and stories.

Further testimony to his weird lifestyle was his work ethic. Each night he had a huge dinner and took a nap before starting to write at 1:00 a.m. He wrote non-stop through the night until 8:00 a.m. This ritual went on for seven days a week. This made him unbelievably productive but exacerbated his emotional problems leading to many breakdowns.

Balzac was manic-depressive, a Type A, obsessive, compulsive, and Machiavellian. He walked that thin line between normality and abnormality. In one introspective moment he wrote, "A lunatic is a man who sees an abyss and falls into it" (Robb pg. 211). He was implying that he was not a lunatic only because he had not fallen in. Balzac prided himself on having the strength and vision to avoid the abysses of life. Another of his unique qualities was an unrealistic self-confidence and optimism that bordered on arrogance. When on the verge of economic disaster and bankruptcy he would buy another company thinking it would save him, but only pushed him further into debt.

Balzac was compulsive to a fault, pursuing each idea to the point of physical and mental breakdown. An example occurred in his twenties when he was compelled to read every entry in Michaud's Biographical Dictionary. He also believed in self-hypnosis saying, "Whenever I like, I draw a veil over my eyes. Suddenly I go back into myself and there I find a dark room in which all the accidents of nature reproduce themselves in a form far purer than they first appeared to my outer senses" (Robb p.16). Bigger debts called for bigger solutions and when facing debtor's prison he wrote a friend saying, "I shall perhaps abandon literature in order to make my fortune. My soul is thirsting for immensity, for the infinite, for nature *en masse*" (Robb p. 300).

POLYPHASIC

Balzac kept more balls in the air than a magician. He was at various times in his life a lawyer, publisher, printer, journalist, novelist, poet, entrepreneur, inventor, con man, interior decorator, philosopher, essayist and playwright. He was many of these at the same time. Balzac had such a fertile mind he would be bombarded with ideas and couldn't decide which to pursue and killed off as many as he used. He wrote his mistress and wife to be Mme Hanka in 1838, "I often finish off a cottage by the light of one of my houses (books) as it burns to the ground" (Robb p. 198).

CRITICAL ACCLAIM

Henry James called Balzac a "towering idol" a man from whom "I have "learned more of the lessons of the engaging mystery of fiction than from anyone else." Oscar Wilde said, "Balzac created life, he didn't copy it." Engels worshipped Balzac. Balzac's French writer comrade Victor Hugo gave the eulogy at his funeral saying, "The author of this enormous, extraordinary work (*The Human Comedy*) belongs to the powerful race of revolutionary writers" (Robb pg. 412). Auguste Rodin immortalized him as Prometheus a sculpture that has become famous in its own right.

Historian Daniel Boorstin characterized Balzac as the writer who documented French society, not of the peasants or workers as Hugo or Rousseau, but the business people, authors, journalists, artists, charlatans, speculators, landowners and women. He wrote, "Balzac's Human Comedy was a grand mosaic of his epoch" (Boorstin pg. 361). *World Literature Criticism* says, "His influence on the development of the novel in France is unsurpassed. He is now considered one of the world's greatest novelists" (1992 pg. 178).

HYPER SUCCESS – What Can We Learn?

Impatience, impulsiveness, and mania are important to achieving. They are also guaranteed to make life in the fast lane less than tranquil. The manic get more done but leave more bodies in their wake. Many of the bodies are family and friends. That happened to Balzac. Mania was his greatest strength, but it also killed him.

Megalomania was central to his work and his success. His need to win at all cost was fueled by his hyperactivity. It also contributed to his insights. In writing *The Human Comedy* his first idea was to depict tragedy in a comedic way, but he ended up depicting life as a tragic comedy. The work was a kind of "mythomania" with himself as protagonist and master. He

257

spoke of himself as the walking Prometheus and biographers have called him the "megalomaniac philosopher."

Balzac's work was created between 1830 and 1850 when he produced the epochal *La Comedie Humaine* – a collection of 100 works. It was banal and a comedy of the absurd. His most noteworthy works in this majestic undertaking were *La Peau de Chagrin* (1831), *Eugenie Grandet* (1833), *La Recherche de l'absolu* (1834), *Le Pere Goriot* (1834), *Le Cure de Village* (1839), and *La Cousine Bette* (1846). All were rife with duchesses, students, usurers, clerks, gangsters and lawyers interacting to describe the essence of mankind during 19th century France.

The enormity of Balzac's work was only possible due to his mania. He wrote more in 24 hours than most writers could write in a week. His Type A behavior caused him to send off manuscripts to the printer prior to their completion. Closure was important to him and contributed to his mania. It made for reliable deadlines, but at the expense of well-thought out and reflective work. Before a work was near complete a need to move on took over and he was off conquering new worlds. He was a perfectionist but with a penchant for the dynamic life that he relegated his need to produce to one to change.

Balzac's protagonists were but thinly veiled reincarnations of his own unique vitality. Biographer Stefan Zweig (1946) called him "the most picturesque, the most absurd, and in many ways the most tragic figure of nineteenth-century France." In most ways his life was a paradox. Here was a man trained as a lawyer who spent much of his life violating the law. He honored convention but was radically unconventional. He wrote incessantly of romance but disdained it. Balzac knew women better than any other writer of his era, understood their passions and motivations, but refused to allow them to be part of his life. He was the ultimate paradox.

Balzac was a hero-worshipper. He wrote constantly of his childhood hero Napoleon and once said, "What Napoleon did not achieve by the sword I shall achieve by the pen" (Robb pg. 142). He modeled his life after the Little General. Both were manic beyond description and were incapable of controlling their passions. And both men paid a dear price for their need for power, fame, and fortune.

Are you willing to sacrifice health and family for fame and fortune? That is the question that must be asked and answered. Not everyone is willing to pay such a high price. Balzac was and he has been vindicated by posterity who has knighted him as the father of the modern novel.

ERNEST MILLER HEMINGWAY
NARRATION & SHORT STORIES
b. Chicago, IL, July 21, 1899
d. Ketchum, ID July 2, 1961

SUCCESS & PSYCHOSEXUAL ENERGY

DOMINANT GENRE
Short stories with a heroic & psychosexual pathos

MOTTO
"What is moral is what you feel good after; what is immoral is what you feel bad after;" "Everything kills everything else in some way."

GREATEST WORKS
The Sun Also Rises (1926)
A Farewell to Arms (1929)
The Old Man & the Sea (1952)
The Snows of Kiliminjaro (1937)
The Short Happy Life of Francis Macomber (1937)

HONORS/AWARDS
Nobel Prize for Literature 1954 – *Old Man & the Sea*

ECCENTRICITIES
Manic-depressive alcoholic and womanizer whom Fitzgerald said needed a new woman for every new book

LIFE CRISES
WWI leg wound 237 pieces of shrapnel, two near fatal airplane crashes and father's suicide contributed to his live-on-the-edge lifestyle

METAMORPHOSES
War wounds armed him with material to pursue heroic stories

13

ERNEST HEMINGWAY – SHORT STORY

Passion & Success

"A man can be destroyed, but not defeated"

Hemingway was a vibrant, hard-drinking, womanizing, and macho male, the same as we find in his novels. His short stories are a study in death, heroism, and psychosexual drive played out between strong and weak men and their women. The most noteworthy was *The Short Happy Life of Francis Macomber*. When Papa could no longer partake in life's pleasures, he ended it all in a dramatic suicide, so often the path taken by bipolar personalities.

After age 55 Hemingway could no longer write, make love, or drink. That was too much for him to take and he ended it all rather than live a life without passion. He had enormous vitality and a limitless libidinal drive, but when Castro confiscated his home, boat, and many unpublished manuscripts in Havana he was emotionally and physically devastated. He walked into his study in Ketchum, Idaho. stuck a shotgun in his mouth, and squeezed the trigger in the likeness of one of his protagonists.

PSYCHOSEXUAL ENERGY & CREATIVE GENIUS

Passion, libidinal drive, or what Freud described as "psychic energy," is often the driving force behind creative output whether it is writing a sonnet, singing a song, starting a business, painting a picture or writing a novel. Passionate people are more vital and use their inner drives to rise above the pack. Passion is not just emotional energy it is a force emanating from within.

ERNEST HEMINGWAY

Is drive for success manifested as libidinal energy? No! But an inordinate libidinal drive is tied to super success. Some people sublimate their passions into work, others like Hemingway use it to drive them, but still chase romance with unabated resolve. As Freud discovered in his analysis of Leonardo da Vinci and Dostoevsky, many people sublimate inner drive into work energy. He admonished us saying, "What is repressed in sexual life will reappear – in distorted form – in daily life." That was the case in Balzac and George Bernard Shaw but not in Hemingway, Camus or Fleming, all womanizers.

Few make it to the very top without passion. Hemingway's life and work are an example of this prescient principle. Passion pervaded every facet of his life. Without his passion for living, loving, and working he would have been a journeyman writer. Those vital people with supercharged energy rise far beyond their genetic predisposition or talent. They become masters of their destiny. It is what elevated a Madonna, by all accounts an average dancer, singer and incompetent actress, to the pinnacle of her profession. How does someone with mediocre ability have $200 million in the bank? Passion is the differentiating element and it can be seen in the world's success stories.

PASSION & PERFORMANCE. Passionate people are better communicators in both words and actions. This can be seen in the frenetic lives and work of Balzac, Dostoevsky, Woolf, Plath and Steel. And their vital characterizations are little else than fantasies of themselves. They imbued their characters with a force and vitality that wouldn't have been possible had they led more ascetic lives. Energy and vitality made their characters jump off the page. Their emotionally charged stories had far less to do with syntax than their own psychic energy. It wasn't an accident that Picasso's mistresses described him as possessing "an inexhaustible passion for work and sex" (Landrum pg. 181). Hemingway had a similar propensity and consequently neither made idyllic mates.

Hemingway lived life on the edge with a penchant for drinking, fighting, females, fishing, hunting, skiing, and writing. While living in Paris he told Thornton Wilder of his hyper-sexuality. Hemingway told Wilder "my sex drive was so strong I had to make love three times a day" (Irving Wallace 1993 pg. 209). Wallace describes Hemingway's raging libido as responsible for his many marriages, mistresses extra-marital liaisons with "Mata Hari, Italian countesses, and Greek princesses."

SUBLIMATED ENERGY. Passion often results in emissions of the pen as has been found in many of these hyper-sexual writers. They have an inner drive or passion that permeates their life and works. Shaw recognized his urges and wrote a book titled *The Philanderer* despite still being a virgin. Twain wrote of a life as a lecher even though one biographer Kaplan (1966) said he was a virgin when married at age 34. Dr. Seuss was a thorough ascetic who released his libidinal energies into his art and words. An example of his inner urges are found in a book that never was published titled *Lady Godiva*.

NEW MATE FOR EACH NEW BOOK. F. Scott Fitzgerald, friend and Lost Generation compatriot, accused Hemingway of "needing a new woman for each big book." Fitzgerald's insight proved to be 20-20. At twenty-two, Hemingway married Elizabeth Hadley, a woman eight years older who nurtured him through his first publication of short stories *In Our Time* (1926) and *The Sun Also Rises* (1926). In this book he labeled himself and cohorts the "Lost Generation" - a group of World War I expatriates living the good life in Paris. One of Hadley's friends, an attractive journalist Pauline Pfeiffer moved in with them and seduced Hemingway. A guilt-driven Hemingway attempted to have the affair take the form of a *menage a trois* relationship. Hadley refused leaving Hemingway the opening to marry his illicit lover. The marriage spawned *A Farewell to Arms* (1929) about a romantic liaison that took place in post WW-I in Paris. Pauline bore Hemingway two sons by caesarian section but as a dedicated Roman Catholic refused to use birth-control methods thereby destroying their relationship.

The couple relocated to Key West and Hemingway began to write the short stories that would become classics. He also embarked on a wild life of fishing and fornicating. His marriage to Pauline lasted twelve years but in reality it was short-lived as he took up with a married beauty named Jane Mason in Key West. Mason was the wife of the head of Pan Am and would be the other woman in many of his short stories. But when a new big book was on the horizon another woman replaced Mason. The third Mrs. Hemingway was journalist Martha Gelhorn, a woman he met in his hangout Sloppy Joe's Bar. The couple relocated to Havana, Cuba, but soon ran off to Spain to cover the Spanish Civil War. This spawned *For Whom the Bell Tolls* (1940). He met and married fourth wife Mary Welsh while in London as a war correspondent for World War II. Mary was the most understanding of his long-suffering wives. She was the catalyst for his masterpiece *The Old Man and the Sea* (1952).

PASSION - CATALYST FOR CREATIVITY

Is high libidinal energy tied to successful writing? No! But individuals with high passion are more driven, more productive, and far more creative than their ascetic counterparts. Such drive finds its way into their work. Fear reigns supreme in most people's lives and it tends to mitigate the free spirit lurking within the raging libido. Biographer Lynn (1987) characterized Hemingway as a man capable of "seducing with words." Charisma and passion are first cousins in the world of creativity and these individuals were all charmers and seductive. Napoleon Hill (1960) wrote, "highly sexed men are the most efficient salesmen and personal magnetism is nothing more nor less than sexual energy."

**THE BIG `T' PERSONALITY.** Sexual prowess is inextricably tied to testosterone and libidinal drive. Frank Farley, past president of the American Psychological Association coined the term Big `T' in reference to high testosterone and high thrill-seeking personalities. According to Farley, Big T's have an inordinately high sex drive, creativity, competitiveness, and risk-taking. He said, "The Big T personality is high in stimulation-seeking and contributes to creative and destructive aspects of society" (Psychology Today 5-86). They are more prone to having frequent sexual encounters and are more creative. Farley wrote (Farley 1986 pg. 46):

> *Big T's, as a group tend to be more creative, and more extroverted, take more risks, have more experimental artistic preferences and*

prefer more variety in their sex lives than do little t's. Their tendency to seek the novel, unknown and uncertain, combined with their risk-taking characteristic further enhances their likelihood of being creative.

Hemingway fits Farley's profile. He had a penchant for romance, aggression, risk-taking, and creative expression. He flaunted his affairs to the distraction of his long-suffering wives. Psychic energy led him to live a life as ski bum, run with the bulls in Pamplona, shoot wild game in the jungles, engage in bar fights, and sail the open sea. He imbued his protagonists with many of these same qualities that would one day be known as the Hemingway *pathos*.

SEX & POWER OF THE PEN. Many writers have raging libidos and use it to draw passionate word pictures. The females in this work tended to romantic forays, the men to seductions. Both were compulsive once turned on. They were also far more prone to admit to their inner urges than the men. Anne Rice wrote, "I am obsessed with horror and the erotic." She told biographer Ramsland, "There is sexuality in art" (Ramsland pg. 212). Sexuality, incest, bisexuality, and passionate affairs pervaded the writing of Virginia Woolf. Danielle Steel's whole life was one long liaison with many lovers and five husbands.

PAPA'S LUST. Hemingway lived a life of wild seductions that brings to mind the actions of lustful Presidents JFK and Bill Clinton. His dangerous liaisons were more important than the seductions. It was as if he was titillated by the danger more than the conquest. There is little question his ego entered the equation as it did Kennedy's and Clinton's. In Papa's case he paid the price for his lecherous nature since none of his wives trusted him. They had met him while he was with another and always suspected the same may happen to them.

Another example of Hemingway's self-destructive lust was his wild fling with the blonde Jane Mason. When they met he took her home to meet Pauline, not the typical move of a rational man. He would immortalize her as Margo in *The Short Happy*

Life of Francis Macomber (1937) and Helene Bradley in *To Have and Have Not*. The affair lasted four years.

The protagonist in *Macomber* was Mason's cuckolded husband Francis who he depicted as a pussy-whipped loser until he killed a buffalo and lost all fear, a classic Hemingway ploy. Hemingway used Mason as the beautiful but unfaithful wife of Francis. Later he would portray his lover as a "rich bitch" in *Art of the Short Story* (1959). He wrote, "Margot Macomber had been invented complete with handles from the worst bitch (Mason) I knew, and when I first knew her she'd been lovely" (Mellow pg. 446). Hemingway's affair with Mason almost ended in tragedy when she was driven to despair by his domination and attempted suicide by jumping from a window. She survived with a broken back but it put an end to their relationship and opened the door for his next marriage.

Why did Hemingway lust after women and then leave them? Because he was more interested in the chase than the catch. The fun ended with the conquest. It frightened him since he had no idea of how to be a husband or father. His son Gregory offered insight into his dad's involvement with Mason. Gregory wrote, "He would feel himself beginning to stagnate after he had been married awhile in the 1930's; he used to cuckold mother unmercifully in Havana" (Gregory Hemingway 1976 pg. 126).

When Pauline could no longer stand his philandering she left for the West Coast. Martha Gelborn then entered his life as wife number three. She was a brilliant journalist on assignment in Key West. She was different than the typical Hemingway woman. She was independent and an indomitable spirit who refused to tolerate Hemingway's womanizing. The 1940 marriage was short lived and ended when Gelhorn accepted an assignment in Spain. Hemingway was furious to be left by a woman and followed her to Spain. But when they returned the marriage was over. Hemingway met wife number four in London during World War II. Mary Welsh was a journalist but a very submissive. The two were married in 1946 and made their home in Sun Valley and Havana.

HISTORY OF THE SHORT STORY

Hemingway was one of America's great storytellers. He was influenced by Twain, Dostoevsky, Dickens, Kipling, and Sherwood Anderson. He wrote, "I thought Kipling was the best short story writer that ever lived." Twain's *Huckleberry Finn* and Dostoevsky's *The Brothers Karamazov* were two favorites. He told his friend Gertrude Stein "No one lasted more than three rounds with Dostoevsky," and "All American literature comes from one book by Twain, *Huckleberry Finn*."

The short story is prose narrative. It can be read quickly and impart a message. It the oldest form of prose fiction originating with the Greeks. Edgar Allen Poe was the first to give it a name calling short stories "an artistic composition controlled to produce a single unified effect."

The first American to master the genre was Nathaniel Hawthorne. His *Young Goodman Brown* (1835) was followed by Poe's supernatural tale *The Fall of the House of Usher* (1839). By 1853 Herman Melville had advanced the art with *Bartieby the Scrivener*. This began a shift from the supernatural to the psychological with a moral encounter – the Hemingway method. James Joyce *Dubliners (1914)* and Sherwood Anderson *Winesburg, Ohio* (1919) influenced Hemingway. Russian writer Anton Chekhov is considered the father of the modern short story. He was trained as a medical doctor but like Hemingway had a writing obsession. He said, "Medicine is my lawful wife and literature is my mistress. When I get fed up with one I spend the night with the other."

LIBIDINAL DRIVE IN LITERATURE

Passion is the fuel that energizes. Oscar Wilde and Colette are two individuals who allowed passion to lead them to the top and to the bottom. Both led scandalous lives and paid the price for their actions. Wilde wrote, "The way to get rid of temptation is to yield to it." In a similar way Colette flaunted her bisexuality and scandalized the Moulin Rouge by appearing on stage nude with her lesbian lover. At the time she was married to a member of French society. The author of *Gigi* wrote, "So many women want to be corrupted and so few are chosen."

In a similar way Lord Byron allowed passion to dominate his life and work. Anne Rice has used fantasy mysticism to reach the bestseller lists. Her obsession with the erotic led her to say, "I'm a sensual person and obsessed with the erotic. I've had sexual fantasies since I was very little." In *Cry to Heaven* she allowed her inner passions to find expression in blatant scenes of oral sex that are little else but pornography. She wrote:

> **S&M to me means games between two consenting adults...I believe most people have some masochism in them. It's the fantasy of attention, of an eroticized authority figure – a balance between cruelty and tenderness – in which a woman could be sexually dominated by a man without fearing for her life" (Ramsland pg. 213).**

Balzac wrote, "My orgies take the form of books." Dostoevsky was passion incarnate. He went through life with a foot fetish. He wrote to second wife Anna Polina, "I go down on my knees before you and I kiss your feet a countless number of times. I imagine every minute and I enjoy it. I long to kiss every toe on your foot" (Wallace p 125). Albert Camus wrote ""sensuality alone ruled my life... artistic creation means to work minus sexuality" (Todd pg. 344). He was incorrigible and never understood why his wife tried to commit suicide over his blatant philandering. He wrote, "Sensuality alone ruled my life. For a ten minute love affair I would have renounced my parents" (Todd p. 344).

The creator of James Bond was a match for Hemingway in terms of libidinal drive and both men wrote classics in the Caribbean while fishing, fondling, and fighting. Fleming had strong sadomasochistic tendencies that were imbued into the character Bond. He wrote, "A writer must be in a state of lustful excitement when writing of love," and was faithful to his aphorism, "Bonds, Blondes, & Bombs" as a philosophy of life in the fast lane.

HISTORICAL EXAMPLES OF SEX & SUCCESS. Eminent psychotherapist writer Wilhelm Reich wrote, "Psychic health depends on orgiastic potency." Passion and performance are inextricably tied together. The lives of the famous offers testimony to high sex drive. The passionate are fun, vital, and eminently interesting even if they are dangerous. Cleopatra crawled nude out of a rug to seduce Julius Caesar. She bore his son so that she could become the Queen of Egypt. Seduction was but a tool to attain her goal as it has been for millenniums.

Catherine the Great was one of the most notorious nymphomaniacs in history. The Russian Empress spoke in her memoirs of "uterine frenzies." She spent the equivalent of $1.5 billion, in 1990 dollars, on paramours. Such excess puts the exploits of Kennedy and Clinton to shame. JFK was convinced he would not be able to sleep if he did not have a new woman every night. He told Presidential advisor Bob Baker, "You know I get a migraine if I don't get a strange piece of ass every day" (Hersh p. 389). Napoleon Hill researched eminent leaders and concluded, "Sex energy is the creative energy of all geniuses. There never has been and never will be a great leader, builder, or artist lacking in this driving force of sex" (Hill 1960).

MOTHER FIGURES. Older women played a key part in the lives of some of these men. Older married women were mistresses to Balzac, Shaw, Fleming and Hemingway. Balzac lost his virginity at 22 to a 45 year-old lover Madame Luare de Berny. Hemingway's Italian nurse Agnes Kurosky was nine years his senior and the heroine in his first novel. Hadley was eight years older.

Shaw was a virgin until twenty-nine when seduced by a friend of his mother's, a woman 15 years his senior. His long-term literary love was Ellen Terry a woman nine years older. Fleming's first mistress was a married woman 17 years older. Fleming seldom slept with woman his age until he was past thirty. Fleming was furious when his doting mother broke up an engagement to his first true love. He told friend Ralph Arnold, "I'm going to be quite bloody-minded about women from

now on.   I'm just going to take what I want without any
scruples at all" (Pearson pg. 44).

Balzac didn't marry until age fifty, Fleming was forty-three, and
Shaw forty.   Shaw and Fleming lived with their mothers until
almost thirty.   Dr. Seuss' first wife Helen was four years older
and functioned as a mother figure writing his checks and
treating him as a child.   One biographer wrote, "she shielded
him from the real world" (Morgan 1995).

HEMINGWAY'S LITERARY INNOVATIONS

Hemingway is most noted for narrative brevity.   Like most
creative geniuses, he simplified the complex.   He wrote,
"Simplicity is key.   Write the truest sentence you know."   He
once said, "I have no style.   I think in simple ways, that is my
style."   John O'Hara called him the greatest writer since
Shakespeare, due to his simple elegance.

Hemingway's brevity of narration peaked with his masterpiece
about an old man fighting for his life to land a big fish.   This
introspective insight into an aging writer struggling against the
vagaries of age tells much about him.   The fish is but a
metaphor and it is he struggling to cope with his aging body.   It
dealt with his personal search for new words, innovative ideas,
the need to mask his failing health and declining masculinity
with booze, younger women, and bigger risks.   Hemingway's
eternal struggle became his classic Nobel and Pulizer Prize
winning book *The Old Man and the Sea* (1952). The Nobel
Committee gave testimony to his mastery of narration saying,
"He achieved a powerful style-forming mastery of the art of
modern narration" (Sanderson pg. 4).

Journalism enhanced Hemingway's narrative brevity.   It taught
him to reduce a sentence to its least common denominator.   In
A Farewell to Arms (1929) Frederick Henry says "the world
breaks everyone and afterward many are strong at the broken
places."   In *The Old Man & the Sea* Santiago says, "Everything
kills everything else in some way."   His concise way with words
have been attributed to his penchant for perfection and many
rewrites. His son Gregory said he rewrote "The Old Man" over

200 times (Sanderson pg. 11). His three short story masterpieces - *The Short Happy Life of Francis Macomber* (1935), *Death in the Afternoon* (1937) and *The Snows of Kiliminjaro* (1936) were all written in Key West are classics in simplistic detail.

WRITING AS CATHARSIS

Hemingway was a hero-worshipper. Literary critics describe his work as "heroic pathos." Biographer Sanderson called his protagonists as "the Hemingway hero." The protagonist of the *Old Man & The Sea,* Santiago remains a hero even after the fish is lost. So were the heroes from his novels, Frederic Henry, Jake Barnes, Robert Jordan, Richard Cantwell.

Hemingway's fears are rampant in his work, especially the short stories. Preoccupation with death pervaded his work as did fear, tragedy, promiscuity, and vitality. Every character was on a mission whether immersed in bullfights, safaris, prizefights, catching fish, or hunting wild game. Self-destruction and conquest dominated *The Short Happy Life of Francis Macomber* (1935), *Death in the Afternoon* (1937), and *The Snows of Kiliminjaro* (1936). *The Fifth Column* (1938) bore the psychic scars of man's duplicity played out in Madrid.

The Hemingway hero always had to catch the biggest fish, bed the sexiest woman, and fight the toughest guy in the bar. All were disguised Papas. Biographer Sanderson wrote, "The Hemingway hero carries both the physical and psychic scars of him. His preoccupation with them is how to live with those scars" (Sanderson pg. 32). Hemingway's own innate fear of impotence is evident in Frederic Henry who is most like Hemingway of any protagonist.

The Hemingway hero always overcame huge obstacles. Man's courage and mettle were tested. He always found a place for women who tested the men's mettle. The *Old Man* is about man's endless struggle with life and the artist's eternal struggle with his art. It was a story of an aging man fighting to survive in a world passing him by. Hemingway was 50 and felt the loss of his virility and vitality. Death was lurking in the wings and he knew it. He was usually as self-destructive as most of his short stories. James Joyce said, "Hemingway was a big powerful peasant, as strong as a buffalo. A sportsman. And ready to live the life he writes about. He would never have written it if his body had not allowed him to live it" (Lynn 1987 pg. 161). And Hemingway knew it, which spawned *The Old Man*. He told F. Scott Fitzgerald in 1934:

> **"We are all bitched from the start and you especially have to be hurt like hell before you can write seriously. But when you get the damned hurt, use it – don't cheat with it. Be as faithful to it as a scientist." (Lynn pg. 10).**

METAMORPHOSES

Hemingway experienced an epiphany at 17. He had been rejected for military service for physical reasons but read Sir Robert Walpole's novel of a man rejected by the military, who then enlisted in the ambulance corps in Europe. *The Dark Forest* proved inspirational for Hemingway who then enlisted for ambulance service in a Red Cross unit. He was assigned to ambulance duty in Northern Italy and narrowly missed death. He was on a hero mission and was given the Medal of Honor after being hit by a mortar shell that deposited 237 pieces of shrapnel in his leg. After release from the hospital he returned to Chicago to regroup and write out his traumas.

PREOCCUPATION WITH DEATH. Back home in Chicago discovered he was emotionally distraught. He had trouble sleeping and retired to a remote cabin in Michigan to put his life in order. He began to write and was given a job as an itinerant journalist with the *Toronto Sun Star* assignment Paris. It was in Paris that he wrote his two masterpieces *The Sun Also Rises* (1926) and *A Farewell to Arms* (1929).

In a doctoral dissertation on creative personalities James Mathew Brodie (pgs. 142-147) describes Hemingway as "succeeding as a result of his traumas." Brodie describes Hemingway as a man with a "heroic self-image...and preoccupation with death." Biographer Sanderson validated the assessment with, "He wrote when there was something he knew (*personal experiences*), and not before (*after injuries*), and not too damned much after (*The Old Man*)" (Sanderson pg. 2).

ECCENTRICITIES

Hemingway overcompensated for his insecurities. He constantly had to prove his manhood. He seduced women, skied down dangerous Alpine slopes, hunted in darkest Africa, drank excessively, and fought at the slightest provocation. He had to be strong. Why? Much of his macho behavior emanated from his bipolar personality. Manic-depressives have super high energy, are Type A's, Machiavellian, often egoistic and very likely to be womanizers.

Hemingway had "boundless energy according to biographer Mellow. He slept little, usually less than five hours a night, exacerbating his depression with liquor. His son Patrick told A & E biography (Sept. 27, 1998) "father drank a quart of whiskey a day for the last twenty years of his life." He held court in a Havana bar, often bragging about an ability to consume sixteen double daiquiris and still walk out. Like most manic-depressives Hemingway was either way up or way down. As he aged he grew deeper and deeper into a state of depression until electro-shock was needed to bring him out of his self-deprecation. Alcohol contributed to his diabetes. After two plane crashes and too much booze and too many fights he was looking mortality in the mirror.

Hemingway had an insatiable need to be the best and to flaunt his valor. During World War II he infuriated military officials by using his influence to outfit his boat Pilar with a two-way radio, fifty caliber machine guns, hand grenades, and a bomb designed to throw down the conning tower of German submarines. Hemingway became a self-proclaimed anti-submarine agent until he got bored, and not enough press, and quit to get into the action in London. Adversaries claimed he used his influence as a ruse to get more than his share of gasoline for his fishing expeditions.

Brodie described Hemingway as brutal and masochistic. He spoke of Hemingway's brutality as a child when the six-year old savagely hacked to pieces a porcupine that he had locked in a woodshed" (UMI pg. 288). This Rankian analysis centered on Hemingway's obsession with death and machismo. Brodie said the bull in *Death in the Afternoon* (1932) "was a symbol of two fears within him; the fear of dying alone and a fear of women" (pg. 134). Hemingway wrote this short story just after his father had killed himself in Chicago. The story was written as a means of immortalizing his dad.

Psychologist Kay Jamison in *Touched With Fire* (1993 pg. 41) wrote, "two-thirds of those people who commit suicide have been found to suffer from depressive or manic-depressive illness." Hemingway was included as were Balzac, Twain, Woolf, and Plath. All had symptoms of rage, grandiosity, excessive enthusiasm, morbid depression, and frenetic energy that contributed to their success as well as their travails.

LIFE CRISES

Hemingway's life was one crisis after another. He was in constant rebellion against his middle-class background and wanted desperately to be a hero. His great need placed him in a position to be a hero or die Italy on July 8, 1918. That was the day he was struck by a trench-mortar bomb near Fossalta di Piave, Italy. A partner was killed and another had his legs blown off and Hemingway came away with 237 pieces of shrapnel imbedded in his leg that would require twelve operations. While there he met and fell in love for the first time.

While recovering in the Italian hospital Hemingway met nurse Agnes von Kurowsky. He fell madly in love with the 5' 8" brunette beauty who was seven years his senior and called him "kid." Nurturing soon turned into passion and they shocked the hospital by consummating their passions in the ward. Such titillation and passion is central to the Hemingway sense of heroism. Love and lust led him to propose, but he was devastated when she rejected him. He left for Chicago and barraged her with poems.

Hemingway had difficulty sleeping and isolated himself in the family cabin in upstate Michigan. He began writing in white heat to remove the emotional and physical scars. His war experiences found their way into two wartime novels and even in *The Old Man and the* Sea. His sense of crisis and creativity is revealed when he has Santiago say, "You can be destroyed, but you can't be defeated."

One of Hemingway's least known traumas occurred during his sojourn in Paris. He wrote obsessively when first sent to France. On one assignment in Geneva, Switzerland he became lonely and sent for his new wife Hadley. He asked her to bring along his manuscripts. She packed two years work and caught the train but when she arrived the manuscripts were missing. Knowing Hemingway's proclivity for rage she feared for her life. Strangely Hemingway did not make a big deal of the huge loss.

According to one of Hemingway's pen pals, Ezra Pound, he had numerous suicidal urges while living in Paris. In 1923 he wrote Pound, "Have felt pretty low and discouraged. Working 14 to 18 hours a day. Can't keep food down. Stomach shot from nervous fatigue. Have insomnia" (Hemingway Review 1995).

Brodie wrote in *The Creative Personality: A Rankian Analysis of Ernest Hemingway (1987)*, "the key to Hemingway's personality and his art was the profound and lasting effect upon the writer of his experience in World War I" (pg. 142). Hemingway was in Key West when his father committed suicide. Later his sister Ursula, brother Leicester, and granddaughter Margaux would end their life by their own hand. As soon as Hemingway was unable to cope with the reality of his physical and professional decline he did the same.

POLYPHASIC LIFESTYLE

Hemingway lived life on the edge and set himself up for a frenetic life. Biographer Mellow (1992) summed up his life as "too much anger, too much drink, too many quarrels, too much of the backbiting literary life, too much jealousy, too many wives, too much of everything" (Mellow pg. 4). Excess was the dominating characteristic of Hemingway's tormented life. He did little in moderation, but it took its toll. Hemingway had difficulty relaxing and was always dreaming up new conquests. In one manic period in Paris he wrote eight of the best stories he would ever write in just three months. Friends and wives were unable to keep up with his 5:00 a.m. to 1:00 a.m. manic lifestyle. He seldom went to bed before midnight and always rose at five to begin a day at his typewriter.

CRITICAL ACCLAIM. Author Sherwood Anderson wrote, "His influence on other writers is incalculable. He has the narration of an inspired reporter. He is one of the great writers of our time" (Sanderson pg. 3). In 1998 the *Old Man & the Sea* placed 32nd in a student ranking by Modern Library of the all-time best books. Hemingway believed "Old Man" to be his best work saying, "it is the epilogue of all my writing." His friend F. Scott Fitzgerald gained fame with his masterpiece *The Great Gatsby* although he admitted to the media, "he is the one true genius of our generation" (Mellow pg. 436).

The Modern Library ranked *The Sun Also Rises* as Hemingway's best work placing it at #18 all time for all books. This 1998 study also ranked *A Farewell to Arms* #20 and *For Whom the Bell Tolls* #30.

Hemingway is arguably the greatest writer of short stories in American history. He is certainly one of the most important for the 20th century. Victory out of potential defeat was his theme, that was exemplified by his classic *The Old Man & the Sea*. When Santiago fights the giant marlin only to have it torn away by the predatory sharks after a long and gallant battle, he is admitting that age and the elements have the ultimate say. A similar theme pervaded his other major works, especially *The Sun Also Rises* where protagonist Jack Barnes is a disillusioned member of the "lost generation." It was central to the Frederic Henry character, the consummate survivor in *A Farewell to Arms*. Hemingway's showed that a person can lose everything but still come away with dignity and courage. Honor must win out even if the big fish gets away. This is the moral message of life in Hemingway's heroic pathos.

LITERARY GENIUS

SUCCESS & PASSION – What Can We Learn?

Hemingway's life validates Gertrude Stein's aphorism "You are all a lost generation." He and pals Fitzgerald, Pound, and Joyce were dislocated. Hemingway peopled *The Sun Also Rises* with those types who had indeed lost their moral bearings. At the time he was a literary bum living off Hadley and idling away the time at Stein's salon when not drinking with buddies on the Left Bank, skiing the slopes in Switzerland, or seducing and dissipating at the bull fights in Spain.

Most who lived in that era paid a high price for their hedonism, but they also used the experience in their works. Vitality set them apart as did their alternative lifestyle. Passion pervaded both work and play. Stein had a love-hate relationship with Hemingway and Picasso. She told Hemingway "You don't have the guts to tell the real story of your life." But he did tell it vicariously through his characters.

Hemingway's estranged son Gregory offers insight into his father's temperament, saying, "Dad had the ability to destroy with words" (*Papa* 1976). Pauline Pfeiffer was Gregory's mother and an heiress to the Sloan's Liniment fortune. Gregory wrote, "In 1951 mom argued with Papa from San Francisco and finally broke down sobbing and died later that night." Gregory never spoke to his father again. Hemingway's passions made him great and in many respects proved to be his worst enemy. He died an unhappy and lonely man due to his contentiousness. He showed us that less can be more and that is his legacy. The irony is that the more he got from women, the less they got.

Mates of the driven always pay a dear price for living life in the fast lane. Hemingway pushed the limits in all things including the truth. Gregory wrote, "My father had a tendency to improve on even the best of stories, and he was uncertain to the point of fear" (*Papa* 1976 pg. 5). But in the end it was awesome ego and libidinal drive that armed Hemingway to write. He had a knack for imparting power and passion in protagonists who always won adulation but lost out in the end. That heroic pathos made his short stories and books entertaining, powerful and passionate, all traits that he bore with pride.

AYN (Alissa Rosenbaum) RAND
PHILOSOPHICAL & POLITICAL NOVELIST
b. St. Petersburg, Russia Feb. 2, 1905
d. New York City, Mar. 6, 1982

VISIONARIES ARE MOST CREATIVE

DOMINANT GENRE
Philosophical & Political Novelist - stories to spawn a whole new philosophy called Objectivism and a Political Party – Libertarian

MOTTO
"I'm a philosophical innovator and radical capitalist"
"I have no other life but writing"
"I am, I think, I will" - "Egoism is rational selfishness"
"When men are rational freedom wins. When free reason wins"

GREATEST WORKS
We the Living (1936) – "Man vs The State"
The Fountainhead (1943) – "The Idyllic Man"
Atlas Shrugged (1957) – "Objectivism – the mind on strike"

ECCENTRICITIES
Virulent anti-establishment in all things including: religion, feminism, marriage, bureaucracy, welfare, fascism, homosexuality and public education

LIFE CRISES
Survived WWI at 9 nearly starved at 12 during Russian Revolution and defected to America at 21

METAMORPHOSES
Escaped into books as a child with Cyrus and Victor Hugo's *Les Miserables;* Red's destruction of family and father transformed her into a passionate epic author of political philosophy

14

AYN (Alissa Rosenbaum) RAND

Visionaries See the Whole Before the Parts

"I'm a hero worshipper; I learn in reverse"

Ayn Rand was a radical visionary who wrote one of the world's great philosophical epics in English despite being Russian and never quite mastering English. Quite a feat, considering when she defected from Stalinist Russia she didn't know one word of English. She had the audacity to attack the heinous system she detested with little training in political science, philosophy, or creative writing, but had a major impact on all.

The Rand approach to the world can be seen in the manner she selected an American sounding name when deciding to remain in the United States. She looked down at her one possession, a typewriter with the logo Remington-Rand. Without further consideration she took the name Rand and refused to change it even when she married a Hollywood actor to keep from being deported. When asked why, this bold and highly opinionated woman said, "I intend to make the name Rand famous."

INTUITION & THE CREATIVE PROCESS

No matter the discipline, to be creative one must tap into their experiential data bank, use that information in an imaginative or innovative way, add a bit of flare, spice it with some fantasy, and draw some conclusion that alters the world in some way. Such a process is not possible if one is buried in the details to such an extent they are unable to suspend belief. The process is what Ayn Rand described as her ability to "learn in reverse."

The starting point should be something like, "I will write a book. The book will be "Man versus the State (We the Living)," "the Ideal Man (*The Fountainhead*(, or maybe "What if the creative minds of the world went on strike? (*Atlas Shrugged*)." That was the starting point for Rand and the manner in which all great concepts begin. No one can reach a goal without defining it, and then gathering the data, or formulating the story that validates it. The premise is critical to the process. In Rand's words from her Objectivist Letters, "I always thought in principles. I don't remember the genesis of my stories, they would come to me as a whole." When she decided to write her opus, *Atlas Shrugged*, on man in pursuit of his selfish best interest she made it into a mystery, not of the flesh, but of the mind with the opening line, Who is John Galt., and proceeded to show that he was the "ideal man" who refused to capitulate to the self-serving bureaucrats who would stifle his creativity.

THE WHOLE COMES BEFORE THE PARTS. Rand's life and work were but an external manifestation of a prescient inner vision. She attacked all questions in a holistic manner, proceeding from the whole to the parts and then methodically back to the whole. Life's details were but a path to the answer, and all logic was father to the goal. She used the parts to validate the answer. The creative genius begins by defining a problem or goal and then quantifies it in an iterative trip to the objective. Such people are *rational visionaries* - Prometheans on a manic journey to realize their dreams. Rand described her writing style as incorporating "organic wholes in which every event and character expresses the central theme" (Sciabarra pg. 18). Rand was a card-carrying Promethean often used by psychologists as an example of intuitive-thinking personalities.

PROMETHEUS LEGEND – A RANDIAN HERITAGE

Hesiod described the mythical Greek Titan Prometheus as a rebel who dared defy the top dog Zeus by stealing fire from the heavens and bringing it back in the form of light for mankind. He paid dearly for his act and had his liver eaten by eagles while chained to a rock. Prometheus has since come down as the metaphorical symbol of entrepreneurial and creative genius.

A classical interpretation has Prometheus a "fore-thinker" with his brother Epimetheus an "after-thinker." Both mythical gods are important for this discussion since the former is typical of right-brain visionaries like Rand, the latter is more akin to left-brain types who prefer certainty. One looks for the new and unique. The other seeks stability, and avoids anything that may prove disruptive to the status quo. Both are valued contributors to society but only one should be leading in the world of innovation or creativity.

Prometheans seek life's opportunities. Epimetheans seek order and structure. Neither is right or wrong just different. Prometheans are easily bored by the mundane and seek novel experiences. Epimetheans fear the new and different and resist it. Prometheans are comfortable with ambiguity and thrive on the unknown. Epimetheans are comfortable with structure and seek surety. Prometheans function best outside the mainstream. Epimetheans function best in bureaucracies.

CREATIVE PERSONALITIES. Promethean personalities like Rand are *intuitive-thinkers.* They see the big picture and deal with what they see very rationally. Their opposites see the details and tend to quantify them even further in what is sometimes referred to by Prometheans as analysis-paralysis. Communism appeals to the Epimethean temperament due to its centralized state and controlled environment, at least as Karl Marx envisioned it. They see man as a part of the more important whole – centralized government – and must sublimate his own desires for a better whole. That is why Rand wrote of the "mind on strike" against such a tyrannical and duty-bound system that destroyed all creativity. Stalin and his henchman were consummate Epimetheans, the types that Rand despised since the had elevated **duty** to an artform, for their own self-serving needs to control.

Many of the world's creative geniuses were Prometheans including Napoleon, Einstein, Frank Lloyd Wright and Bucky Fuller. Like Prometheus they were all renegades with a penchant for defiance. Psychologists describe intuitive-thinkers (Prometheans) as "architects of change." Epimetheans get the label *dependable* due to their preference for sensing and judging. They are the world's traditionalists who label visionaries as *flakes* because of their ungrounded thinking. Visionaries (Prometheans) see bureaucrats as *annals* for the opposite reason. Creative writers are most likely to be Promethean. Why? Because they tend to have a vision and a strong desire to document that vision via word-pictures. Ironically, most editors and publishers tend to be Epimetheans. And so is born a love-hate relationship.

Creative writers tend to opt for unproved risky approaches to their craft. Editors grounded in tradition see the world through an opposite filter. One is driven to change the world. The other is driven to keep it the same. That is why most creative works seldom see the light of day until a renegade is willing to take a risk. It is why George Bernard Shaw's first six novels were never published, why Rand's first book *Anthem* was rejected by twelve publishers, and the Harry Potter series was rejected by nine. All were writing outside convention and were denigrated by the establishment. Socrates was killed by Epimetheans. Men who were furious that he was in defiance of the system and dared ask man to think, a threat to their need for order.

RAND'S RATIONAL SELF-INTEREST

Rand's system of *rational self-interest* validates her arguments against a centralized system of government. She railed against laws that stole man's freedom. She became the poster girl for Libertarians due to her belief that the best government is the least government. Rand despised rules and rituals, and believed that *duty* stole man's right to think. Political correct she was not. But her admonition to pursue, "rational best interest" despite what any government, mate, or parent was central to her *Objectivism*. Her whole premise was a system elevating man to hero status and above any government. She said, "Selfishness is a virtue."

OBJECTIVISM. Rand hated bureaucrats. Her life and work were devoted to elevating free enterprise to a position of godliness with man above the system. Socialism and Communism were enemies and the villains in her philosophy and stories. For Rand Capitalism was the only system in which man could exercise his free will where laws and government were but tools for rational and productive man.

Rand's fiery invective began and ended with Capitalism. Every hero was a passionate Capitalist or venturesome entrepreneur. Objectivism is now taught in most universities. It is an ideology that touches on the social, economic, political, and legal aspects of government. Her protagonists were all male mythical heroes and idyllic free-thinkers – Prometheans if you will, who would rather die than lose their freedom to act as free agents.

She often borrowed characters from real-life heroes. Howard Roark was renegade architect Frank Lloyd Wright in *The Fountainhead* (1943). Roark would rather destroy a building than have it desecrated by self-serving socialists. Rand's invective peaked in her classic philosophic epic *Atlas Shrugged* (1957). In this book she had renegade hero John Galt say, "I swear by my life and my love of it that I will never live for the sake of another man, nor ask another man to live for mine" (Rand 1957 p. 993). Both men fit her model as the quintessential free-spirit in a *laissez-faire* political system.

TREES VS. FOREST MENTALITY. Rand was a visionary writer. She viewed her work in the larger sense of its meaning and moral. In this respect she was at odds with her editors who wanted to be sure they sold. She defied them when they told her they wouldn't sell because they were "too intellectual for the masses." She refused to listen or capitulate and in the likeness of Prometheus, Wright, Roark and Galt she defied them and has been rewarded for her vision with nearly 25 million copies sold. She saw the forest while the editors were more caught up in the trees. Validation of her perspective on the world was seen during her college days in Russia. During a philosophy class in St. Petersburg she brazenly told her professor Nicholas Lossky "I learn in reverse."

All new buildings, products, or books must start with a goal or thesis. Without doing so is akin to jumping into a car and driving without a destination. It may prove interesting, even informative, but if one doesn't know where they are going any road will take them and when they arrive they may not be where they want to be. The destination is the most important part of any journey. This is precisely why press boxes are located on top of stadiums. Those in the heat of battle, are unlikely to recognize what is happening, and will be ineffective in execution. Consider Einstein's theory of relativity. Had he began with Newton's principles he would never have been able to concoct his theories. He had to intuit the answer and then prove work out the physics that validated his answer. Freud kept seeing patterns in his dreams and patients repressions. He took the data and intuitive the answer. There was an unconscious mind that stored or repressed information and only then was he able to embark on his "talking cure" (psychotherapy) as the premise validating his insight.

RAND'S INTUITION. Lossky's *The Intuitive Basis of Knowledge* would prove influential in Rand's approach to life and her work. Professor Lossky taught Rand the Hegelian Dialectic at Petrograd University in St. Petersburg. She would use it to synthesize a whole system of political ideology and then develop a mystery and romantic stories to validate her ideas. She had superhero Howard Roark say, "It is the content of a person's brain, not the accidental details of his life, that determines his character. Reason and emotion must function in integrated harmony, or distortions result in both spheres." This was her way of saying the individual must see the whole or become lost in the muddle. She very adroitly married the mind, emotion, body, and spirit into heroic characters. Biographer Sciabarra said, "Through inductive reasoning and abstractions she broke down the whole into concepts" (Sciabarra pg. 208).

MYOPIA VS VISION. Those who worship at the altar of facts are destined to pay the price of myopia. They seldom, if ever, see the big picture, but become experts on minutia. The world's proof-oriented scientists castigated Einstein for intuiting a Theory of Relativity without formal proof. He had the proof in his head but few were astute enough to see it. Did Einstein care? No! Like most creative geniuses he satisfied his own curiosity and worked out a system that made eminent sense, and left the proofs to those more inclined. The price he paid was fifteen years of torment and rejection until his theories were validated. Einstein preached, "Intuition is the gift of the gods, and logic is its faithful servant" (Gardner pg. 106). He always elevated imagination above logic using concepts like trains and mythical spaceships to arrive at his breakthrough theories. He admonished his doctoral students at Princeton to understand that "Not everything that counts can be counted, and not everything that can be counted counts" (Gardner pg. 106). Creative types are impatient with those that need validation before belief.

Nikola Tesla infuriated his professors by solving complex differential equations in his head and walking to the board and writing down the answers. He had amazingly committed the logarithmic tables to memory and could solve equations in his head. Amelia Earhart had the same ability and they refused to explain how, and may have often not known the traditional paths walked by lesser humans.

A MYOPIC APPROACH. Those people who worship at the altar of numbers tend to get lost in the details and often miss out on the magic of innovation. Such people are dogmatic and resist change, not for any other reason than the fact it doesn't fit into their well-ordered system. As managers or leaders they tend to kill off ideas that lie outside their perspective. They become so mired in the present they often destroy the future, mortgaging the future to guarantee a safe present. Risk is antithetic to their nature making them best suited for bureaucratic organizations where risk is not tolerated.

Epimetheans have a huge psychological stake in tradition. They resist change for no other reason than it disrupts their need for order. Such people do not like books like *Atlas Shrugged* or opinionated visionaries like Rand. They will say they don't like books about railroads when the railroad was but a metaphor lost on their provincial and duty-bound logic. It is imperative that one get outside the box of structure to find the nuances that just might have some prescient approach to problem resolution.

For Rand an entrepreneur is an intrepid warrior and hero. She would have been been disgusted over the United States Justice Department prosecuting Bill Gates for no other reason than being too good. In any other nation of the world Gates would

AYN RAND

have heralded as a hero and defended. But in an ever-
increasing socialized welfare state dominated by legal-beagles,
America has seen fit to attack him for being too successful. In
the words of Abraham Lincoln, "You cannot strengthen the
weak but weakening the strong." Rand called bureaucrats with
such self-serving agendas "second-handers." She labeled
Buckley's *National Review* "the worst and most dangerous
magazine in America" (Sciabarra pg. 349).

Atlas Shrugged was written to entertain and to inform. Rand's
intellectual message was an erudite system of metaphysics,
epistemology, ethics, and politics. This would have been a
Herculean task for a doctoral dissertation let alone for a mass-
market novel. Further complicating her objective was the fact
she was a Russian immigrant, not steeped in the subtle
nuances of American culture. She wrote an epic work on the
philosophy of capitalism without training in those disciplines.

Rand said, "*The Fountainhead* was only written as an overture
to *Atlas Shrugged*," describing it as "an intuitive-system of
thought." It conveyed her "*psycho-epistemology*." Both
Howard Roark and John Galt were mythical superheroes of
Nietzschean proportions. Galt told the world to go on strike,
not a strike of the body, but a strike of the mind against the
welfare state mentality of 20th century mid-America. Her heroes
were merely foils to communicate her political and
philosophical ideology. She "connected economics, psychology,
sex, art, politics, and ideology."

GESTALT. History's most eminent concepts have evolved out
of holistic ideas. Gestalt means "whole" and is a concept
wannabe writers or other creative types should be aware of on
their trek to success. Freud wrote, "Creative activity is not a
direct reflection of deliberate intention. I have restricted
capacities for anything quantitative." Michener said, "I
discovered early that I saw spatial relationships differently than
other children." Stephen King says, "My books are visual
movies in my head. What I write comes from the gut." All great
journeys begin with a destination and then work out the
agenda. Placing too much emphasis on roads and detours is
counter-productive to the process. Rand liked to reverse Rene

286

Descarte's aphorism, "I am therefore, I think." She was intuitive in her world-view if not in her approach. She wrote in the *For the New Intellectual* (1961 p. 96), "Every novelist is a philosopher, because one cannot present a picture of human existence without a philosophical framework." In her prophetic words: (Sciabarra 1995 pg. 194)

> *Creators work intuitively, allowing their subconscious to integrate evidence that not even their conscious minds grasp immediately. Mind is more than the verbal, linear, analytic processes popularly if misleadingly described sometimes as `left-brain' activity. It includes the totality of mental life, including the subconscious, the intuitive, the symbolic, all that which sometimes is associated with the right-brain.*

EXPERTS & MYOPIA. Experts have such a psychological investment in what is they are seldom ever capable of seeing what might be. They should be avoided at all cost when attempting to alter paradigms since they will denigrate the idea for no other reason than it is foreign to their area of expertise. An example comes from a 1997 New Zealand study on the world's worst writers. It showed that college professors had written three of the top five worst books. Why? Probably because they became so caught up in exacting grammar and syntax to the detriment of the story or message. In the inimitable words of Bertrand Russell, "The essence of certainty and revelation comes before any definite belief."

THE PHILOSOPHICAL NOVEL GENRE

Aristotle was one of the first to use philosophy to define a political ideology, elegantly stated as, "The unexamined life is not worth living." *Pilgrim's Progress* was aimed at using Christian metaphors to show the way to the Celestial City. But the use of heroes to tell stories in classics like Dante's *Divine Comedy* (1314), Jonathan Swift's *Gulliver's Travels* (1726), Samuel Butler's *Erewhon* (1872, and Orwell's *Animal Farm* (1945) were the genesis of the genre.

287

Rand raised the genre to another level where heroes were real men, saviors of society, and romantically intertwined with life and women. She wrote cathartically saying, "I can never be in love with anybody but a hero. I have to have a hero." She had been mesmerized with Victor Hugo's masterpiece *Les Miserables* while growing up in Russian and wrote, "Victor Hugo is the greatest novelist in world literature." From that beginning she wrote of heroic deeds and subjugated her own life to her political philosophy. She wrote, "My personal life is a postscript to my novels. Art is but an expression of one's sense of life."

Rand's allegories were aimed at describing truth about life. The more profound the allegory, the greater importance it had to the story. When non-visionaries say, "I didn't care for *The Fountainhead*. I just don't like books about architecture" they just don't get it. In *Atlas Shrugged* she created the ultimate philosophy of life in which she wrote, "The more passionately personal the thinking, the dearer and truer."

A PROMETHEAN NOVELIST

Rand was convinced writers are bred not born. In *We the Living* (1936) she wrote, "No one is born with any kind of talent, and therefore, every skill has to be acquired. Writers are made, not born. To be exact, writers are self-made." She believed the system should be the slave to man. "A great deal may be learned about society by studying man" she wrote, "but nothing can be learned by studying society." This shows her didactic approach to knowledge with heroes the supreme beings. Further testimony is her comment, "When men are rational, freedom wins; when men are free reason wins."

John Galt was a modern day Prometheus and the consummate rational thinker with a mission to stop the world if the bureaucrats should succeed in subjugating man. Galt expressed her philosophy of entrepreneurial freedom:

> *Every man is free to rise as far as he's able or willing, but it's only the degree to which he thinks that determines the degree to which he'll rise ... I swear by my life and my love of*

it that I will never live for the sake of another man, nor ask another man to live for mine. The man who produces an idea in any field of rational endeavor – the man who discovers new knowledge – is the permanent benefactor of humanity, and in proportion to the energy he spent the man who creates new invention receives but a small percentage of his value in terms of material payment, no matter what fortune he makes, no matter what millions he earns. (Rand p. 988).

SUCCESS & INTUITION. Napoleon was an intuitive visionary, a man who refused to fight a battle until he had an overview of the battlefield. Charles Darwin said, "I had a flash of insight" leading to his classic, *Origin of the Species.* He said, "It at once struck me that favourable variations would tend to be preserved and unfavourable ones to be destroyed" (Darwin pg. 120). Einstein attributed all his success to intuition. "The gift of fantasy has meant more to me than any talent for absorbing knowledge." Leonardo Da Vinci said, "The limit of vision is simultaneously the limit of comprehension" (Zubov pg. 168). Nikola Tesla wrote in his autobiography, "I could visualize with the such facility. I needed no models, drawings, or experiments. I could picture them all in my mind."

Catherine the Great was precognitive in the sense she unconsciously predicted the coming of Napoleon. In mid 18th century when Napoleon was still a child living on the island of Corsica she wrote, "If France survives she needs a superior man, greater than his contemporaries. When will this Caesar come? Oh! Come he will, make no doubt about it. Everything depends on that!" What prescient vision!

LITERARY INNOVATIONS

Rand's most important literary innovation was her psycho-epistemology delivered in novel form. In *The Fountainhead* (1943) she effectively portrayed individualism over collectivism in a story that was just commercial enough to inspire Hollywood to immortalize it in a movie starring Gary Cooper.

Her plot was based on a fictional Frank Lloyd Wright, an iconoclastic architect who dared to defy the establishment rather than compromise his creativity. Wright was known at the time as "The Anarchist of Architecture," an arrogant renegade who was a hero to Rand. Self-esteem was at the root of all ethical conduct and at the core of the Randian "ethical egoism." It was her as Dominique Francon telling superhero Roark, "To say I love you one must first know how to say the I." She admitted, "Dominique is myself in a bad mood." She has Roark say, "I do not recognize anyone's right to one minute of my life, nor to any part of my energy. I am a man who does not exist for others." Such intellectual dialogue was her trademark for delivering to the thinking reader a moral message.

After twelve publishers turned down *The Fountainhead* as "too intellectual" until one intrepid editor, Archie Ogden at Bobbs-Merrill took it on. But he ran into tremendous resistance from his boss in 1943 and was forced to bet his job to publish it. An archenemy of Rand's philosophy, Nora Ephron of *the New York Times Book Review*, wrote in 1968, "It is one of the most astonishing phenomena in publishing history" (*Contemporary Authors* pg. 397). The book that should not have been written sold 2.5 million copies and by the 90's had sold five million.

Atlas Shrugged pushed the envelope of intellectual dialogue even more than her previous works. And it was a *tour de force* of 1200 pages in eight-point type. It was an epic work that took her fifteen years to write. It was an appeal to the masses to stand up and be heard, a virulent attack against socialism written in scholarly rhetoric. The book found even more enmity from Random House editors. They told Bennett Cerf he was crazy to publish it. The irony is the masses loved it more than the classes who were upset by Rand's opinionated invective on everything including politics, education, religion, welfare, and the left and right. The book hit the bookstores at a time when social-welfare systems were at their peak. Rand's rational self-interest and atheism were too far right for the nuclear family of the 50's and 60's. And her anti-mass education, anti-government and anti-gay stances were too far left. Rand's long-time lover and protégé, Nathaniel Branden called *Atlas Shrugged* "a mystery story, not about the murder of man's body, but about the murder – and rebirth – of man's spirit." Most critics agree she succeeded in her task but most violently disagreed with her radical ideas.

Rand was opinionated to a fault, seldom acknowledged opposing views, and managed to piss off all factions. She was dangerous to interview due to her brilliant insights and political ideology. She was cynical, arrogant, highly articulate, and capable of destroying with words. Random House editors were instructed to leave her alone. She refused to have one word changed on her massive manuscript. The famous John Galt radio speech took two years to write and went on for 200,000 words. It comprised sixty pages and when asked to pare it down Rand responded caustically, "Would you cut the Bible?" The editors predicted, "It will never sell despite its potential for genius. It is too long, too intellectual, too inflammatory, and a personal vendetta against Russia."

WRITING AS CATHARSIS

Rand began *Atlas Shrugged* saying, "My personal life is a postscript to my novels." In *We the Living* she said, "I am only writing to get Russia out of my system." She admitted in the Forward the book was little else but "My autobiography. Kira the heroine is me." She was also the prototype for both Dominique Francon in *The Fountainhead* and Dagny in *Atlas Shrugged.* "Dagny is myself with any possible flaws eliminated." Later she wrote, "I have never had a personal life in the usual sense. My writing is my life."

The Russian radical told Barbara Branden, the wife of her young protégé Nathaniel, that she began believing she was special as a young girl in Russia and her life would "involve doing great things." In *Atlas Shrugged* she said, "I decided to be a writer at age nine and everything I have done was integrated to that purpose." When a college professor asked if she agreed with Plato she replied, "No, I don't." When asked why, she responded, ""My philosophical views are not part of the history of philosophy yet. But they will be" (Sciabarra pg. 85).

Rand passionately wanted to destroy Communism and used a philosophy of Capitalism as a foil to do it. When she left Russia for America she vowed to get even with a system that had destroyed her father and broke up her family. Her words were virulent and vindictive, words like "vile users," "losers," and "exploiters living off the productivity of others as second-handers." She wrote "When the first creator invented the wheel the first second-hander responded with the word altruism." (*Fountainhead* p. 684). Rand argued "a man who consumes without producing is a parasite, whether he is a welfare recipient or a rich playboy" (*Philosophy* p. 154). She told Phil Donahue, "Russia is the ugliest, and incidentally, the most mystical country on earth" (*Contemporary Authors* 27 pg. 395).

METAMORPHOSES

Rand began writing screenplays at ten and toyed with a novel at twelve. Books were her escape from the vile Russian winters and turbulence of WW-I and the Russian Revolution. After graduating from college she applied for a visa on the ruse to visit a cousin in Chicago. She intended to defect, but made it appear a vacation by carrying nothing but a few clothes and a typewriter. On leaving relatives asked, "What will you tell them in America." She said, "I will tell them of the horrors of Communism." Her promise became her mission. The voyage became her epiphany and spawned many books, the Libertarian Party, and the Objectivism philosophy. There is little question her books contributed in some small way to the fall of Communism in 1990. The monumental event took place just eight years after her death. She was buried under a giant 10' dollar sign of flowers befitting the Mistress of Capitalism.

We the Living (1936) was an exorcism of the fears and torment of Russia, that demonic system she depicted as a "vast cemetery" where "bodies, minds, and spirits" were deteriorating from the loss of freedom. She was careful to attack the system not the state for fear of retribution against her living relatives. But it launched her career as a writer of political philosophy.

LITERARY GENIUS

AN ECCENTRIC RUSSIAN RADICAL

Rand was a renegade from her childhood as Alissa Rosenbaum in St. Petersburg. She was the first child of a successful Jewish merchant. She grew up lonely and escaped into books. Her reading led her to embrace atheism rather than religion at age eleven despite being raised in an Orthodox Jewish family. She admitted to being, "a philosophical innovator and radical capitalist." Rand was always brighter than most of her peers and soaked up Nietzsche and Hegel at the University of Petrograd where she earned a degree in History. Rand's New York City lawyer said, "Dealing with Ayn Rand was like taking a post-doctorate course in mental functioning." He was correct based on her statement, "I do not recognize anyone's right to one minute of my life, nor to any part of my energy."

Rand was writing screenplays in Hollywood when she met future husband Frank O'Connor. He always knew he was a distant second to her work, but for thirteen years was even second to her love affair with a young protégé Nathaniel Branden. It started in 1947 when she had just begun to write *Atlas Shrugged*. Branden was a psychology major at the University of Southern Californian and had become enamored of her book *The Fountainhead*. They became friends and collaborators on the Objectivist philosophy. He would head up her fan club and then become acknowledged as her "intellectual heir." But they found an emotional attraction even though both were well married. In the inimitable style of Rand she called for a meeting between Branden's young blonde wife Barbara, her artist husband Frank and her intended lover Nathaniel. Rand thought all conflicts had to be discussed rationally and could be resolved without emotional intervention.

Rand's Galt-like rationality was captured by Barbara Branden in her 1982 biography on Rand. Branden wrote, "Ayn never lived or loved in reality. It was theater or fantasy of Ayn's dream world" (Branden p. 260). The couples agreed that a liaison of the mind and body was appropriate and that Ayn and Nathaniel would meet weekly in a very regulated love affair in her Manhattan apartment. At the appointed time Frank would take a discrete departure for Central Park and Nathaniel would show up and consummate the mating of the souls between their alter-egos Dagny and John Galt. This scene was pure Hollywood and would still play as a perversely entertaining sitcom. Rand's ethical reasoning made this weekly *affaire d'amour* all very rational aimed at accommodation their physical and emotional needs. This weekly relationship continued for thirteen years until Branden met and fell in love with younger woman. He dumped Ayn at age sixty-five and she never forgave him.

To say that Rand was not politically correct is a gross understatement. She referred to Republicans as "Reagan's Militant Mystics," the *National Review* as "the most dangerous magazine in America, and gays as "not normal with psychological flaws." She antagonized conservatives with comments like, "Devotion to the family is an obsession and at the root of tribalism." Pro-welfare groups were no better than wannabe communists and described as "losers" and "users." The religious were "witchdoctors and mystics, worse than revolutionists." Her belief that "the best government is the least government" rankled all politicians. Feminists hated her for saying, "Men are superior to women." Educators approved of her "enlightened self-interest" but were turned off by her statement that "mass-education molds mediocrity and is anti-cognitive and anti-conceptual."

LIFE CRISES

Rand was born in Russia during one of the most turbulent periods in history. She survived a number of near-death experiences from childhood until she left. By the time of the Russian Revolution her successful merchant father had been relegated to a number and the family nearly starved to death. Then the Communists took over had to beg in the streets for food. The family fled to Crimea for some months and during the trip they were accosted by thieves and almost killed. After graduating from college Alissa decided to flee to America. She packed little for fear of being stopped. Her early traumas armed her for the trek and nothing later would ever come close to the devastation she had encountered growing up.

POLYPHASIC

Rand dabbled in various forms of literary expression including plays, non-fiction novels, documentaries, screenwriting, essays, and ultimately published an Objectivist Newsletter. She fashioned herself a playwright, philosopher, political essayist and romance novelist. In each of these mediums she espoused her ethical system of *laissez-faire* capitalism. She was highly focused but also capable of multi-tasking.

CRITICAL ACCLAIM

World Literature Criticism wrote, "The ingenuity and artistry of Ayn Rand as a plot writer creates a sense of drama and conflict, and a matchless integration of philosophy and action" (Branden pg. 2879). On release of *The Fountainhead* (1943) the *New York Times Book Review* lauded Rand as a "rare woman writing about ideas." They went on to describe her as a "writer of great power with a subtle and ingenious mind and the capacity of writing brilliantly, beautifully, bitterly" (*Contemporary Authors* 27 pg. 397). Helen Beal Woodward did not like Rand's philosophy, but wrote in the *Saturday Review,* "She is a writer of dazzling virtuosity" (*Contemporary Authors* Pg 398).

After the release of *Atlas Shrugged,* Rand became a cult hero on college campuses. Her philosophy of heroic independence and individualism were the buzzwords of the period and she was a guest of Johnny Carson, Tom Snyder, and Phil Donahue. She was interviewed by *Playboy* and became a free-lance contributor to the *Los Angeles Times.* Her influence was pervasive with the free-love disciples of Fritz Perls and the rebels of the 60's who became the virulent anti-government protestors. Her *Objectivist Newsletter* and *laissez-faire* philosophy gained a loyal following of notables including Allan Blumenthal, Dick Randolph, Edith Efron, Billie Jean King, Alan Greenspan, Leonard Peikoff, Mickey Spillane, and even Margaret Thatcher. Psychologist writer/lover/confidante Nathaniel Branden became the editor of her *Objectivist Newsletter* until their break.

The Rand philosophy is controversial, but controversy sells. *Atlas Shrugged* was demeaned by William Buckley's *National Review.* Writer Whittaker Chambers called it "remarkably silly, bumptious, and preposterous. Out of a lifetime of reading, I can recall no other book in which a tone of overriding arrogance was so implacably sustained. Its dogmatism is without appeal" (*Contemporary Authors* Pg. 398). The *Catholic World* described it as a "shrill diatribe against non-productive people." They were right. She had hit a sensitive issue on welfare of the non-productive and the do-gooders found it highly distasteful. But posterity has been more kind. Rand's philosophy has recently been adopted. The producers, aka John Galt, have metaphorically gone on strike against the non-producers and illegal immigrants. It has spawned bills like Proposition 209 in California. They have adopted Rand's theory of "rational selfishness," and revolted, saying enough is enough.

Contemporary Authors – New Revision Series (pg. 398) described *Atlas Shrugged* "a multi-million selling phenomenon" and compared it to *Uncle Tom's Cabin* as a book that "had fueled a movement." That it did. The Libertarian Party was borne out of the passionate rhetoric of this epic philosophical work. John Galt has become a Promethean hero of intellectuals. The Objectivist philosophy has taken longer to ferment but is now taught on most college campuses.

PROMETHEAN VISION – What Can We Learn?

Ayn Rand believed everything in life is either black or white. Such inflexibility elicits either positive or negative emotions with few on the fence. People either loved her or hated her with the majority in the latter camp. But she succeeded in communicating her epistemological message via passionate words in romantic plots.

Freedom for mankind was her aim and it will go down as her legacy. Rand's intractable belief in the right of man to exist without governmental intervention was an idyllic notion that she was able to communicate in novel form. Not an easy task but instructive for those of us wanting to deliver a message.

Did success come without a price? Hardly! She never had children and by her own admission had little life beyond writing. Writing pervaded her whole being. She didn't believe in living to another's agenda and lectured on this extensively. She wrote in *Philosophy Who Needs It* (pg. 97), "Duty destroys reason, Duty destroys values, Duty destroys love, Duty destroys self-esteem, and Duty destroys morality." To Rand "duty" and "welfare" were pornographic and despicable concepts that were adversarial to innovative man. It was only "rational self-interest" that held any reason for Rand. And she applauded any man who dared take on the world. This was never more apparent than in John Galt's words, "The man who produces an idea in any field of rational endeavor, the man who discovers new knowledge, is the permanent benefactor of humanity" (pg. 988). Rand's disciples were visionaries. Her enemies were bureaucrats from the school of exactitude. She described these enemies with passionate invective in: *Philosophy* (pg. 171)

> *Today, originality, integrity, independence have become the road to martyrdom, which only the most dedicated will choose, knowing that the alternative is much worse. A society that sets up these conditions as the price of achievement, is in deep trouble... Any man who says, 'Just listen to my prophet, and if you hear him speak of sacrifice run, run faster than from a plague. Where there's sacrifice, there's someone collecting. Where there's service, someone is being served."*

Books are like people in that their greatest strength tends to be their greatest weakness. The strength of *Atlas Shrugged* is its intellectualism, and it was its weakness. Those unable to relate are those unable to see the meaning beyond the words. They don't care for messages that attack sacred icons. That is fearful. Such people describe Rand as a rebel intent on destruction. What her critics don't seem to get is that one doesn't necessarily have to agree with her philosophy to enjoy the trip. She makes people think and that is good even if you don't agree with the destination. Welfare types and gays might object to her strong opinions, but they would be best served to consider the message rather than burning her books metaphorically. That is akin to poisoning Socrates. The people Rand labeled altruists.

Any creative work of art, product, novel, poem, or drama must be visualized as a totality before it can take on a life as a complete entity. This demands beginning with the answer and then making the parts agree with the whole. Confusing the map with the territory is dangerous in such an undertaking. The pieces are only important in the context of the whole and what that message is intended to impart. Those unable or unwilling to start with the whole are destined to remain forever mired in minutia. This was never stated more succinctly than in John Galt's profound statement, "An inventor is a man who asks Why? of the universe and lets nothing stand between the answer and his mind" (Atlas Shrugged p. 950) or:

> *The thinking child seeks equals. The conformist seeks protectors. There is no anonymous achievement. There is no collective creation. Every step in the development of a great discovery bears the name of its originator. There is no collective achievement involved. There never has been. There never will be. There never can be. There is no collective brain. ... I submit that any man who ascribes success to luck has never achieved anything and has no inkling of the relentless effort which achievement requires.* (Rand 1982 pg.107)

The digital world at the millennium worships at the world of numbers where modeling becomes godly. It is not godly, because the world is not digital it is analog. Life is best lived in a gestalt manner where one can pursue dreams without an accounting. Rand wrote what she wanted, how she wanted, and the way she wanted and refused to change for anyone including her editors. That was based on her Promethean spirit, what proved in the end to the panacea for her success. Quality will always be more important than quantity.

ALBERT CAMUS
ESSAYS, PLAYS, & PHILOSOPHY
b. Mondovia, Algeria Nov. 7, 1913
d. Paris, France Jan. 4, 1960

INSECURITY BEGETS ACHIEVEMENT

DOMINANT GENRE
Non-fiction existentialist philosopher, novelist, and playwright, who introduced a moralistic philosophy to a world in chaos

MOTTO
REVOLT – FREEDOM – PASSON! "I revolt therefore we are"

GREATEST WORKS
The Stranger (1942) An Absurd world is meaningless
The Plague (1947) Search for the meaning of life
The Fall (1956) Guilt and nihilism – a self-portrait

HONORS/AWARDS
Nobel Prize for literature 1957; 2nd youngest winner at 44

ECCENTRICITIES
"Sleeping is a waste. I have a mad, avid thirst for everything";
"Sensuality alone ruled my life. For a ten minute affair I would have rejected my parents."

LIFE CRISES
Father died when one, raised as foundling; TB at 15, a death sentence in 1929 Algiers; married drug addict at 19

METAMORPHOSES
TB as teenager transformed him into a frenetic overachiever who lived life in the fast lane; he was searching for truth in an absurd world

15

ALBERT CAMUS – Non-Fiction

Insecurity Breeds Greatness

"I'm pessimistic, ignorant and don't know how to write"
(months after receiving Nobel Prize)

Camus was born on a bus in Algeria, lost his father before age one, was diagnosed with Tuberculoses at fifteen, and never had a permanent residence until he married at nineteen. No wonder he was insecure. But he used his afflictions as motivators not inhibitors. An on-the-edge lifestyle shortened his life but few men have ever lived with more gusto than this French philosopher who was dealt a poor hand but played it with style and panache.

SELF-DOUBT AS INSPIRATION

Alfred Adler said, "We cannot develop unless we struggle." Few other comments better describe the life and work of Albert Camus. Adler was the first psychologist to use insecurity as the basis of overachieving. To him insecurity was overcompensation that lead to greater success than would have been possible if the inner fears were non-existent. He wrote, "The more intense the inferiority, the more violent the superiority." Adler came about his conclusions from his own struggle at age five when doctors declared him terminal. When medicine helped him live he said, "My decision was confirmed. I must become a physician." He soon turned to psychology and wrote, "inferiority is central to understanding human nature" (Hoffman p. 176). Adler felt that early fears and inferiority led inextricably to overachieving. Camus confirms Adler's thesis. He wallowed in internal fears of failure much of his life. Just after receiving the Nobel Prize for Literature he wrote, "I'm pessimistic, ignorant, and don't know how to write."

ALBERT CAMUS

The Algerian born existentialist began life in the gutter and life proceeded downhill from there. Confirmation of his struggle with life and negation was immortalized in his classic work *The Fall* (1957). This turned out to be a classic, but he described it as "ugly." But his true nihilism came to the fore after winning the most prestigious award possible for a man of letters. In 1957 he came off stage in a dejected state and told a friend, "The Nobel gives me more doubts than certainties."

Camus was not the only writer in this book who lived with self-doubt. James Michener wrote in his memoirs, "For forty years I awoke at 4 a.m. in a state of dread, nobody will want to read this. It won't work. I'll never fool em" (Michener 1991). Dostoevsky also wallowed in self-doubt. When he finished *The Idiot* he sat back and said, "My dissatisfaction with my novel amounts to disgust." Maya Angelou spoke of being discovered as a fake since she didn't think she could write. Such is the nature of insecurity. It can motivate or debilitate and the only difference lies in the underlying self-esteem of the writer.

CARTESIAN ERA IS OVER! Rene Descartes, the father of modern philosophy was lauded for creating the scientific method. Historians have labeled those who live by the numbers as Cartesian – the consummate rationalists. In some academic circles this is called Cartesian Doubt because Descartes questioned everything to derive his philosophy of life. He was highly inquisitive and threw out anything that didn't have sensorial proof. If you couldn't see, touch or feel it, it didn't exist. Rationality was his god summed up by the expression *Cogito ergo sum* – "I think therefor I am." It's nihilistic alternative could read, *Dubito ergo sum*, "I doubt therefor I am."

In a Cartesian world, man is but a machine and this worked well through the Industrial Revolution but in a world where man has been elevated above machines it is now an obsolete concept. However, Camus lived through the transitional state and helped with the transformation. Those who worship at an altar of numbers would still have us believe that the world is digital. It is not. It is analog. We have long since passed the point where quality exceeds quantity, at least in the Western world. We should not be concerned with how many words, but the quality of the words to fulfill our premise, just as the food we eat should be more qualitative than quantitative.

Descartes' skepticism was rampant in the writings of Camus who said, "I don't believe in anything" and elevated *doubt* and *revolt* to a state of deity. His overwhelming doubt brought on by many childhood foibles and debacles makes him our poster boy for insecurity. If insecurity can breed greatness, then Camus is validates the premise. Camus' inferiority drove him to excess. Those excesses pervaded his life from the day he was given the death sentence diagnosis of tuberculosis at fifteen until he died in a car wreck at age forty-seven. Obsession with early death made drove him to become one of Europe's great philosophers and playwrights. He has been called the most successful French writer of the 20th century and has had an enormous influence on existential philosophy.

FEAR, SUCCESS & WILL. How did fear lead him to the top? The fear of dying before he had the opportunity to express his innermost ideas and philosophy made him into a frenetic writer, a man on a mission. Since he believed he would die early he saw life as unfair and doubt became central to his thought. But more importantly, the self-doubts drove him with a passion not found ordinary men. Insecurity and fear spawned a "philosophy of doubt and absurdity." After being diagnosed with tuberculosis at fifteen he expected to be dead by twenty-one. Many men would have checked into a sanitarium and awaited death. He didn't. Camus took on life as a challenge and lived it as if double-parked on a busy highway. Life for him became more important and he truly believed "sleeping was a waste." He wrote, "I have a mad and avid thirst for everything (Todd p. 49).

Nietzsche and Schopenhauer described *will* as central to man's drives. We now know individuals who allow insecurity and self-doubt to dominate their thoughts are destined to a life of mediocrity or worse. Those who use life's roadblocks as temporary obstacles to bypass will rise above the pack. It isn't the roadblocks that defeat us but the inner belief that they can. Those who use fear as motivators get better from the experience. Those who allow them to win will see themselves as victims and blame the roadblocks. The only difference between the two is *attitude* and a Nietzschean *will-to-power*.

British psychiatrist Anthony Storr (*The Dynamics of Creation* 1993) described creative geniuses as armed with a "divine discontent." He said, "man's discontent is his most precious attribute which spurs him on to creative achievement" (p. 244). Examples are eminent people like Charles Darwin, Karl Marx, Sigmund Freud, Carl Jung, Nikola Tesla, and Madam Curie. All suffered nervous breakdowns, contemplated suicide, and used their infirmity as a springboard to success. Woolf, Twain, Plath, Hemingway, and Fleming were pathologically insecure.

Ted Turner admitted to being raised to be insecure by an alcoholic father who felt that "insecurity bred greatness" (Whittemore 1990). Whittemore said, "Turner was beset by an "extreme form of insecurity and vulnerability... the driving force behind his inexhaustible need to achieve" (Landrum pg. 222). Buckminster Fuller was fired for being more visionary than prudent as a businessman. He never worked again, at least for any firm. The rejection led him to the brink of suicide at twenty-seven. He regained his composure at the 11th hour and vowed never again to listen to another human being. He became introspective after two years of speaking to not one individual including his wife. His epiphany changed him into the creator of the geodesic dome, 2000 patents, and 25 books. Martin Luther King offers further insight with his aphorism, "The children of darkness are frequently more delusional and zealous than the children of light."

ANXIETY & SUCCESS. Anxiety and fear leads to superior performance. Breakdown leads to breakthrough. Hegel saw this and wrote in *Phenomenology of Mind* of "growth through struggle." Playwright Eugene O'Neill was thrown out of Princeton and turned into an alcoholic sleeping on park benches. Like Camus, in 1912 he was diagnosed with TB and landed in a sanitarium. He wrote about his traumas as a catalyst for his Nobel and four Pulitzer Prizes for literature.

Studies on anxiety and stress show that fear releases adrenaline enabling a person to fight harder which in turn leads to higher performance both physically and emotionally. Reneau A. Peurifoy wrote a book titled *Anxiety, Phobias, & Panic* (1997) in which he said, "high levels of creativity, extreme competence, and manic work ethic are the by-products of anxiety" (*USA Today* Aug. 18, 1997). Sports psychologists preach about the high value of stress on athletic performance. *Arousal Theory* shows that stress and anxiety improve athletic performance up to a point when it will start to decline. This theory argues in favor of a "state anxiety" to arouse the central nervous system. In other words, fear can spawn passion, which in turn improves performance. Getting *psyched-up* is dependent on anxiety.

UNHAPPINESS AS CATALYST. Camus was so insecure he threatened to quit writing. He was still so inclined after having won the Nobel Prize for Literature in 1957 at age 44. After receiving the prestigious award he told a friend, "I want to give up writing," (Todd pg. 366). At his acceptance speech he told the audience, "Success is a balm, but a temporary one, and an artist's discontent remains incurable" (Todd p. 373). A friend who attended the ceremony described Camus' speech "more like a eulogy than a happy event" (Todd pg. 373). This was not unexpected from a man who claimed, "my only riches are my self doubts." Anthony Storr validates Camus' words in a study of great writers titled *Dynamics of Creation* (pg. 2). He wrote, "Writing is not a profession, but a vocation of unhappiness. I don't think an artist can ever be happy."

Fear of failure is often manifested by overachieving, especially for those with a strong will. Freud confirmed this with his admonition "a happy person never phantasies only an unsatisfied one" (Storr 1989 pg. 81). Storr said, "writers create via distress rather than by any excess of joyful vitality" (Storr 1993 p. 2). He described Sir Isaac Newton as "anxious, insecure, hypochondrical and self-disparaging" (p. 97). Beethoven's greatest symphonies (8th & 9th) were written after he was deaf. In a similar way Chairman Mao's physician Dr. Zhisui said, he "had delusional symptoms of paranoia with debilitating illness just prior to any political upheaval."

INSECURITY & SUCCESS IN LITERATURE. Fear engulfed Virginia Woolf. She feared insanity and the anxiety was personally debilitating but professionally motivating. Woolf vacillated between euphoria and hysteria that is apparent in her dream sequence in *The Waves (*1931). In the dream volatility was the only constant with her on precipice with "waves rising and spreading over me." Ten years later she would be engulfed by the haunting waves of the River Ouse that took her life. As she walked knowingly into the water she was casting aside those inner demons that tormented her. Creative narrative written in a stream of consciousness was to be her legacy but it was spawned by an obsessive fear of insanity.

Plath also lived life on the brink of despair and self-depredation. In one period of anguish she wrote, *Johnny Panic* (1958). It was a way of documenting her inner fears and doubts over not being perfect. She had to be the very best or die trying. These fears drove her frenetically. Despite a 160 IQ, graduating with honors from Smith, a Fulbright scholarship to Cambridge, and successful publishing at a very young age, Plath was tormented by fears of failure. This made no sense but it was real and validated by her journals and passion-laden lyrics. Plath spent her short life questioning her ability with flagellating self-doubts with journal entries like, "You can't teach, write, think, do anything" (Stevenson p. 114).

How could someone with so much talent be so insecure? Unrealistic expectations! But as we ramble through life we become more aware that there is really no true perfection. Writers like Plath were really attempting the impossible. And such actions can only lead to stress, anxiety, and self-denigration that manifests itself in drugs or suicide. Such are the classic symptoms of the Type A perfectionist – consummate overachievers who never able to placate an inner need for excellence. Overachievement is inextricably tied to self-worth.

Self-doubt also pervaded the life and work of Irish wit and playwright George Bernard Shaw. He was so insecure he wrote to Ellen Terry, "I wish I could write a play, but unfortunately I have not the faculty." This was after he had already written six novels and ten plays (Holroyd pg. 392). The *London Times* wrote, "Shaw was unable to take even his own work seriously." Dr. Seuss was even more insecure than Shaw. Even after the publication of *A Cat in the Hat* (1957) he said, "I've lost it. I can't write anymore." He attempted to burn his first book *Mulberry Street* feeling it was a loser. His wife stopped him just as Stephen King's wife recovered his *Carrie* from the garbage.

Ian Fleming's brother-in-law Hugo Charteris, described the egocentric creator of James Bond as "a self-doubting hypochondriac." He told the media, "There is no limit to Ian's capacity for feeling inferior" (Lycett p. 206). After Fleming wrote *Casino Royale* he didn't even bother to show it to a publisher. He said, "It is all nonsense and nobody will be interested" (Lycett p. 226). He was a lifelong hypochondriac with an obsession for psychosomatic afflictions, and succeeded by overcompensating via pomposity and arrogance.

EXISTENTIAL PHILOSOPHY GENRE

Camus said he learned more from Dostoevsky than any other writer. His idolatry led him to produce a play based on Dostoevesky's *The Possessed*. He said of the word, "It is a prophetic book – it predicts nihilism. It has nourished and educated me" (Todd pg. 395). Dostoevsky's *Notes from the Underground* (1864) documented his alienation against rational humanism. It was the basis of his existentialist motif of subjugation, control, and destruction. He then furthered the message with *Crime & Punishment*. Nihilism permeated the lives of both men who performed a self-destructive dance through life. The two were strangely similar relative to their idiosyncrasies, libidinal urges, and bipolar afflictions.

Other existentialist writers preceding Camus were Arthur Schopenhauer, Soren Kierkegaard, Karl Jaspers, Paul Tillich, Martin Buber, and Frederick Nietzsche. A major influence, albeit questionable and highly volatile, was friend and adversary Jean Paul Sartre. Sartre has been credited with coining the word *existentialism,* although it had been previously used by Karl Jaspers to describe a movement he called *existence philosophy.* He and Sartre admonished man to make choices and take responsibility for their actions through control of the *will*. Camus wrote, "Suffering is nothing. What counts is knowing how to suffer" (Todd p. 26).

Sartre described the existential movement as "human freedom." Camus was obsessed with freedom based on being raised in a colony of France where freedom for natives was non-existent. Freedom was fundamental to Camus' whole system of moral philosophy causing him to write, "Life is absurd." A biographer called him a "personal freedom addict." It must be remembered the era in which he lived and worked. Camus grew up in an era when Communists were taking over nation after nation, the Great Depression relegated people to bread lines, WW-II led to the occupation of Algeria and France, followed by the Cold War that threatened nuclear holocaust. These threats led to his statement, "The only coherent philosophical position is revolt," and his philosophy of the absurd where "revolt is happiness."

Sartre's definition of existentialism was *essence* exceeds *existence,* one that Camus came to refute, but his words tell a different story. He was deeply committed to essence over existence based on the negativity that dominated his whole life. This can be seen in the three works that define him and his form of positive negation: The novel (*The Stranger* 1942), play (*Caligula* 1944), and essay (*The Myth of Sisyphus* 1955). By age twenty Camus had found work as a free-lance writer for an Algerian magazine. While in that job he wrote an article with these words, "I don't believe in anything, and its impossible to live like this, having killed morality inside me, I have no more purpose, no more reason to live and I will die (Todd pg. 21).

The existentialist movement peaked in popularity during the beat generation of the 50's and early 60's. It died out during the revolutionary student outbursts of the late 60's. An early branch was Kierkegaard's religious existentialism, what Camus called *philosophical suicide* (he was an vocal atheist). He felt it was everyone's freedom to worship as they saw fit, but strongly opposed any dogmatic system that recommended blind obedience. His influence may have contributed to the decline of organized religion of the masses to the more personal nature that has evolved in the last forty years. He was a fan of Kierkegaard's and lived to his aphorism, "To venture causes anxiety, but not to venture is to lose oneself."

AN INSECURE NOVELIST & PLAYWRIGHT

Anthony Storr said, "Writers, particularly poets, are commonly afflicted by severe, recurrent depression and their work can often be interpreted as a way of relieving their distress" (Storr 1996 p. 1996). This was true of Camus whose raging insecurity was manifested in cathartic words of passion.

Camus began life in the whole. He had no father, no home, knew only poverty as a child, and then was told he only had a few years to live when in his mid-teens. Not the idyllic way of building a positive view on life. The death sentence of tuberculosis pushed him over the edge into nihilism. He loved literature and learning and had decided on a career as a college professor but Algerian laws prohibited anyone with a life-threatening disease to teach. Destiny had intervened and he was thrust into the role of writing out his frustrations and telling the world about its absurdity. Words were suddenly used to exorcise his demons. Then in an impulsive move at age nineteen he met and married a drug addict Simone Hie. The marriage was predestined to fail. After the divorce he left for France. France was then occupied by the Nazis, and Camus was unable to return to Algeria. He had no means of livelihood and began writing for an underground newspaper, and lived in daily fear of German retaliation that meant instant death. Is it any wonder Camus became an existentialist?

There was no limit to Camus' self-flagellation. After completing his finest novel - *The Stranger* – he wrote to his wife, "I've just reread all that I've written of my novel. I was seized with disgust and it seemed to be a failure from the ground up" (Todd pg. 108). Even after a highly successful writing career that included winning the Nobel Prize for Literature he wrote, "I have no imagination" (Todd pg. 380). Despite self-castigation he continually wrote, rewrote, and rewrote every manuscript. Then he would discard them and start the process over again. He was introspective about his compulsions, "I must start things over again if I want to do them really well" (Todd pg.

153). Self-doubt still dominated Camus' life in January, 1960. It was just one month prior to his fatal automobile accident that he wrote to one of his many lovers Catherine Sellers and said:

> *I get desperate about writing rubbish, and then start over again, only to throw it all away, and go around in circles, and ask myself what do I want to do, not knowing the answer, but trying anyway, and screaming for a little genius that will cure nothing but at least stop this endless suffering ... To work one must deprive oneself, and die brutally, so let's die, because I don't want to live without working* (Todd pg. 410).

DOES INSECURITY BREED GREATNESS? People often succeed more due to a fear of failure than insightful inspiration. Why? Because they are more interested in proving their value and self-worth and that energy catapults them beyond where they may have been without such motivation. They are more inspired by the negativity of losing, than any positive aspect of grabbing the brass ring. What is it about *insecurity* that makes people strive to be better? It is about ego. Many people won't strive for #1 but will die before allowing themselves to be last. Fear therefore, becomes more motivational than desire. Internally, the whip is more of a motivation than the carrot. Anyone who has witnessed the last point in a highly combative tennis or racquetball match can see this. If the contestants had played the whole match with such ferocity they couldn't lose.

Examples of this are pervasive in history. Stephen J. Cannell, writer/producer of such winning shows as Adam-12, The Rockford Files, Baretta, Hunter, Wiseguy and The Commish was a loser until mid-life. He flunked the first, fourth, fifth, and tenth grades and was asked to leave for ineptitude. He told the media, "Deep down I figured I wasn't the brightest guy around. My attitude was always, who cares? But writing became my passion" (IBD p. A8 6-14-99). Ted Turner told David Frost in October 1991, "You won't hardly ever find a super-achiever anywhere who isn't motivated by a sense of insecurity." The creator of the Great Gatsby, F. Scott Fitzgerald tacked the 122 rejection slips on the walls of his small apartment to motivate him. Perseverance paid off and after his first publication many of his others were finally produced.

Balzac gave up writing on numerous occasions in total disgust. The father of the modern novel often referred to his writing with "a sense of shame." Agatha Christie told the media, "I regard my work of no importance. Perhaps one day they will find me out and realize that I can't really write at all" (Robyns pg. 204). Sylvia Plath was consumed by an obsessive fear of failure. She wrote, "I walk the razor's edge of tragedy...I am now flooded with despair, almost hysteria, as if I were smothering. "You can't teach, can't do anything. Can't write, can't think" (Stevenson pg. 134). Stevenson said she was in a battle "waged constantly with her dark self," that led to self-deprecation.

LITERARY INNOVATION

Camus was an anomaly. Before him there was never a great philosopher who came from a Third World nation beset by abject poverty. Philosophers are typically born in professional families and reared in sophisticated environs. Philosophers just do not have peasant fathers, illiterate mothers, and a milieu like Algiers for molding their prescient vision. Metaphysics and epistemology are born of people like Karl Marx whose father was a lawyer, and he was educated to be a college professor. Philosophers tend to write for the intellectual elite not the common man. Camus' upbringing and lack of formal education caused his break with the upper-class bred Sartre and led to his philosophy of freedom for the working classes.

Camus wrote, "I am not a philosopher, because I don't believe in reason enough to believe in a system" (Todd p. 408). By his adamant denials he was confirming his passion for philosophy and epistemology. Could a non-philosopher write something like "The spirit of rebellion can exist only in a society where a theoretical equality conceals great factual inequalities" (The Rebel p. 20) or "Suffering is nothing, what counts is knowing how to suffer" (Todd p. 26). This is a man predisposed to questioning the plight of man on a perilous journey.

MYTH OF SISYPHUS. Camus found success with his first novel – *The Stranger* (1942) followed shortly by his classic essay *The Myth of Sisyphus*. These two works would become models for the budding existential movement just after WWII. Camus' contribution is found in defining the freedom of mankind that is manifested in a kind of optimistic nihilism. He wrote, "Sisyphus is the happiest man alive," a cynical comment about him not knowing that he was in a no-win struggle. His metaphorical use of the Greek myth about pushing a rock up a hill and having it come back down in a futile struggle that could not be won, was based on his theory of a world gone power mad. It must be remembered that Camus grew up without electricity or running water and was expected to die. Struggle was endemic to his life and survival inherent in his soul.

Camus reached adulthood during the Great Depression. After Nazi's occupied France he wrote for the underground paper *Combat*. When the allies liberated Paris he was fired and forced to live by his wits. His mother and brother lived in daily fear of their lives in Algiers due to the Algerian revolution. It is little wonder Camus saw the world in "negation." His asked "man to rebel or revolt" against the absurdity of it all and "strive for a kind of humane stoicism." His legacy will be "absurd" and "futile" reflections on life that were immortalized in his works like *The Plague* (1947), *The Rebel* (1951), *The Fall* (1956), and *Exile* (1957).

WRITING AS CATHARSIS

Existentialism for Camus' was a way to cope. His life was caught up in the passion of a world gone berserk and they give testimony to his inner anxieties, hopelessness, fear and rebellion. He wrote of this inner turmoil, "I don't believe in anything and it's impossible to live like this having killed morality inside me. I have no more purpose, no more reason to live, and I will die" (Todd pg. 21). His whole output was little other than a long series of cathartic inspirations based on life on the edge. His inner sense of despair and fatalism comes through with nihilistic invective. Camus was keenly aware he was dealt a poor hand. He played it with panache and zeal that would leave many female bodies in its wake.

On graduation from high school Camus was awarded a prize for French composition and philosophy. He had finally decided, "I don't want to live without writing. I've made a wager that forces me to create something meaningful, otherwise my life will be totally absurd" (Todd pg. 66). A Roman Catholic upbringing influenced him. Such people either buy into the dogma or become radical renegades. He became a renegade writing, "I have a deep-seated attitude against religion" (Todd pg. 29). During college he discovered Nietzsche and bought into the superman thesis of *will-to-power*. Nietzsche alerted him to the possibilities of life beyond mere survival. He adopted an ideology similar to his mentor and wrote, "To the question of how to live without a God who does not exist – live, act, write" (Todd pg. 45). He spent the rest of his life attempting to find the meaning of life lived without control.

METAMORPHOSES

Camus' illiterate mother was a cleaning lady who sent him to live with relatives. Food was scarce and life was cheap. After many moves he began living with his uncle Gustav, a well-read butcher with a passion for books. Camus devoured the books in his uncle's library as an escape and by seven had decided to become a writer to emulate his heroes Balzac, Dostoevsky, Hugo, Zola, Voltaire and James Joyce. By high school he found a mentor - teacher/author Jean Grenier. Grenier was instrumental in getting him a job as a free-lance columnist for *Sud* magazine. This transformed him from a fearful teen into a writer capable of free expression.

But his epiphany took place when diagnosed with TB. After that he wrote, "I am in a hurry to live a lot, with lots of experiences" (Todd pg. 49). He was still young but was now intent on living in double time. Mortality drove him. While still in school he wrote, "I've only four years to write the works I want to write due to my illness." Success did not materialize immediately. His first novel - *The Stranger* (1942) was complete when he was 21, but wasn't published until he was 29. He wanted desperately to sit for a philosophy-teachers exam in Algiers, but his illness didn't allow it. That forced him to take up the free-lance life of a journalist-writer where he would not have to be in contact with others. Such are the vagaries of life.

ECCENTRICITIES

Camus was an iconoclast who wrote, "I feel one must revolt to arrive at happiness – I revolt therefore we are" (Todd pg. 296). He lived life outside convention but with the insight that rebellion is tied to innovation and creativity. This is expressed in his strong invective, "The only coherent philosophical position is revolt" (Todd p.145). His life is defined by his classic *The Rebel*. But rebellion was not just a philosophy for him. It pervaded his very being, both personally and professionally. Most existentialists live well outside tradition but Camus, lived outside all established values when it came to his love life.

He often wrote of wanting a conventional life. But his actions cast a different light on his values. He was a man of excess whether smoking, driving, working, romancing, or philosophizing. Passion was pervasive in his blood. He was afflicted with panic attacks, severe depression, mania, and obsessive-compulsive behavior. He lived, loved, and drove like a man possessed. Womanizing is too soft a word to describe the complex love trysts of Albert Camus. One woman or even two was never sufficient to quiet his raging libido.

Camus married a gorgeous brunette named Francis Faure. She adored him but was never faithful. His philosophy of marriage was, "One must live with her, shut up, or sleep with them all." He slept with them all. Two or three women were never enough. In a poignant moment of introspection he wrote, "Sensuality alone ruled my life. For a ten minute love affair I would have renounced my parents." His trysts included Parisian actress Maria Cesares, American journalist Patricia Blake, French singer Catherine Sellers, a young protégé Mi, plus a plethora of women throughout France. He was incorrigible and recognized it saying, "It is painful for me to admit that I would have exchanged ten conversations with Einstein for a date with a pretty walk-on extra. But after ten dates with her I would usually be longing for Einstein, or serious books (Todd pg. 344).

Francine Faure willingly shared him with mistress Maria Cesares, and American journalist Patricia Blake but when he took up with the 21-year Mi she had reached the limit and attempted suicide. It is amazing he could live with one woman, keep a mistress, and carry on a perpetual series of one-night stands. He was irresistible to women and even slept with Sartre's long time mistress Simone de Beauvoir. She said, "I was seduced by his charm." His lechery destroyed his wife Francis Faure. In justification he wrote, "We always deceive ourselves twice about the people we love – first to their advantage, then to their disadvantage." He justified his behavior with "to love someone is to accept to grow old with them. I am not capable of that kind of love. Women inspire in us the desire to create masterpieces, and prevent us from finishing them" (Todd pg. 185).

LIFE CRISES

Life for Camus was traumatic from birth to death. It would have destroyed a lesser man. He was born to an illiterate cleaning lady, Spanish Catherine Sintes. His father Lucien was killed in the Great War, leaving Camus to be raised by distant relatives. Growing up without parents gave him no role model and led to his own poor record as a father and husband. When diagnosed with TB, a death sentence in 1930 Algiers, he began to see life as cheap and went for the gusto. The trauma led into an early marriage with Simone Hie, a brilliant beauty and drug addict. When war interceded to disrupt his life he left for Paris and never returned except for occasional visits.

POLYPHASIC

Camus lived life like a double-time. Freneticism defined him. He was intense and always had many balls in the air at once. His work ranged across many genres including novels, plays newspaper articles, essays screenplays, and short stories. He worked as a journalist, publisher, writer, actor, playwright, and philosopher. Camus wrote all three of his major works simultaneously - *The Stranger, The Myth of Sisyphus,* and *Caligula..* One was a novel, the other a play, and the third a philosophical essay. Work was godly to him as seen by his words, "Man's most dangerous temptation is inertia, sleeping is a waste; eternal liveliness is the essence of life" (Todd pg 220).

CRITICAL ACCLAIM

The Nobel Prize for Literature was the highlight of Camus' life although he never admitted it was important. He was broke at the time as he lived life on the edge and money was but an instrument of his hedonism. The $42,000 award came at a time when he needed the funds to keep writing. A friend witnessing him walk on stage said he appeared to be a schoolboy undeserving of the prestigious award.

Literary critics attacked him unmercifully. In the early fifties when his novel *Revolt* appeared, a critic named Rebatet denigrated it saying, "Camus has been diagnosed with arteriosclerosis of style" (Todd pg. 373). Longtime friend and drinking buddy Jean Paul Sartre turned on him with the most ruthless and callous attack. Sartre was probably venting some unconscious rage over the dashing romantic Camus who contrasted Sartre's short, fat and ugly stature. Sartre wrote, "You are afflicted with somber self-importance, bourgeois attitudes, are philosophically incompetent, your reasoning is inaccurate, and you are vague and banal" (Todd p. 309).

Posterity has been much kinder to Camus than Sartre. Camus is now considered a major contributor to the existentialist movement especially for documenting the nihilism of Fascist-torn Europe. He is credited with postulating a positive and optimistic viewpoint on a philosophy of negation - *The Absurd*. Camus has outlasted most of his critics by becoming the most widely read French author of the 20th century. He is also considered the most gifted of the French journalists writing for the resistance during World War II. His success has dwarfed that of his turncoat friend Jean Paul Sartre.

SUCCESS BASED ON SELF-DOUBT – What Can We Learn?

Self-doubt and insecurity were critical to the success of Camus. Why? Fear of failure motivated and inspired him, and he used his self-doubts as stepping-stone to a successful philosophy of life. It is important that we recognize that what happens to us is insignificant to how we deal with it. Camus used his fears as the basis of a whole philosophical system of thought.

EXTERNALIZE FEAR. Did Camus have a secret? Not that he was aware of but Anthony Storr has defined it as, "divine discontent" – an inspirational motivator for the creative writer. In such a system of belief the writer must place blame externally, never internally. Camus blamed his predicament on a stupid world in chaos. His negation became a positive one aimed at showing universal chaos doesn't have to be personal. The person exceeds the environment. Had Camus internalized his trauma it would have devastated him. He blamed an "absurd world" and went on to create the chaos as an enemy to be attacked rather than something to be feared. This proved to be the genesis of his existential philosophy.

The Greek mythology *Sisyphus* was adopted by Camus to explain the futility of mankind during the mid-20th century. It was arguably the most violent in the history of man tantamount to a man attempting to push a rock up a steep grade and expecting it to stay while he rested. Such an act was pure folly leading to "futility" and "absurdity." He justified his life as a hedonist by saying, "Only an absurd man will spend a life pushing rocks up hills with a preordained outcome." He predicted failure for any man so inclined. Any man so stupid should lose due to being uneducated or unthinking.

Camus relegated fear of failure into a nihilistic philosophy. Without such a system of thought, he may well have ended it all in suicide, insanity, or drugs – all of which he contemplated at various periods in his turbulent life. He took the negative and used it to make a bunch of positives. That is the essence of creative genius. Revolt was his only escape and he took it. He was a man attempting to sublimate his greatest fears into philosophic dialogue. Camus' achievements are akin to the cancer patient who takes huge doses of chemotherapy to kill off the cancer cells. There is a delicate balance between killing the disease and killing the host. He taught us to never allow fear to defeat us but force it into a corner where it can be defeated.

DANIELLE STEEL
THE QUEEN OF ROMANTIC FICTION
b. New York City, Aug. 14, 1947

MISTRESS OF CHARISMATIC POWER

DOMINANT GENRE
Prolific romance novelist: charismatic skill & cathartic style

MOTTO
"The mind can create its own reality" - "Strong people cannot be defeated"; "I'm a conservative rebel"

GREATEST WORKS
The Promise (1978) – movie, TV serialization - 3 million sold
Mixed Blessings (1992)
The Gift (1994)

HONORS/AWARDS
Publishers Weekly (May 27, 83) "Steel is a masterful plotter;"
1981 record of 390 consecutive weeks at #1 on *New York Times*
list. By 2000 had sold in excess of 400 million books of 77
titles

ECCENTRICITIES
Manic-depressive, Type A and obsessive traits; said
"I'm a write-aholic." Married rapist in prison and after another
arrest divorced him to marry a convicted drug addict

LIFE CRISES
Polio at 12, hepatitis at 16 – ensconced in boarding schools
"My parents never once came to see me"

METAMORPHOSES
Teenage marriage as trophy wife; devastated she wrote it out of
her system in *Going Home* (1973) - she didn't know a comma
from a colon; "being an introverted observer made me a writer"

318

16

DANIELLE STEEL – ROMANCE

CHARISMA CAN MOVE MOUNTAINS

"The mind can create its own reality"

COMMUNICATIONS SKILL & LITERARY GENIUS

The ability to effectively communicate via the spoken or written word is more important than virtually all other skills. The quintessential example of charisma in her dress, style, charm, sophistication, and words and actions is Danielle Steel. Steel is the Mistress of Romance and her power is not steeped in writing skill or intellect, but charisma.

Steel writes about what she knows and she knows a lot about the jet setting life in Paris, St. Tropez, Rome and Monaco. She has lived and vacationed in the romantic places of which she writes. To her fans these playgrounds of the rich and famous are merely mythical, but Steel is able to make them real, and that talent has resulted in 100's of millions of book sales.

Communication is a skill critical to all those interested in getting to the top in any discipline, but it of paramount importance to a romance writer. Look at the leader in any major organization in the world and you will see someone with magnetic appeal. Such people are able to effectively communicate via the spoken and written word.

Charismatic power is key to finding a mate, getting a job, managing others, attracting friends, securing an agent and getting published. For the entrepreneur, it is critical to getting funded and attracting key individuals to follow your dream. Anyone with sufficient charm can rise above the pack. IQ, work ethic, storytelling talent, and narrative brilliance are critical to the process, but all pale in comparison to the need to effectively

319

communicate a message. Rising to preeminence in any domain is always a function of getting your message across to those who can help or are willing to follow. Danielle Steel personifies this in her personal style, image and articulation as well as her thrilling accounts of love lost and found.

Despite being demeaned by literary critics for writing inane fantasies for the escapist reader most would agree that Steel is a master storyteller and wordsmith. She knows how to communicate her message and does it with style and grace. Mary Warner Marien of the *Christian Science Monitor* (Sept14, 1987) wrote about her books, "The pleasure of the text is the pleasure of your mom's tapioca pudding." *Contemporary Popular Writers* said, "reading Steel is equivalent to a roller coaster of emotions." A *Detroit News* article described her style as "a flair for spinning colorful and textured plots out of raw material." Others acknowledge her work as entertaining.

CHARISMATIC POWER. Charisma is an inner energy that encompasses all you touch. It is internally generated but externally used. It can move mountains if used properly. Those with such power attract disciples who will follow them anywhere. The power demands a common purpose, a concept that Steel has mastered adroitly. Those with charisma can attract legions off faithful followers, or in the case of books devoted fans. Millions are looking for *the way,* and will follow anyone who believes they have a map. Alexander the Great had this power. So did Napoleon, Martin Luther King, John F. Kennedy and Mother Teresa. Their expertise:

- *ENORMOUS EGO & SENSE OF SELF*
- *A MEGALOMANIACAL MISSION OR DRIVE*
- *ENTHUSIASM TO THE POINT OF MANICNESS*
- *USE OF POWERFUL & PASSIONATE WORDS*
- *ARTICULATION ABILITY - BOTH INTELLECTUALLY AND EMOTIONALLY*
- *USE OF A COMMON GOAL TO PERSUADE*

Other sources of power like *money* (financial power), **authority** (position power), or *even muscles and guns* (physical power) are external and therefore fleeting. A person can make money but can lose it overnight. The same is true of a politician who wins the election. His power is in the position and once he no longer has the position the power is gone. The same is true with force or muscles. There is always someone bigger so relying on such power is fleeting. Anyone who has been rich and lost the money knows how fleeting such power can be. The only true power emanates from within, and that is what charisma power offers to those looking to excel.

Charisma can be verbal or non-verbal. It is sometimes delivered in a tone or command, or by eye contact, or a function of body language like dress or posture. Sometimes non-verbal charisma can be more powerful than verbal, just as one word can convey much more emotion than another. The passion emanating from within can be seen in the words of Steel, Hemingway, Fleming and Plath. That is why they were so successful at writing books picked up by TV and Hollywood. They drew passionate word pictures that were able to capture the reader's imagination.

Is charisma inherited? No! Psychologists have known for some time how to train a person to be more charismatic. Are some people better able to learn it? Sure! Look at Hitler, a loser who was trained in the art. He was bipolar and since emotion and enthusiasm is critical to the process verbally he was a good prospect to teach. Napoleon was similar since he was also bipolar. The same was true of Balzac, Dostoevsky, Twain, Woolf Hemingway, and Plath.

CHARISMA'S DARK SIDE. The dark side of charismatic power can be found in cultists Jim Jones, David Koresh and Marshall Applewhite. Attila the Hun had it as did Mussolini. The debacles at Jonestown and Waco were traced to the charismatic powers of mesmerizing evangelists Jones and Koresh. These men attracted a zealous following of rabid disciples and used their charismatic powers to lead them to their own self-conceived nirvana. Both employed the oldest form of deception to gain a following. They frightened their followers with a common enemy and promised to save them. To achieve their objective they had to elevate themselves into the role of messiah. Such power is needed since they tend to pick on the weak and disenfranchised who are in desperate search for a leader. The cultist uses fear as a weapon, frightening the weak with a common enemy and then promising to save them.

LEGITIMATE CHARISMA. The Queen of Romance utilized a similar methodology to Jones and Karesh. Her ploy is to frighten her readers with the loss of love and then show them the way to find it. Despite the fantasy of the journey, the reader enjoys the redemption. Steel creates a scene of unhappiness featuring dysfunctional people and then insures they live happily ever after, with the woman always getting the man.

The charismatic style of Steel has worked. Her legions of loyal fans wait for her next sojourn into a world devoid of love and then look forward to a happy ending. Steel writes of what she knows, futility and loneliness experienced as a child and in a number of disastrous marriages. The cultists used spiritual and political fears, where she used loneliness, but the result was the same. Hitler adopted the threat of the Red Menace as his enemy and promised the German people he would save them. And his ploy worked!

HITLER & CHARISMATIC POWER. Hitler is the consummate example of someone being taught to be a rabid communicator. A German intellectual - Dietrick Eckart decided to mold Hitler into a compelling speaker and leader. It worked! Eckart believed in mind-control and an ethereal concept called Thulism. After the first war he convinced Hitler to become a protégé. Consider the difficulty of such an undertaking. Hitler was lazy, pathologically shy, manic-depressive, had not even graduated from high school and never held a job. Eckart groomed this unemployed flake to take over a nation. Powerful and passionate words were key. By 1923, Eckart had finished his project and wrote to a friend on his deathbed:

> *Follow Hitler! He will dance, but it will be to my tune. We have given him the means to maintain contact with the Masters. Don't grieve for me. I have influenced history more than any other German.* (Scwarzwaller pg. 60).

322

German Socialite Elsa Bruchman said, "I would have done anything for him." A young German hearing him speak said, "I experienced an exultation that could be likened only to a religious experience" (Landrum 1996 pg. 258). A German worker who admitted to disliking Hitler's racist ideology said, "I felt I had come face to face with God. The intense will of the man flowed from him into me. When he spoke men groaned and hissed, women sobbed" (Landrum p 259).

THE ROMANCE GENRE

Love and chivalry began to find their way into literature in the Middle Ages. The first art form was aimed at entertaining. Languages soon became linked with romanticism and they still are. Italian, Spanish and French are known as the romance languages. Words like *love* and *chivalry* began cropping up in literature to describe hero protagonists. During this period Sir Gawain and the Green Knight influenced Elizabethan literature. That soon led to Nathaniel Hawthorne's 19th century novels featuring heroes and heroines. Hawthorne was convinced romance writers should be free to pursue psychological truths and wrote in this way with such classics as *Scarlet Letter* (1850) and *The Seven Gables* (1851). Romance prior to Hawthorne had been limited to novels; but after Hawthorne romantic realism would come to be identified with the novel. Colette ahd a French influence with her *Claudine* series culminating in her classic work *Gigi*..

By the 20th century romance became linked with escapist fiction. It featured a light narrative form so the reader did not have to work too hard. Work and pleasure in books are diametrically opposed. Some books, like romance, are dedicated to entertaining, those like this one is more for informing and is significantly more work. Balzac altered the genre from pure lighthearted stories to meaningful plots. Brit Dame Barbara Cartland was called the Queen of Romance due to her incredible output of 635 books that sold 750 million copies. Like Steel, Cartand tapped into the subconscious to contrive exotic stories of the heart.

DANIELLE STEEL

Steel is America's answer to Cartland. *Newsday's* critic Marvin Kitman accused her of being "too heavy and realistic for me with her psychological studies" (Hoyt pg. 377). Others competing in this arena are Jackie Collins, and Judith Krantz. Critics estimate 22 million American readers of romance novels. Most literary critics do not care for the genre. L.J. Davis of the *Chicago Tribune Book World* described Steel's 1983 book *Changes* "as the sort of basilisk prose that makes it impossible to tear your eyes from the page even as your brain turns slowly to stone" (*Contemporary Authors* New Revision Series 65 p 330).

A CHARISMATIC ROMANCE NOVELIST

If Charisma is about magnetism, titillation and "divine grace" (the Greek translation) then Steel is the poster girl. Charisma was first defined by sociologist Max Weber as, "manifesting passion, vitality and intensity." Such a definition is consistent with Steel's life and writing. Her personal life story is far more fascinating and titillating than any of her best-selling books. In March of 1998 she married for the fifth time at age 50. Her new significant other was a man named Thomas Perkins (66) a Silicon Valley entrepreneur who helped launch Sun Microsystems and Netscape. The marriage ended as the first four since Steel, like most driven people, are not inclined to have two masters in their life.

EARLY LIFE. Steel's escapist writing was born of a traumatic early life. She was the only child of two jet-setting parents who dragged her through the trendy capitals of Europe. She was placed in boarding schools in Switzerland, France, Italy and New York while her parents lived the good life. This led to an unhappy life for the lonely girl who escaped into the fantasy of books. She became enamored of the Colette novels. Colette was a role model to some degree since she wrote while living elegantly. Both were renegades and wrote for people outside their class structure. Colette was a bisexual and Steel married one bisexual, a San Francisco playboy who became her fourth husband.

Steel was so engrossed in books in her teens she would walk into walls. She got lost in an imaginative world with happy endings, a place she desperately wanted to be but could only find in stories.

Danielle was never taught, or expected, to clean, cook, or sew. She lived the life every girl dreams of traveling between San Francisco, New York and Paris. Illness plagued her constantly. She once spent two months in Denver recouping. At twelve as diagnosed with polio, had hepatitis at 15, and was hospitalized with a tumor at 16. She called her parents "self-indulgent" and told the media "I had a disastrous childhood. I was an unwanted child" (Bane & Benet pg. 11). She escaped by marrying Claude-Eric Lazard a wealthy international trader but that proved just as dysfunctional since he was only buying a teenage trophy wife and was a chauvinist in her words.

By twenty-one Danielle had become weary of the social scene and was "very bored and disenchanted." She answered an ad in a Manhattan newspaper for a secretarial position at Supergirls, a high-flying public relations firm. When she was hired her husband was furious since he had forbidden her to work. It was during this period that she met John Mack Carter who encouraged her to write about what he considered an interesting and provocative jet-setting lifestyle. That proved to be the genesis of her writing and resulted in her first book *Going Home* (1973). She told *People*'s Nancy Faber (People 2-5-79) "every woman falls in love with a bastard at least once in her life." She told *Women's Day* (June 1990) "I am never lonely when I write. You concoct dream men because they are no men in your life." Although that defies the reality since she has always had men. But her exacting standards are hard to meet and her manic lifestyle makes her a difficult mate.

CHARISMATIC SUCCESS. History gives us many famous leaders who used charm and charisma to climb to the very top. Cleopatra and Catherine the Great used their feminine charms just as Napoleon did. Napoleon's mortal enemy was Wellington who would give Napoleon the ultimate compliment saying, "The Corsican's presence on the field of battle was equivalent to 40,000 men." Napoleon's greatest moment occurred when he escaped from St. Elba with a small band of men and marched on Paris to regain the throne. Hearing of Napoleon's escape

King Louis XVIII dispatched General Ney to arrest him or kill him. Ney encountered Napoleon at Grenoble.

Seeing that all was lost the intrepid Napoleon dropped his sword and walked into the midst of the enemy and proclaimed, "Kill your emperor if you wish, but follow me to the Promised Land" (Landrum 1996 pg. 132). Ney ordered him to surrender and when he didn't he ordered them men to fire on their former emperor. Suddenly the troops lowered their muskets and started chanting, "*Vive l'Empereur!* Napoleon had won with guts and gusto. Ney and his troops joined Napoleon in the march on Paris where he regained the throne. Balzac immortalized the moment writing, "Before him never did ever a man gain an empire simply by showing his hat." Napoleon wrote in his memoirs, "Before Grenoble, I was an adventurer; at Grenoble I was a reigning prince."

Margaret Mead was another eminent writer who used charismatic power as a tool. Her second husband Reo Fortune said, "She is life force incarnate." While making a speech in New York, a young male was so enthralled he said, "The sex appeal of her mind was absolutely captivating. If she had pointed at me and said, you! You are the one I choose, I would have gone with her anywhere" (Landrum 1999 pg 54).

LITERARY INNOVATIONS OF A ROMANCE WRITER

Publishers Weekly lauded Steel's ability to sell books calling her, "a masterful plotter" (March 27, 1983). They saw what her faithful followers saw, a powerful persona that comes through in word-painted pictures of elegant motifs peopled with sophisticated heroes and heroines. Her plots tend to educate middle-class readers on the nuances of the rich and famous. Since Danielle grew up in these sophisticated circles she is a master at drawing word-pictures that describe the jet set world that others can only imagine. Danielle comes armed with the words to back up her style. She speaks French, Spanish, Italian, German and Japanese.

Literary critics admit that she brings the psychology of the chase into her tales of love and romance. She has raised the romance novel to another level. The Danielle Steel story is about jet-setters rendezvousing in elegant playgrounds where yachts, diamonds, silver, tuxedos, and butlers reign supreme. Such settings are but fantasies to her loyal fans mesmerized by trappings they have only heard or seen in the movies. Using Worth Avenue, Rodeo Drive, Park Avenue, and the Champ Elysees are exciting to those who will never visit them. *People* magazine says, "She writes mushy paperbacks that are almost as exotic as her own life" (Bane & Benet 1994 pg. 186). Steel told *People* "I make a world peopled the way I want my life to be." She has now sold 400 million books. This gives some validity to her power of the pen since she has influenced a large segment of the book-buying public.

MANIA & AURA. Steel says, "I become totally crazed" when describing her writing style. Her work has been described as "passionate realism" and "cathartic drama." Biographer Nicole Hoyt says, "She has an aura about her." Energy and emotion make up her dialogue and exotic rendezvous like Capri, Vail, Paris, Athens and Rome. Illusion and imagination are the tools that have made her successful. Reading Steel is akin to taking a vicarious journey into netherland where the beautiful people live and love and the girl always gets her man but not until she pays a horrible price.

WRITING AS CATHARSIS

Few writers ever allow their true inner feelings out. Most use metaphors. Steel's are but thinly veiled romantic longings from within. She is a woman in love with love, desperately in search for that love she never had as a child. Her vicarious explorations are but fantasy longings, and her love-starved heroines are her in disguise. Ex-husband Danny Zugelder says, "She creates the fantasy she wants to live and that is how she lives. And if any little things don't fit into that fantasy, it either doesn't exist or she changes it to fit the fantasy. That's just Danielle." (Bane & Benet pg.148)

Steel sees life as a process. She is optimistic, humanitarian, and nurturing. Her books all fit one profile with the exception of the 1998 book about her son Nick Train's tragic suicide. *His*

Bright Future was her first attempt at non-fiction, but it was really a way to write out her trauma. In 1981 she published *Love Poems. Publisher's Weekly* Oct. 5, 1984) panned them saying, "These are not poems, they are adolescent scribblings, filled with simplistic emotions and cliches." They were but cathartic expressions and the only time she dared bare her inner feelings in words. All the rest of her work has been thinly disguised as other women.

Women are drawn to her majestic style of emotional traumas searching feverishly for Mr. Right. "I just write what is in my head," she says. What is that? A desperate need for love. Danielle has lived this vicarious life of mythical romance for so long it is inextricably ingrained in her stories as it is in her subconscious. Her own life is being run in reverse. She married at seventeen to escape from an unhappy life in Manhattan. Her first husband was a chauvinistic French banker. They had homes in Paris, San Francisco and New York City. When not entertaining or partying she found herself shopping in the world's elegant boutiques. She hung out at Saks and Tiffany's, presumably every teenagers dream. But she was unhappy and left. The experience proved better than any Ivy League education, at least for grooming a woman for life as a romance writer.

Steel's books delve into the fantasyland of every woman's dream of having it all. All of her protagonists have careers, but are never quite complete until they capture that perfect male. The paradox of this highly successful career woman is that love and romance is the thing she has never mastered. She manages her career and family with the precision of a corporate executive, her organizational skills are those of drill sergeant, but she is totally inept when it comes to men. She writes about having it all – career, family and love - but the bottom line is that when you are as driven as Steel you cannot serve two masters. Thus she has to keep writing to survive.

Steel has written for "18-hours a day" for many years. She says, "It is my all-consuming passion" (Holt pg. 326). She told one biographer that she locks herself in a room and refuses to leave until finished with a story, beginning to end. She said, "I forget to get dressed or to comb my hair" (Holt 326).

Steel's real-life romances always end up in a novel. Her first book was about her first failed marriage. The fictional prisoner in her second novel *Passion's Promise* (1977) was about husband #2 convicted rapist Danny Zugelder. He was also the role model for the protagonists in her next two books *Now and Forever* (1978) and *Season of Passion* (1979). *Fine Things* (1987) was written about a friend who died of breast cancer and her 1998 book was about the traumatic death of her son Nick. Her fifth husband Tom Perkins was the protagonist character in *The Klone* (1999) and is testimony to her need to document what she finds attractive in men. It appears she is in constant need of new relationships as fuel for new romance books.

METAMORPHOSES

The Queen of Romance married French banker Claude-Eric Lazard but was divorced by age twenty and was given custody of their daughter Beatrix. Life with Lazard was miserable but it led her to escape into books and then to write out her misery in the form of a romance novel. She admitted to having no story outline or writing method. She just sat down and attempted to exorcise her anxieties through the medium of words. As her marriage deteriorated she escaped more and more into the fantasies of fiction. Her writing was becoming a form of therapy. She new about romance novels since she had consumed them "by the trillions." In her frenetic escapes she rode into the night to exotic places with princely men who worshiped her and treated her like a princess. Georgette Heyer had been a favorite writer and she would mimic her style.

Going Home was published when she was 22. Danielle admitted that she didn't even know enough to include paragraph indentations or punctuation. Her first submittal earned her the admonition, "go home and learn to cook." She ignored the advice and now says "I never did learn to cook." It was at this time that Danielle discovered a lump in her breast. Awaiting a biopsy she experienced a personal transformation. She packed up her baby daughter, packed her sizeable wardrobe, and headed west for San Francisco. The City by the Bay was the epicenter of avante-guard lifestyles. She fit right in, filed for divorce, and lived in a commune during those flower-child days of 1972. She finally found a publisher and *Going Home* was published by Bantam in October 1973. She was given a $3500 advance. It was her only book written in the first person and according to her account, it was revised so many times she hardly recognized it in its finished state.

ECCENTRICITIES

Steel is overtly shy but a self-proclaimed "write-aholic." She lives in perpetual search for love even after five marriages. Few women would consider speaking to a murderer living in a maximum-security prison let alone carrying on a torrid love affair with him. She was making a talk in the prison when she met Danny Zugelder and was bold enough to have relations with him in the men's room whole his buddies stood watch.

She married Danny despite his history of rape and robbery and used her influence to have him released. But while living in her house he committed another heinous crime and she had the marriage annulled. Testimony to her renegade nature she met a drug addict during the period awaiting the annulment and married him. That marriage was doomed from the beginning and ended in divorce. She married playboy shipping magnate John Traina but that marriage failed although it produced a number of children and lasted the longest. Her next attempt at marital bliss came with venture capitalist Tom Perkins. It lasted but a year.

Steel's writing style is more bizarre than her love life. She describes herself as "becoming totally crazed. I'm in a trance and will go a month without leaving the room. I can't leave it or I'll lose it. I'm terrified" (Hoyt p. 324). She told reporters, "When I'm working on a book I pretty much work around the clock. Every 20-22 hours I take a two to three hour sleeping break, then I go back at it" (Hoyt pg. 326). Her methodology includes producing the first draft in a flurry of ideas without any organization. This takes approximately twenty hours. She then spends the next year rewriting. As only a perfectionist can do, she then toils over every word and phrase to make it work.

Steel is such a control freak she plans her books years in advance. When her kids were at home she scheduled their activities six months in advance. Her Christmas shopping is always complete by October 1st. And she always orders a Christmas tree for the next year in January. The Romance Queen admits to publishing a family register each Monday that must be followed by each family member for the balance of the week. To maintain tight control over her eight children she has a beeper and cell phone. Third husband Bill Toth told a reporter, "I had to tell her I loved her, not once but what seemed like fifty times a day. Every time I passed her she said `I love you,' and I had to say it back. When I didn't we got into arguments" (Bane & Benet 184). When she was dating Danny Zugelder in Lompac Prison she would write him voluminous love letters. He said, "I'd get two or three or five a day and once a record seventeen" (Bane & Benet pg. 50).

LIFE CRISES

Steel is still paying the price for a very unhappy childhood and parents she described as "self-indulgent." Illness plagued her constantly. She once spent two months in Denver recouping. At age twelve she contracted polio, hepatitis at 15, and was hospitalized with a tumor at 16. She was devastated when her parents failed to visit her. Life in boarding schools led to an escapist marriage at seventeen to a European banker - Claude-Eric Lazard a wealthy international trader who acquired a teenage trophy wife for his social engagements. She played bore him a child and lived the jet set life for two years before rebelling. When that marriage ended she promised herself to never again fall prey to the social set disease that had plagued her all her life. It is no wonder she married down, way down, the second and third times.

Steel displays all the symptoms of a manic-depressive personality. This affliction is heritable and the suicide of her son Nick Traina at age 19 offers some insight into her own ups and downs. Nick was diagnosed manic-depressive and his death prompted her book *His Bright Light.* She speaks at length about his manic-depression as a strange neurological disorder, strange for a woman who exhibits many similar traits.

POLYPHASIC

Few people could keep up with Danielle Steel. She is pure freneticism and walks, thinks, writes, eats, talks, shops, drives and even sleeps at double time. Friends describe her at a picnic writing on her side, turning over and writing another plot on the other side, and maintaining this flip-flop vigil all afternoon. Biographers describe her working on three plots simultaneously and writing ideas all over the house, on mirrors, on napkins, in restaurants and at times on toilet paper.

Danielle is the classic Type A personality who feels barren without when not faced with a deadline. Keeping many balls in the air – polyphasia – is her forte. And she must finish what she begins even when it isn't interesting. She locks herself in a room and refuses to leave for fear of not finishing.

In the midst of her fifth divorce to Tom Perkins she finished her 47th book titled *Irresistible Force* (Nov. 1999). Each book has been completed as a *tour de force.* While the book is being edited she is fast at work on another and when that draft is complete will stop and begin editing the first. Such is the life of a woman with energy incarnate. An example of this routine is the time she wrote four books and a screenplay while waiting for her first book *Going Home* to be published in 1972. Danielle dabbles in escapist fiction, non-fiction, magazine articles, childrens books and poetry.

CRITICAL ACCLAIM

If success has any correlation with success Danielle Steel has surely made the grade. Now approaching 50 books with sales in excess of 400 she has made it despite being demeaned by literary critics. Critics are paid to criticize and that doesn't appear to alarm Steel. She has altered the romance genre and along the way has given her fans the ultimate in escape entertainment. *Washington Post* writer Susan Dooley says,

"Danielle Steel is a very bad writer" (March 3, 1985). The opposite comes from David Ball who wrote in the *Wall Street Journal* (March 11, 1985), "She is one of the high priestesses of escapist fiction." Critics often demean her for having her women "purr contentedly" and "look up adoringly" at their men.

In 1981 the student body of Southern California University voted her one of the world's most influential women for her work *Remembrance*, that gave her seven titles on the paperback romance list at the same time. Critics call her books "escapist soap opera." That may be the case but she appears to have learned her craft well. She provides her audience interesting and provocative fantasies that give them hope if not escape. And compared to other escapist tripe such as Dennis Rodman's erotic stupidity, the spaghetti westerns like Louis L'Amour, and Zane Grey Steel she is not bad.

SUCCESS & CHARISMA STYLE – What Can We Learn?

Charisma is the ability to attract a following to your vision. Steel is a master. The intent is to communicate, motivate and titillate, and she certainly does that. A charismatic is able to make their disciples believe they are "special." Steel seems to succeed in this as well.

Passions of the pen like Steel's work should entertain and this is not possible without flare and charisma. Steel empathizes with lonely woman, since she is one, and therefore is able to write with total identity with her reader. Steel *is* the consummate romantic protagonist portrayed in her books. They are but realistic fantasies popping out of her inner needs and desires.

Albeit trite, knowledge does build enthusiasm, and consummate knowledge, that knowledge of belief that says you are special and have a unique message, can only come from a person who believes passionately in their work. Steel is such a person. And when you believe the world will follow you just as Steel's fans have faithfully followed her through almost fifty books. Exaggeration, extravagance, excess, titillation, diamonds, jewels, exotic travel and flamboyant scenes of opulence are the cornerstones of flights of fancy. These are critical for romantic fiction. Steel is the personification of all these. How many people order jeweled cigarette cases and exotic diamonds over the phone? The next day she will call Rome or Paris and have a dress delivered from a favorite courtier. Beauticians come to her home to do her hair. She shops on-line for designer couture dresses costing $10,000 each, and once had Dior designer bring dresses to the house for her kids birthday party. All her parities are catered even for another couple. She once surprised John Traina with a $145,000 Lamborgini for his birthday. This is not quite the lifestyle of Miss Jane Secretary. It is one of their fantasies. But it is not fantasy to Steel making her the charisma queen.

In *Having a Baby* she wrote, "I like bringing the mountain to Muhammad," in describing her penchant for ordering products costing hundreds of thousands of dollars by phone. Steel lives in the posh Pacific Heights district of San Francisco in the Spreckel's mansion. She purchased the home in 1990 for $7 million but it had no guest facilities so she bought the adjoining house for another $2 million. Such is the opulence of a rich lady who dares be different and writes as she lives. Living the life of illusion makes it easier to write illusory stories. She people's her stories with characters right out of her own glamorous and ostentatious lifestyle.

The secret of charisma is tapping into your inner passion and pursuing it at all costs. If you believe, it will often come. In writing the words must connote the passion of your dreams or chance being ineffective. Readers sense when something is faked. Cult leaders have long understood this. Successful charismatics align themselves with *cause celebre.* Shaw and Hemingway used hero-worship as their vehicle and Anne Rice chose immortality. They imbued the reader with a cause and then captured them with powerful and passionate word-pictures. Rice told the media "I'm sure of one thing, if I get as weird as I want to get, and as crazy as I want to get, readers will go with me." Fleming found the same in his Bond fantasies. Readers would suspend belief to go with him into bizarre scenes that were nonsensical but empowering to couch potatoes seeking titillation for a mundane life.

17

SUCCESS IMPRINTS & LITERARY GENIUS

"Exceptional individuals are impelled by their inner nature to seek their own path" Carl Jung

PARADIGM SHIFTS & SUCCESS

Socrates was poisoned for teaching people to think. Galileo was imprisoned for writing that the sun, not the earth, was the center of the universe and it only took Mother Church another 300 years to admit they were wrong. Gordon Bruno was burned at the stake for daring to teach the earth moves. Guttenberg was ostracized for inventing type. Charles Darwin was charged with heresy for his work on evolution. Thoreau was jailed for having ecological ideas. Freud was hated for writing that many illnesses originate in the unconscious. And Professor John Henry Popper pronounced Edison's electric light bulb as the "work of a charlatan." J.P. Morgan said Bell's telephone idea "had no commercial value."

The prestigious *Scientific American* pronounced the Wright brother's flight a "hoax." In 1925 a young visionary inventor, Milo Farnsworth, showed up with his new radio picture invention (first TV), but they sent a secretary down to get rid of the radical and told the secretary to "watch for guns, knives and bombs." Buckminster Fuller was fired for being too innovative. Walt Disney's first animated film *Snow White* was called Disney's Folly. The same myopics who poisoned Socrates have now attacked Bill Gates for being too good. What message can we find in all this? The price of creativity is dear indeed. Challenging the status-quo can be dangerous if not lethal.

The creative are best served to ignore the establishment. Why? Because traditionalists often have a self-serving agenda. They almost always sacrifice the future for a better present, when all innovation demands the sacrifice of the present for a better

335

future. This is true of any dynamic system. Such systems require a visionary to lead them to the Promised Land, because the world is not *digital it is analog; it is not quantitative it is qualitative; it is not fixed it is dynamic, it is not limited, it is boundless; and the path is inductive not deductive.* Few understand this fundamental truth, but Prometheans understand it better than most since they begin with the end and use the detail to justify their prescient vision.

TASTE & SUCCESS. The publishing industry is self-serving. They usually take on books guaranteed to sell with merit relegated way down the list of importance. Decisions are made by executives who are motivated by numbers never quality. Why? Because continued employment lay in the balance.

Consider the incredibly popular Harry Potter children books by J. K. Rowling whose work was turned down by no less than nine publishers. Then her first four books reached sales of $100 million in revenue and her fifth book, *Harry Potter and the Goblet of Fire* released in July 2000 enjoyed a first printing of 3.8 million copies. What did the tenth publisher know that escaped the first nine? Nothing! The first ones made decisions predicated on how they would look, what the book would potentially do to the bottom line, and how acceptance might impact their own personal future, none of which has anything to do with the merit of the manuscript.

An inverse relationship often exists between what is worthy and what is published. Acceptance and rejection has a long history across many venues. The most shining examples are found in food, music, and entertainment. French wine, classic music, designer dresses, and elegant cuisine have the ultimate quality, but the least acceptance. Why? Because, quality always comes in second to quantity. French cuisine may be superior to a McDonald's Big Mac, but the dollar sweepstakes always go to the Golden Arches. Symphonies and opera provide a better cultural experience, but the Jimmy Buffet wins this game and the opera holds bake sales to survive. Natural foods are far more nutritional, but they lose out to the purveyors of fast food. In TV the A&E Biography program educates and inspires, but loses out in the rating wars to Jerry Springer's inane talk show.

The *National Enquirer* outsells *Architectural Digest*. What does this say to writers? The demand for knowledge is less than the demand for entertainment.

WRITING PARADOX. The preeminent storytellers in this work validate the above. Those who made the most money were the best storytellers - Twain, Christie, Hemingway, Fleming, King, Michener, Rice, and Steel. These writers sold close to 4 billion books with countless movies, TV specials, and stage plays to their credit. The books earned billions. Of these only Twain and Hemingway were considered literary. And Twain had to die to get that label. All the others have been criticized for writing tasteless drivel for the masses. Ironically, all of these writers wrote real page-turners.

Those who wrote with a message, moral, and intellectual bent were Shaw, Woolf, Camus, Campbell, Plath and Rand. Of these Woolf and Camus achieved the greatest acclaim, but they starved. Rand is the greatest paradox. *The Fountainhead* was made into a 1947 movie that gained a cult-following by the intellectual college set. It was despised by the literary community for its inflammatory philosophy. Remember it was published during a period sympathetic to socialism, a concept she detested. When the students grew up to be leaders she was granted some modicum of acceptance but that didn't happen until the rebellious 60's and 70's. Intellectual books by Campbell and Plath, found moderate acceptance, but were never commercially successful. Balzac, Dostoevsky, and Dr. Seuss married superb story telling with a philosophical message with Dr. Seuss enjoying the greatest success.

WHAT PRICE GENIUS?

The price of creative genius is high indeed. Three of these subjects committed suicide – Woolf, Hemingway, & Plath. Balzac, Camus and Fleming died young due to their dissipative lifestyles dominated by women, booze, and life on the edge. The above six were manic-depressives.

Most sacrificed their families for their career. Balzac died from his own frenetic work ethic that didn't allow time for sleep or rest between *tour de forces* that ended in 100 volumes. He refused to allow a mate interfere with his grand scheme and wrote, "If I am not a genius I am done for. Demons drive me" (Robb pg. 60). Robb described his self-destruction a "self-induced madness" (pg. 24). Such fury is born of an inner drive to prove oneself worthy. Dostoevsky had a similar predilection. He was forced to deal with the "fiend" (epilepsy), alcohol, and a gambling habit that kept him on the brink of bankruptcy. Both he and Balzac wrote to avoid life in debtors-prison.

Bernard Shaw lived with his mother until almost thirty. Once married when nearing forty he never consummated the marriage. Virginia Woolf and Sylvia Plath wrote as a means to escape imminent insanity. Both lost the race and did themselves in. Hemingway did the same while Fleming used an alternate method, cigarettes and booze.

PERSONAL VS PROFESSIONAL. A writer is not able to serve two masters. That is especially true for anyone looking to climb to the very top. You can be a good mate, or the best at your profession, but you can't have both at the same time. Why? Because the price is too high for either to have a fair chance. Only three women, Woolf, Rice, and Rand lived a reasonably normal family life. had a normal marriage. (Woolf's inclusion is questionable since she had a female lover for many years) Rand stayed married to one man but engaged in a thirteen-year affair with a young protégé. Anne Rice has enjoyed the most normal marriage, but it was dotted with life in those turbulent years in Haight-Ashbury and Berkeley.

Of the men Joseph Campbell came closest to normal marital bliss. But he and his professional dancer wife Jean Erdman agreed that children would not interfere with their careers. They jokingly agreed to spawn "spirit children not earthly children." Dr. Seuss and first wife Helen led a relatively uneventful life until he became involved with the wife of a friend and she committed suicide. Hemingway, Fleming and Camus led tumultuous personal lives with women more pawns than mates. Stephen King and Mark Twain were faithful husbands, but their lifestyles were anything but normal. Almost half -

seven of seventeen (Balzac, Campbell, Michener, Shaw, Dr. Seuss, Rand, and Woolf) – went childless.

Most of the males believed as Freud, that sexual activity was counter to creative activity. Balzac had one illegitimate child by a mistress, but otherwise lived a barren life. Fleming had one child, but the boy became a drug addict and committed suicide as a teenager after his father's untimely death. Shaw and Campbell had pre-nuptial agreements that forbade children. Dr. Seuss adored children but his first wife was unable to conceive and he was too old by the time he remarried.

Hemingway was a flagrant womanizer who was never faithful to any wife, lover, or mistress. He was estranged from his son Gregory for the last ten years of his life. Danielle Steel had everything - beauty, money, culture, and the good life ensconced in a San Francisco mansion. But on closer inspection the Romance Queen has lived a tortuous personal life with five divorces and a son who committed suicide. Dame Agatha Christie's unfaithful husband left her for a younger woman causing her to suffer a nervous breakdown. Her second marriage was without the passion of the first. Mark Twain's personal life was a tragedy. One daughter committed suicide, another was institutionalized, and a son died due to his parental neglect. His wife was gravely ill much of her life.

TYPE A WORKAHOLICS. The majority were Type A personalities (see table 5). Over half were A+ types functioning like megalomaniacs on a mission. Such people confuse self-worth with achievement and live life in the fast lane. They have a time fixation and seldom take vacations or allow themselves to relax. Balzac, Dostoevsky, Twain, Woolf, Hemingway, Dr. Seuss, Plath, and Steel were the A+++. They got a lot done but left many bodies in their wake. Balzac was off-the-scale. He regularly worked 18-hour days in a *tour de force* that ultimately killed him. He began work every night at 1:00 a.m. and wrote non-stop until 8:00 a.m. He rested for a few hours before starting the next day around noon. Huge amounts of coffee were consumed to maintain his frenetic pace. In a moment of introspection he wrote, "The days melt in my hands like ice in the sun. I'm not living, I'm wearing myself out in a horrible fashion" (Robb 25).

Danielle Steel often fell asleep at her desk during a self-imposed need to complete a book before leaving her room. She often wake up with typewriter marks on her face. Her obsessive behavior has resulted in a long string of romance novels that have now reached 400 million in sales. Steel says, "If I'm working on a book I work pretty much around the clock – every 20 to 22 hours, I take a two to three hour sleeping break then I go back at it" (Hoyt pg. 326).

The Type b's in the book were Campbell, Christie, Michener, and Rand. But even they had traits of the Type A as they refused to take a vacation for fear of losing out on productivity. Joseph Campbell wrote, "No misfortune can be worse than the misfortune of resting permanently static" (Larsen 1991). Even the low key Agatha Christie wrote wrote one new book or play, each year for 57 straight years. By virtually any definition of work ethic she was driven. Michener also has the traits of a Type b but a look at his work ethic tells a different story. The master of the historical novel refused to take a vacation for thirty years. When in his 70's he refused to take time off for personal enjoyment, and toiled seven days a week on his typewriter. One literary adversary wrote, "Michener is the hardest working American author."

RISK-TAKING PROPENSITY. All but one male and one female lived an adventurous life that was risky at best and downright dangerous at worst. Few were as self-destructive as Balzac who wrote, "I am the gambler without cards, Napoleon without troops, the investor without capital." His excesses were legend. To stave off bankruptcy he would go out and buy another business to try and save the first incurring so much debt he was never able to recover. With cynical humor he once wrote, "Debt is a countess who is a little too fond of me" (Robb p. 128).

Virtually all regularly bet the farm on their dreams. Risk and creativity were never stated more eloquently than by Lord Attenborough who said, "Unless it is daring and risks failure, any artform will wither and die." Philosopher Soren Kirkegaard offers further validation with his aphorism, "To venture causes anxiety, but not to venture is to lose oneself."

LITERARY GENIUS

Dostoevsky, Twain, Hemingway and Fleming were compulsive gamblers. Dostoevsky once sold all of his future royalties for $1000 rubles to pay off his debtors. Instead of paying his debts he retired to a casino and lost every ruble on the spin of a roulette wheel. The next day he had to borrow money to eat. He wrote to Turgenev. "I have lost everything. I am completely broke. I even gambled away my watch" (Boorstin 666). But the loss became a catalyst for *The Gambler* (1867) written to get enough money to eat. Mark Twain lost millions in wild ventures that he labeled "my fatal addiction." Ian Fleming tested the limits of the fastest sports cars and did the same in Alpine skiing adventures. Hemingway loved the thrill of deep-sea fishing and wild game hunting in the wilds of Africa. He was also infamous for barroom fights.

Campbell, Hemingway, Camus and Michener all ran with the bulls at Pamploma. The majority drove fast cars and generally lived life in double-time. What they considered safe most people would have found risky. They thrived on the chance of winning big and lived life with a kind of death-wish mentality. Fear is the enemy of all innovation not its friend. Hiding behind fear or waiting for lady luck to appear is the pathway to mediocrity just as locking your child in a room will insure they never get a bloody nose. They will also never learn to cope.

RENEGADE NATURE. These subjects were renegades if not radical. Most were thought of as eccentric. Refusal to conform made them special, and also separated them from the pack. There is always a fine line between being different and being thought of as dangerous. Twain, Shaw, Rand and Rice were radical but talented enough to cover their bets. They adroitly used their renegade reputations as an asset instead of allowing it to become a liability. Stephen King admitted to being a recovered alcoholic and drug addict. Dr. Seuss and Agatha Christie were highly reclusive. Balzac, Twain and Dostoevsky filed bankruptcy. Fleming was sado-masochistic and Woolf was bisexual. Normalcy was not one of their qualities.

George Bernard Shaw was about as radical as you can get. The Irish dramatist was an atheist in the Victorian era, a vegetarian long before it was in vogue, a Marxist who co-founded the

British Labor Party, and lectured extensively against the evils of marriage and doctors. He labeled doctors and their profession "witchcraft." When awarded the Nobel Prize for Literature and the Order of Merit he turned both down as "valueless." As an elder statesman during World War II he outraged those fighting to save Britain. He told the press, "I would welcome a German attack on London." His contentious behavior is found in his masterpieces, *Man & Superman* and *Pygmalion* (My Fair Lady).

Dr. Seuss, aka Ted Geissel wrote, "I'm subversive as hell. I've always mistrusted adults. It is the one reason I dropped out of Oxford. I thought they were taking life too damn seriously" (Morgan p. 248). His advice to aspiring writers was "always do something as different as you can."

CHARISMA. All these subjects were great communicators. Effective communications skill is critical to any success especially for anyone trying to get published. Balzac said it wasn't how well you write but how well you can talk that is important. He believed that selling and marketing were more important that writing. And it is true that one cannot find an agent, get published, or promote their work with charisma. Campbell, Twain, Rand and Fleming had evangelistic qualities.

Great people are superb communicators. This was true of Catherine the Great, Napoleon, Sigmund Freud, Carl Jung and most cult leaders. George Bernard Shaw had a remarkable following considering he was highly introverted. After having his first eight works rejected he took to the lecture circuit and made over 1000 speeches to build a reputation of a man deserving to be published or produced. It worked! He was hired as a newspaper critic for drama, art, and music and elected to public office. Only then were his plays produced.

The word *charisma* comes from the Greek meaning *Gift of Divine Grace*. When Balzac walked into a room his energy pervaded it. When he spoke the aura was all-consuming. When he laughed the room exploded with a kind of celestial energy. Such is the stuff of legends emanating from within a driven person.

LITERARY GENIUS

Author William Dean Howells said, "Mark Twain had a mythic dimension that set him apart from the rest of our sages, poets, seers, critics humorists" (Kaplan p. 190). Part of his speaking ability was staged. "He wrote, "No man will dare more than I. I used to play with the pause as children play with a toy" (Kaplan 86). A media critic said of Shaw, "His words were a ray of light such as we seen once or twice in a century" (Holroyd pg. 192).

Joseph Campbell was spellbinding. Disciple Lynn Kaufman said, "He was radiant, the aliveness of the world came through him" (Larsen p. 565). Erudite individuals selected him as their mentor and were in awe of his mythical vision. One example was *Star Wars* creator George Lucas who said, "If it were not for Joseph Campbell I might still be writing Star Wars" (Larsen p. 541). An editor of *Psychology Today*, with had a doctorate degree, heard him speak at Esalen and proclaimed, "Joseph Campbell didn't know more than any of us, he knew more than *all* of us. I think he was the encyclopedia – all by himself" (Larsen p. 490). Ardent disciples included John Steinbeck, Bob Dylan, Jerry Garcia, Alan Watts, George Lucas, Marianne Williamson and Bill Moyers.

PASSION. A number of these subjects were so passionate they dominated any forum in which they were invited. Ardor defined them for the most part. If doors were closed they knocked them down, if they were not accepted once in they altered the situation, or changed the motif. Bipolar illness afflicted many including Balzac, Dostoevsky, Twain, Woolf, Camus, Fleming, Hemingway, Plath and Steel. When in a euphoric state they were unstoppable, but when they came down they were incapable of the simplest acts. Psychic energy pervaded their very being with eghty-three percent classified hypomanic (euphoric) and eight manic-depressive. When up they were above the world. When down they went underground.

To summarize, the literary genius is a maverick. They must be to create. But they must also have a huge ego to thwart those that would destroy them for daring to be different. Another quality is having a big picture view of the world. They must have an inner picture of the journey before defining the road that will lead there. Such people have a penchant for operating at various points on the personality continuum and prefer breaking new ground to treading the old. They seek life's opportunities no matter where they may lead. These type people are driven beyond the norm and are opportunists who use what they have to break down the barriers to the top. They have **High Self-Esteem, Work Ethic, Manic Drive, Risk-Taking Propensity, Vision, Non-Conformity, Charisma, Machiavellian Behavior,** and **Passion.** Let's discuss those that haven't already been covered.

SELF-ESTEEM – BELIEVE AND THE WORLD WILL FOLLOW

One of Balzac's mistresses told him, "You are pretending to be god." His justification was that he had decided to be great and knew no other way than to assume a messianic manner. He told her, "If I am not a genius I am done for." Similarly, Virginia Woolf, Sylvia Plath, and Anne Rice dreamt they were God and wrote with messianic fervor. Dostoevsky admitted to being an egotist. He wrote, "I am a braggart." Such self-esteem led to his monumental works of psychological insight. The most confident writer in this book was the creator of James Bond, Ian Fleming. One long-term mistress described him as a man "who was obsessed with himself." It takes supreme confidence to create scenes that are outlandish and super heroes like 007 who violate all rules and regulations. After his death Fleming's wife Ann told a biographer "He was egocentric."

Hemingway was nearly as egotistical as Fleming. Papa was a self-absorbed boar to those not enthralled by his charms. The most arrogant female was Ayn Rand. She wrote extensively on the value of pursuing one's "selfish best interest." She wrote, "High self-esteem is at the root of ethical egoism." Few talk-show hosts would interview her for fear of being destroyed by her acerbic commentary. Rand wrote a book on the philosophy of selfishness titled *Anthem,* in which she elevated "rational selfishness" to a godly state. This confident woman refused to have one word of her work changed by an editor. When her sixty page speech by John Galt speech in *Atlas Shrugged* was questioned she responded, "Would you change the Bible?" Further testimony comes from Sciabarra (pg. 305)

The man who accepts the role of sacrificial animal, will not achieve the self-confidence necessary to uphold the validity of his mind, and the man who doubts the validity of his mind, will not achieve the self-esteem necessary to uphold the value of his person.

G.B.S biographer Holroyd (1988) wrote, "Shaw's greatest creation was himself. He could not wait until he was famous to behave like a great man." Shaw would have agreed. He wrote, "The man who is modest is lost, my prodigious conceit towers over all ordinary notions of success" (Holroyd pg. 246).

The more contrite Michener wrote, "I am an incorrigible optimist." He admonished aspiring writers to become self-assertive and to work on their self-esteem "Without a solid self-confidence, I do not see how young people will have the courage and determination to undergo the disappointments of apprenticeship in the arts" (Michener 1991 pg. 327).

INSECURITY AS MOTIVATOR. Despite strong self-esteem many of these writers were beset by self-doubt. Shaw, Camus and Fleming were consumed by insecurity. Others lived in mortal fear of failing. They could question themselves but god forbid if someone else challenged them. Dr. Seuss, Sylvia Plath and Stephen King all burned their most famous manuscripts. Even those who had been dealt an awful hand like Dostoevsky, Woolf and Plath flirted with insanity and feared the abyss.

Despite repeated rejections by friends, mates, and publishers these writers maintained a remarkable inner confidence. They abided by Afred Adler's admonition, "inferiority causes overcompensation." Inferiority proved a catalyst to make them try harder. Bucky Fuller wrote, "I am the world's most successful failure" meaning that he was successful despite his self-flagellation and many failures.

HYPOMANIA & HIGH PRODUCTIVITY

Most of these seventeen were *hypomanic*. The DSM-IV definition of this state is "a psychopathological state falling between euphoria and mania." Eight-eight percent (88%) fit this definition. They did most things fast including eating, walking, talking, driving, and even sleeping. They were in a hurry and always scheduled more than they could possible finish. Dostoevsky was both hyper and epileptic. He called his epileptic seizures his "Mystic Terror," and blamed them on his "volcanic eruptedness." He described his inner demons as a scourge of the driven personality. But the drive that he felt was ruining him was also the very thing that made him. Without those inner demons it is unlikely he would have been so productive. He certainly wouldn't have written some of his books such as those dealing with his excesses *The Gambler, The Idiot,* or *Crime and Punishment.*

Hypomania is one of the symptoms of bipolar illness. Eight, or nearly half were manic-depressive and three of these committed suicide. Their mania was a positive as well as a negative in that it was a major contributor to their awesome productivity. Hemingway is an example of a manic personality who used it to improve his writing. He was over fifty when he finished his classic Nobel Prize winning *The Old Man & the Sea.* His manic need for perfection caused him to rework it over 200 times. Hemingway averaged about four hours each night as did Balzac, Woolf, Dr. Seuss, Camus, Steel, and Plath. Most felt sleeping was a waste of time.

Sylvia Plath was both manic and obsessive. She spoke of her inner demons as an "out-of-control beast," and wrote, "It is as if my life were magically run by two electric currents: joyous positive and despairing negative – whichever is running dominates my life, floods it. I am now flooded with despair almost hysteria...I am as mad as any writer must be" (Stevenson p. 134).

TABLE 5

Behavioral Data Of Literary Genius

SUBJECTS	EGO-Mania	TYPE A/B	HYPO MANIA	BIG T/t	REB. DVR	Char-isma	HIGH MACH	SEX Drive
MALES								
BALZAC	E+++	A+++	M/D	R+++	I+++	C+++	M	S+++
CAMPBELL	E+	B	NO	NO	I++	C+++	NO	NO
CAMUS	E++	A+	M+	R	I+++	C+++	NO	S+++
DOSTOEVSKY	E	A+++	M/D	R+++	I++	C+	M	S++
FLEMING	E+++	A++	M/D	R+	I+++	C+++	M	S+++
HEMINGWAY	E++	A+++	M/D	R+++	I++	C+++	M	S+++
KING	E	A++	CUSP	R+	I+	NO	NO	NO
MICHENER	E+	A+	M+	R++	I+++	NO	NO	NO
SHAW	E+++	A	NO	R+	I+++	C++	M	NO
DR SEUSS	E	A+	M+	R+	I	NO	NO	S
TWAIN (CLEMENS)	E+	A+++	M/D	R+++	I+++	C+++	M	S++
MALES **(11)**	E= 11 100% E++=5	A=10 91% A+=6	M=9 82% M/D5	R=10 91% R+=5	I=11 100 I+=9	CH=8 73% C+=7	MC=6 55% LM=5	SX=7 64% S+=6
FEMALES								
CHRISTIE	E	B	M/D	NO	NO	NO	NO	NO
PLATH	E++	A+++	M/D	R++	I++	C++	M	S++
RAND	E+++	B	M	R	I++	C++	M	S+
RICE	E+++	A++	M+	R++	I+++	C++	M	S+++
STEEL	E+++	A+++	M/D	R++	I+++	C+++	NO	S+++
WOOLF	E+	A+++	M/D	R++	I+++	C+	M	S+++
FEMALES **(6)**	E = 6 100% E++=4	A= 4 67% A+=4	M= 6 100% md=4	R= 5 83% R+=4	I=5 83% I+=5	CH=5 83% C+=4	Hm=4 67% LM=2	SX=5 83% S+=4
TOTALS **(17)**	E=17 100% E+=9	A=14 82% a=10	M=15 88% m/d9	R=15 88% R+=9	I=16 94% I+14	C=13 76% C+=11	M=10 59% LM= 7	S=11 65% S+=7

Mark Twain was restless and traveled extensively to quiet his inner engines. He said, "I was born excited." Virginia Woolf also suffered from mania. She spoke often in her journals about a "racing pulse, excitability, rages, temper, and severe mood swings." Danielle Steel's first boss described her as having, "the most astonishing energy. She was ten times faster than anyone I know."

MACHIAVELLIANS – THE ENDS JUSTIFY THE MEANS

Ten subjects were High Machs, meaning a person who allows the ends to justify the means. Such people use others to attain their goals. It has a negative connotation in business and politics since Nikola Machiavelli wrote his book *The Prince* as a means of destroying from both within and without. He admonished Italian princes to attack before being attacked and use power to control the masses.

These writers were more into sacrifice and achievement than power, but Hemingway was a classic user as was Fleming. Most sacrificed family, friends, health, and money for their passion. The least capable of this were Michener, Campbell, and Dr. Seuss. No sacrifice is ever too great for a High Mach. Woolf gave credence to this with her statement, "Writing is the synthesis of my being" (De Salvo p. 1989). GBS said, "I have a wicked tongue, a deadly pen, and a cold heart" (Holfoyd 1988 111). Stephen King told the media, "If I wasn't writing I'd probably commit suicide or might be a mass murderer." Plath wrote in her journal, "If I don't write I will die." With such admission it isn't hard to see why they were willing to sacrifice the personal for the professional.

Balzac was the consummate High Mach. The father of the modern novel sacrificed his health and welfare for his own genius refusing to consider marriage because it would interfere with his creativity. He told his friend Alexander Dumas, "a night of love cost half a volume. No woman alive is worth two volumes a year" (Robb p. 179). Consequently, Balzac didn't marry until a few months before he died at age fifty due to his megalomania. Dedication to their writing caused these authors to have few close friends.

HIGH LIBIDINAL DRIVE & OBSESSIONS

Passion ruled the lives and work of these subjects. Sometimes that passion was sublimated in work as in the case of Balzac, Campbell, and Dr. Seuss. Balzac's biographer Robb said, "Sperm for him was an emission of pure cerebral substance filtering through the penis a work of art" (Robb 179). Others expressed their passions more normally through aggressive pursuit of romance. An example is the two-thirds (see Table 5) who were psychosexually driven (they qualified if married at least three times or spent an inordinate amount of time seducing members of the opposite sex as did Dostoevsky, Hemingway, Fleming, and Camus or Woolf, Rice and Steel who wrote about little else).

Balzac, Hemingway, Fleming and Camus were womanizers with a capital W. Sex and seduction dominated their existence. Fleming was the most nefarious. He used and abused women in real life almost as bad as his alter-ego James Bond. Rice wrote pornographic books and Woolf wrote obsessively about her illicit affairs with both sexes. She called this "autoanalysis." Her stories were autobiographical probes into being molested by half-brother George Duckworth and various lesbian relationships with her sister Vanessa and writer/lover Vita Sackville-West. She also wrote about an adulterous affair with Vanessa's husband Clive Bell.

Danielle Steel and Hemingway were similar in many perverse ways. Both wrote heroic fantasies that took place in exotic European settings, neither was able to find any permanent relationship that worked, and they were the most married of all the subjects. Both were needy to a fault, impossible to live with, attractive, passionate, and had a flare for the perverse. Hemingway had three children by two different women while Steel had eight by three different men. Hemingway attempted to interest his wives in menage-a-trois relationships and was never faithful. Steel appears to have remained faithful to a point, but was crazy enough to have a liaison in the men's bathroom in a maximum-security prison with a convicted criminal who she later married. Both wrote cathartic stories of lost love and fantasies beyond them in real life. Their words were often titillating with a realistic bent since they were based on their own provocative experiences.

18

CREATIVITY & GREATNESS

"The limit of vision is simultaneously the limit of comprehension"
Leonardo Da Vinci

BOOKS & MYTHICAL HERO/MENTORS. Books have a huge impact on the great and especially eminent writers. But the influence is not what one might expect. It is not reading skill, vocabulary enhancement, or what is learned on the journey, although all of these are beneficial. It is the power of hero-mentors, protagonists who are larger than life that, when identified with are capable of removing inner limits to success. That is the overwhelming benefit of books, even comic books, and why they should be a fundamental part of the life of every child. Why? When a child adopts a hero that is bigger than life and identifies with them totally they are removing self-imposed limits that inhibit growth and success in life.

Why is this? Our major limitations are never external. They are internal - in our heads and hearts. When we identify with a hero, even if mythical like Superman or Wonder Woman, they allow actions beyond the purview expected. It was no accident that Shaq O'Neill won the 2000 MVP and World Championship in the NBA with a tattoo of Superman on his arm. Is he naturally good? You bet! But that special edge must emanate from within where all limits are born.

Anne Rice became obsessed with the occult and supernatural after seeing the ghost scene in *Hamlet*. And after reading Dicken's *A Christmas Carol* "more times than anyone in history. I wanted to go into the supernatural persona of Scrooge." Young George Shaw attended a performance of *Faust* at age 15, went home and decorated his room with symbols of

351

Mephistopheles. His internalized devil would emerge thirty years later in his classic play *Man & Superman.*

BOOKS, SUCCESS, & FANTASY HEROES

There are numerous examples of great leaders modeling their life and actions after some hero from books. Since most of our limits are self-imposed it is obvious adopting a hero who is larger than life, an Alexander the Great, Napoleon, Superman, or some eminent writer, will arm one to overcome adversity and become greater than otherwise possible. Emulating a hero can elevate you above mere mortals and overcome the rejection that is part of the journey to creative genius. Alexander is an example. He carried Homer's *The Illiad* with him to the far ends of the world and fought as his mythical hero Achilles would have; which allowed him to conquer the world before age 35. Henry Schlieman was a poor German boy who had one book as a child - Homer's *The Illiad.* He reread it many times until the story of Troy was part of his very being. When he retired and decided to find Troy, the world's archeologists scoffed at his chase of fool's gold. They said he was chasing a myth. He was, but he found it buried in Western Turkey. Carl Jung says, "All our concepts are mythological images. It is not Goethe that creates *Faust,* but *Faust* who creates Goethe."

Joseph Campbell spent his life on mythological heroes. In a 1988 TV special he told Bill Moyers "Myths are powerful guides to the life of the spirit – our ticket to the passages of life. They are models for understand your life. All our images are masks – a myth is a metaphor that makes heroes out of those who heed them" (Segal pg. 18). Quotes from various creative geniuses are shown in Table 5 on the next page.

CRITICAL ACCLAIM & SUCCESS

The success of these subjects was pervasive. Many took years to find success. Others found it quickly, but none ever considered quitting when rejection was the only constant in their life. Table 6 offers insight into the time line and their contribution to the genre.

TABLE 6

BOOKS AS INSPIRATIONAL TOOLS

MAYA ANGELOU	"*CRIME & PUNISHMENT* changed my life"
JOSEPH CAMPBELL	"*The Romance of Leonardo Da Vinci* changed my life"
ALBERT CAMUS	"*The Possessed* nourished and educated me"
FYDOR DOSTOEVSKY	"I read like a fiend, and would rave deliriously about Anne Radcliff's novels inmy sleep"
THOMAS EDISON	"I didn't read a few books, I read the library"
ALBERT EINSTEIN	"I had read Kant and Darwin by age 12"
BILL GATES	"My favorite hobby is reading"
ERNEST HEMINGWAY	*THE DARK FOREST* altered his life
STEPHEN KING	"Lovecraft's fantasy horror fiction opened the way for me. I lived and died with *Dr. Jekyll & Mr. Hyde*"
JAMES MICHENER	"By 12 I read 40 volumes of Balzac's *Human Comedy*"
OPRAH	"Books changed my life"
AYN RAND	"Hugo's *LES MISERABLES* is the greatest book ever written"
ANNE RICE	"Shakespeare's ghost scene in *HAMLET* obsessed me as did Dicken's *A Christmas Carol*"
DR. SEUSS	"It was Belloc's *The Bad Child of Beasts* that introduced me to the hypnotic joys of ryme"
GEORGE B. SHAW	"*Das Kapital* was the turning point in my career"
DANIELLE STEEL	"I walked into walls reading romance novels in school"
NIKOLA TESLA	"Mark Twain changed my life"
MARK TWAIN	"I read Kipling's *Kim every year*"
VIRGINIA WOOLF	"My nicest presents as a child were books"

CREATIVITY

AUTHOR, GENRE Major Influential Work	CRITICAL ACCLAIM
Honore Balzac – Modern Novel *The Human Comedy* (1841) Father of the Modern Novel	Engels wrote, "I've learned more from Balzac than all the professional historians, economists, and statisticians put together." Influenced Marx, Dostoevsky, Michener & 1848 French revolution
George Bernard Shaw –DRAMA *Man & Superman* (1905) *Pygmalion* (1913)	Irish dramatist and winner of Nobel Prize for Literature and Knighthood and turned both down; the consummate renegade who saw a Nietzschean "Life Force" or *Superman* as fundamental to all success.
Albert Camus – Non-Fiction *The Stranger* (1942) Existentialist philosopher	Nobel in Literature for "The Plague" (1957); An insecure Algerian peasant who altered French philosophy via plays and novels; absurdity and positive nihilism his contribution
Fyodor Dostoevsky – Psychology *Crime & Punishment (1866)* Father of psychological novel	"I learned more about psychology from Dostoevsky than any other person." (Nietzsche); Freud, Gide & Bennet wrote, "*The Brothers Karamazov* (1880) is the greatest novel ever written"
Ian Fleming – Spy Thrillers *From Russia With Love* (1957) Master of Playboy Fantasies	*Forbes* (1993) "Bond is a phenomenon, the most popular film series ever. In every man born after 1930 there surely still exists a part of his psyche which dreams of being James Bond."
Mark Twain (Clemens) - Humor *Huckleberry Finn* (1884) Father of American Literature	"All American literature comes from one book by Mark Twain called *Huckleberry Finn* … There was nothing before. There has been nothing as good since." (Hemingway)
Agatha Christie – Mystery *Murder of Roger Ackroyd* (1926) Queen of Detective Crime	British housewife wrote one book for 57 straight years with 2 billion sold in 103 languages. *The Mousetrap* (1952) longest running play in history. "I regard my work of no importance. I simply entertain."
Ernest Hemingway–Short Stories *The Old Man & the Sea* (1952) *Death in the Afternoon* (1932)	"Hemingway is the greatest writer since Shakespeare." (John O'hara); Pulitzer Prize (1952) & Nobel Prize (1954); *The Short Happy Life of Francis Macomber* (1935) and *The Snows of Kiliminjaro* (1936)
James Michener- Historical Novl *South Pacific* (1948) Master of Historical Novel (41)	1947 Pulitzer Prize for literature and most prolific American writer of historical fiction. A classic illustration of perseverance paying off. He didn't begin writing until age forty and never worked again.
Joseph Campbell – Mythology *Hero With Thousand Faces* (1949) Father of Mythology (45)	Major influence on Lucas' Star Wars who said, "Hero was very enlightening to me," due to Campbell's thesis, "Myths create heroes out of those who heed them" and "Follow your bliss."
Ayn Rand – Philosophical Novel *Atlas Shrugged* (1957) Greatest philosophical novel	Libertarian Party elevated her to sainthood by adopting her philosophy as its fundamental doctrine and it became a new philosophical movement known as Objectivism.
Sylvia Plath – Poetry *The Bell Jar* (1961) Cathartic Realism (29)	First posthumous winner of Pulitzer Prize for introspective work that has made her into cult figure. Her passionate prose is "fierce and enduring" according to *Time* (April 1994)
Danielle Steel – Romance *The Promise* (1979) The Queen of Romance	Writeaholic who has become most prolific producer of romantic novels in American history with 400 million in sales. She creates the romantic life she personally needs to live as cathartic release
Stephen King – Horror *Carrie* (1974) The Master of the Macabre	Rolling Stone wrote, "Stephen King is a one-man horror industry," with an inexhaustible imagination for macabre tales. "Has the artistic sensibility of a clever 14 year old." (Time Dec. 1992)
Theodore Seuss – Children's *Mulberry Street* (1937) *The Cat in the Hat* (1957)	*And to Think I Saw it on Mulberry Street* (1937) led to 48 zany books with over 200 million sold. Dr. Seuss was a mediocre artist defining anarchic youth culture of 60's via "Cat in the Hat"
Virginia Woolf – Innovator *Mrs. Dalloway* (1925) *To the Lighthouse* (1927)	One of the 20th centuries acclaimed innovators in the stream of consciousness style who revolted against traditional narrative techniques with perceptive observations on the human psyche
Anne Rice – Occult *Interview with the Vampire* (1976) Queen of the Occult	Publisher's Weekly wrote, "Interview is an extraordinary first novel." "Interview is an existential gothic … due to Rice's kinky fatalism." (Newsweek Nov. 1994). Existential nihilism striving for immortality.

There are times in life when all seems lost. The person pursuing their dream has many chances to call it quits after being devastated by some personal tragedy or rejection. It is not what happens to us in life but how we deal with it. And the winners appear to be able to write off tragedy to some external factor that keeps it from debilitating them personally. One of the factors discussed throughout this book is chaos and trauma. Actually, bad stuff can be a blessing in disguise.

CHAOS & CREATIVITY THEORY. Dr. Ilya Prigogine won the Nobel Prize for his work on chaos and creativity. He showed that emotional trauma can be an asset as well as a liability. In *Order Out of Chaos* (1984) he wrote, "Psychological suffering, anxiety, and collapse can lead to new emotional, intellectual, and spiritual strengths. Confusion and death can lead to new scientific ideas." Prigogine's Dissipative Structures Theory says, "All structures are teetering perpetually between self-destruction and reorganization." He argued that when bad stuff happens we hit a "bifurcation Point" where a person or system either dies or reemerges. But if they use it to learn they actually can become better than prior to the chaos. An example is breaking a bone in your arm. You can never break it at that spot again. Why? Because the bone becomes stronger at the break point. Prigogine's model says the emotional system functions similarly. He wrote, "Many systems of breakdown are actually harbingers of breakthrough."

When a writer hits the wall or experiences total rejection they can either die (quite writing) or reemerge better. When F.Scott Fitzgerald received 22 rejections for his first novel he tacked them around his apartment for inspiration to keep going. Many others may have taken them personally and quit. Prigogine says that psychological suffering, anxiety, and collapse can lead to enhanced productivity. That happened to Fitzgerald who later wrote the classic *The Great Gatsby* as it did with Balzac, Shaw, Dr. Seuss, and Stephen King.

Even more telling are the personal tragedies of Dostoevsky, Michener and Rice. Dostoevsky wrote to his brother on his near death and ten years in a Siberian prison saying that the experience was both devastating and enlightening:

*Prison destroyed many things in me and
created the new. I won't even tell you what
transformations were undergone by my soul,
my faith, my mind, and my heart in that four
years. The escape into myself from bitter
reality, did bear its fruit.* (Gide pg. 63)

For those wishing to tap into their creative side it is imperative
to review the path taken by these creative visionaries. After
much research on the methodology of people attempting to
succeed in a left-brain world - one that worships at the altar of
mediocrity not innovation - I have come up with some laws that
appear to be critical to the process.

TABLE 8

DR. GENE'S LAWS OF CREATIVITY

1. **PERSISTENCE PAYS**
   What if George Bernard Shaw had stopped writing when
   his first six novels and an equal number of plays were
   rejected? What would have happened to Danielle Steel if
   she had returned home and learned to cook as one
   publisher advised? Rand had her first novel turned
   down by 12 publishers, the same number that rejected
   J.K. Rowling's sensational books on Harry Potter. If you
   never quit and you can never be defeated.

2. **NEVER, EVER, EVER LISTEN TO AN EXPERT!**
   Why? Because experts have such a psychological
   investment in what *is* they are never able to see what
   might be. History has much validation of this principle.
   Edison went to his grave denying the value of AC. Why?
   Because he had invented DC. For the same reason
   Einstein refuted quantum physics, and many publishers
   are so steeped in past success they seldom are able to
   accept the new and innovative. Experts poisoned
   Socrates and burned Joan of Arc at the stake.

3.   ITS OKAY TO BE DIFFERENT

Why? Because there are few wins where the masses live.
Virtually every innovative breakthrough comes from the
fringe by visionary renegades who dare challenge
convention. Shannon's Law tells us that, "the adoption
of information is inversely related to its credibility."
Biographers have used the Law to describe the irascible
Dr. Seuss who adamantly refused to conform and
thereby revolutionized children's books. Mediocrity
reigns supreme in traditional venues. Victor Hugo
violated every rule of French literature but his style soon
became the accepted way. In the inimitable words of
George Bernard Shaw, "Reasonable men adapt to the
world. Unreasonable men attempt to adapt the world to
them. Therefore all progress depends on the
unreasonable man."

4.   NEVER WRITE OR DO ANYTHING JUST FOR $

Chasing money is counter-productive to getting it. We
keep score in capitalism with money and if you execute
well money will be delivered in trucks. Bucky Fuller,
authored twelve books, held a Chair in Poetry at
Harvard, and created the extraordinary geodesic dome.
He said, "You have to decide whether you want to make
money or make sense, because the two are mutually
exclusive." How right he was. Stephen King told 60
Minutes, "I've never written for money even when I didn't
have any." The world's richest man – Bill Gates never
did anything for money nor do literary geniuses.
Dostoevsky is an exception since, paradoxically he wrote
The Gambler, to pay off his gambling debts. Mark Twain
said, "I published *Jumping Frog* simply to advertise
myself, not with the hope of making anything out of it."
The book cost him $2000 but led to his literary career.

5.   IDENTIFY YOUR GREATEST WEAKNESS & ATTACK

You are only as good as your greatest weakness. It is the
only thing that can destroy you, so identify it and attack.
If you hate detail, get immersed in it. If you don't know
how to promote your work, take a marketing class. If
pathologically shy go out and make a speech. If

uncomfortable with risk, go bungie jumping. Becoming comfortable with weakness disarms it. Anne Rice told *Rolling Stone* (July 13, 1995), "When I write, I explore my worst fears and then take my protagonist right into awful situations that I myself am terrified by. It is therapeutic and helps me to continue."

6. LIVE ON THE EDGE – JUST DON'T FALL OFF!
Big wins without big risks don't exist. The eminent people of the world tend to live life right on the edge but have a prescient insight into when to back off. They understand that risk and reward is a zero-sum game with rewards declining in direct proportion to the risks taken. Safe is not best unless security is the driving force within you and you are searching for exactitude and mediocrity. Look for the greatest risk you can manage and take it. Life is far too short to live it in the slow lane. Risk pervaded the work and lives of Michelangelo, Leonardo, and Picasso, as it did with Dostoevsky, Twain, Woolf, and Stephen King. Even the matronly Agatha Christie lived on the edge. She violated the most sacred laws of writing by daring to have the culprit be the storyteller. Her temerity led to two billion books sold and her label as the Queen of Mystery.

7. TAP YOUR GUT & INTUITION & WORK BACKWARDS
Allowing your imagination free reign, and fantasies to enter your work, is the beginning of creative genius. Einstein said, "The gift of fantasy has meant most to me. Everything that counts can't be counted and everything that can be counted doesn't count." What was he saying? That the world is dynamic and qualitative and getting lost in the trees of numbers can destroy any chance at true innovation. George Bernard Shaw said it well, "Some men see things the way they are and ask, Why? I see them as they are not and ask, Why not?" Creativity is born of unrestrained exploration into the surreal and life's possibilities. Campbell recommended we adopt a mythical-mentor. "Myths are models for understanding your life. They create heroes out of those who heed them." Don that cape and go where the fearful

fear to tread. It is imperative to have a vision and quantify it, not the other way. Start at the end and "learn in reverse" as Ayn Rand recommended. Or as J.K. Rowling told the Associated Press in July of 2000, "My characters come fully formed. I knew Harry was a wizard. And then it was a process of working backwards to find out how that could be, and forwards to find out what happened next."

8. **FOLLOW YOUR BLISS!**

Joseph Campbell admonished us to live by our own agenda. And to never live to another's, including mate, parent, teacher or editor. He wrote, "Each individual must find the myth fundamental to his internalized need and follow it. Follow your bliss for an emotionally stable life. Bliss is miraculous, follow it and don't be afraid and doors will open where you didn't know they were going to be." Many creative geniuses live a long life. Why did Plato live until eighty when the life expectancy was less than half that? Because his labor of love at The Academy left little time for sickness or even death. That was also true in the long productive lives of Michelangelo, George Burns, Irving Berlin, Bob Hope, Helena Rubinstein, Picasso, Frank Lloyd Wright, and George Bernard Shaw. These individuals never retired and were productive right to the end. They saw life as a process and once you stop being a part of the process it ceases to be pleasurable and you succumb to illness.

ITS NEVER TOO LATE TO BE GREAT. The mind, like a muscle, atrophies without use. The creative seem to understand this better than most. Frank Lloyd Wright was broke at 60, designed *Fallingwater* at 69 and the Guggenheim Museum at 91. One-third of his life's output was produced after he was eighty. Goethe didn't complete *Faust* until he was 82. Copernicus wrote *Revolutionary Heavenly* Spheres at 70, Cervantes published *Don Quixote* at 68, and Hugo wrote *Les Miserables* at age 60. Shaw wrote until almost mid ninety. Michener was still writing when he pulled the plug on his dialysis machine at age 92. Dr. Seuss created *The Cat in the Hat* at age 57 and lived to be 87. Agatha Christie wrote until she died at 86, and Campbell had just begun a series of eight new books at 83.

CREATIVITY SELF-ASSESSMENT

The following self-assessment exercise is meant to give the reader an indication of their propensity for a creative life. The score will not guarantee anything whether high or low. It is simply another barometer that will allow you to see how you compare to others on a scale relative to research findings of other creative individuals.

DIRECTIONS: *Rank yourself low (1) if you have little likelihood for the behavior; in the middle (2,3,4) if that best describes you, or high (5) if you have a strong likelihood for the behavior. Your score will vary depending if you use a professional or personal perspective. Be candid and honest in order to find your propensity for creativity. One mark should be made for each question depending on how you see yourself. Total the scores on each dimension and see answer key below.*

A. FLUENCY (COMMUNICATIONS ABILITY)   1-2-3-4-5
   1. HAVE RICH AND FLUENT VOCABULARY   _____
   2. SPEAKS MIND ON MOST TOPICS   _____
   3. ARTICULATES STYLE, COLOR
      & COHESION ON NEW IDEAS   _____
   4. ATTRACTS FOLLOWERS TO IDEAS   _____
   5. HAS PERSONAL MAGNETISM   _____

B. SPATIAL ACUITY (INTUITIVENESS)
   1. SEES BIG PICTURE IN MOST THINGS   _____
   2. QUALITY EXCEEDS QUANTITY   _____
   3. PURSUES THE "POSSIBILITIES" OF LIFE   _____
   4. PREFERS MATH TO ACCOUNTING   _____
   5. LONG-TERM EXCITING   _____

C. IMAGINATION (INNOVATION)
   1. DAILY FLIGHTS OF FANTASY   _____
   2. INQUISITIVE TO A FAULT   _____
   3. INVETERATE NEED TO KNOW   _____
   4. PREFERS NEW RESTAURANTS   _____
   5. INTOLERANT OF USELESS CONFORMITY   _____

D.   COMFORT WITH AMBIGUITY   _____
   (RISK-TAKING PROPENSITY)
   1. THRIVES ON THE NEW & UNKNOWN   _____
   2. GETTING LOST IS EXCITING   _____
   3. LIKES DIFFICULT PROBLEMS

    4. PREFERS NEW VENUES TO OLD   _____

    5. SELDOM DOES ANYTHING FOR MONEY   _____

E. PASSION & PRODUCTIVITY (DRIVE)
    1. IMPATIENT & INTOLERANT OF OTHERS   _____

    2. PREFERS TO WORK INDEPENDENTLY   _____

    3. ENTHUSIASM APPROACHING MANIA   _____

    4. TAKES ON UNREALISTIC TASKS   _____

    5. EATS, TALKS, WALKS & THINKS FAST   _____

F. SELF-ESTEEM (EGO-STRENGTH)
    1. INTROSPECTIVE   _____

    2. NEEDS FEW SUPPORT SYSTEMS   _____

    3. GUILTY OF UNREALISTIC EXPECTATIONS   _____

    4. BELIEVES ANY GOAL IS ATTAINABLE   _____

    5. FELT SPECIAL AS CHILD   _____

G. INDEPENDENT (ICONOCLASTIC)
    1. RATHER BE DIFFERENT THAN PERFECT   _____

    2. ASKS MANY QUESTIONS IN LECTURES   _____

    3. REDUCES THE COMPLEX TO THE SIMPLE   _____

    4. SEES PROBLEMS AS OPPORTUNITIES   _____

    5. VORACIOUS READER OF NON-FICTION   _____

H. NO SACRED COWS (AUTONOMOUS)
    1. SELF-SUFFICIENT IN ALL THINGS   _____

    2. ACHIEVEMENT VERY IMPORTANT   _____

    3. PREFERS VARIETY TO STRUCTURE   _____

    4. PATHOS FOR THE PROVOCATIVE   _____

    5. LOVES MAXIMUM RESPONSIBILITY   _____

TOTALS   _____

CREATIVITY CQ: CREATIVITY IS IN THE MIND OF THE BEHOLDER. SOME INDIVIDUALS ARE BEST SUITED TO WORK IN STRUCTURED ENVIRONS AND NOT ATTEMPT TO ALTER THE STATUS-QUO. OTHERS SHOULD NOT LIMIT THEMSELVES AND ARE BEST SUITED TO WORK IN A FREE-FORM SETTING WHERE THEY CAN ALLOW FREE REIGN TO THEIR CREATIVITY.

SCORE	CREATIVE CQ
175-200	HIGHLY CREATIVE
140-174	VERY CREATIVE PERSON
100-139	ON THE CUSP OF CREATIVITY
75 - 100	GET A JOB
< 74	GET A BUREACRATIC JOB

ADDENDUM

TABLE 9

ENVIRONMENTAL DATA OF LITERARY GENIUSES
5 Women, 11 Men, 6 Europeans, 10 Americans from 16 Genres
Three from 19th century; Six from 1st half 20th century, Seven
from Last half 20th century

SUBJECTS	Birth order	Self-Empl Parnt	Forml Educ.	Move Travel	Class Lower Upper	Chaos death	Religion
	First		Coll.	5-move	L-M-U		
MALES							
BALZAC	1ST	YES	BA	TR+	M CL	YES	YES
CAMPBELL	1ST	YES	MA	TR++	M CL	NO	AGN
CAMUS	2ND	YES	MA	TR	L CL	YES	ATH
DOSTOEVSKY	2ND	YES	BS	TR	M CL	YES	YES
FLEMING	2ND	YES	15TH	TR++	UP CL	YES	ATH
HEMINGWAY	2ND	YES	HS	TR	M CL	YES	NO
KING	1ST	YES	BA	TR+	L CL	YES	NO
MICHENER	1ST	YES	MA	TR++	L CL	YES	NO
SHAW	3rd	YES	8TH	NO	M CL	NO	ATH
DR. SEUSS	1ST	YES	BA	TR	UP CL	YES	NO
TWAIN (CLEMENS)	LAST	YES	5TH	TR++	M CL	YES	NO
MALE TOTALS (11)	1ST=5 45%	Y=11 100%	HS=3 BA=5 MA=3	TR=10 91%	UC=2 MD=6 LC=3	CR=8 80%	REL=2 NOT=5 AGN=4
FEMALES							
CHRISTIE	2ND	YES	8TH	TR	UP CL	YES	YES
PLATH	1ST	YES	15TH	TR	M CL	YES	NO
RAND	1ST	YES	BA	TR++	M CL	YES	ATH
RICE	2ND	NO	MA	TR++	M CL	YES	AGN
STEEL	1ST	YES	HS	TR+++	UP CL	NO	YES
WOOLF	7TH	YES	Home	TR	M CL	YES	AGN
FEMALE TOTALS (6)	1ST=3 50%	Y=5 83%	HS=3 BA=2 MA=1	Y=6 100%	U=2 M=4 L=0	CR=5 83%	REL=2 NOT=1 AGN=3
GRAND TOTALS (17)	1ST=8 47%	Y=16 94%	HS=6 BA=7 MA=4	Y=16 94%	U=4 M=10 L=3	C=13 76%	REL=4 NOT=6 AGN=7

CREATIVITY

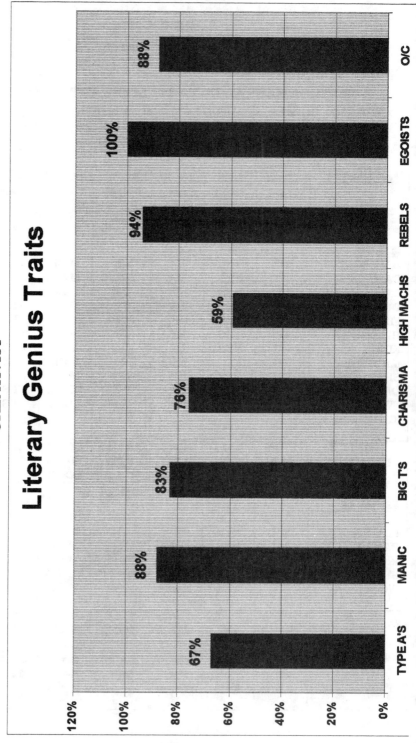

Literary Genius Traits

LITERARY GENIUS BIBLIOGRAPHY

SUBECT CRITERIA RESEARCH

Boorstin, Daniel. (1992). The Creators. [Balzac, Dickens & Dostoevsky section in particular]. Random House, N.Y., N.Y.

Draper, P. Joseph. (1992). World Literature Criticism., Gale Research, Detroit, MI

Hart, Michael. (1978). The 100 - A Ranking of the Most Influential Persons in History. Citadel Publishing, New York, N.Y.

Hodges, Jack. (1992). The Genius of Writers. St. Martin's Press, N.Y., N.Y.

Magell, Frank. (1994). Great Women Writers.

Pickover, Clifford (1998). Strange Brains & Genius, William Morrow, N. Y.,

Storr, Anthony. (1993). The Dynamics of Creation. Ballantine Books, NY

Wordsworth Poetry Library. (1995). The Metaphysical Poets. Wordsworth Editions Ltd. Herfordshire, England.

Young, Thomas & Fine, Ronald. (1968). American Literature: A Critical Survey. American Book Company, N.Y., N.Y.

GENERAL BIBLIOGRAPHY

Adler, Alfred. (1979). Superiority and Social Interest. Norton & Co. N.Y.

Amabile, Teresa. (1989). Growing Up Creative, Crown Publishing, N.Y.

Barzun, Jaques. (Summer 1989). "The Paradoxes of Creativity". The American Scholar.pg 337.

Boden, Margaret. (1990).The Creative Mind, Harper-Collins, NY, NY

Branden, Nathaniel. (1994). Six Pillars of Self Esteem. Bantam NY

Clark, Barbara. (1988). Growing Up Gifted, Merrill Publishing, Columbus,Ohio

Frankl, Victor. (1959). In Search of Meaning. Pockey Books, N.Y., N.Y.

Freud, Sigmund. (1925) On Creativity & the Unconscious. Harper, NY

Gardner, Howard. (1983). Framing Minds - The Theory of Multiple Intelligences. Basic Books - Harper, N.Y., N.Y.

Ghislin, Brewster. (1952). The Creative Process. Berkeley Press,

BIBLIOGRAPHY

Gillespie, Marcia. (Dec 1992). Essence pg 49 "Maya Angelou"

Gordy, Berry. (1994). Berry Gordy – To Be Loved, Warner Books, NY.

Goleman, Daniel & Kaufman, Paul & Ray Michael. (1992). The Creative Spirit. Dutton, N.Y., N.Y.

Hannah, Barbara. (1997).Jung. ChironPublications, Wilmette, IL

Hershman D. & Lieb, J. (1994) A Brotherhood of Tyrants, Prometheus, Buffalo,

Hoffman, Edward. (1994). The Drive for Self - Adler and the Founding of Individual Psychology, Addison-Wesley, New York, N. Y.

Horn, Thelma. (1992). Sport Psychology. Human Kinetics, Leeds, England

Hutchison, Michael. (1990). The Anatomy of Sex & Power. Morrow, N.Y.

Jamison, Kay. (1994). Touched with Fire - Manic Depression, Macmillan, N. Y.

Jung, Carl. (1976). The Portable Jung ["The Stages of Life"] Penguin, N.Y., N.Y.

Keirsey, D. & Bates, M. (1984). Please Understand Me. Prometheus, Del Mar, CA.

Landrum, Gene. (1993). Profiles of Genius. Prometheus, Buffalo, NY

Landrum, Gene. (1994). Profiles of Female Genius. Prometheus, Buffalo, NY

Landrum, Gene. (1996).Profiles of Power. Prometheus, Bufallo, N.Y.

Landrum, Gene. (1997) Profiles of Black Success. Prometheus, Buffalo, N.Y.

Landrum, Gene. (1999) Eight Keys to Greatness. Prometheus, Buffalo, N.Y.

Leman, Kenneth. (1985). The Birth Order Book. Dell Publishing, N.Y.

MacKinnon, David. (1965). American Psychologist. "Personality and the realization of creative potential". pg 273-281

Noll, Richard. (1997). The Aryan Christ Random House, N.Y., N.Y.

Ornstein, Robert & Thompson, Richard. (1984). The Amazing Brain. Houghton-Miflin, N. Y., N. Y.

Pearsall, Paul. (1991). Making Miracles. Avon Books, N.Y., N.Y.

Peterson, Karen. (12-15-92). USA Today pg 3C "Angelou has Brave words for UN bash"

Pickover, Clifford (1998). Strange Brains and Genius, William Morrow, NY

Pierce, Ponchitta. (Aug. 6, 1995). Parade pg 4, "Who are our heroes?"

Prigogine, Ilya & Stengers, Isabelle. (1984). Order Out of Chaos.
    Bantam Books, N.Y., N.Y.

Simonton, Dean Keith. (1999). Origins of Genius – Darwinian
    Perspectives on Creativity. Oxford Press, N.Y., N.Y.

Storr, Anthony. (1989). Freud, Oxford University Press, Oxford, England

Storr, Anthony. (1996). A Study of Gurus – Feet of Clay, Free Press, N. Y., N. Y.

Taylor, I & Gretzels, J. (1975). Perspectives in Creativity. Chicago, Ill.

Wallace, Iriving, Amy, Sylvia & Wallechinsky, David. (1981). The Secret
    Sex Lives of Famous People, Dorset Press, N. Y., N. Y.

LITERARY SUBJECT BIBLIOGRAPHY

AGATHA CHRISTIE

Christie, Agatha. (1977). Agatha Christie - An Autobiography. Berkley, N.Y., N.Y.

Gerald, Michael. (April 14, 1994). The New England Journal of Medicine.
    "The Poisonous Pen of Agatha Christie. Texas Press, Austin, TX.

Gill Gillian. (1990). Agatha Christie -- The Woman and Her Mysteries.
    Maxwell Macmillan, N. Y., N.Y.

Magell, Frank. (1994). Great Women Writers. "Agatha Christie" pg 94-97

Robyns, Gwen. (1978). The Mystery of Agatha Christie - An Intimate
    Biography of the Duchess of Death. Penguin Books, N. Y., N.Y.

Shenker, Israel. (Sept. 1990). Smithsonian. "The Past Master of Mysteries"

HONORE BALZAC

Draper, P. Joseph. (1992). World Literature Criticism., Gale Research, Wash,

Maurois, Andre. (1965). Prometheus - The Life of Balzac. Harper & Row,

Robb, Graham. (1994. Balzac - A Biography. W.W. Norton, N.Y., N.Y.

Wallace, Iriving, Amy, Sylvia & Wallechinsky, David. (1981). The Secret
    Sex Lives of Famous People, "Balzac" pg. 87-90, Dorset Press, NY

Zweig, Stefan. (1947). Balzac. The Viking Press, N.Y., N.Y.

Zweig, Stefan. (Nov. 1947). Balzac. "Book of the Month Club"

BIBLIOGRAPHY

JOSEPH CAMPBELL

Campbell, Joseph. The Inner Reaches of Outer Space. Harper & Row, N.Y.,

Campbell, Joseph. Transformations of Myth. Harper & Row, N. Y., N.Y.

Larsen, Stephen & Robin. (1991). A Fire in the Mind - The Life of Joseph Campbell. Doubleday, N.Y., N. Y.

Lefkowitz, Mary. (Summer 1990). American Scholar "Mythology – The Myth of Joseph Campbell"

Moyers, Bill. (1987). The Power of Myth - Joseph Campbell's Theories of Life & Myth. PBS TV shown in four series October 1995

Segal, Robert. (1987). Joseph Campbell. Mentor Books, NY

Toms, Michael. (1989). An Open Life: JosephCampbell. Perennial Library

ALBERT CAMUS

Camus, Albert. (1951). The Rebel. Vintage Books, New York, N. Y.

Literary Review (1990); "Camus the Outsider" page 225

Reiter, Joseph. 1995 Grolier Electronic Publications. "Albert Camus"

Solomon, Robert. 1995 Grolier Electronic Publications. "Existentialism"

Todd, Olivier. (1997). Albert Camus – A Life. Alfred Knopf, New York, N.Y.

World Literature Criticism. Pg. 384-385, "Albert Camus"

FYODOR DOSTOEVSKY

Dostoevsky, Fyodor.)1946). The Gambler. Bantam Books, N.Y., N.Y.

Dostoevsky, Fyodor. (1950) Crime & Punishment. Random House, N.Y.

Draper, P. Joseph. (1992). World Literature Criticism. "Fyodor Dostoyevsky" p 969, Gale Research, Detroit, Michigan

Frank, Joseph. (1976). Dostoevsky 1821-1849. Princeton Press, Princeton, N.J.

Frank, Joseph. (1995). Dostoevsky - 1865-1871 Princeton Press, Princeton, N.J.

Gide, Andre. (1923). Dostoevsky. New Directions, N. Y., N. Y.

Morson, Gary Saul. (Winter 1995). American Scholar. "A Writer's Diary 1873-1876 By Fyodor Dostoevsky". Northwestern University Press

IAN FLEMING

A&E TV SPECIAL. (Jan 9, 2000). "The Story of James Bond"

Lycett, Andrew. (1995). Ian Fleming : James Bond. Turner Publishing, Atlanta,

Pearson, John. (1966). Ian Fleming, McGraw-Hill, N. Y., N. Y.

Stacy, Mitch. (Oct. 23, 1998). Associated Press "Top 10 Movie Quotes"

Swann, Christopher. Contemporary Popular Writers. Pg. 148

Symons, Julian. Contemporary Literary Criticism. Pg. 159CLC

Weller, Anthony, (Nov. 22, 1993). Forbes. "Bond at 40" pg. 1

THEODORE GEISEL (Dr. Seuss)

Contemporary Authors. "Theodore Seuss Geisel" p 168-171

Morgan, Judith & Neil. (1995). Dr. Seuss & Mr. Geisel.   Random House, N.Y.,

Seuss, Dr. *Random House* (1999). Tom Peters, New York, N. Y.

ERNEST HEMINGWAY

Brodie, James Matthew. (1987). Dissertation Ernest Hemingway. UMI
      Dissertation

Hemingway, Ernest. (1926). The Sun Also Rises. MacMillan, N.Y., N.Y.

Hemingway, Gregory. (1977). Papa - A Personal Memoir, Pocket Books, NY

Lynn, Kenneth S. (1987). Hemingway. Fawcett Columbine, N.Y., N.Y.

Mellow, James. (1993). Hemingway.Addison-Wesley Publishing,   Boston, MA

Sanderson, Stewart. (1961). Hemingway. Oliver & Boyd, Edinburgh, Scotland

Young, Thomas & Fine, Ronald. (1968). A Critical Survey. "Ernest
      Hemingway" p. 315, American Book Co, N.Y., N.Y.

STEPHEN KING

A&E TV SPECIAL. (Jan. 17, 2000). Stephen King., Harry Smith, Wolf Films

Beahm, George. (1992). The Steven King Story. Andrews & McMeel, Kansas
      CityMO

BIBLIOGRAPHY

Contemporary Literary Criticism Vol. 12 pg. 309-311 "Stephen King"

Contemporary Authors. New Revision Series, Vol. 52, pg. 231-243, "Stephen King"

Draper, P. Joseph. (1992). World Literature Criticism. "Steven King" p 309, Gale Research, Detroit, Michigan

60 Minute CBS TV Interview on Aug 2, 1998, "Stephen King"

Minzesheimer, Bob. (9-17-98). USA Today pg. D1, "Horror's Home Run king"

Roush, Matt (9-24-96). USA Today "King's Double House of Horrors Sect D PG-1 TLC TV SPECIAL. (Jan. 7, 2000). Chuck Verrill interviewed on "Stephen King – Master of the Macabre"

Wohlber, Curt, (12-95). American Heritage Magazine. "The Man Who Can Scare"

JAMES MICHENER

Donahue, Deidre. (Oct. 17, 1997). *USA Today* pg. 4A, "James Michener dies"

Hayes, John P. (1984). James Michener – A biography. Bobbs-Merrill Co.,

Michener, James. (1959). Hawaii. Random House, N. Y., N.Y.

Michener, James. (1992). The World is My Home. Random House, N.Y.

Michener, James. (1993). Literary Reflections. Tom Doherty & Associates, N.Y.

Rosselini, Lynn. (June 17, 1991). *U. S. News & World Report* pg 3

MARK TWAIN - SAMUEL CLEMENS

Clemens, Samuel. (1990). The Autobiography of Mark Twain. Harper, N.Y..

Draper, P. Joseph. (1992). World Literature Criticism. "Mark Twain" p 3712, Gale Research, Detroit, Michigan

Devoto, Bernard. (1964). Mark Twain Fawcett Publications, Greenwich, CN

Kaplan, Justin. (1966). Mr. Clemens & Mark Twain - A Biography. Simon & Schuster, N. Y., N.Y.

World Literature Criticism. "Mark Twain" pg 3712-3713

Young, Thomas & Fine, Ronald. (1968). American Literature: A Critical Survey. "Mark Twain" p. 223, American Book Company, N.Y., N.Y.

SYLVIA PLATH

Contemporary Authors – New Revision Series Vol. 34 pg. 353-357" Sylvia Plath"

Hayman, Ronald. (1991). "The Death & Life of Sylvia Path". Birch Lane

Hughes, Ted & Frances McCullough. (1991). The Journals of Sylvia Plath. Ballantine Books, N.Y., N.Y.

Iannone, Carol. Contemporary Literary Criticism Vol. 62 pg. 382-383 "Sylvia Plath"

New Republic (June 6, 1996). "The Bell Jar" pg 34

Sachs, Andrea. (April 18, 1994). "Poets in Suicide Sex Shocker - Janet Malxolm explores the lurid obsession with Sylvia Plath". Time

Schwiesow, Deirdre. (10-24-96). USA Today pg 6D "The Bell Jar"

Stevenson, Anne. (1989). Bitter Fame. Houghton-Mifflin, Boston, Ma

Wagner-Martin, Linda. (1987). Sylvia Plath St. Martin's Press, N.Y.

AYN RAND

Branden, Nathaniel. (1962). "Who is Ayn Rand". Random House, N.Y., N.Y.

Branden, Barbara. (1986). "The Passion of Ayn Rand - A Biography".

Branden, Nathaniel. (1989). "Judgement Day - My Years with Ayn Rand". Houghton-Mifflin. Boston, Ma.

Branden, Nathaniel. (1992). World Literature Criticism pg. 2877, "Ayn Rand Critical Commentary"

Contemporary Literary Criticism. (1975). CLC-3 "Ayn Rand". pg 423

Draper, P. Joseph. (1992). World Literature Criticism. "Ayn Rand" p 2877, Gale Research, Detroit, Michigan

Rand, Ayn. (1982). "Philosophy: Who Needs It". Signet, N.Y., N.Y.

Rand, Ayn. (1957). "Atlas Shrugged". Signet, N.Y., N.Y.

Rand, Ayn. (1993). "The Objectivist Newsletters - 1966 thru 1971". Second Renaissance Books, Oceanside, Ca.

Toffler, Alvin. (March 1964). Playboy Interview of Ayn Rand. "Playboy".

ANNE RICE

Contemporary Literary Criticism, Vol. 41, pg. 361-366

Contemporary Authors. New Revision Series, Vol. 53, pg. 398-404

BIBLIOGRAPHY

Gilmore, Mikal. (July 13, 1995). Rolling Stone , "The Devil & Anne Rice" pg

Ramsland, Katherine. (1994). Prism of the Night. Penguin Books, N.Y., N.Y.

Riley, Michael. (1996). Conversations with Anne Rice. Ballantine Books, N.Y.

Tartt, Donna. (Nov. 1898). US, "Anne Rice" pgs. 84-90

GEORGE BERNARD SHAW

Adam, Ruth. (1966). What Shaw Really Said. Schocken Books, N. Y., N.Y.

Draper, P. Joseph. (1992). World Literature Criticism. "George Bernard
Shaw" p 3184-3200, Gale Research, Detroit, Michigan

Holroyd, Michael. (1988). Bernard Shaw - The Search for Love. Random
House, N.Y., N.Y.

Holroyd, Michael. (1989). Bernard Shaw – The Pursuit of Power. Random
House, N. Y., N.Y.

St. John, Christoper. (1932) Ellen Terry & Bernard Shaw.Putnam & Sons
N.Y., N.Y.

Tehan, Arline. (Nov, 90). Smithsonian. "The Playwright and his `Mollissima'"

World Literature Criticism. "Bernard Shaw" pg 3184-3186

DANIELLE STEEL

Contemporary Authors, New Revision Series, Vol. 65, "Danielle Steel" pg.   329-31

Contemporary Authors, New Revision Series, Vol. 19, "Danielle Steel" pg. 438-440

Bane, Vickie & Benet, Lorenzo. (1994). The Lives of Danielle Steel, St. Martins, N.Y.,

Hoyt, Nicole. (1994). Danielle Steel. Windsor Publishing, N.Y., N.Y.

VIRGINIA WOOLF

DeSalvo, Louise. (1989). Virginia Woolf - The Impact of Childhood Sexual
Abuse on Her Life and Work. Ballantine Books, N.Y.,N.Y.

Draper, P. Joseph. (1992). World Literature Criticism. "Virginia Woolf" p
4043, Gale Research, Detroit, Michigan

Dunn, Jane. (1991). A Very Close Conspiracy: Vanessa Bell & Virginia
Woolf, Little, Brown, N.Y., N.Y.

Economist. (Aug. 29, 1992). "A Bart in Woolf's Clothing." pg 24

Gordon, Lyndall. (1984). Virginia Woolf - A Writers Life. W.W. Norton , N.Y., N.Y.

Marder, Herbert. (Spring 1993). The American Scholar. "The Biographer & Angel"

Rudikoff, Sonya. (Spring 1991). American Scholar. "The Unknown Leonard Woolf".

Tynan, William. (Dec. 5, 1994). Time "Love Letters - Virginia Woolf corresponds with Vita Sackville – West"

Wallace, Iriving, Amy, Sylvia & Wallechinsky, David. (1981). The Secret Sex Lives of Famous People, "Woolf" pg. 483-485, Dorset Press, .

Willis, J. H. (1992). Leonard and Virginia Woolf as Publishers - The Hogarth Press 1917-1941. The University Press of Virginia

Woolf, Leonard. (1954). A Writers Diary - Virginia Woolf. Harcourt Brace,

INDEX